GLOBAL CATHOLICISM

In Memory of
Richard Gray (1929–2005)
Mentor, Scholar, Friend

IAN LINDEN

Global Catholicism

Diversity and Change since Vatican II

Columbia University Press
New York

Columbia University Press
Publishers Since 1893
New York

Copyright © 2009 Ian Linden

Library of Congress Cataloging-in-Publication Data

Linden, Ian.
  Global Catholicism : diversity and change since Vatican II / Ian Linden.
    p. cm.
  Includes bibliographical references (p.   ) and index.
  ISBN 978-0-231-15416-1 (cloth : alk. paper)
  1. Catholic Church—History—1965- 2. Vatican Council (2nd : 1962-1965) I. Title.

BX1390.L54 2009
282.09'045—dc22

                                    2008048765

∞
Columbia University Press books are printed on permanent and durable acid-free paper.
This book is printed on paper with recycled content.
Printed in India

c 10 9 8 7 6 5 4 3 2 1

References to Internet Web sites (URLs) were accurate at the time of writing. Neither
the author nor Columbia University Press is responsible for URLs that may have
expired or changed since the manuscript was prepared.

CONTENTS

FOREWORD & ACKNOWLEDGEMENTS

History is often written with questions about today and tomorrow, as well as the past, in mind. It always requires difficult choices about what to leave out and what to put in, and where to focus attention. This book is no exception. I do not believe you can understand the history of Catholicism in the last one hundred years, least of all since the Second Vatican Council, without understanding the changing political context which shapes it and which, at times and in many ways, it shapes. Neither can the story of a Eurocentric Church becoming more global be told without striving to view the world and the Catholic Faith from the "global South". Nor is the development of the Church's theology unimportant to what happens.

The belief that work for justice is a constitutive dimension of the Church's mission for the redemption of the world and that this is the core business of Catholicism is mainstream Catholic doctrine. It has certainly determined choices about the content of this book. So I would deny that my choice of content means that I have "an axe to grind". Or, at least, it is the same axe ground by the world's Catholic bishops gathered at Synods in Rome during the 1970s. Indeed if writing Church history does not show some trace of the bias implied in an "option for the poor", it has to be asked in what sense it is Catholic.

I became a Catholic just as Vatican II was getting underway. The purpose of this book is to celebrate the fiftieth anniversary of Pope John calling the Second Vatican Council on 25 January 1959. A lifetime later I am not at all sure I have understood the Council's significance. So the following chapters are not a Whig history of Catholicism, merely a personal attempt to understand what the Council meant, its impact, and what it might mean in the future.

I got married soon after the Council began. So it is fitting that my principal acknowledgement is to my wife, Jane, who edited this book with a minimum of pain to me, and with great patience and insight, and who shows far more of the common-sense of Catholicism than I do.

Many people inspired me to dare write these chapters. To reflect on the post-conciliar Church is to think of Mildred Nevile, Sue and Geoffrey Chapman and Albert Nolan who, through good times and bad, "preached the Gospel and sometimes used words", words always carefully chosen, full of love and vision. And during the 1980s how can I forget being blessed by crossing the paths of Frank Chikane, Mandlenkhosi Zwane, Beyers Naude and Denis Hurley? Julian Filochowski brought his much needed experience and wisdom to bear on the Latin America chapters. Denys Turner and Nicholas Lash taught me how theology, an integral part of the life of the Church, must be an integral part of its history. The other acknowledgements and thanks go to far too many long suffering friends and colleagues to name all of them. Their wisdom, insights and experience enrich the text. But they cannot be held responsible for it.

1

THE LEGACY OF ANTI-MODERNISM

There are four Roman Catholic Churches. The first is that vast and diverse gathering of different cultures and nationalities in all their particularity, touched, turned and sometimes transformed by Christian faith, so that some 1.3 billion people may be said to share a common religious identity in a global community.[1] Defined by baptism, the celebration of a shared Eucharist and acceptance of the Petrine office of the Bishop of Rome, this community comprises 17.4% of the world's population and half of its Christians.

The second is the Church as it ideally hopes, and sees, itself to be, the story it tells "the world" about itself. Here is a purely theological construct rooted in a belief that this body of people, this nation of pilgrims, in and for the world, is a fundamental part of God's plan in history, guided by the Holy Spirit. And here are to be found accounts of sacraments, charisms, saints and martyrs—not to mention sinners—in a drama of salvation, a divine mystery, of which Catholics understand themselves to be, however insignificantly, however distantly, a part.

The third, the product of a more mundane vision, is the Church as it really functions, how things are in all their human frailty: a body whose fluid boundaries carry heavy traffic between a "City of God" and an "Earthly City", a Church which lives a different life from its head, the Pope and Vatican, in the heart of the political and cultural capital of Rome. Here is the Church's Curial government where conflict appears as common as consensus, power relations as obvious as the ideal of humble service.

From this "panting heart of Rome" derives the tendency—contested by many bishops and priests—to behave as if the vast array of living Catholic communities were an adjunct or passive recipients of goods

1

and services provided by an exclusive hierarchical power structure. And here the gap between what is happening in these communities, predominantly sustained by women, and the pronouncements, encyclicals, and decisions of the male hierarchy, is striking. Indeed it creates a "two-speed" Church, at best complementary in a fruitful internal dialectic, at worst divided.

Finally, the fourth, is how "the world" sees and places this Church in the order of things, often an ideological construct, rooted in a combination of historical and personal experience, fitted—sometimes shoehorned—into secular, or rival religious narratives, a Church characterised in a few graphic reference points that evoke contestation or admiration, and sometimes both, firm views on the beginning and end of life, bells, incense and vestments. It is not easy to click onto each of these Churches, to drag them from one historical folder to another; they are largely inter-linked and coterminous. Together they make up the contemporary identity of Roman Catholicism.

So seeking a truthful presentation of the Roman Catholic Church as a coherent historical entity entails a process not unlike tuning in to a long conversation in which four people talk at once. What might be true in one discourse gets drowned out, or contradicted, by another. Moreover each account smuggles in, or openly proclaims, its particular vision of what is essential to Catholicism, thus importing its own brand of essentialism, how it wants to identify the Catholic Church from any other conglomeration of people who might see themselves as inter-related in a global community, like for example the Muslim *umma*. To make matters more complicated, what is meant and signified by all four of these accounts of the Church undergoes historical change, and not necessarily all at the same time or pace. And the content of this long conversation, and the intensity at which the discussion takes place, change over time.

An Ecumenical Council of the Universal Church

The end of the 1950s is the real starting point of this book, marking the beginning of a seismic shift, the end of a distinct period in the life of the Church, heralding partial resolution of a number of longstanding arguments. It is important to delve back earlier to discover their origins. The symptom of transition was that, after a time of enforced silence, the volume was unexpectedly turned up—as if interlocutors for the four Churches had all begun talking at once. The Church no longer conversed in *sotto voce* mode, with muffled cries off stage, but resolutely in public, or at least as public as its inveterately secretive Curial government in Rome would tolerate.

This was a conversation dominated by Europeans but with many different voices intervening from Churches around the world. In the background was the clear and present danger of communism, witnessed as a major threat in the experience of missionaries, bishops and Christians in China, and bishops and Catholic communities in Eastern Europe. Catholicism was on the verge of creating a world Church but it had not yet done so. The Church managed to be parochially Roman and international at the same time. Yet change was coming. It did not come out of a clear blue sky, though it was unexpected.

The cause of this change was, at its most proximate, a simple granting of permission to sort things out. This consent was given with the authority and apparent insouciance of John XXIII, a new Pope, a remarkable man schooled in a traditional faith who embraced the role of father of this dysfunctional family with warmth and charisma. Moreover, during his short pontificate, John was blessed with a serene certitude that the long overdue "sorting out" could reliably be entrusted to the Holy Spirit working in the Church, whatever the failings of its members, or his own. Exactly what was to be "sorted out" was initially far from clear; that too, he believed with a humble spirituality, was up to the Holy Spirit to determine.

The framework in which this debate was to occur was soon known as the Second Vatican Council; though John himself tellingly called it an Ecumenical Council of the Universal Church, indicating an event in which diversity was acknowledged—not necessarily positively—and unity affirmed. The Church's commitment to mission and the building of new local Churches had been a consistent feature of its life since the nineteenth century, but its pretensions to universality were combined with an all too human desire for uniformity. The prodigious event of a Council was inevitably first understood in the narrow context of unfinished European business. It would be a continuation of the First Vatican Council that was abruptly terminated in 1870 with unfortunate consequences: most notably that the only account given of the Church was in terms of the primacy and infallibility of the Pope. Put more positively, the First Council curtailed a dangerous move towards the personal infallibility of the Pontiff; his role was primarily to adjudicate within the context of the infallibility of the Church. But the second Council turned out in practice differently: it attempted both to speak the Christian message anew to the diverse and fast-changing world of the 1960s, and to give a theological account of such a Church speaking anew to the world.

The impact and consequences of one man's decision to open a structured and public debate are extraordinary. It was far from a foregone conclusion at the end of the 1950s that the Church, a nascent global community, could find the resources to do so. Nothing very obvious indicated that the Church would be able to reflect on the four discourses that made up its identity—though its ecclesiastical leaders did not see matters in that way. For many the idea of a Council came as a threat, or simply a totally bewildering surprise. Nobody quite knew what to make of it.

It would have been understandable had the unfinished business of the first Vatican Council formed the exclusive content of the Second. But this was never likely. In the post-war world there were enough Catholics who saw the urgent need to say something new about the relations between the Church and the "world", and several theologians who had been doing so to great effect within the constraints imposed by the Vatican. Some wanted very much to talk about change, even if only a few had precise ideas about how they might go about the task. Indeed it could be said that there was nothing on the final agenda of the Council that had not been incubating in local Churches, in local or wider initiatives, for biblical renewal and liturgical reform for example, or as small movements. These previous developments were part of a wider network of innovation, and coalesced during the Council years, 1962-1965, during a historic transition in global Catholicism.

A Chinese proverb says that when a tree falls it makes a big noise, when a forest grows nobody hears anything. A number of small coppices had been growing for several decades in the Church and making very little noise. Initiatives in ecumenism, catechetics and liturgy were known about only within limited circles of pioneers and networks of supporters. Tentative suggestions amongst a small number of theologians for thinking in a different way about the Church and the world had been consolidated in a body of writing. The Christian life of the "people of God" had been slowly changing. The metaphor for the

Church, formerly a "perfect society", now the Mystical Body of Christ, was changing correspondingly.

These modest antecedents make some sense of the surprising outcomes of the Council. Its Constitutions, Decrees and Declarations, formulated in the unique ecclesiastical culture of Rome, seemed remarkably new and fresh; their content both shocked and invigorated the Catholic world. To understand why this should be so requires going back to a time when mobs of *sans-culottes* in Paris hacked priests to pieces in scenes repeated during the Rwandan genocide.

From Emigrés de l'intérieur to Dialogue: 1789-1918

The French Revolution spread by Europe-wide war, and the later rise of liberalism and Italian nationalism, along with the loss of the Papal States swept away by the *Risorgimento*, produced a massive decline in the temporal power of the Catholic Church reducing it from a belligerent State with active troops to a besieged enclave in Rome with a decorative Noble Guard. The Revolution decapitated the French Church and seemed to threaten its very survival. Some thirty thousand clergy fled France, leaving behind over a thousand dead. Pope Pius VI, a man in his eighties, was captured by the French army in 1796, deported by Napoleon and died in captivity in Valence; his successor, Pope Pius VII, by way of a penalty for refusing to hand over English troops seeking sanctuary in the Papal States, was taken prisoner in July 1809.[2]

By 1829 there were 646 dioceses in the Latin Church around the world but only twenty-four of the bishops heading them were directly appointed by the Pope. States controlled appointments to 555, and local Church chapters appointed sixty-seven.[3] Intermittent Republican and Liberal together with growing working-class anti-clericalism continued throughout the nineteenth century, keeping Church leaders on the defensive. In 1849 the Pope fled the Quirinal Palace in Rome disguised as a servant after his secretary was shot dead by a revolutionary mob. Rome was occupied in 1870 and in 1878, Pope Pius IX's funeral procession was pelted by mud on the Ponte Sant' Angelo, and the bier narrowly escaped being thrown by the crowd into the River Tiber.

The Church suffered greatly as a result of anti-clerical programmes in Liberal Europe. In Germany between 1873 and 1878, Bismarck's *Kulturkampf* — suppression of Religious Orders and take-over of Catholic schools — was partly a response to the provocative declaration of Papal infallibility in the first Vatican Council. Things did not improve with the passage of time. In 1901, under the French Third Republic, some 30,000 members of Religious Orders were dispersed and, in 1905, the Law of Separation ended the Concordat with Rome and with it state-supported Catholic education, not to mention other financial benefits of ecclesiastical establishment.[4] This had profound effects nationally but also in the French colonies, Senegal for example, where the closing of Catholic schools had an even greater impact as missionaries involved in education were obliged to leave. The historical memory of persecution and martyrdom had become by the mid-twentieth century one of quiet but fierce pride.

Under great pressures, Rome developed a siege mentality; its internal disagreements were not to be made public, nor were they to develop into obvious divisions. Ultramontanism, the quest to shore up the Papacy with greater notional powers, was a natural corollary to loss, insecurity and fear of disunity, and a powerful current in the nineteenth-century Church. No less symptomatic were outbursts and intemperate anathemas against contemporary "errors" and "*isms*", Liberalism and Socialism, directed at a world that was far from attentive. The "*isms*" condemned, particularly Modernism, sometimes seemed inventions of a Roman imagination verging on the pathological: eclectic ideas aggregated into a new amalgam by ecclesiastical authorities who inhabited a mental world of conspiracies against the Truth.

The Church's boundaries were sharply drawn against a multitude of supposed enemies without, and some within, none more hated than secularism in its many "satanic" forms. Correct thinking was asserted—and demanded—by the teaching authorities of the Vatican, the Magisterium. The "Deposit of Faith" was handed down, as from a decrepit Leninist vanguard always a little late in getting news from the front, often working with unreliable intelligence, spawning fearful rumours. The language was strident and defensive, the tone authoritarian, with little concern for arguing a case. Pope Pius IX's 1864 *Syllabus of Errors* was a sad monument to the genre. The rejected proposition, eightieth on the list of errors, that "the Roman Pontiff can and should reconcile himself to progress, liberalism and recent civilisation" sums it up.[5] Dissent in the ranks was quelled; assent or silence were demanded. The teaching Church reacted with an intellectual Pavlovian reflex: rejection of new developments in science, philosophy and politics. The faithful listened. And piety required that, on the whole, they did not answer back. The *Syllabus* would leave the Fathers at the Second Vatican Council with an uncomfortable papal precedent—one of many—to ignore or fret about.

The nineteenth and early twentieth century Catholic faithful were loyal to a fault. "This devotion was a kind of passionate, fervent emotion, afire with repressed indignation, which is offered to an abandoned wife, an abused mother, a dethroned queen", wrote Ida Goerres of the French Catholic world into which St. Thérèse of Lisieux, the "Little Flower", was born.[6] Exceptions to this mind-set appeared as threats to Rome and, only much later, as antecedents to the theology of the Second Vatican Council.

Catholics inclined to the conviction that with the armies of anti-Catholicism at the gates, a united front and discipline were imperative. Legalism was not considered a defect but a bulwark against compromise. Nothing could be allowed to threaten the juridical carapace of the institutional Church from within. Never was the detail of Church law so loved. This was Goerres' harsh verdict: "and yet how much narrowness and intolerance, how much injustice and falsehood, how much servile renunciation of responsibility, how much mental laziness and cowardice...assembled in the course of time behind the broad shield which those faithful warriors held out to protect their endangered heritage".[7] Nonetheless, Women Religious were finding a significant if limited freedom—very limited if they were working class—founding new schools for the poor, staffing clinics and hospitals, working in the missions around the world.

There was simply no place for home-grown dissidents. The Church did not—with exceptions such as the worker priest movement of the 1950s, one of the intimations of the Council ferment—have a body of working class intellectuals, schooled and rooted in the Catholic *masses populaires*. Future theologians and thinkers with promise, whose views and understanding were destined to be influential, were fed—mostly smoothly—from lowly local seminaries into strictly controlled elite colleges, theological courses and universities in Rome, where they absorbed an etiolated and restricted version of the Church's intellectual tradition, along with elements of the culture of the Vatican administration, the Curia, and Canon Law.

A seminary theological textbook from the 1950s would have read much the same as one from the 1750s. Theological scholarship was largely an elaboration of this tradition within a particular philosophical framework. The art of the establishment theologian might pejoratively be described as "colouring in", an orderly filling out of the tradition; creative insight, doing something new on the canvas, was hazardous and likely to have adverse consequences, silencing, banning or even excommunication. The primary theological task was to make sure that the deposit of faith, the Church's theological capital, was not threatened and eroded.

Despite the widely acclaimed and subtle reflections of the English theologian, John Henry Newman, on the historical development of Catholic doctrine, the theologian's task was not the discovery of new truths implicit within a live and developing tradition dating back to the Biblical canon. Least of all was the task to learn from other intellectual traditions or to express faith in a more accessible language, it was the circumscribed articulation of old formulas, the "tending of a walled off supernatural garden". An unchanging ahistorical Church required ahistorical doctrines. To say something new—and permissible—a theologian had to derive it from preferably a recent papal utterance or document, in such a way that, when challenged, it could be plausibly presented as saying the same thing. Such restrictive thinking remained alive and powerful until the Second Vatican Council, with enervating consequences.[8]

There was little reason for hope of change from the educated laity. Many beleagured French Catholics—and not only French—adapted psychologically to the Church's trauma by becoming *émigrés de l'intérieur*, (retreating into an interior spiritual life), adopting a spirituality that avoided intellectual engagement with modernity; Goerres floridly described them as "exiles who have remained at home and who nevertheless have emigrated from the prevailing order, who are fugitives from the whole life of the nation, left-overs of a vanished era, quietly longing for a return to or restlessly bent upon reconquest of the past".[9]

For genuine *émigrés*, the past, that other country, was there to be reconquered in the mission territories, and here Catholics were to find a refuge from modernity. Thanks to the dispersal of the French religious teaching orders, 1901-1904, and their flight abroad, theirs was a spirituality that travelled around the Catholic world. Many new converts

were educated by French nuns. African and Asian converts were expected to cut themselves off from their own "pagan" culture as a result
of conversion. And from the 1860s a great new wave of missionary expansion found Protestants and Catholics in competition with each other, and with Muslims, for converts to the two monotheistic religions.
Meanwhile in Latin America, as in other parts of the world, there was a
massive growth in the number of domestic *émigrés* to celibacy, poverty
and obedience, into new Religious Orders, most of them led by women.
Half of today's Latin American Religious Orders were founded during
the nineteenth century, a staggering 261 new Religious congregations,
many, despite different degrees of enclosure and rigorous prayer discipline, dedicated to the education and welfare of the poor; the same
picture could be replicated in Europe and North America. Philadelphia
born Mother Katharine Drexel founded the Sisters of the Blessed Sacrament for Indians and Coloured People in 1891. In France the number
of Women Religious rose from 12,300 in 1808 to 128,000 in 1901.[10]

The inner world painted in Goerres' passionate prose was part and
parcel of what the missionaries brought as their intellectual and cultural
luggage, and often formed the political background to their evangelisation. Many were mesmerised by the shimmering vision of a "Christian
kingdom in Africa"...or, for that matter, a compliant monarchy any-
where else. And in those parts of Europe or Latin America where the
Church had been accustomed to the State docilely reflecting its views
on social and ecclesiastical policy, the liberal solution of separation of
Church and State was seen as betrayal, an end to establishment and
privilege. Nor did the Vatican fully understand the difficulties of the
bishops of the USA. The recognition that the State was more than a
pliant instrument under the instruction of the Church, in pupillage for
carrying out its divine purposes, was a long time in coming. Indeed
a Vatican rearguard clung onto to it until routed during the Second
Vatican Council.

But if this were the whole story, the Council could not have launched
the Church, as it did, on a new trajectory in the space of three years,
from 1962 to 1965. Debates had been underway for decades, often in
a form of Catholic *samizdat* emerging from small theological pockets,
and the arguments had been honed over the years. If non-establishment
theologians had not courageously and faithfully borne their banning
orders and imposed silences in order to refine their thought, better to

prosecute their argument within the arcane symbolic universe of the Catholic establishment in Rome, the Second Vatican Council would not have been a turning point between two historical epochs. It would have been another, possibly terminal, though defiant, shout from a teaching Church that could not bring itself to converse with pluralism and "modernity".

Early Antecedents to the Council. The search for the origins of the conciliar debates, emerging in the years leading up to the Second Vatican Council, sheds a distinctly dappled light on the Council's theological antecedents. The beginnings of serious conflict about modernity—or as Rome called it "Modernism"—go back to before 1843 and John Henry Newman's Oxford University sermon and seminal essay on the theory of development in religious doctrine. It began with attempts to reconcile Catholicism with the ideas of the French Revolution and, later, with Liberalism. From the perspective of Rome, both presented the Janus faces of Modernism.

The first major airing of what became the modernist controversy took place in the turbulent 1830s. In Poland the Russian Czar Nicholas was crushing the Uniate Church which was in communion with Rome. Monarchical rule now seemed to threaten the freedom of the Church and winning back freedom for the Church was the aim of Catholic liberalism. Liberal Catholics led by a prodigious Breton priest, Félicité de Lamennais, saw the way forward for a Church suffering under anti-clerical regimes in separation of Church and State, Liberal freedom of conscience, democracy and a free press. This Liberal religious populism was a genuine conviction rather than a tactical manoeuvre, and incurred the wrath of the anti-Republican French bishops and a sizeable faction of French conservatives and Bourbon monarchists.[11]

Lamennais, a fervent ultramontane believer in the Papacy as a counter-force to anti-Catholic regimes or to supine, state-funded clergy, sought support from Rome. It was not forthcoming. The Pope saw in the power and principle of absolute monarchy, a sacred alliance between throne and altar, an indispensable bulwark against Liberalism and at the very least a practical necessity for the protection of the Papal States against demands for popular sovereignty. *L'Avenir*, the flagship publication of the Catholic Liberals with its stirring theme of "God and Liberty", but no money, was obediently wound up.[12] However, there was more to papal belief in absolute monarchy than that. Forty years later, the absolutist monarchical principle was to be asserted within the Church in the proclamation of Papal infallibility.

The net consequence of Lamennais' brand of accomodationist theology was to focus Rome's attention on the broad collection of views that he articulated. The mish-mash of ideas summarised by the heading "Liberalism" was something of a moving target, but thanks to *L'Avenir* it took concrete shape—in its Italian form initially—as a distinct and threatening amalgam of errors in the mind of the Pope, Gregory XVI. In *Mirari Vos*, published in 1832, he condemned the fundamental tenets of political Liberalism which were later to form the basis of the democratic project. Liberty of conscience, according to Gregory, was "madness", freedom of the press "loathsome", and the idea that Church and State should be separate, anathema.[13] Liberalism was viewed as a revolutionary creed that would destroy the good order of society. The Church conducted a ruthless counter-insurgency campaign against the Catholic Liberals on a wide intellectual front. "Especially after they had been condemned, opposition to them deteriorated into a shameful heresy hunt, complete with a cunning system of espionage, a secret code and a campaign of slander," writes the Dutch Dominican, Mark Schoof. [14]

Despite holy pictures appearing on the 1848 barricades alongside socialist slogans, conservative Catholic reaction to the revolutionary outbreaks that rid France of King Louis Philippe won the day. The death in Paris of Archbishop Affre, shot while mediating between the two sides, played its part in hardening positions.[15] For forty years until Pope Leo XIII's efforts at reconciliation with the French Republic, conservative intransigence held sway. On 20 September 1870 the nationalist Royal Italian Army entered Rome. The world of the *anciens régimes* finally disappeared. The Pope was left without support, a "prisoner in the Vatican".[16]

The brutalities of the 1871 Paris Commune and its suppression brought back fearful memories and widened the gap between the European working class and the Church. The Roman Curia simply banned Catholics from voting or standing for election in the new Italian State and this state of affairs prevailed until the ruling was abrogated by Pope Benedict XV. Pope Leo XIII saw the dangers and called on clergy to concern themselves wholeheartedly with the workers, the poor and people of the lower classes. His 1891 encyclical *Rerum Novarum* reflected his fears about the growing fault lines in society subject to socialist manipulation, between employers and workers, but he eschewed Catholic involvement in political solutions. Bold enough to insist on accommodation with the Republican state and on engagement with workers, Pope Leo XIII's attitude to modernism was ambiguous and tentative; enough for a few flowers to bloom, but he was always ready to prune them hard in pursuit of Vatican policy.

There was to be no Catholic revolution until 1926 when Mexican Catholics, bands of *cristeros*, revolted against the brutal anti-clerical regime of President Plutarco Calles with applause from Church leadership. Mexico was a proof that Liberty spelt anarchy and led to the cemetery.[17] The idea that social upheaval with its attendant violence was almost invariably against the common good, and spelt disaster for the Church, was now firmly entrenched in the ecclesiastical mind.

Seventy years after Catholic Liberalism and Lamennais were condemned in *Mirari Vos*, Monsignor Alfred Baudrillat, rector of the Liberal-leaning Institut Catholique in Paris—and a future Cardinal—could say of Lamennais in 1903, that he was "the man who stands at the beginning of the intellectual movement of the French Church and to whom all those great currents of thought at the close of the nineteenth century owe their origin". The best known thinkers associated with this intellectual movement, Alfred Loisy and Maurice Blondel, and his pupil Lucien Laberthonniére in France, and in England the Jesuit George Tyrrell—born a Protestant in Dublin—and Baron Von Hugel, born in Germany, had already emerged as significant voices by the turn of the century. Their ideas were picked up in North America. The founder of the Josephites, John Slattery, a zealous promoter of Black American seminarians whom he hoped one day to see evangelising Africa, met Loisy and Von Harnack in 1902. He left the Church four years later.[18]

However weighty the proponents of new thinking in turn of the century Catholicism, the Vatican did not budge. Pope Pius X simply reverted in July 1907 to bald condemnation with 65 theses contained in *Lamentabili*, and, that September, in a follow-up "anti-modernist" encyclical, *Pascendi*. In 1910 came unadulterated intellectual repression, an oath of allegiance against modernism for all theology teachers, and candidates for theology degrees. "Modernism", this eclectic assemblage of ideas, was called "the receptacle of all heresies". The enemy was within the Church; "the partisans of error...lie hid in her very bosom and heart", it was announced. Councils of vigilance were required to be set up in every diocese.

Pius X declared himself adamantly opposed to "dubious alliances" and against Catholic movements wanting co-operation with those fired by "liberty, equality and fraternity", such as those clustered around the French Catholic Republican periodical, *Le Sillon*. Established as a response to Leo XIII's opening to the worker movement, *Le Sillon* was condemned in 1910. A universal society could only be created by, and under, the Church's direction. And that meant it could not be led by lay activists, nor the innovative priests found in such social movements as the *Semaines Sociales*, but only under the direction of the Vatican. The model was the missionary, obedient to Propaganda Fide, exporting a distinctly *Roman* Catholicism around the globe. In a world of 1.6 billion people in 1900, only 558 million were Christian. There were 8.7 million Christians and 34.5 million Muslims in Africa. The missions offered a heroic model and an epic objective. Cardinal Charles Lavigerie's International Missionary Sisters of Our Lady of Africa and his pioneer Missionaries of Africa were prime examples. African Christians outnumbered African Muslims by 1985.[19]

The Vatican's by now routine condemnations—though those of Pius X seemed particularly intransigent—targetted three of the most significant themes being developed by "modernist" thinkers and which came to inform the theology of the Second Vatican Council: that renewal of the Church meant going back to the Gospel and Patristic sources; that the Church needed to make contact with the variety of contemporary— "secular"—experience, and to incorporate feelings and needs as well as rational explanations of God's existence; and that by doing so she would be able to hear and respond to the human "cry for the transcendent".

The tragedy of this missed opportunity had multiple causes and consequences. The Church interpreted the intimation, suggestion, or forthright claim that she was as subject to history as any other institution as an assertion of the relativism of Christian doctrine. So instead of a scholarly historical inquiry into the thought of Thomas Aquinas— alongside Augustine the main philosophical and theological support for contemporary Catholic thought—the Church adopted "neo-scholasticism", a lifeless creed created from a degenerate remnant of Thomism. The result was that large numbers of Catholics were presented by

Rome, and thus by their local clergy, with the spiritual equivalent of a car manual.

Pope Leo XIII went so far as to proclaim neo-scholasticism as "the" Christian Philosophy. This left in some doubt what might have been "*the*" philosophy of the Church before its invention.[20] So it was that the object of the Church's concern remained a particular way of expressing the Faith as a system of ideas and propositions. And concern for preserving this system was substituted for concern about how the Faith might be the key to understanding all reality. This was to turn on its head the position of Aquinas, who had roundly said in the *Summa Theologiae,* "the terminus of the act of faith is not the proposition but the reality".[21]

Biblical scholars were *a fortiori* in the firing line. Alfred Loisy, a pupil of the celebrated French atheist philologist Ernst Renan, but a loyal public defender of the richness of the Catholic tradition against Protestant reductionism, was on dangerous ground, delving back into the historical context of the Gospels in the same breath as writing about the Church "The 'deposit of faith' is not merely a symbol or creed", he wrote, "but it is a concrete religion left by Christ to his Church; it is perhaps in some sense more directly a *lex orandi* than a *lex credendi* [a law of prayer more than a law of belief]; the creed is involved in the prayer and has to be disentangled from it; and the formularies are ever to be tested and explained by the concrete religion which they formulate."[22] In other words theology must arise from the lived experience of the faith. The insight was to be taken up much later in two different ways: firstly in the liturgical renewal movement and, most notably, by Marie-Dominique Chenu—both influential in the Council—and then in liberation theology. Loisy, who in some ways triggered the anti-modernist witch-hunt with his 1902 book *L'Evangile et L'Eglise*—informing a vulnerable Church that it had not been Jesus' intention to found any such organisation—came to reject Scripture as revealed by God, and was driven out and excommunicated.

The natural path to religious renewal, a return to origins, was thus temporarily blocked. The second and—correlated—consequence was that, as George Tyrrell correctly indicated in the title of his unfinished book, Christianity was at the Crossroads. Not least this was because of the Church's loss of the working class at a moment when Marxism was about to mutate from theory into potent political practice. The problem as Tyrrell saw it was that the theological Christ presented by Rome "lived in a blaze of certainty about everything—like a Roman Cardinal". But Humanity about to embark on the rapid and dramatic changes of the twentieth century needed a Christ who "shared all our groping and darkness and uncertainty and blameless ignorance".[23] And a Church that could share and understand this deep vulnerability, not hide in the walled garden of neo-scholastic propositions, might have been more attractive to many in search of a spirituality for their time. For a while, and perennially for some, certainty would be seductive. Marxism and then Nationalism Socialism played on this need. But for many more in Europe the stance of the Roman Church was profoundly alienating.

What saved the Church was that the foreign missions provided an opening for powerful spiritual energies that might have been destructively turned inwards. Women Religious and missionary orders provided an outlet for adventurous women seeking big horizons. Pope Benedict XV's 1919 encyclical on the missions, *Maximum Illud*, championed the missionary vision of the Church, calling for new regional seminaries and the promotion of an indigenous clergy, setting up the "Ethiopian" College in Rome, while retaining the Vatican's distrust for nationalism. A year later Benedict beatified the Uganda martyrs. When the Cathedral of the Sacred Heart of Jesus and Mary, Rubaga, Uganda, was consecrated on 31 October 1925 in the presence of thousands of Ugandan Catholics, product of a vibrant and growing African Church, no-one present was worrying about Modernism.[24]

2

DOMINICAN AND JESUIT PIONEERS

On 17 March 1920, eleven missionaries from the newly founded Missionary Society of St. Columban went from Ireland via San Francisco to Hunan province in China. They took a new-fangled cine-camera with them to make a movie promoting the China mission. *The Cross and the Dragon* featured a little known crooner singing 'Silent Night'. The Columbans went on to produce a successful mission magazine, *The Far East*, and Bing Crosby sang "Silent Night" to greater acclaim elsewhere. Less than three months later, two Ugandans both of whom were "confessors of the faith", Joseph Nsingirisa and Denis Kamyuka, the former imprisoned with the Uganda martyrs, the latter spared the pyre at the last moment left the Basilica of St Peter's in Rome where they were met by a throng of bishops, priests, and assembled laity "eager to embrace them, touch them or to kiss their hands". The occasion was the beatification of twenty-two young African men, servants in the Buganda court, burnt to death for their faith by the Kabaka in 1885-1886. In Naples the two confessors were refused a berth to Mombasa by a British steamboat company on racial grounds, and under pressure from the White Fathers were finally accepted by an Italian company but only in the lowest class available.[1]

The two vignettes show the Catholic Church on the cusp of globalisation, with its strong roots in the past, entering a world of rapid technological change with a certain confidence. Catholicism and modernity, Church life and Society, were not neatly divided. But the differences are worth noting.

The hubris of secular Europe had died on the Somme. The Church had been less undermined spiritually by the slaughter. The international missionary society of the White Fathers was seeing growing numbers of

17

ordinations of African clergy in their Tanganyika, Rwanda, Congo as well as Ugandan vicariates. Colonial society saw them through a black and white prism; "confessors", deacons, priests, were one or the other and treated accordingly. It was a time of Catholic breakthrough in Africa as seminaries filled up, new African priests proved their worth, and the Church began to focus on education. The missionary impulse of the Church, theology, strategy, and dogged perseverance, were being rewarded.

During the first half of the twentieth century Religious women gradually became involved in new forms of evangelisation. Education of "pagan" women and children drew the Sisters of Our Lady of the Mission to New Zealand in 1865, but they were diverted by the bishop to education of Christian settler children. In 1901 they opened St Joseph's Maori Girls College in Opunake and, in 1950, the first young Maori woman sought admission to the noviciate. American Maryknoll Sisters started a mission in Hong Kong in 1921 and their work soon included social welfare, raising women's awareness of their rights and combating foot-binding.[2] Their status as nun and missionary, not the same as other whites or foreigners, whether in Asian slums or black ghettoes in the USA, enabled the poor to approach Religious Women. The nuns were also able to relate both to colonial and local elites. Ethnic and asexual ambiguity created by dress and partial enclosure opened doors in class or race divided societies.

Latin America was "the Catholic Continent", but it also attracted Religious orders with a missionary vision. The Maryknoll priest, John Considine's, *Call for Forty Thousand*, published in 1946 strengthened the commitment of the US Church to Latin America. The pace of arrival of North American and European Women and Men Religious—about a third of them from Spain—continued unabated in the first half of the twentieth century until after the mid-1950s when it began to slow. By the end of the 1960s the continent numbered 9,030 foreign Women Religious (out of 130,190) and 6,659 foreign Men Religious (out of 39,810), not to mention the many expatriate Latin American Religious, most notably working in Guatemala, El Salvador and Panama. As pre-war Catholics put their coins in the red boxes of the Pontifical Mission Societies, read mission magazines, or contemplated the plight of black babies' souls, they had a sense of a community growing around the world, and a quiet pride in a Church nourished by the blood of martyrs and the sweat of missionaries, a universal communion that was much more than a theologian's construct.

Life after Modernism

But no matter where they lived, until the Second World War, Catholic theologians had to exercise caution in confronting ideas and practices that blocked renewal in the Church, and they wrote in neo-scholastic terms. As Dom Cuthbert Butler, an influential Benedictine in the English Church, put it to Baron Von Hugel after the Papal condemnation of modernism in 1907, the Church ran like a train on neo-scholasticism; if on arriving at a station you were not following the line, you were by definition derailed. Papal condemnations of modernists proved conclusively that the alleged renegades were not neo-Thomists, but failed to prove that they were not Catholics. The atmosphere of the witch-hunt was only dissipated by Pope Benedict XV in his letter *Ad Beatissimi* in 1914.[3]

Despite the pressures, by the 1930s, fragmented dissent was beginning to coalesce around two schools of reformist theological thought in which new approaches, branded *"la nouvelle théologie"*—by its opponents—were institutionally promoted. Hitherto new ideas had sometimes been cast in the form of existentialism or personalism—most notably that of the philosophers Emmanuel Mounier and Maurice Blondel. Or, more commonly, in a fervent assertion of the values of Reason and the Enlightenment creating a stand-off between "blind faith" and faith as an objective form of knowing. Increasingly the battles had to be waged purely within the terms of neo-scholasticism even if on a wide front. As Dom Cuthbert Butler pointed out, there was no other way. Catholicism did not lend itself to a Bultmann or a Tillich, far less to the great symphonic dogmatic synthesis of Karl Barth, soaring aloft in innovative theological harmonies.[4]

At the same time the mish-mash branded "modernism" was beginning to diverge into a number of distinct if inter-related questions and sites of intellectual debate. Most importantly the major political issues—ultramontanism, monarchy, papal states, the French Republic—that had created complex currents and counter-currents between Rome, national hierarchies and European governments of different political hues, and were also tangled up with the conduct and content of

19

the philosophical debates, began to fade into the past. In their place came one overarching concern: atheistic Communism.

Communism in the Soviet Union, Eastern Europe, Italy and then after 1949 China programmatically attempted to inculcate atheism and a vision of a new Man and a new Society that was in direct competition with the Church. It was a different form of totalitarianism from fascism. Both saw themselves as representing different visions of a "perfect society", as did the Church. But Church-State relations with communist governments amounted to the Church trying to resist an inexorable drive to destroy it as an institutional, public, social and sometimes even private, reality. Repression might ease according to circumstances and political expediency, bishops might undertake different strategies for survival and the continuation of Church life, but the goal of communist states soon became clear. There was an initial hope after the Bolshevik Revolution that by degrees of accommodation things might get better. They got worse.

The French Church

France having lanced its revolutionary boil was only at moderate risk of potential communist infection. French Catholics had a "good war" between 1914-1918 with thousands of French priests going to the front as medical orderlies, stretcher-bearers and chaplains to fight in what many saw as a Holy War for civilisation against—what was co-incidentally Protestant—Germany. The White Fathers alone were decorated with 84 Croix de Guerre for feats of bravery. Catholic patriotism was rewarded by a thaw in relations with the Republic, and a distinct softening of anti-clericalism. In a change of tactics, both Pius XI and Benedict XV showed willingness to strike deals with the French "laicists", a return to Leo XIII's policy of accommodation. But the aristocratic and military Catholic conservatives who rallied to the banner of *Action Française*, an organisation that promoted the idea that France was under the thumb of "foreigners", Jews, Protestants and Freemasons, continued to live in the past. They were damaged though far from quelled, by a Papal condemnation in 1926, placing them under the threat of excommunication.[5]

In the face of such atavistic lay movements and the new communist menace, Pope Pius XI set out his ideas in two encyclicals: *Ubi Arcano* (1922) and *Maximam Gravissimamque* (1924), on the lay apostolate, called *Catholic Action,* the Church's outward deployment in pursuit of a "New Christendom". In response to his call for Catholics to establish "the social reign of Christ", Canon Joseph Cardijn formed *Jeunesse Ouvrière Chrétienne (JOC)* in Brussels, and similar movements for students, rural youth, the middle-class and sailors. The *Jocistes* in Young Christian Worker and Young Christian Student groups fanned out across France and, via mission personnel, into Latin America, Africa and Asia where the "see-judge-act" methodology, rooted in experience in a variety of social milieux, was to play a vital role. This methodology had extraordinary resonance around the world.

This revival in the French Church was accompanied by the acquisition of celebrity converts: Léon Bloy, his convert Jacques Maritain, and Paul Claudel. Growing self-confidence made possible the special apostolate of the "worker priest", immersed distinctively in the daily life of industrial labour. Maritain produced a framework for Catholic political engagement based on "integral humanism" that fed into the thinking of Christian Democrats such as the future Chilean President, Eduardo Frei.[6] The decades of lay flight from the world into private spirituality and individualism, what had almost become a Faustian pact with secularism to evacuate public space, was officially ending.

This was the encouraging context in which a French Dominican House of Studies at Le Saulchoir, and a Jesuit theological faculty at the foot of the Fourvière hill in Lyons, began training a new generation of priests and formulating key theological questions. The scholarly and extensive writing of Marie-Dominique Chenu OP, Yves Congar OP, and Henri de Lubac SJ, was treated with the greatest suspicion by Rome; the two Dominicans, Chenu and Congar, were silenced, sacked or censured and their publications frequently banned. De Lubac, better protected by his Jesuit Superiors and teaching the history of religions and fundamental theology at the University of Lyons, fared better. In the thirty years leading up to the Second Vatican Council, together they formulated a theological framework for change. Whereas condemnation had resulted in major reformers of the nineteenth century, more often that not, spinning intellectually out of control and sometimes out of the Church, a hundred years later a resilient loyalty prevailed. Condemnation was simply endured. Enforced silences resulted in even more earnest study and application to the task.

Given Chenu's role as the driving intellect and magnet for students at Le Saulchoir, it was perhaps surprising that his primary expertise was in mediaeval Church history, but this gave him two vital insights. First he saw that the life of the Church was, and always had been, in constant movement and interaction with the world, and second that the original thinking of Thomas Aquinas was nothing like the desiccated and static set of propositions taught in official neo-scholasticism. Inspired by the *jocistes* and influenced by the worker priest movement, he sent some of his Dominican students for their training into the mines to experience the life of workers underground. But Chenu's vision was wider than merely an apostolate to workers. "To do theology is to be present to the revelation given in the present life of the church and the present experience of Christendom", he wrote in the influential periodical *La Vie Intellectuelle*.[7] He saw the dynamism and autonomy of the secular world as giving a whole new perspective to the role and responsibilities of lay people.

Yves Congar, ten years his junior, came to teach at Le Saulchoir in 1931 elaborating a theology of the lay vocation, as well as developing his own intellectual foundations for an ecumenical theology.[8] The Dombes group—an annual meeting of 40 Catholics and 40 Protestants—led by Abbé Couturier and the future Cardinal Gerlier began work in France in 1937. In turn the Dutch Dominican Edward Schillerbeeckx came under Congar's influence before moving on to teach at the Dominican House in Louvain (Dominicans were at the time forbidden to teach at the University). The Dutch Church was developing ideas which were to be influential in the ecumenical thinking of the Council.[9]

The ecumenical movement had its origins at the beginning of the century, and was to prove a powerful lobby before the Council. It was in the Netherlands in 1952 that Father Jan Willebrands and Father Frans Thyssen set up the Catholic Conference on Ecumenical Questions with Father Augustin Bea—Pope Pius XII's confessor—to shadow the World Council of Churches (WCC) in Geneva. The Catholic Conference was later to form the nucleus of the Secretariat for Christian Unity. Such was the ecumenical climate of the day that Rome forbade the group from attending the 1954 WCC meeting in Evanston, near Chicago, though the Dutch links through the WCC General-Secretary, A.Visser 't Hooft, ensured good relations.[10]

The New Theology

The inspiration of the reformers came from the early Church and they saw their "newness" as a reversion to the authentic tradition rather than a conversion to a novelty. Fourvière, the Jesuit theological faculty became known for its retrieval, and reflection on, Patristic writings, the thinking of the Early Fathers of the Church during the first few Christian centuries, a second important source of new insights into the historical development of the Church. Henri de Lubac's finished his seminal work *Catholicism* there in 1937. Dom Christopher Butler, Abbot of Downside, described how "paragraph after paragraph, startling perhaps *in its apparent novelty* (author's italics) rests on the basis of converging teachings of Fathers or Schoolmen".[11] Only in 1943, after Pope Pius XII's encyclical *Divino Afflante Spiritu,* were Catholic scholars allowed to engage freely in historical biblical studies.

Rather like Chenu who became seen as the theologian of the worker priest movement, De Lubac learnt of the clergy's most seminal experiences of wartime France through his friend Yves de Montcheuil, who was chaplain to resistance fighters and executed in 1944. The few priests sent by the French bishops who survived the German munition factories and labour camps also had a positive experience of "secularity" in the solidarity and life of some 800,000 deported French workers. De Lubac's fellow French Jesuit, Father Victor Dillard, took this path and perished in Dachau concentration camp.[12] The new solidarities of these environments fed an understanding of the modern world and the urgent challenge facing the Church. Similar insights pushed Cardinal Emmanuel Suhard of Paris into speaking of France as a mission territory. Suhard supported and defended the *Mission de France* to French workers from 1941 until his death in 1949.[13]

The future Pope John XXIII was nuncio in Paris during this critical period, and through his conversations, and disagreements, with Suhard, and his wider experience in the French Church, he was brought into contact with "Social Catholicism".[14] Likewise the future Pope Paul VI was a friend of the Catholic convert philosopher, Jacques Maritain, who was grappling with issues of pluralism. Maritain saw the promotion of democracy and the free competition of different ideas", in the light of totalitarianism, as the fundamental "needs of the times". The Church, he argued, was not opposed to a pluralist society which itself had a basic faith and inspiration of its own. Church and State represented different fields of endeavour, not opposing self-contained "perfect societies"—a formula used until the time of Pius XII. "In any case the responsibility of nurturing, strengthening and enriching a common democratic faith would belong no less to the priest, dedicated to the preaching of the Gospel, than to the teacher, dedicated to the scientific spirit, if both of them came to a clear awareness of the needs of our times".[15] This repositioning of the Church and rejection of a sterile and abrasive dualism was to inform, twenty years later, the Council's *Constitution on the Church in the Modern World*.

The dialectic between contemporary experience and theological insights into the historical development of the Church's consciousness of its faith generated a threatening series of questions for the Roman theologians. Europe's agony, amidst competing totalitarian states, and the secular horror of war and its aftermath, encouraged the Vatican to turn defensively inwards, as the new theological movements turned outwards. A privately circulated edition of articles on theology from the Dominican house of Le Saulchoir was put on the Roman Index of banned books in 1942. The French Dominican, Réginald Garrigou-Lagrange, an influential Professor at the Angelicum university in Rome, Pius XII's confessor and a co-founder of the Ecole Biblique in Jerusalem, Chenu's Professor, repudiated his pupil's "historicism", and denounced the architects of *la nouvelle théologie* as "modernists" in 1946.[16] The Jesuit paleontologist, Pierre Teilhard de Chardin, took a growing historical consciousness into deeper waters with his flamboyant and mystical reflections on human evolution, the Eucharist, and the Cosmic Christ. Pope Pius XII saw him as an author of unadulterated heresy and he was exiled to New York.[17]

The 1950s: eddies but no big currents

What Congar described as "one of the finest moments in the life of the Church", the 1946-47 renaissance in French Catholicism, challenged Pope Pius XII at a number of levels.[18] The magisterial sweep of a wideranging pastoral letter from Cardinal Suhard, much influenced by the pastoral and theological ferment in the French Church, evoked wrath in Rome in 1947.[19] In February 1948, under the reactionary influence of two powerful Curial figures, Archbishops Alfredo Ottaviani and the Sicilian Ernesto Ruffini, Pius XII began to toy with the idea of holding a second Vatican Council to unify the Church after a divisive world war, and to deal with the unfinished business of the First Council. The Pope wanted to condemn existentialism, and Teilhard, and to have the Blessed Assumption of the Virgin Mary into heaven acclaimed as sacred dogma. Then communism needed an anathema or two, canon law required an update, and the future conduct and direction of "Catholic Action" needed to be controlled. Secret exploratory commissions were set up. But the financial cost of a Council, and the consequences of prolonged absences of busy bishops from their dioceses, were seen as outweighing the advantages of holding one.[20] So nothing came of it. Instead Pius XII settled for a Holy Year and published *Humani Generis* on 12 August 1950 with the help of Garrigou-Lagrange. It was widely read as an attack on the new theology, and as an attempt to regain the high ground from the upstart French bishops and their lamentable brood of theologians. The French Church's outstanding Jesuit and Dominican theologians were purged. Yves Congar was considered sufficiently dangerous to be banned from entering any "House of Formation" where he might "corrupt young seminarians and monks". In exile, sitting on the wall of St John's College opposite Blackfriars Dominican House in Oxford and thus enabling young Dominicans across the road to continue their training uncorrupted, the poor man could be found eating his lunchtime sandwiches.[21] The vision of the Church in *Humanae Generis* was both unreformed and irreformable.

The reformed Catholicism of Le Saulchoir and Fourviere was not a rival quest for Cartesian "pure facts" of faith, unchanging truths expressed in clear formulas, God's own discourse as it were. There could only ever be an analogous grasp of the Divine. For, as St Thomas wrote, "what is known is adapted in the knower to his mode of knowing"; God's mystery was always filtered to the faithful through human words and understanding.[22] Chenu did believe that the concrete history of faith illuminated how this understanding, these words, could become more "numinous and explicit".[23] History and tradition mattered for *la nouvelle théologie* not because it revealed an unchanging number of truths in pat formulas—or failed to as the case may be. Rather Revelation was "first and foremost—and will always be", he declared "the manifestation of a Person, of the Truth in Person... God's invitation to salvation in Christ as handed down in concrete forms from generation to generation within the community of the 'people of God on the way."[24]

Those who opposed this thoroughly Biblical approach were thought-lessly labelled "conservatives". It was plain misleading, though, to call a group clinging to nineteenth-century neo-scholastic propositions and twentieth-century innovations in the Papacy and Church government "conservative". Nor was dubbing as "progressive" those refreshing the Catholic tradition at the wells of St Thomas, early Patristic and Biblical writing, the proponents of returning to early theological sources, *ressourcement,* particularly helpful. This compounded the misunderstand-ing. As did a polarised account of all debate as a stereotyped conflict between "conservatives" and "progressives", for neither of the group-ings were homogeneous.[25]

Theology was an academic pursuit. But to touch liturgy, the Latin Mass, was to touch the heart of Catholicism. To change liturgy, to think historically about its development, was to suggest that change was possible throughout the body of the Church.

The quest for *ressourcement* was greatly reinforced by the historical study of Catholic worship, liturgical practice, associated with a Ger-man school of which the Benedictine Odo Casel was the best known. An Anglican monk, Dom Gregory Dix, published his study of the his-tory of the Mass in 1943, as pastoral centres for liturgy were being founded in Paris and Trier. The Austrian Jesuit Josef Jungmann's *The Early Liturgy,* arising out of lectures given in Notre Dame, Indiana in 1949, established him also as a leading liturgist with his emphasis on the "kerygmatic" theology embedded in the Mass. *On the Spirit of the Liturgy* by the future mentor of Cardinal Joseph Ratzinger, Romano Guardini, was much read and put the Eucharist at the heart of spiritual life. The intention of the liturgical movement was plainly not relativism but an attempt to reinvigorate worship and reinstate its role as a form of perennial catechesis.[26]

The *Institut Supérieur de Liturgie,* founded in Paris in 1956, the litur-gical and catechetical centres in Camby, Vietnam, the *Centro di Azi-one Liturgica* in Italy, the Missionary Liturgical Congress in Nijmegen in 1959, and the bishops' conference of the Congo which produced a detailed programme of liturgical reform in 1961, were among several meetings and bodies around the world bringing liturgical change to the fore prior to the Council. Correspondingly the catechetical movement drew on Biblical studies, the most notable meeting being the Eichstatt Catechetical Study Week of 1960 led by the Jesuit expert Father Johannes Hofinger whose base, in the first intimations of a genuinely global Church, was the East Asian Pastoral Institute in Manila.

The minority Rites of the Middle Eastern Churches were often over-looked or forgotten. For the vast majority of Catholics the obligatory Latin Mass on Sunday and Holy Days was the core of their identity as a worshipping community, their primary encounter with the mystery of their faith, and with the Church, the *fons et origo* of their religious ex-perience. The Mass was part of a richer tapestry of ritual and celebra-tion involving uniquely Catholic forms of worship inside and outside the church building, such as exposition and veneration of the Blessed Sacrament, Stations of the Cross, processions with statues, the Corpus Christi procession, prayers at grottoes and shrines, Holy Water sprin-klings, lighting candles and kissing crucifixes, scapulars and spiritual bouquets, and a plethora of private prayerful devotions at home, accre-tions of many centuries of popular yet formally sanctioned piety. Most notably saying the Rosary was strongly promoted in the 1950s.

The other great pre-conciliar contribution of Jesuit scholarship came out of Germany and was led by Karl Rahner, Joseph Ratzinger and Hans Urs von Balthasar. Karl Rahner emerged as a prolific scholar of international repute in the 1950s. Well established at the University of Innsbruck as professor of dogmatic theology from 1948 until the 1964, he set about three main tasks. Each was to prove of great impor-tance for the future Council. Rahner placed Christology at the centre of theology, tried to make theological debate accessible to the general public, and, seeing a "transcendental foundation in people's search for self-realisation", tried to establish a Christian anthropology of Grace. To do so he introduced some of the language of Martin Heidegger's philosophy—with whom he had studied in Freiburg—and the insights of historical theology, into a Catholic intellectual scene dominated by neo-scholasticism.[27]

Rahner undertook forensic theological investigations and asked questions—not ducking the hardest, the evolutionary origins of human-kind—creating a refreshing climate of exploratory work in progress, rather than magisterial proclamation. His theological work, as the Do-minican Mark Schoof puts it, was of "higher specific gravity" than that of his French contemporaries; which meant, amongst other things, that Rahner wrote very long sentences.[28] Moreover he was settled in an Austrian university, outside Rome's target zone of the French Church, and had the support of Cardinal Julius Döpfner, Archbishop of Munich and President of the German Bishops' Conference. His position as editor of the encyclopedia *Lexikon für Theologie und Kirche* put him in an exceptional position to influence the thinking of the powerful German Church. A whole new second front exploring modernity was allowed to flourish relatively freely by the Vatican.

While the encyclical *Humanae Generis* checked what might have become a powerful current of historical theology in the Church, it did not stop Biblical and liturgical scholarship developing apace in the 1950s. Rahner published and gained acclaim and a large following of students. His writing packaged his thinking in protective and refined subordinate clauses that could not readily be turned into a series of simplistic, refutable propositions. But he was cordially mistrusted in Rome, not least because he was among the first serious critics to describe the Church as "sinful" in its conduct during the Third Reich, an assertion that highlighted the omissions and vulnerability of Pius XII.[29]

Humanae Generis did not stop the thinking of silenced theologians, or those out of favour, crossing the Atlantic. Away from the Vatican, the premise of intellectual freedom in democratic cultures played its part. Excerpts of works frowned on in Rome were translated into English. Several were included between 1953-1964 in the monthly bulletins of the Sister Formation Conference (SFC) in the USA, and used in renewal courses for Women Religious.

The SFC was formed after Pius XII's Congresses for Religious in Rome, called to promote minor reforms in training. These were long overdue. Under the 1918 Code of Canon Law, the model of Religious life was based on enclosure, a "self-sufficient community cut off from the world outside", a microcosm of the Church as *societas perfecta*. Nuns were supposed to be either contemplative or, if they served the Catholic community, to keep "partial enclosure". Almost none had advanced theology training. Some 68,000 women passed through these SFC formation courses bringing to their high school and college teaching elements of *la nouvelle théologie*. Some became the best educated nuns in the world, with doctorates in social sciences, psychology and theology. Concerned by the Cuban revolution and the possibility of other Marxist advances in Latin America, the Vatican urged the North American bishops in 1959 to respond to the pastoral problems of socio-economic deprivation in the south of the continent. In 1963, the SFC was invited to initiate a similar Sister Formation Conference for Latin America, widening the penetration of the writings of Chenu, Congar, Maritain and the Toronto based philosopher, Etienne Gilson. They later worked with Religious in India and Africa.[30]

Yet, closer to Rome in Europe, the current of *la nouvelle théologie* was forced into something akin to an underground stream. In the words of Yves Congar, who was released from the German prison of Colditz in 1945: " from the beginning of 1947 to the end of 1956 I knew nothing from [Rome] but an uninterrupted series of denunciations, warnings, restrictive and discriminatory measures and mistrustful interventions". Indeed the mid-1950s saw three French Dominican Provincials dismissed. Cardinal Giuseppe Pizzardo, Secretary of the Holy Office, ordered Emmanuel Suarez, the Master-General of the Dominicans, to "root out indiscipline"; Chenu and Congar had to be dealt with "to save the Order".[31]

Rome was now working in the context of strong Catholic political leadership in Europe, De Gasperi in Italy, Adenauer in Germany, Bidault and Schumann in France. Christian Democracy flourished. Indeed its core Catholic vision had provided the motivation and intellectual architecture of the post-war European project. But, far from this relaxing Vatican minds and central control, or creating tolerance for critiques of post-Tridentine theology and spirituality, Rome remained as uncompromising as ever. The Vatican now condemned what it called "opinions" rather than "errors", but the result was much the same. In 1954, Monsignor Giovanni Battista Montini, the future Pope Paul VI, considered "soft" on several issues, was summarily moved from his post in the Secretariat of State and sent to Milan as Archbishop.[32] In retrospect this resembles nothing less than the authoritarianism of a dying regime, a Brezhnev era prior to the new Gorbachev; at the time it seemed like an antediluvian Church in virtual stasis behaving with predictable defensiveness.

The Roman World-Church

There was no brake on the Church's growth and expansion. The Holy Year of 1950 brought a wave of pilgrims to Rome: 570,000—non-Italian Europeans came, 46,000 North Americans, 16,000 Latin Americans, 6,400 Africans, 3,460 Asians and 1,350 from "Oceania", many from Australia.[33] The figures give a remarkably good snapshot of how,

29

overall, the Church *seemed* to be: a vast organisation—soon to reach 500 million members—with its centre of gravity in Europe and subsidiary and less important communities worldwide. But reality was more complex. Catholicism was becoming international and global. The flow of ideas was no longer simply Rome broadcasting *ex cathedra* to the Catholic world, but the beginnings of a more interactive, though embryonic, network with nodes concerned with liturgy, biblical studies, catechesis, ecumenism and *nouvelle théologie*.

What the relative number of pilgrims from different parts of the world does not tell us is how the centre of gravity of the Catholic Church was about to shift. And correspondingly nothing about the degree to which the Church was still centralised with power vested in a bureaucracy led by the cardinals, congregations and consistories in Rome. Or to put it another way, the degree to which the power and perceptions of the Catholic Church were Eurocentric. The figures did not, of course, reflect how much local Churches were indigenised and had bishops of their own. Moreover, travel costs and other practical difficulties, and differences in national wealth in each region, skewed attendance in Rome.

The African continent, six years away from the independence of Ghana and a wave of decolonisation around the continent, had a fast growing Church but with an overwhelmingly European Church leadership. The only black bishop was Joseph Kiwanuka who had been vicar-apostolic of Masaka in Uganda for eleven years and was consecrated in Rome in 1939.[34] He was a product of a Catholic community dating back to the Church of the Uganda Martyrs. Africa was still thought of as "the missions" and fell under the authority of the Sacred Congregation for the Propagation of the Faith in the Vatican. Less than 15% of the clergy, some 800 priests, were Africans; the rest were missionaries. It offered an uncomfortable parallel with colonial rule.

On the other hand, China, where six indigenous bishops were appointed in 1926 had a flourishing Asian Church. Before the impact of the Communist takeover was felt in 1951—when the government required all contact with the Vatican to be severed—there were 3 million Catholics led by thirty-five Chinese bishops out of a total of 146 and 2,500 Chinese priests out of a total of 5,500. Fu Jen, the international Catholic University in Beijing, was closed but restarted in Taipei in Taiwan with Archbishop Yu Pin as director. This level of indigenisation compared well with that of the Latin American Church; on the "Catholic" continent about half the clergy were still missionaries.

But even to consider the Church on a continental, or sub-Saharan Africa scale neglects the enormous differences between countries and dioceses, the lack of phones and the vast distances that still separated them, overcome only by hedge-hopping aircraft for those that could afford it. Thanks to Katigondo Seminary in Uganda, Bishop Kiwanuka's Masaka diocese was soon entirely African-run with African Sisters, priests and brothers, parish councils with lay participation and a steady stream of vocations to the priesthood. And there were thriving dioceses in Tanganyika, Rwanda, Burundi and the eastern region of Nigeria with strong contingents of African priests and Sisters. But the Congo was still a Belgian enclave with more than 3,000 missionaries, priests, Sisters and Brothers, almost all Belgian, and in this vast territory only some 300 African priests and Sisters. Angola and Mozambique were even more an extension of the national heartland with Portuguese secular priests serving Portuguese settlers and negligible numbers of African priests and Sisters. As a goodwill gesture to Portugal after the signing in 1940 of a Concordat with the fascist regime of Salazar, the Vatican had appointed Africa's only Cardinal, the Portuguese Archbishop of Lourenço Marques, Clemente Teodosio de Gouveia.[35]

So when the two Apostolic Delegates for Africa, Rome's men for East and West Africa, the missionary bishop, Archbishop Marcel Lefebvre of Dakar later to form a schismatic Church and Archbishop David Mathew—who in 1960 chose Laurean Rugambwa as the first African Cardinal—brought their 6,400 pilgrims to Rome in 1950, it was the first time that the vast majority of the travellers from Africa would ever have met. The international Church they encountered was recognisably familiar even if the grand surroundings of ecclesiastical Rome were very different from the parish church back home.

Whatever his professed intentions, Pope Pius XII's 70-strong College of Cardinals and the Roman Curia continued to be dominated by Italians. When his successor Angelo Giuseppe Roncalli, the son of peasant farmers from Bergamo, was elected Pope John XXIII, his first consistory increased the numbers of Cardinals and included the first of Archbishop Mathew's African appointees, Laurean Rugambwa, Archbishop of Dar-es-Salaam, Tanzania, with Japan, Philippines and Mexico also getting their first Cardinals. The future Pope Paul VI, Giovanni Battista Montini, John's friend and ally from Milan, was top of his list.

Looked at from the perspective of its lay membership, the Roman Catholic Church was at the same time international, European and Italian. But from the perspective of its Church hierarchy, and particularly its centralised direction from the Roman Curia, it was formidably and almost exclusively Italian and European. Moreover much of the political life and spirit of clerical Rome was pre-occupied with Italian rather than global politics. The post-war slings and arrows of a corrupt Christian Democracy, in the context of the Church's major pre-occupations, the struggle against Communism and the need to control Catholic lay movements, figured large. While Catholics and Communists in resistance movements had shared a common struggle in Nazi-occupied Europe, their strategic agendas differed, and there had been little love lost. After the liberation of Rome, Italian Communist partisans in Emilia killed scores of priests. The enemies were at the gates. With the lights going out in Eastern Europe and the Pope in depression and panic, the Vatican supported a massive Christian Democrat mobilisation during the 1948 Italian elections. In 1952, frightened that Togliatti's Communists would come to power through municipal elections, Pius XII unsuccessfully tried to push the Italian Christian Democrats, replete with dollars, to ally with the neo-fascists to form a right-wing bloc.[36]

In the early 1950s, as CIA money poured clandestinely into the coffers of anti-Communist political parties abroad, Senator Joseph McCarthy launched his witchhunt against Communist infiltration in the USA, supported by Cardinal Francis Spellman of New York and many clergy. After the war, the major centres of Catholicism under Communism, in Czechoslovakia, Hungary, and Croatia, as well as in Soviet Lithuania, and to a lesser degree the powerful Church in Poland, suffered grievously. Many priests spent years—some decades—in prison, or worse, were killed; by 1955 some 5,000 priests and 10,000 nuns had been imprisoned or otherwise restricted in Eastern Europe alone. But none of these countries experienced the massive and overwhelming losses and virtual public extinction experienced in Albania and the Soviet Union, nor the problematic creation of a "Catholic Patriotic Association" and severance with Rome as in China. The outbreak of the Korean War in 1950 left American missionaries, and others by association, as enemy aliens in China and North Korea, and local Catholics as "imperialist collaborators" sent to forced labour camps. Sometimes willingly, sometimes not, the Church was in the front line.[37]

The foliage and texture of the newly planted Churches in Africa, Asia and "Oceania", now rooted and growing strongly, were at least superficially European—more western than eastern—and Italianate, whether the faces of its Church leaders were black, brown or white. The Church was badly placed therefore to gauge the significance of anti-colonialism and "Third World" nationalism. The Vatican, too financially dependent on the Italian state for its own good, supported the invasion of Abyssinia; likewise European clergy in the African Portuguese territories and in the Belgian Congo were very close to the colonial authorities whose nationality they shared. In July 1950 Pope Pius XII extended his general excommunication of Catholics supporting Communists to include those working with Communists in anti-colonial movements. In 1956 Ermelinda, the mother of Nobel Prize winner Bishop Carlos Filipe Belo, prayed on the little island of Timor in the Indonesian archipelago for the people of Hungary; the Pope had asked for prayers and the request had been passed on by the missionaries. Whether in Rhodesia or East Timor, in the eyes of Rome, anti-colonialism was suspect, a possible handmaid of Communism, and Communism was the common enemy of the universal Church.[38]

An important element of the local Church leadership shared the political preoccupations of their European fellow bishops. They feared that anti-colonialism was opening the gates to the Trojan Horse of Communism, so Catholic reactions to anti-colonial nationalism were ambiguous and divided. The local political context might have been expected to dominate the theology coming out of Africa, but it was rarely directly reflected in theological and ethical thinking. South Africa in the context of apartheid, and in the person of Archbishop Hurley, was an exception, though he never raised the issue at the Council. Instead, in the place of a political theology emerged questions of culture, Africanisation, and a quest for an authentically black expression of Christianity as the principal themes for theologians.

It was only in 1957 in *Fidei Donum* that the rights of colonised people to their Independence were given some support, though Benedict XV, some forty years earlier, had foreseen many of the problems of the African and Asian Churches in a post-colonial world.[39] The English Cardinal, Arthur Hinsley, in the 1930s saw the importance of Catholic education in the creation of an African Catholic elite capable of assuming government functions in the British colonies, but the Papacy was slow to think through the full implications of decolonisation beyond developing an indigenous priesthood. Pius XII built new seminaries in Rome to make sure that the best of this clergy, the new indigenous clerical elites, toed the theological line, and he promoted them. Meanwhile it was mission elites, including those of the Catholic Church, who formed the leadership of the nationalist movements.

The superiors-general and heads of the missionary provinces and Religious Orders, most notably in Africa, were forces for globalisation in their own right. The first international Congress of Religious met in Rome in 1950 with renewal as its theme. Some of the Mission Orders had considerable power and personnel, so that many of the new indigenous clergy sought emancipation from missionary tutelage through appeals to the Vatican. If some of the new African bishops were more Roman than Rome, it was often because this stance brought them powerful allies in their dealings with the missionaries in their dioceses. The different Missionary Societies and Orders, though often adopting different strategies shared much in common culturally. They built the same kind of mission buildings in East Timor as in East and Central Africa; they brought with them from Europe and North America much the same devotions, theological eddies and minor currents, and a pervasive clericalism, and passed it on to men and women Religious, priests and laity from a different culture. The educational gap between priest and laity in Africa was significantly bigger than in Europe. The missionaries who became seminary teachers trained indigenous clergy in the same old curriculum dominated by the neo-scholasticism they had received themselves in pre-war Europe, and tried to replicate a Church they had left behind.

But at village level the cultural transmission belt from the European Church passed through indigenous catechists who translated the imported Europeanised Faith—both linguistically and culturally—into something more meaningful and rooted in their communities. The local catechist was the main agent of inculturation, although by the 1950s policy dictated that the catechist was beginning to play second fiddle to the school teacher. And at the same time many of the missionaries, particularly new ones, were realising the importance of local cultures for effective evangelisation. This growing cultural sensitivity was also slowly developing in Latin America (and is discussed in Chapter Nine) though Mayan Indian culture had a surprisingly hard struggle before it was taken seriously as integral to faith.

The Catholic Church was changing, obviously in the development of local indigenous clergies, subtly in other ways, but rapidly throughout much of the underdeveloped world, save the Middle East. Yet its heart in Rome was gathering more power to itself. An entrenched centralisation, the continuing balance of power favouring Europe, and the historic role of the French Church, are the backdrop to the tiny schools of thought, in Le Saulchior and Fourvière, driving what became the future theological agenda of the Second Vatican Council. Big ideas have a strange way of emerging from small and apparently insignificant places when the conditions are right. The Jerusalem of Jesus the Nazarene, hardly the throbbing heart of the Roman Empire, is a case in point.

The struggles of a young Cardinal Rugambwa in Tanzania or a Bishop Stanislas Lokuang of Tainan, in Taiwan, or even a Bishop Helder Camara in the poverty-stricken north-east of Brazil, their problems in building their local Churches and preaching the Gospel were real and important, but their stories were not to form the main narrative of the Council's proceedings. Nor could they have done. The first generation of indigenous Archbishops and Cardinals in the South were not required to demonstrate assertiveness, creativity and innovation but piety, obedience, and conformity—not necessarily in that order. Like all bureaucracies the Vatican dowsed youthful fires in the belly with urbane and sophisticated distaste and disparagement. Achieving the transition from a missionary to an indigenous Church required a safe pair of hands. Only a few slipped through the vetting to go on, with prayer book in hand, a closeness to the people, and great vision, to champion the needs of an impoverished "Third World" Church, a Church of the Poor.

In the mid-1950s a number of Francophone African priests were training in Rome. Jean Zoa from Cameroon, Vincent Mulago from Congo, Bernardin Gantin from Dahomey, Robert Dosseh from Togo and the Tutsi intellectual, Alexis Kagame from Rwanda, attracted others. Together they began to address and to analyse the relationship between African religion and culture and the Gospel. They produced a challenging book, *Des Prêtres Noirs s'intérrogent*, in 1956. It certainly did not go unnoticed, but tellingly it did not draw down the kind of censure reserved for challenges from the French Church. Unlike the

Latin Americans studying abroad they were not absorbing "*la nouvelle théologie*" at source.[40] A similar Anglophone grouping developed around the *African Ecclesiastical Review* that began publishing from 1959 at Katigondo seminary in Uganda, the centre from which the catechetical movement was launched for Africa five years later.[41]

With some notable exceptions the leaders of the young African Church were neither influential in setting the agenda for the Council nor, with the exception of the Decree of Missionary activity of the Church, in influencing its outcome. In this they were no different from the rest of the representation from the developing world who came to Rome not knowing what to expect, many wondering if they would have enough money to survive beyond the First Session.[42] The Churches of the Middle East in communion with Rome were different. Their Patriarchs spoke with the authority of ancient and venerable Churches. They particularly dominated the debate about the Church's relationship with Jews and Muslims. Otherwise the Council illustrated how Eurocentric, and North American was the thinking, and funding, of the Catholic Church.

Inside the Church of Pius XII

That the Church of Pius XII was nurturing something more than missionary expansion, planting of new Churches around the world, and very minor reforms was notable only in hindsight. Indeed there is a whiff of Whig history in focusing on the rise of *la nouvelle théologie* from the 1930s to the 1950s as the intimation of great change. Nobody at the time knew where it was all heading, or had such a firm sense of a growing *movement* of theologians. Moreover, there were important differences between the theologians later lumped together as a vanguard, and not all were "progressive" about the same things.[43]

One of the perennial features of Catholic thought is that key thinkers have not necessarily combined "liberal " views about society with "liberal" views about doctrine and Church order. Nor have "conservatives", who might be vehement about a particular understanding of the Papacy deemed "conservative"—though usually some recent innovation—been necessarily politically conservative. Some have had radical views about Christianising society. Nor, as their political consciousness or theological insights have grown and developed, have their views remained static. Cardinal Pierre Gerlier of Lyons, who worked with the "Third World" group in the Council, supported the Vichy regime in wartime France.[44] The courageous anti-apartheid champion, Archbishop Denis Hurley had been on the side of Franco, "protector of the clergy", in the Spanish civil war, and the no less saintly Dom Helder Camara Pessoa, later Archbishop of Olinda Recife and champion of the Church of the Poor in North East Brazil, had been one of the founders of the *October Legion,* a Brazilian "integralist"—fascist—organisation.[45]

The Spanish civil war was important in shaping Catholics' political views. But the massive backdrop of the Soviet Union where all religious instruction was banned in 1929, active atheism promoted, and some 200,000 Russian Orthodox nuns, priests and monks killed, was the primary determinant in forming political preferences. Like so many other seminarians in the late 1920s and 1930s, Dom Helder and Denis Hurley were young, inexperienced swimmers in the intellectual eddies of the time. Fascist thought entered the seminaries in the guise of a corporatist mediaevalism, a utopian refuge from class struggle and Communism. The publication of the Papal encyclical *Quadragesimo Anno* in 1931 did nothing to divert the flight from Communism away from this dangerous line of thought. An unhealthy flirtation with Fascism among some European Catholic intellectuals, and some ugly weaving and ducking undertaken in the short-term temporal interests of the Church with Mussolini, incurred hefty political costs, and left a bitter aftertaste.

Church leaders from around the world were at liberty to join in European theological debates, such as they were, but generally did not—unless this impinged on the particular problems that they faced at home. Political contexts varied enormously as did, correspondingly, the relevance of what Rome was saying. Joining in was no simple matter. There was no forum for theological debate besides books, and the Catholic universities, and these were controlled by the Vatican's fiercely defensive Holy Office, later to be called the Sacred Congregation for the Doctrine of the Faith.

Women Religious, though highly controlled, were assumed to be "safe" since theologically mute. But in the USA the Sister Formation Conference created a generation of Sisters who rapidly became both theologically and sociologically "literate". Straining at the leash of enclosure, and other canonical constraints on their freedom of movement and action, they avidly read the Belgian Cardinal Joseph Suenens' *The Nun in the World: Religious and the Apostolate*—translated into English in 1963. They shared their experience with missionary Sisters around the world. Backed by the Franciscan Cardinal Juan Landázuri, at the Catholic University of Lima in Peru, US Sisters set up Regina Mundi, a high-powered centre to prepare women and Sisters for university entrance, and to disseminate the thinking of the Council from 1963 to 1967. Many went on to engage with contemporary social issues most notably the civil rights movement and racial justice through the National Catholic Conference for Interracial Justice, and later, feminism and women's role in the Church. Travelling Workshops on race relations led by "Sister-Professors" in mini-vans were far from the stereotype of the "Good Sisters" tidied away in the cloister, or safely labouring in parochial schools. Their theological vision remained largely unchallenging to bishops and Rome. The theological rationale for working with the poor in inner city missions was a concept of renewed community, the desire to break down divisions in society, drawn from Pius XII's 1943 encyclical *Mystici Corporis Christi*, the Church understood as the Mystical Body of Christ.[46]

The Catholic bishops of the USA, with a fast growing flock of 26 million Catholics, and steady post-war vocations to the Religious life, might have been expected to exert the kind of influence in the Council that their country did in world affairs. This was not so. The USA was a strongly Protestant country. In 1951 President Truman, for example, was unable to get the appointment of a US ambassador to the Vatican through Congress. The US bishops had to contend with antiquated rhetoric from the Roman Curia opposing separation of Church and State, a key foundation of a revered constitution, along with opposition to freedom of conscience under the old rubric of "error has no rights"—not unlike some Islamic "integralism" today. Defeating these ideas was the US bishops' most important Council contribution. They were guaranteed to alienate the strongly Protestant Christian US public and encourage them to see Catholics as perfidious universalists with no allegiance to the flag promoting a mediaeval understanding of a Catholic State. So much so that John F. Kennedy spent time finessing his Catholicism in his 1960 campaign in order—only just—to capture the Presidency. Following the lead of the illustrious Cardinal Spellman, the strongest card Kennedy had to be play was a staunch Catholic anti-Communism.[47]

If Rome was relatively indifferent to the North American predicament, and the US bishops had difficulty in navigating their way around the Curia—they contrived to present a robust "country boys come to town" image in Rome—how much more was this going to be the case for the less wealthy Latin Americans? They had been forced to abandon the integration of Church and State only in the 1930s after inroads from Liberalism. Here were representatives of a continent-wide Catholic culture dating from the time of the *conquistadores* whose conquests provoked the great sixteenth-century debates on natural rights which reverberated around Europe. They ought to have been taken seriously. But Latin America was a heterogeneous set of nation states, from the rural backwaters of central America to urbanised, industrialised Brazil, from the large Mayan communities of Bolivia, Peru and Guatemala, to the *ladino* and Europeanised cities of Chile and Argentina, from the low mass attendance of Cuba and Honduras to the crowded churches of Colombia. And all these disparate Catholic communities were a long way away from Rome.

Monsignor Giovanni Montini, then second in command at the Vatican Secretariat of State, encouraged the setting up of new national coordinating structures, the Bishops' Conferences, and seemed to welcome the local insights that grew out of them. Bishop Helder Camara led the Brazilian Episcopal Conference from its inception in 1952 until 1964. The continent-wide regional conference, CELAM (*Consejo Episcopal Latinamericano*), though strongly influenced by the Chilean bishops, set up its general secretariat in Bogotá, Colombia, in September 1955. It was later to be a key player in the spreading of liberation theology and the promotion of a universal "option for the Poor". The work of CELAM slowly generated a Latin American identity amongst its member bishops, and strengthened Dom Helder Camara's status and contribution to the Council. He was the dynamic force alongside the ageing Cardinal Gerlier in the Council's offstage "Third World group".

What characterised Catholic sentiment in Latin America, particularly in Brazil and Chile, was the convergence of a felt need for change in both Church and Society. The economic growth of the 1940s was causing rapid urbanisation. Industrialisation in Brazil created consistent and phenomenal growth of over 5% annually but was unable to draw into employment the large number of urban migrants. Dangerous divisions were growing up within society. The growth of radical rural

39

movements such as the *ligas camponesas*, the Brazilian peasant leagues, and the accompanying rise of Marxist thinking, alerted the Church that something needed to be done.[48] Christian Democracy might look like a solution but it could not integrate societies polarised between rich and poor, and it did not, for a variety of reasons, get off the ground in Brazil and Argentina. The political consequences for human rights of the emergent rule of the oligarchs and military dictatorships, arising out of underlying socio-economic change, were to be dire.

The pastoral letters and statements of the Brazilian bishops of the north-eastern dioceses throughout the 1950s left no doubt that they saw poverty as a challenging *religious* problem. "For man, as a union of body and soul, the relationship between material and spiritual questions is constant," they underlined.[49] The two went together. The Church placed "itself on the side of the downtrodden, to co-operate with them in the task of rehabilitation and redemption," they proclaimed.[50] And note this was not a call for charity, nor for the Catholic corporal acts of mercy, but for an active engagement in economic, social and political transformation, or—the key word was not long in appearing—"liberation".

This awareness of injustice and poverty as urgent problems grew out of two related processes: the transformation of Catholic Action in Brazil under the influence of the Cardijn methodology of see-judge-act (see above, p.21) and Church leaders' experience of the plight of rural workers in their dioceses. Here is Dom Inocencio Engelke, the Bishop of Campanha, Minas Gerais, writing on the need for rural reforms in 1950: "Do the shacks in which they live merit the names homes? Is the food they eat really nourishment? Can the rags they wear be called clothing? Can their unhealthy vegetative existence, without expectations, vision and ideas, be called living?"[51] Dom Helder Camara took this experience into CELAM and defined for the Latin American Church its implications. "The Church should denounce our collective sin—the unjust and stagnant structures—not as someone who judges from the outside, but as someone who accepts a share of the guilt. She must be bold enough to identify with the past and thus feel herself more responsible for the present and the future."[52]

This was not an insight that preoccupied the Europeans in the midst of the "golden" 1950s post-war boom, and nor did it touch Africa and Asia in quite the same way. Here the urgent preoccupation was material and spiritual decolonisation, an imposed cultural uniformity and, not least as an aggravating factor, the financial dependence of the local Churches that left parishes more outposts of receding Empire than centres of a self-supporting African or Asian Church.

At the end of the second century, St Irenaeus of Lyons had spoken evocatively about the four winds from south, north, east and west that formed the Catholic wind blowing through, in and from the Church. But the globalisation of the Church was still far from being realised. To quote Karl Rahner, the Council was "in a rudimentary form still groping for identity, the Church's first official self-actualisation as a World Church". Here the emphasis should be put on "rudimentary".[53] Rahner was presenting one of the four faces of the Roman Catholic Church with which this book started, the Church described in theology, a Church of intent, the *terminus ad quem*. There was a long way to go before there was a full metamorphosis into a real World Church, as diversity in universality, as a network of salvation rather than a centre with lines out into a distant periphery.

To become a global Church required a new enabling language to define its structure. And for that to occur, it would take the death of Pius XII, a Pope who had faced the unprecedented horrors of totalitarianism and in retrospect—that harshest of judges—had been found wanting. In his 1933 Concordat with Hitler, he had cut the ground from under the German Church.[54] An unambiguous, clear, public denunciation of the Nazi Holocaust of the Jews, commensurate with the significance for humanity of the most terrible genocide in human history, had not been uttered. At all levels in the Church there had been Catholic collaborators and guilty bystanders to Nazi tyranny.

Yet, from parish priests and parishoners to bishops and Cardinals, the Church did speak out against National Socialism—and several suffered as a result. But the number who did so was not impressive. The Austrian Frans Jaegerstetter, a family man of deep piety from the Diocese of Linz, for reasons of conscience went to the guillotine in Brandenburg as a war resister. The Catholic chaplain who accompanied him to the door of the execution chamber said that he had met a saint. Jaegerstetter was beatified in 2008. The Dutch bishops in May 1943 publicly banned Catholic police from joining in hunting down Jews; but to no avail; 80% of the Jewish population was deported to death camps, a greater percentage than in the other Western occupied territories. Many Catholics hid Jews; papal nuncios helped hundreds of thousands to escape. Some 1,000 Catholic priests died in Dachau concentration camp alone, sharing the plight of millions of the innocent.[55]

Catholics ardently defended Pius XII as peacemaker and friend of the Jews and just as passionately berated him as complicit in the Shoah. The implications of these terrible years for the theology and direction of Catholicism were as contested as the facts and the judgements based upon them. The Holocaust questioned the integrity of the European Church, particularly its leaders, and called in question its fundamental beliefs.

Pius XII shifted the Church away from its self-image as a "perfect society", not in the above sense but understood as a self-sufficient body with all the means to achieve its end. The more flexible image of "Mystical Body" opened up possibilities that were to be seized at the Council. He encouraged biblical scholarship up to a point. He endorsed minor liturgical reforms in 1946 (*Mediator Dei*), re-introducing the permanent diaconate and the Easter Vigil liturgy, easing the fast before Catholics received communion and allowing evening masses, but blocked the vernacular and concelebration of the Eucharist at the 1956 Pastoral Liturgical Congress in Assisi controlled by the Roman Congregation of Rites. He gave lukewarm support to ecumenical contacts in *Ecclesia Catholica,* to secular institutes for lay spirituality and the lay apostolate—beyond that of the Legion of Mary—most notably through the World Congresses of the Laity in 1951 and 1957, and sought minor reforms in Religious life. He used radio to great effect, broadcasting during the war on the "rights of persons", but failed to endorse clearly the UN Declaration of Human Rights, already ten years old when he died. Nor did the rights of persons extend to the worker priest movement that he hobbled and curbed when priests became more involved in trades union leadership.

"We who were brought up in the Church of Pius XII", wrote Cambridge Professor Nicholas Lash, no admirer of an overblown centralised papacy, " know that it was a world neither of tranquil certainties and quiet obedience disrupted by dissent, nor a dark place of clerical oppression from which the Council set us free."[56] Pope Pius XII should not be caricatured as the motionless still centre of a motionless Church. There was nothing motionless about the mission Church, the radical pacifist Dorothy Day and her Catholic Worker movement in the USA, nor the indefatigable Abbé Pierre and his Emmaus communities of *chiffoniers* in France, none of which could be described as operating below the clerical radar. Nor was Pius XII's "obsessive anti-Communism" without justification. He had even personally been held at gunpoint by a detachment of the Bavarian Red Guard during the abortive Bavarian Soviet Republic of 1919. Arguably however the Holy Office decree of 1 July 1949, declaring Catholics who "profess, defend and propagate" communism "apostates", and his special prayer services "to save the world from Communism", had many of the immediate negative consequences for the Church that he feared would stem from a forthright denunciation of the Holocaust.[57]

The Church all around was slowly changing from below. Yet Pius XII never moved into a theology of life in all its historicity beyond what a reforming young German theologian and the future Pope Benedict XVI, Joseph Ratzinger, called "encyclical theology"—some twenty large volumes of it, endless allocutions and writings about everything and nothing.[58] A fastidious and ethereal Pope, whose oddities have been charitably interpreted as holiness, he remained steadfast and uncompromising on the truths of the faith to the end, leaving the intellectual immobilism of the Roman Curia largely untouched. Within three months of his death the Church was on the move again. In the words of the Council historian, Giuseppe Alberigo: "A season of Catholicism in which liberating ferments had been in constant danger of being suffocated by a uniformity inspired more by ideology than by the gospel" was ending.

3

THE VATICAN COUNCIL
EARLY STAGES

Cardinal Angelo Roncalli, Patriarch of Venice, was elected Pope John XXIII on 28 October 1958, nineteen days after the death of Pius XII, and after eleven ballots of the assembled cardinals. A warm, gentle and charismatic leader, he had a gift for improvisation stemming from a holy trust in the future, and a freedom of spirit that shone out of a rigidly traditional spiritual formation. All manner of things would be well. He was far from naïve; he knew the opposition that awaited any Pope who allowed "a thousand flowers to bloom". He was seen, even by many of his supporters, as a stop-gap. Giovanni Battista Montini, Archbishop of Milan, still had to be made a cardinal. Then he might be elected Pope.[1] From a peasant background, with a solid spirituality and formation, Angelo Roncalli would be a safe pair of hands in the interim. Little did they know.

John XXIII faced a daunting task. The First Vatican Council had given the Pope powers akin to those of an absolute monarch. But his directions required people to carry them out. And those people ran the Vatican. They were an introverted and sclerotic bureaucracy, the Roman Curia. However pious and well-meaning, in the words of the future Pope Benedict XVI, Joseph Ratzinger, their attitude to change was an "almost neurotic denial of all that was new".[2] Moreover, during the 1950s the Church did not apparently have very much of relevance to say to the world outside, *ad extra*—at least no one paid much attention—nor much capacity for internal reform, *ad intra*, the two categories of concern within an emerging framework for the Second

Vatican Council.[3] To a great degree it was Pope John's faith and trust that generated that capacity, or at least acted as its starter-motor.

The hesitations before John XXIII's election reflected the indecision of the Catholic Church's leadership. There was no consensus about how they understood the Church and what needed to be done. A priority for some was to improve relationships with the "Eastern" Churches, the Orthodox family. Another contender for the Papacy had been Cardinal Gregorio Agagianian, as the name indicated an Armenian, though one thoroughly Romanised after many years living in the Vatican. John himself had been for nine years, from 1935 to 1944, an Apostolic Visitor and Delegate in Bulgaria, and with his additional experience in Istanbul and Athens fulfilled the Orthodox requirement, and much more. More important, as the Italian National Director for the Society for the Propagation of the Faith, he had a keen sense of colonialism coming to an end and the needs of the Church around the world. Latin America was of particular concern, in need of "rehabilitation". Once Pope, he called for 10 per cent of the Church's mission personnel to be pledged to the continent's renewal, and set up a Pontifical Commission for Latin America, diverting funds and rapidly increasing the number of dioceses and bishops. The worry was Communist and Protestant encroachment. Yet he shared the wider concern for greater Christian Unity, and was probably aware of the Orthodox Patriarch of Constantinople, Athenagoras' proposal in the early 1950s for a "Pan-Orthodox" assembly based on their conciliar pattern called *sobornost*. On 29 January 1959 the world learnt that Pope John XXIII was summoning a General Council of the Church. There was also to be a Roman Synod of bishops to discuss Church life in Rome, and an *aggiornamento*, updating, of the Church's Code of Canon Law.[4]

According to his private secretary, Monsignor Loris Capovilla, no stranger to presentation and spin, the Pope was talking about holding a Council within two days of his election. As a Church historian John XXIII enjoyed his new access to the Vatican archives and had been browsing there on 2 November 1958, apparently looking up the documentation generated by Pius XII's transient interest in a Council during the period 1948-1951.[5] The new Pope's meetings with the Cardinals departing Rome after the electoral conclave would have given him indications of the range of problems confronting the wider Church. Most noticeably the discussions offered the non-Romans an opportunity to express their dislike of the Curia's intrusive oversight of the local Churches around the world. They were looking for support and under-standing, not finger-wagging. By 8 January 1959 the Pope had prob-ably taken the decision that a Council should be held. He consulted his Secretary of State, Cardinal Domenico Tardini, with no certainty of finding support, on 20 January.[6] Calling a Council was an act of spiritual discernment by a holy man not, as was later made out by its opponents, the rash action of a simple soul, a rustic out of his depth.

The first announcement was made on Sunday 25 January 1959 in the Basilica of St. Paul's-without-the-Walls, on the feast of the conversion of St Paul, at the end of the—widely ignored in Rome—annual Octave for Christian Unity. Seventeen cardinals attended. The Pope's sermon had been billed as a reflection on the "Church of Silence", code-name for the persecuted Church in communist countries, and it was indeed silence that greeted his announcement, a frozen silence some thought, an "impressive and devout silence" others later wrote. The official Vati-can paper *Osservatore Romano* printed his strictures on Communism on the front page relegating the announcement of the most important event in the life of the Roman Catholic Church for almost a century to the centre pages. The official Vatican newspaper, the organ of the Cu-ria, often behaved like the mirror image of the enemy's *Pravda*.[7]

The announcement shocked the future Pope Paul VI, Archbishop Giovanni Montini in Milan. "This holy old boy doesn't seem to realise what a hornet's nest he's stirring up," he told a friend.[8] There were very few indications of what might be the nature and agenda of the Council at this stage. The Pope had described it blandly as for "the edification and joy of the Christian people". Only the ecumenical dimension of the project was clear: an "invitation to the faithful of the separated Churches to participate with us in this feast of grace and brotherhood for which so many souls in all parts of the world aspire".[9] Many bish-ops thought that Councils were only called to proclaim a doctrine or when there was a crisis. But what crisis? What doctrine? There were many historical precedents for thinking Councils meant confusion and trouble, or to be more precise, schism of one sort or another. Cardinal Spellman in the USA declared it was "destined for certain failure".[10]

The vagueness was in some ways protective. An imprecise promise of a forthcoming General Council—it was soon known as an Ecumeni-cal Council but only in July described by the Pope as Vatican II—would arouse great expectations of reform and renewal among some, and in others comforting hopes that Pius XII's vision of a Council would be revived, and "*la nouvelle théologie*", the latest brand of modernism as they saw it, condemned. Likewise the Pope gave no sign that ecumenism meant more than the traditional call for other Christians to "return", an opinion reinforced a month or so later when he used the unfortunate phrase in a speech to the Association of Catholic Universities, to the general consternation of non-Catholic Christians. His main interest was of course in reconciliation with the Orthodox Churches. The lack of clarity was frustrating for those excited by the prospect of a Council, but his proceeding at slow and measured pace, waiting for reactions and proposals, made it less likely that all the Vatican hornets would swarm at the same time.

Ante-preparatory or anti-preparatory commissions?

It is in this context, keeping the Vatican bureaucracy on-sides, that the events of 1959, or relative lack of them, may be explained. If the Pope created shock waves by announcing a General Council within three months of taking office—and shock waves customarily were muted by decorum—he was to take a long time in doing anything concrete. Symbolically choosing Pentecost to make the first significant move, the creation of an Ante-preparatory Commission, he appointed his Secretary of State, Cardinal Domenico Tardini, to lead it. Tardini was a key figure whose support was essential if the Vatican bureaucracy was to be reassured.

When the Pope addressed the small, entirely Curial, and largely Italian Commission at its first meeting in June 1959 he emphasised a focus on consolidation laced with a stout defence of the past pleasing to Curial ears. But in his bland first encyclical *Ad Petri Cathedram* on Christian unity and peace they might have been alarmed to read a citation by the Pope from John Henry Newman. Like the troublesome theologians of France and Germany, John XXIII did not shirk from dealing with history nor with the clash of ideas, nor even more threateningly with the development of doctrine—"such controversies do not disrupt the Church's unity".

A Council acceptable to the Curia was one that spelt out the central doctrines of the Church, repudiated the latest versions of modernism, then quickly moved into the practical ordering of Church life. Like any bureaucracy, the Curia relied on controlling—and manipulating—the rules and in the Roman Catholic Church these were expressed in a Code of Canon Law. An obscure professor of Canon Law at the Lateran University, Monsignor Pericle Felici, was appointed by Tardini to be secretary to the Ante-Preparatory Commission.[11] The Lateran, Gregorian and Angelicum Universities were—rival—centres of theological scholarship that *de facto* defined theological correctness within the framework of neo-scholasticism, and passed it on to an elite group of seminarians deemed worthy to be students on what was the fast-track to the episcopate. If Rome wanted to field intellectual pugilists against avant-garde upstarts it was to these universities that it would turn.[12]

The first task of the Ante-Preparatory Commission was to consult with the formal and intellectual leadership of the Church, with the bishops and with the leaders of Catholic Universities, Institutes and seminaries, and the Curia, about the Council's agenda. The replies with their suggestions were due by September 1959 but many bishops missed the deadline and Felici extended it to the March 1960. There were 2,150 replies from around the world, the vast majority with suggestions limited to minor reforms.[13] This was not necessarily because the bishops only thought about the nitty-gritty of diocesan life; Rome gave no encouragement to believe that broad strategic thinking and "big topics" were needed.

Archbishop Denis Hurley in Durban, South Africa, twelve years a bishop but still only in his 40s, was far from being a "Pius XII man" and welcomed the Council. He read widely: Congar, Chenu, the liturgists Clifford Howell and Jungmann, Teilhard de Chardin, John Courtney Murray on religious freedom, F.X. Durwell on the resurrection, Emil Mersch on spirituality and Jacques Maritain on Christian Humanism. His reply to Felici emphasised four thematic areas/desiderata: creation of Episcopal Conferences; use of the vernacular in the liturgy; worries about the slow take-up of Catholic Social Teaching in the Church, and how to move Catholic Action forward. They neatly fitted the "practical" requirements of the Curia but opened up wider issues: collegiality, the role of the laity, and the Church's role in social justice. More common replies requested minor reforms such as more faculties, (powers), for bishops, and few were the examples of consultation even within national hierarchies.[14]

On 5-6 June 1960 the members and presidents of the Preparatory Commissions were announced. They were almost completely Curial controlled, led by the prefects of the Curial congregations. A central Commission was under the direction of Cardinal Alfredo Ottaviani, head of the Holy Office, the Vatican's doctrinal watchdog, along with sub-commissions corresponding to the Congregation or dicastery structures of the Vatican, and led by their Rome heads. The massive central body, onto which Archbishop Hurley was invited, contained 58 Cardinals, 5 Patriarchs, 29 Archbishops, 5 Bishops and 4 Superiors-General of Religious Orders. It was an intimidating body for a young bishop. One of the recently appointed Cardinals, the former Superior-General of the Dominicans, Michael Browne, had taught Hurley at the Angelicum. Seniority structured all the proceedings of the Council, and it took courage for younger bishops to contradict older, and for older bishops to oppose Cardinals. But the Central Commission's authority was soon whittled down. It did not meet until June 1961 but the relationships formed in it were important in making possible co-ordinated responses from the bishops at the opening of the Council. The pace was painfully slow.[15]

Even as the Curia were moving their pieces strongly to the middle of the board, flanking manoeuvres were being prepared. The second slate of cardinals made by Pope John included the name of Augustin Bea, the Jesuit rector of the Biblical Institute (Biblicum) in Rome. The German confessor and adviser to Pius XII, he was to play a brilliantly strategic bridging role between the Curial old guard and those committed to reform, not least Pope John himself, and the powerful German/Austrian Church.

There were opportunities for those prepared and in the position to take strong initiatives. Thanks to Bea it was the ecumenical movement which was first off the mark. He sought the help of Bishop Lorenz Jaeger of Paderborn, who had a long association with the Ecumenical Centre for Dialogue with Lutherans in his diocese in Germany. Jaeger and Bea formulated a plan for an "ecumenical commission" which was to be sent to the Pope. Bea's second in command was Father Jan Willebrands, who had laboured since 1946 in the ecumenical movement in Netherlands where he had become President of the St Willibrord's Association. Williebrands was a tireless traveller and campaigner who had studied John Henry Newman for his thesis at the Jesuit Gregorian

University in Rome. He sought and was granted permission to attend the WCC's Faith and Order Commission in St Andrews.

After some skirmishes with Ottaviani, official Catholic observers later attended the WCC General Assembly in New Delhi in 1961, and, another Faith and Order WCC Conference in 1963, this time selected by the Secretariat for Christian Unity. This was a major ecumenical breakthrough. So "when the Holy See emerged from semi-absenteeism in ecumenical matters, it found the ground tilled", and this was in no small measure the work of committed ecumenists like Willebrands and his co-worker, Bishop Emile-Joseph de Smedt of Bruges.[16] Meanwhile the Pope had been strengthening his relationships with Patriarch Athenagoras and the Eastern Orthodox Churches.

The announcement of the preparatory commissions came in a Papal directive *Superno Dei Nutu*; it established a Secretariat for Promoting Christian Unity (SPCU), a new sort of Vatican body able to some degree to operate under the Curial radar. It was later made into a full ecumenical commission. The Secretariat, set up June 1960 in poky offices in the Via dei Corridori in a decrepit Roman *palazzo*—there was chronic shortage of meeting rooms—was at times treated like an irritating NGO. But it was under Bea's direction and safely outside the Curial structures, and had the right staffing to work successfully on the Council document on ecumenism.[17] Moreover it was able to feed into debates on Council documents other considerations arising from the wider ecumenical context and Christian world.

It was only on 13 June 1960, one year before the first session of the Council, that the "Jewish question" entered the Pope's mind. On recommendations from the French ambassador to the Vatican, he met with Professor Jules Isaac, Director of Education in France and promoter of the Paris-based *Amitié Judéo-Chrétienne*. The problem of what to do about Judaism, along with several insistent requests to speak out on anti-Semitism after the Shoah, landed surprisingly in Bea's lap in September for the first meeting of the Secretariat for Christian Unity. With the Pope's agreement, he set about preparing a document with the utmost secrecy. It was to prove the most political and fraught of all the Council documents, with, at one point, the government of Jordan approving a demand from Bethlehem Christians that Bishops who absolved Jews of the guilt of Christ's death be banned from the Holy Sites. Bea's draft was finally transformed into a new but brief document on non-Christian religions begun only on 12 May 1965, shortly before the close of the Council. Before it could be approved by the bishops, there was a "prudential" removal of any reference to "deicide" in relation to the Jews.[18]

Meanwhile in December 1961, Willebrands and Bea had gained an audience with the Pope for Geoffrey Fisher, Archbishop of Canterbury, head of the Anglican World Communion, and one of the six presidents of the WCC. Tardini was annoyed; Bea was forbidden from attending the meeting; no cameras were allowed. Just in case there was any doubt that the invitation was made in more than the name of the Secretariat for Christian Unity, under no circumstances was the limousine bearing the leader of the Anglican Communion to carry Vatican license plates. After a cordial but somewhat furtive meeting with the Pope, Fisher had tea at Bea's private residence in the Brazilian College.[19] So much for the role of the Secretariat, set up to "show in a special manner our love and good will towards those who bear the name of Christ" and for the Pope's "search for unity" with the separated brethren. This arch-Curial edict was fairly typical of a supercilious culture where hierarchical distinction had become an obsession and knocking on the right door essential. A closed culture, demanding fluent Latin, extraordinary perseverance and subtle debating and diplomatic skills, it reduced some to hopeless fury and frustration. Bea was not one of them.

The other main outflanking movement was extramural. It consisted of a plethora of books, pamphlets, talks and broadcasts by those strongly in favour of a "reform and renewal" Council. Archbishop Thomas Roberts SJ, formerly of Bombay, was a strong advocate for one of the Council's proposed themes, peace.[20] The debating weapon of choice was historical scholarship. Bishop Lorenz Jaeger wrote a high density tome called, in English translation, "The Ecumenical Council, The Church and Christendom" that left in no doubt that Councils could be, and had been in the past, whatever a Pope and contingent circumstances made of them. The Swiss theologian Hans Küng, about to become the youthful and provocative Professor of Theology in Tübingen, entered the fray in 1960 with *Konzil und Wiedervereinigung. Erneuerung als Rüf in die Einheit* (Council, Reform and Reunion) which boldly set out steps to reform the Church, which, he suggested, would have the additional benefit of leading to Christian unity.[21] Küng's arguments had weighty Franco-Austrian endorsement from Cardinal Achille Liénart of Lille and Cardinal Franz König of Vienna. The Dutch bishops produced in the same year a pastoral letter on the theology of the episcopate, influenced by the reformist writings of the Dominican theologian Edward Schillerbeeckx, a lecturer at Nijmegen, responding to the announcement of the Council.

The Struggle for Control

In the final year before the Council the battle of ideas was joined between what might best be described in shorthand as curialists versus non-curialists, those who behaved as if "tradition" extended no further back than the Council of Trent in the sixteenth century, and those who studied the Bible and Patristics and saw tradition as a springboard not a comfortable sofa. Senior churchmen, scholarly and retiring, not naturally attracted to the mass media, began to use the remaining time available to promote their ideas. In the nine months leading up to the opening of the Council, Augustin Bea gave twenty-five talks and published interviews.[22] Others issued pastoral letters to their dioceses or wrote articles in Catholic periodicals.

But the non-curialists could make little headway in the ten Curia-controlled preparatory commissions. Their monthly meetings made heavy demands on prelates in charge of large dioceses, and proficiency in Latin was unequally distributed between the contending tendencies. There was the overriding sense among prelates visiting Rome that "they" had the ball and were not going to give up possession. Cardinal Ottaviani, a baker's son from the working quarter of Rome, Trastevere, and a doughty protagonist for his vision of the Church, seemed to see the Central and Theological Commissions as an emanation of the Holy Office giving them a right of veto over the work of every other commission. Position papers, schemata, proliferated and elderly men with multiple responsibilities got very tired.[23]

Pope John addressed the first meeting of the Central Commission about the need to sort out practical matters, voting, role of experts, conduct of debates and so on. The Council was about updating and for reunion of the Churches "the recomposition of the whole mystical flock of Christ", he said.[24] Such sessions were august occasions beneath the tapestries in the great Hall of Congregations in the Vatican, a time for lofty monologues. The agenda was narrow and dominated by the preoccupations of the Holy Office: a new formula for the profession of faith; a schema on the sources of Revelation, decisions on non-Catholic observers; and support for parishes. Despite the Pope's subtle warning that the Council "should dissipate errors by the force of truth", the curialists were still pushing for some kind of denunciation of *la nouvelle théologie*.[25] Archbishop Hurley caught the mood in an acerbic comment on their proposed new profession of faith: "I suggested that it was inviting us to believe against rather than in".[26]

Perhaps the most disconcerting feature of the deliberations was that lack of direction reduced much of the proceedings to skirmishing on minor matters. Only the Liturgical Commission, with the inestimable Vincentian Monsignor Antonio Bugnini as secretary, backed up by a number of competent liturgists, with centres of liturgical excellence in several countries, worked successfully as a group with something akin to a common vision.[27] Liturgical reform had already had a long gestation. *Veterum Sapientia,* a paean of praise to the Latin language from Pope John issued in February, insisting on its continued relevance as the medium of instruction in seminaries, looked ominous but did not deter. No one outside the top curial officials knew clearly what was going on in Commissions other than their own; this greatly strengthened the hand of the key Curial players in the Central Commission. A bureaucracy that does not control the documents is, after all, no bureaucracy at all.

Where the Curia were at a loss was in controlling the Pope who moved, within the framework of Catholic Social Teaching, in a direction that they saw as dangerous: the "opening to the Left". *Mater et Magistra*, produced in July 1961, accepted the Welfare State—formerly opposed—and used one of Teilhard's key words, "socialisation", in the encyclical's translations from the Latin. It brought the concept of the Common Good to the fore again and championed the idea of—what was not then called—"civil society" as a bulwark against totalitarianism. French Dominican and Jesuit influences that the Curia loved to hate, and the thinking of Jacques Maritain, were in evidence.[28]

Tardini died in July 1961. An Italian Cardinal, Amleto Cicognani, from the Congregation of Oriental Churches—whom John had got to know in Bulgaria—was appointed as Secretary of State and charged with conciliar preparations. In his solemn convocation of the Council at Christmas 1961, *Humanae Salutis*, Pope John set out his objectives: the

Council was to be outward-looking, at the service of the whole world, and the Church should learn how to "read the signs of the times".

The signs were not reassuring; there was a palpable sense of danger and pending crisis. Khrushchev and Kennedy were testing each other's wills against a background of possible nuclear war, tension over Berlin and their status in East and West Germany. But John retained a sense of hope and highlighted the positive. Nature and Grace did not stand in radical opposition to each other; human beings were not doomed to an eternal dualism—rather "the light of Christ...leads them to discover in themselves their own true nature, dignity and purpose".[29] This differed significantly from the vision of Holy Mother Church confronting the sinful world with a series of ultimatums concerning salvation. And it introduced, implicitly at least, a question that had to be resolved. How much of the Council was to be *ad extra*, dealing with the world's problems, and how much *ad intra*, focussed on the internal life of the Church? Catholics were, for John, part of the Church but they were no less "citizens of the whole world".[30]

This dilemma is probably the reason Pope John got in touch with Cardinal Léon-Joseph Suenens of Malines, Belgium in March 1962. A former Vice-Rector of the University of Louvain, and a member of the Central Commission since February, he had written a pastoral letter on the Council that dovetailed with much of John's thinking. "Who is attending to the making of an overall plan for the whole Council?" Suenens asked the Pope. *"Nessuno"* (nobody), came the reply. It was a revealing and shocking answer with the opening of the Council three months away.[31]

Pope John was as far away from being the CEO of a vast transnational corporation as can be imagined; he was standing back from practical preparations. Suenens put forward his suggestions for discussion: permanent deacons, pastoral training as well as private study for seminarians, and the idea of post-conciliar Commissions, permanent bodies to carry the work forward and a special role for Bishops' Conferences—these were evidently going to be a threat to the Curia. He was also concerned about fundamental social issues: "there is practically nothing written on the obligation to give one's surplus to others, nor the social application of goods created for the use of everyone". Overall he underlined the need for balance between the *ad extra* and *ad intra* cocerns of the Council recommended by theologians at Louvain.

His key question for the Council was "how the whole Church could be put into a state of mission?"[32]

The second main source of support for the Pope was Archbishop Montini in Milan who nailed his colours to the mast in a magisterial Lenten Pastoral, *Pensiamo al Concilio* (Thinking about the Council). The great conciliar theme had to be the mystery of the Church not the juridical reality of its ordered life as an institution. " It is the whole Church that expresses itself in the Council," Montini declared, and "we are the Church." Moreover, the Church wanted to address the world as "sister and mother"—not as chastising father—with exhortation rather than anathema. He wanted "positive rather than punitive reforms". The emphasis had to be on renewal and *aggiornamento*; the modern world demanded "simpler forms" of Church life than the seigneurial Church of the past.[33] The Curia was facing a serious challenge.

Montini's position would not have surprised the curialists but Suenens was more of an unknown quantity. Cicognani circulated Suenens' plan around the Commission heads. The powerful German Cardinals, Joseph Frings of Cologne and Julius Döpfner of Munich, had wanted the Council postponed due to the poor quality of the preparatory documents; they then joined with Franz König of Vienna, and proposed to the Pope that a smaller think-tank sub-commission might be formed to give the Council some shape and sense of direction. Informal meetings in the Belgian College with such key cardinals as the Franciscan Giacomo Lercaro of Bologna, a liturgical reformer and a volatile force, and Paul-Emile Léger of Montreal, a passionate and radical man, led by Julius Döpfner, began in July 1962 but it was becoming apparent that a formal sub-commission was a non-starter. Without the gentle prodding of Montini and Suenens, the Council was in grave danger of drifting into chaos.[34] This largely European influential inner group goes some way towards explaining the Eurocentric perspective of the Council's documents. Intended for universal application, in many instances they read like reflections on the Church in the developed world.

The 1962 May and June sessions of the Preparatory Commissions laboured with a massive agenda and multiple and rival schemata doing the rounds. And then that was it. The Curia collected the cards from the table and disappeared with them. *Rien ne va plus*. Four months later, at the first session of the Council in September 1962, the ordinary members of the Commissions received the modified final drafts of the documents. Only seven draft texts out of seventy had reached the bishops by the opening, all with the Curia's fingerprints on them. All, except that on liturgy, were to be thrown out by the Council fathers.[35]

Finally, in a broadcast on Vatican Radio on 11 September 1962, the Pope publicly adopted the *ad intra* and *ad extra* division suggested by Suenens as a conceptual framework for the Council. By so doing he inadvertently emphasised the comparative lack of preparation on *ad extra* questions, particularly the study of contemporary world problems. This was most starkly evident in relation to "Third World" issues. The Brazilian Bishop Helder Camara was telling everyone willing to listen that the real question for the Council was development in the underdeveloped world. Yet few were willing to listen despite the Pope's making the third theme in his broadcast the Church's image in the underdeveloped world and the injustice of poverty.[36] Poverty was only briefly addressed prior to the Council even though it featured again in the Council's "Message to the World" on 20 October 1962.

John in his September radio address returned to the question of poverty, bringing it in to sharper focus: "the Church presents herself as what she is and wants to be, as the Church of all, and particularly, as the Church of the poor". The underdeveloped countries revealed the "miseries of social life that cry out to God for vengeance in the sight of God". These broadcast words gave great encouragement to the anti-poverty lobby among the bishops. They were no mere rhetoric; actions backed up his words. During 1962 John canonised Martin de Porres, an illegitimately born Peruvian of mixed race and a champion of the poor from Lima, and appointed new archbishops to Conakry, Dakar, Lome, Bamako and Madagascar. He raised the Collegium Urbanum for African clergy to the status of a Papal university. And with the world six weeks away from the Cuban missile crisis, the Pope proclaimed the message of the Church to be perennially *"pacem in terris"*, a task he saw as a goal of Mission.[37]

In the event, neither peace nor poverty was to feature in the final Council documents as major themes and a truncated analysis of the world's problems was only just included before the Council finally closed in December 1965.[38] Given the inertia and resistance of the Curia, real impact during the Council relied on movements having had time to build up, together with previous networking. Liturgy and ecumenism had made some headway, partly for this reason, and partly because of the Eurocentric weighting of the preparatory commissions. But the third theme, poverty, had been barely studied by theologians.

The Council's First Session; the turning point

From 1962-1965 Council sittings amounted to four annual periods of ten weeks, with Commissions working with varying degrees of effectiveness in between. The Second Vatican Council gathered together some 2,500 prelates from around the world. Missing were the episcopates from China, North Vietnam and North Korea. Representation from Eastern Europe was sparse. There were in addition over fifty official observers from some thirty-five other Churches—the number more than doubled before the end of the Council—and, largely offstage, at least initially, countless advisers and the 200 theological experts, the *periti* in the entourage of the Council Fathers. These influenced the outcome of deliberations to varying degrees, with the Lutherans often seeing eye to eye with the German Augustinian theologians.[39] The *aula* where they met for formal debate, and all the Commissions' proceedings, were dominated by Europeans, not least by an inert and "incurably myopic" group of some 430 Italians who were poorly if at all coordinated. There were some sparkling exceptions.[40]

The axis of intellectual dynamism lay in northern Europe with almost 200 French bishops plus the Belgians and Dutch, and the German-speaking Fulda conference, which brought together bishops and heads of Religious Orders. The key grouping had its roots in countries which had experienced the Second World War as a moral as well as a political crisis—this had been reflected in the pivotal role of their statesmen in forming the European Economic Community. Open to, and attracting others, by the second session this loose alliance ran a co-ordinating committee that met in the *Domus Mariae* on Friday evenings. They linked up with Asian and reform Latin American bishops through Cardinal Frings and the German Catholic aid agencies, Misereor and Adveniat. They met at intervals and had access to such influential theologians as Karl Rahner, invited by Cardinal König in October 1961 to review the conciliar preparatory drafts, and there was the ubiquitous and indefatigable Congar on hand. Rahner's and Congar's views converged with those of Edward Schillebeeckx, who demolished the official schemata in the widely circulated form of *Animadversiones*, and had influence beyond the Flemish-speakers. The alliance made good use of their national Catholic media.[41]

Yet, despite entrenched differences of opinion and perspective, status and wealth, the proceedings of the Council were remarkably good-humoured and courteous. The contending bishops showed respect for each other both in their civilised public discourse and the warmth of personal relationships. Though there was a high degree of residential sorting into national groups—many countries had their own national colleges in Rome—there was some mixing of nationalities in the over ninety residences crammed with bishops around the city.

Bishops from the developing world began to discover each other at the Council and to develop some joint thinking from the perspective of the "South". They relied predominantly on the help of the European *periti*; fewer than 5 per cent of the Council *periti* were drawn from the "Third World". Thanks to their meeting together in the regional Bishops' Conference of Latin America, CELAM, the 530 Latin Americans already had some degree of regional cohesion. The six Arabic Eastern Rites Churches, Melkites, Maronites, Syriac, Coptic, Chaldean and Armenian formed a joint executive committee, and Nagpur missionaries from the Syrian Malabar rite were also represented, but they found it almost impossible to agree joint positions. The 300 or so bishops from Africa comprised only one third Africans—the rest were missionary Bishops or represented Religious Orders. Like the Indians, the Nigerian and Madagascar bishops put forward lists of candidates for the commissions as national Episcopal Conferences. The bishops from Africa were otherwise united enough to form a pan-African group with a general-secretary—and on several occasions, agreed unanimously—allowing a single speaker to represent them in an intervention in the *aula*, a tactic that gave a greater chance of their man being called to speak. They later formed a "Committee of Theologians for all Africa" as an advisory group. This did not amount to the creation of regional voting blocs. Bishops from the South only came into their own as a powerful grouping in the Commission on Missions. with nine out of sixteen members and Bishop Stanislaus Lokuang of Tainan, Taiwan, as Vice-President. The Asian bishops played an important role and were bunched in three separate groups: India led by Cardinal Valerian Gracias of Bombay, Sri Lanka and the Far East/Philippines led by the Indonesians, Vietnamese and Taiwanese who wanted a strong emphasis on cultural adaptation, religious freedom and interreligious dialogue. There were 800 missionary bishops in all some of whom met in a group founded by Monsignor Tarcisius van Valenberg, a former Apostolic Vicar of Dutch Borneo. None had arrived geared up for lobbying. They learnt how as they went along.[42]

The English-speaking bishops outside the Franco-German and Dutch axis were at first none too adept at getting their views across either. The North Americans, poor at Latin, enjoying their customary creature comforts by renting three luxurious hotels, were, according to Archbishop Hurley, not much accustomed to in-house "horse-trading".[43] They punched below their numerical weight, some 217, and their financial clout which was believed to be considerable. But on their big domestic issue, religious liberty and relations between Church and State, they came out in force, clustering irately around the altar in St Peter's after one reverse. The British, Irish, Australians and New Zealanders with some exceptions played the role of extras, with some fine English character parts, for example the curmudgeonly Cardinal Jack Heenan, a progressive player on ecumenism, and the wily Bishop Derek Worlock, who worked effectively behind the scenes in the laity commission; few of them were remotely prepared for or had swum in the currents of *la nouvelle théologie*, or if they had, they did not care for it.[44] This was not a Bandung conference with geographical political blocs, though regional identities had a broad overall significance in how the individual Fathers saw things.

When Pope John XXIII opened the Council in St Peter's on 11 October 1962, he knew he was dying of stomach cancer. His opening address not only clarified his own hopes for the broad direction of deliberations, but also illustrated the distance of the curialists from his own position. His references to "those who although consumed with zeal do not have very much judgement or balance" and for whom the modern world was "nothing but betrayal and ruination", could not have been misunderstood. He spoke graphically of "these prophets of misfortune who are forever forecasting calamity" who "go on as though they have learned nothing at all from history—and yet history is the great teacher of life". "Christians and Catholics of apostolic spirit all the world over", he went on, "expect a leap forwards in doctrinal insight and the education of consciences in ever greater fidelity to authentic teaching. But this authentic doctrine has to be studied and expounded in the light of the research methods and language of modern thought. For the substance of the ancient deposit of faith is one thing, and the way in which it is presented is another." It had to be "adapted to our own times". He not only summoned the vision of a dynamic and pilgrim Church boldly seeking the truth but pointedly downplayed "errors", comparing them to a "mist before the sun", quick to disappear. It was a masterly performance, unexpected and revolutionary. The Vatican Radio Latin text was doctored by officials before appearing in the official collection of Papal utterances, but the Fathers had heard the message, and the majority heeded it.[45]

The Curia handed down 180 names for membership of the sixteen conciliar commissions. The Council Fathers began on 13 October as they meant to continue; the French Cardinal Achille Liénart called for time for consultation and then they rejected the Curia's proposal. It was in many ways a turning point; the assembled bishops suddenly sensed their communal authority. *They* would elect Commission members. The search for names set off countless caucuses and meetings, as prelates lobbied and tried to discover each other's views and preferences; this pattern continued into the theological discussion of the preparatory documents, schemata. Who got to speak in the great *aula* was hierarchically ordered—as was the seating itself—with Cardinals speaking first; no interruptions were countenanced. But time was rationed; there was an 8-minute warning, then at ten minutes the microphone was cut off. Such "belling" of famous Cardinals could elicit schoolboy glee from younger frisky bishops in their 50s. It was not a recipe for dialogue. Most of that went on in the coffee bars set up around St Peter's Basilica; two favourites were nicknamed "Bar Jona" and "Bar Abbas".[46]

Rome was full. Any vacant building available was used for large meetings. English-speaking bishops from the African continent met in a hall in the Via della Conciliazone. Prelates from the Church in Eastern Europe had to join up with bishops from France, Germany, Austria, Belgium, and Holland if they wanted to get involved. Within the first few weeks Yves Congar was lecturing in French on theological topics to the Latin Americans. "Rome was one big theological 'think-in' or at least 'listen-in'", wrote a Protestant observer. "Though we did not realise it then we were present at perhaps the greatest theological concourse the Christian world has seen".[47]

Suenens' question about who was running the Council remained pertinent. The Pope privately thought the Council could be over by Christmas and showed little realistic grasp of what the vision set out in his opening peroration would entail. It may be that his cancer was affecting his perspective; more likely he shared the widely voiced anxiety that the Church's bishops would be kept away from their dioceses too long. And there was also the expense. Many of the Third World bishops from Latin America, Africa and Asia did not think they could afford to return for a second session.

The Pope may have deliberately stood back from the planning of the Council's agenda. But there were two bodies who should have taken responsibility. A Council of Presidents had overall control of procedure. And a Secretariat for Extraordinary Affairs led by the moderate Cicognani, an ex-nuncio to the United States and now Secretary of State, had been appointed to adjudicate on difficult new issues that arose and to liaise with the Pope. It contained representatives of all factions and none. Both were ineffectual, and barely met, although the Council of Presidents decided that the liturgy should be the first item for debate, taking up the first month of deliberation.

It made sense tactically to tackle the best preparatory document first, one capable of gaining some consensus, and a topic that involved the whole Church. But in terms of setting the work of the Council in a clear, sequenced and inspiring theological framework, the decision highlighted the lack of any plan. What could be said for it was that it gave the theologians time to get across their views on the fundamental issues of Revelation and the Church, due for debate later. In the event the discussion of the liturgy became embroiled in a conflict about the use of Latin, splitting the Council down Curial versus non-Curial lines with a large majority in favour of change.[48]

Archbishop Hurley, a relative outsider, was soon reflecting on the Council's "aimless drift".[49] So was an insider, Montini, who had enormous influence with the Pope. In a letter dated 18 October he set down his own worries and suggested in detail how the Council might sequence its schemata. It was a canny letter referring first to the "completion" of Vatican I and casting the central theme of the Council in terms of Pius XII's *Mystici Corporis*, as the "mystery of the Church". But he also supported Suenens' *ad extra* agenda underlining that the Council must not be "too introspective". The second theme for consideration should be what the Church did, her mission, and thirdly relationships *ad extra* from civil society, to peace and war, and to the world of work. Montini, Suenens and Lercaro of Bologna henceforth formed a triumvirate trying to steer the Council and attempting by their interventions to provide it with a logical conceptual framework.[50] No less important were the German-speakers, Bea and König, who had the Pope's ear.

November saw little change in the battle lines drawn in the discussion on the liturgy. The Council now began addressing the sources of Revelation, a theological debate that allowed the head of the Holy Office, Cardinal Ottaviani, to wheel out his brainchild, a schema on the "Two Sources of Revelation" which proved to be a turning point for the Fathers. At first glance an unpromisingly dull topic, Ottaviani's position struck at the heart of the ecumenical question by defining how the Church reached the truths of faith. The Curialists asserted, as every Catholic schoolchild at the time was supposed to know, that the teaching authority of the Church, the Magisterium, determined the criteria for discerning the truth, and that when it did so it used two sources of Revelation: Scripture and Tradition. This way of talking about the problem effectively shut down ecumenical dialogue; much of contemporary Protestantism of course started out from a premise of scripture alone as the source of Revelation.

Ottaviani's sally from the Holy Office brought out in force the bishops from the northern European "mixed countries", Germany, Netherlands and Belgium. His focus on the teaching Church opened the door to opposing themes of "*la nouvelle théologie*": the truth was a Person, Jesus Christ, not a check-list of propositions, and, moreover, the Church was always in a state of *fides quaerens intellectum* (faith seeking knowledge).[51] In Congar's measured words: " We must strive to move beyond the comfortable and settled possession of a truth that involves no problems, and attain an idea of doctrine that is equally traditional, but broader and able to integrate those aspects of truth which the questions of our separated brethren compel us to treat more seriously."[52]

Fathers Karl Rahner and Joseph Ratzinger, the present Pope, already had an alternative schema prepared in which God's presence in the "history of mankind" was asserted as another source for the Church's quest for the truth. They had the ear of the powerful German-speaking contingent. Bishop Karol Wojtyla from Poland, the future John Paul II, speaking for the first time in the *aula* declared that the only real source was God speaking to humanity—everything else was derivative, a neat way of avoiding the clash but one that no one was going to settle on.[53] Ottaviani had made a strategic blunder: there were several different reasons for rejecting his approach as a basis for discussion and there resulted, in consequence, a heavy vote against it. His prestige and influence were damaged. The "progressives", as they now were beginning to be called, actually the moderate centre, gained heart and confidence.

This was a second turning point. Pope John, pressed to act by Bea and the Montreal Cardinal, Léger, now stepped in decisively and committed the topic to a new balanced Commission in which Curialist marked non-Curialist at all levels of hierarchical authority from its co-presidents, Bea and Ottaviani, downwards. This balancing between two tendencies was to be the Pope's approach until his death. On 5 December, against the express wishes of the Holy Office, which had been systematically blocking Rahner's access to the official meetings and structures of the Council, Cardinal König simply defied Ottaviani and escorted Rahner into the meeting of the new mixed Commission. In February 1963 Rahner was formally named as a *peritus* for a seventeen-strong group working on the document on the nature, role and structure of the Church.[54] A very large Trojan horse had entered the citadel. Chenu, Congar and others followed later.

By now the Council had achieved certain fragile *acquis*, some agreed principles and procedures. The Council would be *pastoral*, not *legal*, in tone and intention; in other words it sought a loving openness not a rule-bound closure. Old style neo-scholastic thinking would have to live up to that challenge or be rejected. And it was to be ecumenical in scope not a narrow internal dialogue. In a remarkable way the observers from the other Churches, who could not speak in the sessions, were, as if by remote control, influencing the work of the Council, most notably on ecumenism and the nature of the Church. They had a great deal of contact with participants outside the *aula* and avidly listened to lectures by prominent *periti*. The Pope, although terminally ill, had succeeded in getting key aspects of his vision accepted as normative.

The defeat of the Curialists' schemata meant that the long preparatory work for the Council had virtually to start again. There were major tasks to accomplish. But most of the bishops now knew what they did not want. Before the first session of the Council broke up and its members went home, Pope John announced the formation of a weighty Co-ordinating Commission to control the revision of the different schemas and to hold the fort during the long break before the second session. Montini and Suenens delivered keynote speeches setting out the framework for the new vision: *ad extra*, on "modern problems", and *ad intra* on the Christ-centred nature of the Church. Suenens itemised in particular social justice, war and peace, poverty and the Church of the poor, and "the population explosion" for consideration, and received an ovation from the assembled fathers, but these items were never given the attention they needed. Montini drew on his Milan pastoral letter and the ideas he had agreed with the Pope to set out a vision of a missionary Church. The Council at last had a sense of direction.[55]

Cardinal Lercaro of Bologna speaking on behalf of the Third World group broached the third theme, poverty, and proposed the "Church of the Poor" as the organising principle of the Council. Congar in his talks had been emphasising a "Church of service" as the basis of authority. Lercaro spoke of a Church of *kenosis*, self-emptying, exhorting the Fathers to follow Christ who "though being rich, became poor for us".[56] This won no applause. Though Lercaro as a Franciscan practised what he preached, and had turned a comfortable diocesan villa into a home for orphans, passionate appeals about poverty never did cut much ice among bishops. Archbishop Hurley who knew something about poverty in Africa wrote tongue in cheek: "it sounded like too strong an invitation to self-denial".[57] Indeed, the very passion of Lercaro's approach risked driving the question of the Church of the Poor off the agenda, despite the lobbying and concerns of men such as Helder Camara who referred repeatedly to Pope John's own appeal during his September Vatican Radio broadcast. As with the question of peace, poverty was to be dealt with in the form of a major Papal encyclical outside the Council deliberations. More importantly it was later to motivate the theology of an entire continent, Latin America. This future movement of the Church's intellectual centre of gravity is the topic of Chaper Five.[58]

4

THE VATICAN COUNCIL
A NEW VISION

It is no exaggeration that the first session of the Council was, for a significant number of bishops, a conversion experience. They held the destiny of the Church in their hands and glimpsed a new, if vague, vision of what it might become. Over 500 spoke during the first session, and out of their encounters inside and outside the *aula*, came a collegial sense of themselves as a gathered world-wide episcopate. "Collegiality" was thus an experience of the Council as much as one of its primary propositions. Many of them, back in their dioceses between sessions, gave talks or sermons on the Council and its purpose. The theological *periti* were even more active spreading their ideas far and wide. A palpable sense of breakthrough had occurred but what would replace the curialists' vision was still far from clear. Confidence had grown. "We have learned to walk with our own legs", Cardinal Valerian Gracias, Archbishop of Bombay, declared.[1] He wanted major structural change. He thought it was sometimes necessary to demolish a house that was falling to bits and build a new one—but many felt that it was not that easy, the result might be bricks scattered all over the place.

As always shifts in the Church's theological core were associated with more superficial, and political, realignments. The curialists, and a cabal from Opus Dei led by the inept Cardinal Arcadio Laraona, Prefect of the Congregation of Rites, a friend of General Franco and Fascist Spain—and a "hopeless protagonist"—plus the more wily Cardinal Giuseppe Siri of Genoa, pushed for the Council to condemn Communism.[2] The eastern European bishops knew how much damage this would do to fragile relations with the Church, though the Taiwanese bishops were keen. The Pope and Montini were both highly sensitive to the problems of the Church in Eastern Europe and the Soviet Union. John, with his long experience of communist governments, warmly received Khrushchev's daughter and son-in-law, Alexis Adjubei, and their young family, ignoring fears that this symbolic hand of friendship would damage the Christian Democrat vote in Italy. Montini summed up John's feelings about the Church's *pastoral* position on Communism perfectly in the words: "They experience our harshness not our charity".[3]

The issue of Communism was raised in the last encyclical issued by John before he died on 3 June 1963, *Pacem in Terris*. It in some ways made up for his absence from the sessions of the Council that followed and he may even have intended it as his last attempt to lead the latter. It was a clarion call to change attitudes towards the world. The Pope saw himself no longer as embattled Defender of the Faith but as "interpreter of the most ardent wishes of the whole human family" engaged in a joint pursuit with the secular world for the "universal common good". For this reason he sought the creation of a political expression of this good, a "world authority", and was encouraging of the work of the United Nations and its component organisations.[4]

A meeting ground with the secular world lay in its "most ardent wishes". These were foremost a checklist of human rights which *Pacem in Terris* endorses and categorises in a logical order. Social and economic rights come before civil rights only because they are most easily derived from natural law, and logically because eating comes before voting. Moreover rights come before duties; states are responsible for ensuring the rights of their citizens and the model of relations between state and citizen forms the model of inter-state relations in entailing a nexus of rights and duties. War is the antithesis of human rights as well as their graveyard; armed conflict between states heralds massive human rights violations. There is no mention of a just war presumably because the destructive potential of atomic weapons ruled out the regulation of the conduct of war, *jus in bello*; it no longer made sense "to maintain that war was a fit instrument to repair the violation of justice". He was not arguing in the abstract; he had been a medical orderly during the First World War, at the Caporetto Hospital, and had never forgotten the screams of the wounded.[5]

Pacem in Terris was a clear and practical application of John XXIII's admonition to read "the signs of the times"; the Church's old condemnatory rejection of modernity was missing. As Suenens told the 119 member States at the United Nations in a speech lasting more than an hour while presenting the document on 13 May 1963: "If respect for the person dwells within our hearts we can devise a social, political and economic system that will enshrine respect".[6] Of course, Communism had to be condemned but "people have a value far above whatever views they may hold", and a distinction had to be made between an ideology—bad—and its historical manifestation in the action and intentions of people—sometimes good.[7] Here was a minor miracle. The Church was speaking and the world was listening, not excluding the right-wing Catholic press in the United States who were appalled and could find solace only in the belief that the Pope was a naïve Italian peasant. The rupture with the past and its customary alliances could not have been greater. The dying Pope was asking Catholics to become citizens of the whole world not *émigrés de l'intérieur* living in a Catholic ghetto.[8]

Discarding the "Dry Bones"

When Pope Paul VI opened the second session of the Council on 29 September 1963, there was a profound sense of continuity linked to real hope of progress. He had been a key figure quietly steering the Council and had only intervened when the agenda became grid-locked. As a close adviser to Pius XII, Paul also articulated the new ideas in ways more acceptable to the "old guard" who were showing signs of acute anxiety and disaffection. Now he appointed four moderators: Suenens, Lercaro, Döpfner, and Agagianian, adding to the complexity of the Council's leadership structures, in an attempt to direct the Council more firmly. The qualification *"more"* is relative; not all wished to follow. Some twenty-five Cardinals out of eighty-one still refused to budge an inch, and most of these had voted against Paul VI at the conclave that elected him Pope. So he still needed to find some way of carrying the Curial vote in the Council, and may already have made some concessions to them during the conclave.[9] By framing his ideas in the language of continuity with Pius XII's thinking and encyclicals, he could garner some added legitimacy in their eyes. Unassailable legitimacy, of course, came from the authority of the Petrine Office which he was quick to emphasise in his speeches.

It was easy for critics to characterise Paul's ambiguities, telling amendments to schemata, and the subtleties of his public positions apparently supportive of the disaffected minority, as a watering-down of positions taken by the late "good Pope John". His "watering down" was often a continuation of his predecessor's balancing act carried out with greater diplomatic skill and often more sensitivity towards the troublesome minority. Thus, for Paul, the task of the Curia was to be a watchdog of received truths "while transforming them into a language capable of dialogue with human minds".[10] There was something for everyone. Eastern Churches were "Sister Churches" and Protestants were not rudely asked to "return"; ecumenism was all about a "reintegration of all Christians in unity".[11] And that could be interpreted as convergence or asymmetric movement towards unity. These subtleties of a refined and strategic mind meant it was not always clear—perhaps deliberately unclear—where the Pope stood.

On the question of the Church, the position was distinctive. Paul started out using the "Mystical Body" language of Pius XII. The Church was the mysterious instrument of Christ in the world and shone forth as a people "made one with the unity of the Father, the Son, and the Holy Spirit"—in St. Cyprian's trinitarian formula. So the "nature" of the Church was pure communion. The Chilean bishops insisted on this key communal element in the Catholic understanding of salvation, in the words of *Lumen Gentium*, they were saved "as a people, not as individuals without any bond or link between them".

But—and here was the breakthrough—the Mystical Body was not a bounded society whose members were co-terminous with the members of the Roman Catholic Church. The Mystical Body subsisted (*subsistit*) in the Roman Catholic Church; there was no complete identification between the two. Completeness, the fullness of the Truth, had to await the end of time. That "many elements of sanctification and truth can be found outside her visible structure" was the corollary.[12] It was a question of degree not of either/or, more of the Mystical Body here rather than there, but not all of it here. This unlocked the door to future ecumenical dialogue. The dynamism of the trinitarian symbol was reflected in the Church's "going out" to the world in mission and this required it "to some extent to assimilate the forms of life of those to whom we want to take the message of Christ", a clear message of "inculturation" for the missionaries from Africa and Asia.[13]

Given this vision of the Church it is surprising that Paul was unhappy with the proposed—and definitive—ordering of the vital Constitution on the Church, *Lumen Gentium*. In the Constitution the "People of God" came first and the hierarchical structures of the Church—bishops, archbishops and so on—came afterwards. No doubt this expressed in many ways the most radical re-visioning of the Church to come out of the Council. Congar had been a key influence in the theological work of preparation. He preferred the term "a messianic people", and it also appeared in the text.[14] For Cardinal Suenens, the Holy Spirit was given to the whole Church not just to its pastors, and a variety of *charisms*, gifts, were spread throughout the Christian community among the laity. But it was Bishop de Smedt of Bruges, speaking for the Secretariat of Christian Unity in a speech condemning triumphalism, clericalism and legalism, that became rightly famous, who most contrasted the antinomies at play in the Council. He wanted the document to reflect the nature of the Church's purpose as the "bearer" of the Word of God. Certain bearers came first. Alongside reasserting authority structures, Pope Paul saw the apostles and their successors as first and foremost missionaries. "I understand the People of God to be structured", he complained.[15]

Karl Rahner, theologian to Cardinal König and an adviser on the Commission on the Church, gave great weight to building the local Church. St Paul did not found missions but local Churches. This dovetailed with a widespread concern about collegiality, that there should be a shared governance of the Church by the whole college of bishops with, and under, the Pope. Paul VI had emphasised collegiality in a dry speech opening the second session but, again, the contents had been tailored for the Curia. This was not collegiality from the perspective of the many local Churches but in the context of Papal primacy. His top down approach was countered by several speeches in the *aula* which emphasised, as it were, collegiality from below. This was of passionate concern to some of the Oriental Churches, most notably the outspoken Melkite and Maronite Patriarchs, who saw their Churches as apostolic foundation stones making up the building of the universal Church. The key Council vote in favour of shared governance, collegiality, was won on 30 October 1963. It was a major advance in thinking about how the Church worked but it was never to be fully implemented.[16]

So where were this "People of God", the lay people, to be found? In ludicrous secrecy some lay experts provided evidence for Commissions on the Lay Apostolate and Church in the Modern World. Articles by Professor Rosemary Goldie, a lecturer in the Pastoral Institute of the Lateran University, were circulating amongst the Council Fathers. Finally Pope Paul formally invited lay representatives to attend the Council as "auditors". But they were needles in the clerical haystack. Patrick Keegan, an international president of the Young Christian Workers (YCW) addressed the Third Session of the Council. Pope Paul vetted his relatively bland speech and wanted, somewhat redundantly, reference to the "laity's submission to the hierarchy" to be inserted. Esuebe Adjakplay, regional secretary for Africa of the World Federation of Catholic Youth, spoke on the role of lay missionaries. Meanwhile discussions were proceeding to decide the contents of a Decree on the Laity, and whether a future Secretariat should be "of" or "for" the laity. Bishop Eugene d'Souza of Bhopal in India raised hackles by wanting strong lay representation in the Vatican Curia and diplomatic corps. The Tanzanian Archbishop Laurean Rugambwa must have caused consternation with his suggestion that the Catholic principle of subsidiarity should apply to the lay apostolate.[17]

And where were half the Catholic population, women? They were after all the main practitioners, both lay and Religious, of the Catholic Faith. Only from the third session of the Council onwards were some female "auditors" admitted, eight Religious—representing 1.2 million Women Religious—and seven lay, permitted to attend sessions "of interest to women". "Good" was the response of Sister Mary Luke Tobin, Superior-General of the Loretto Sisters, "then I can attend them all". Two were from the developing world: Sister Marie de la Croix Khouzam, president of the Union of Teaching Religious in Egypt, and Sister Marie Henriette Ghanem, president of the Assembly of Major Religious Superiors. They were assigned a special coffee bar to avoid mixing of the sexes, soon dubbed the Bar-Nun. None were permitted to speak in the aula. Cardinal Suenens advocated their participation but the majority of the Council Fathers were simply unquestioning and accustomed to the male *status quo*. There was to be no major breakthrough here.[18]

The schema on mission, *Ad Gentes,* drew strongly on Congar and Ratzinger's theology of the Church, and not unnaturally elicited the highest level of intervention from bishops from the developing world. The indigenous bishops on its conciliar commission were from Cameroon, Tanzania, Ivory Coast, Philippines, Vietnam, Indonesia, India, Mexico and Guatemala . Most of the 25 "consultors" were missionary bishops. Both Asian and African bishops made strong bids for "adaptation" to local culture, implantation not transplantation, what was later to be dubbed "inculturation" of the Church. Bishop Elias Zoghby, the Melkite vicar-general from Egypt, placed the debate within the context of the mission of Christ, "an epiphany, and eruption of the divine light upon the work of creation". The vital role of the catechist was highlighted by Bishops Youghbare, Upper Volta and Kihangire, auxiliary in Gulu, Uganda, as well as the exiled Bishop Massa from Nanyang, China; the former wanted a special Papal body dedicated to the work of catechists.[19]

The Commission was poorly led by Cardinal Gregorio Agagianian, Prefect of the Sacred Congregation for the Propagation of the Faith (SCPF), in charge of the mission territories. The members as usual reached agreement that the preparatory document needed complete rewriting, but met only once during the first session for a friendly get-together. Finally four sub-commissions were formed to work on doctrinal principles, the reasons for the missionary apostolate, formation and co-operation. Between sessions, thirty-two of the bishops and apostolic prefects of West Africa met in Dakar led by Archbishop Gantin of Cotonou. They had particular concern for how to evangelise in the context of rapid social and economic change, and underlined the role of both the catechist and the bishop.[20]

The problem was that the SCPF did not want a special document on Mission and there were bubbling tensions: the competing needs of the vibrant young Churches, the Missionary Orders and the Propaganda's archaic central control. The latter came under attack particularly from a group of Francophone African bishops who saw the Congregation's relationship with them as colonial, imposing a foreign culture, and wanted it divested of its authority. Its role as a financial donor to the mission territories could remain. The battle later came down to a proposal for a new Central Council for Evangelisation within the SCPF, but would this be consultative or decision-making and who would be on it? Positions in the Commission tended to be irreconcilable on the broad issues and between those wanting a broad theology of mission, and those seeking a tightening up of the practical and legal administration of Church life in the mission territories. In the Amazon, for example, half the new Churches fell under the authority of the Propaganda, the other half did not. But the basic question was whether the document should be about the mission of the Church or "the missions", about "Christianisation"—which for Congar could equally well be in the Paris slums—or territorial expansion and the planting of new Churches in distant lands.

The Pope made matters worse by insisting that the schema should be reduced to a few tidy propositions, and given only a "short discussion". This was one of the clearest examples of growing Papal anxiety about the net impact of the Council resulting in ill-advised interventions. The general secretariat of the Pan-African Episcopal Conferences, eleven national and regional conferences, led by Archbishop Jean Zoa of Yaounde were lobbying for a proper debate. They got one—and in muted defiance of the Pope—a full final document. It placed Mission as a responsibility of all the Church not narrowly that of a minority organised as missionaries in mission societies.

The approach of the key documents, *Lumen Gentium* (LG) and *Gaudium et Spes* (GandS), and a Declaration on the Church's relations with non-Christian religions, *Nostra Aetate*, tended to put the Mission Orders on the defensive. "Those who, through no fault of their own, do not know the Gospel of Christ or his church, but who nevertheless seek God with a sincere heart, and, moved by grace, try in their actions to do his will as they know it through the dictates of their conscience— these too may attain eternal salvation (LG 16)." This was because "we must hold that the Holy Spirit offers to all the possibility of being made partners, in a way known to God, in the paschal mystery" (GandS 22). These propositions finally scuppered the ancient position "outside the Church there is no salvation" in favour of a carefully modulated acceptance of the action of Grace in other religions—"All Grace has a communitarian quality and looks towards the Church"—and a clear assertion that Muslims "along with us adore the one and merciful God". But the suspicion lurked that to "acknowledge, preserve, and promote the spiritual and moral goods found among these men, as well as the values in the society and culture" implicitly meant that mission in the normal sense, proclamation of the Gospel, converting people, was redundant. The task was now dialogue.[21]

The day of the main debate on mission opened with an Ethiopian mass, with drumming and clapping presided over by Bishop Haile Cahsay of Adigat, which generated considerable excitement in St Peter's Basilica. The drama was heightened when Pope Paul took the unprecedented step of coming into the *aula* to attend the session, taking his seat at the top table between the two presiding cardinals. He had made a first visit to Africa in July-August 1962 to visit the Milanese consortium IMPRESIT working on the Kariba Dam, and to see the work of the Lombardy Mission. He had just canonised the Uganda Martyrs. His commitment to Africa was manifest but his presence in the *aula* underlined, in his words, "the special seriousness and greatness of the subject". An astonishing 100 speakers had put in a bid to address the assembly. Many of them had been asked to speak by the Superiors of the Mission Societies led by Father Leo Völker of the White Fathers (Missionaries of Our Lady of Africa). The day showed off the Church at its most international.[22]

The subsequent debate and that of the final plenary session on 7 October 1965 threw up most of the themes that were to preoccupy missiologists in the coming years. Archbishop Jean Zoa was insistent that "native clergy" should get exactly the same formation as other clergy—while integrating it in their own culture—and his anguish over the chaos in the Congo and Chinese penetration of Africa was evident. He placed theology of mission at the heart of the Church's life. "Mission is the unique movement which has its origin from the Trinity and returns to it after it has passed through the world and history". Congar was so excited to hear echoes of his own thinking that he enthused about Zoa in his diary "as wonderfully open-minded, intelligent and, as always, with such integrity", (*"toujours aussi magnifiquement libre, intelligent et vrai"*). The Most Reverend Elias Zoghby from Egypt re-inforced Zoa's position, insisting that mission must not impose a "pre-fabricated Christ, a Christ of one people, or some determined civilisation" but respect for the *"Germe du Verbe"* (seed of the Word) placed in each human heart. "The peoples who accept Jesus Christ must be able to express Him in their image, to re-incarnate Him in their likeness, so that he can be everything for everyone", he said. This wonderful oration was delivered provocatively in French, not in the required Latin.[23]

The Irish Carmelite missionary Bishop of Umtali and later redoubtable opponent of the Smith regime in Rhodesia, Donal Lamont, had been polishing up his Latin, and rejected no less eloquently the "*ossa arida*" (dry bones) approach of the schema.[24] A vote was taken to retain some of the dry bones, out of respect for the Pope, but nonetheless to revise the schema totally, allowing new *periti* to become involved. Seventy Missionary Orders combined to request Yves Congar. Johannes Schütte, expelled from China in 1951 and Superior-General of the Divine Word missionaries, brought in Joseph Ratzinger, theologian to Cardinal Frings.[25] "Happily there is Ratzinger", wrote Congar in his diary, "He is a great help, reasonable, modest and with no axe to grind".[26]

The revamped Commission held its meetings in the Divine Word Missionaries' Summer House on Lake Nemi, South of Rome. With the missiologists in the major missionary orders staking out their own ground, the celebrity *periti* did not have things all their own way. Did mission imply a general movement of the whole Church or a special ministry? The Commission Vice-President, Bishop Lokuang of Tainan, Taiwan, supported Congar's position that used Mission in the patristic sense of the Mission of the Divine Persons, and thus the whole Church. As did Alfred Silva, the Rector of the Catholic University in Santiago, Chile. The Latin American bishops wanted the duty of mission to apply also to the Christian faithful. The broadly acceptable compromise formula was that missions were a "peculiar exercise of the universal mission of the Church". So there were *missio*, an all-inclusive and constitutive dimension of the Church, and *activitas missionalis*—what missionaries did among unbelievers.[27]

The final document *Ad Gentes,* to which a wide spectrum of people made a significant input, was in some ways a triumph for the conciliar process despite its cumbersome machinery. Some of its Trinitarian theology was clearly derived from the thinking of the "Oriental" rather than Western Churches. Speakers from the developing world, Africa, Asia and Latin America, made major contributions and their views were reflected in what finally emerged, with some of the Church's best theologians working on the wording and ideas. The emphasis had moved from competition between European missionaries, to collaboration, and to the importance of supporting the young Churches. The Council Fathers had wrested the ball from the canon lawyers of the Preparatory Commission, or as Congar, at his most French, wrote in his diary, things had moved *"du purement juridique à l'ontologie surnaturelle"*, ("from the purely juridical to the realm of supernatural ontology"); in short the theologians had prevailed.[28] The largest vote in favour of any Council document, 2,394, was recorded, but it took until November 1965 to get there. Missionary theology was placed on a sound footing for future generations; the Church had moved from missions to Mission, and this meant none other than co-operation with the Mission of the Son and the Holy Spirit.[29]

The headline debates: Liturgy and Religious Freedom

Had it not been for the Constitution on the Sacred Liturgy promulgated on 4 December 1963, and a dull decree on the mass media, the Council would have had nothing concrete to show for its first year of deliberations. Fear of the Council running into the sands generated a growing momentum. By the time the Council ended in December 1965, four Constitutions, nine Decrees and three Declarations were completed and approved. During this time the trajectory of the Council's thinking, despite counter-attacks and last ditch stands, was clearly away from that of the small Curial minority. They did not lose completely. The result of their opposition usually showed in the ambiguities found in final drafts of documents approved by the assembly and signed by the Pope. And these ambiguities gave them ammunition to block reform when the bishops went home.

The Constitution on the Liturgy was the first of such victories for the majority. *Sacrosanctum Concilium* had a reforming word to say on the totality of worship, from the Divine Office, the daily prayer of the Church, to private devotions, and most notably on the way mass was celebrated. The vexed question of Latin in the canon of the mass was handled with a characteristic balance and caution: the decision was delegated to Bishops' Conferences. Latin *could* continue as the language of the mass—in the Latin Rite of course—but local Bishops' Conferences were to decide to what degree the vernacular would be used instead. The criterion for deciding on any such change was the principle of achieving "full and active participation" by the laity, enabling them, God's gathered people, to realise their "royal priesthood" in the central act of worship of the Church.

It had been obvious from the *aula* interventions that such enabling provisions would open the gates to the removal of Latin from the mass, and result in other changes. In short it would make what happened at the altar more integrated with the prayer and life of the faithful. Good translation into the vernacular was vital. English-speaking bishops, led by Archbishops Denis Hurley of Durban and Paul Hallinan of Atlanta, were already getting together to create an International Commission on English in the Liturgy (ICEL). Catholics would henceforth be given a wider selection of Biblical readings and the Liturgy of the Word, with the homily, would form a significant part of the celebration of the mass. Reflection on the Scriptures, as in the Protestant Churches, was, at least theoretically, back at the heart of Catholic Christian life. An interim, and then a new, Lectionary was the material expression of an interim and then a new—more Biblical –spirituality.

The Constitution on the Liturgy was important at a number of different levels. It empowered both bishops and laity, in equal measure though in different ways, and was a tangible expression of collegiality. This power came not from the Pope but from the formative event of the Eucharist that founded the universal Church anew at, and in, each celebration in a local parish. It was what made a global Church fully local, rooting it in the different cultures of the human family.

From 1959 to 1963, a significant number of dioceses around the world had been tentatively renewing the liturgy. They were now given the green rather than amber light. But, above all, the Constitution intended to reconfigure the mass from something that only the priest did, representing Christ, into a more active communal celebration by God's gathered people, full of theological meaning and catechetical potential for the life of the assembled congregation. This was particularly the vision of Pope Paul VI who took a personal interest in the evolution of the liturgical texts.[30]

Not an arcane—beautiful—language muttered at the altar by a distant priest in colourful vestments, but the Catholic belief that the consecrated bread and wine became the Body and Blood of Jesus Christ, offered up by the worshipping community as a whole, expressed the ineffable mystery of the mass. And it thereby redefined the identity of Catholic Christians as the people of God who both heard and acted on God's word. In this sense liturgical change prefigured and led to the new emphases in the Council's understanding of the constitution of the Church as well as the role of the laity.

But for many around the world the Council became synonymous with these changes in the liturgy, and very little else. For some, sadly but understandably, the loss of Latin as a liturgical language emptied the mystery out of their regular Sunday worship.[31] The timing of the Constitution on the Liturgy and its impact on the laity perhaps made this inevitable. It was much reported on, this most contentious issue for pious worshippers, and was quickly felt in ordinary parish life. The vernacular changes were permitted from the first Sunday of Lent 1965, and the new Missal came into force in 1970.

The Latin mass also became a touchstone of a conflict now cast in the form of "progressive versus conservative", either to conserve the Tridentine liturgy or progress to vernacular worship. Of course this mixed up the instrumental with the substantial and thereby missed the point. In some ways the obsession with Latin was a convenient diversion from the real significance of the Council, the wider role of the Church and the laity in the modern world, what it had to say about politics, modernism, pluralism, the development of doctrine. Or for some, what it did not have to say—at least at enough length—about peace, poverty and underdevelopment. Canon F.H. Drinkwater, writing in the *Catholic Worker* before the close of the Council, described the dispute about liturgy baldly as "an unconscious effort to avoid the more urgent problems confronting the Christian".[32]

But liturgical reformers were as socially aware, if not more so, than any other Catholics. There was no conspiracy to keep the modern world at bay. Those whose priorities prevailed at the Council had rudimentary movements and came from better organised networks. The liturgical movement had made some ground before the Council and the submissions of some 25 per cent of the bishops had expressed interest or concern about it. *Sacrosanctum Concilium* cleared the hurdles early for this and another very simple reason: it had canny, as well as expert, members of its commission and it did not demand any revision of doctrinal principles. Any issues that challenged doctrine were contested repeatedly by the Curial minority throughout the Council. If they saw their guardianship of the truth directly challenged, it became their religious duty to oppose to the end. And so they mustered their forces around the Doctrinal Commissions.

The Declaration on Religious Liberty fell into this doctrinal category. As its champion, the Jesuit theologian John Courtney Murray, later observed, it highlighted the fundamental role of the Council: "to discern the elements of the tradition that are embedded in some historically conditioned synthesis that, as a synthesis, has become archaistic". But this theme evoked the Curialists' nostalgic love of "national Catholicism", a confessional State and a State Church with special privileges. They saw the Liberal State as carrier of an ideology that placed conscience as the sole arbiter of religious precepts and moral truth, drastically diminishing the role of the Church in society. They approved of the position of the Church in fascist Portugal and its colonies, and in Franco's Spain. The Spanish bishops enjoyed the Vatican Concordat with government that blocked any advance by Spanish Protestants. Likewise some of the Latin Americans feared the new evangelical Protestant sects.

Most other Bishops, the North Americans, the Germans and eastern Europeans—Archbishop Joseph Beran, in exile from Prague, and the Polish bishops, notably Wyszynski and Wojtyla, put great store by Religious Liberty—played an important supportive role at critical moments. Like Lammenais, they thought of Liberal institutions as the guarantors of protection for the Church in as much as such institutions protected the freedoms of all. This was both when they were absent—under Communism—and when they were juridically present—as in the USA. Some of the African bishops saw religious liberty in the light of the pressures of local religions and cultures on their new Christians. To some extent the main difference in attitudes was a product of the difference between Southern European and "Anglo-Saxon" attitudes to Liberalism.[33]

Dignitatis Humanae and the treatment of religious liberty had a chequered passage, starting as a question for the Secretariat for Christian Unity, moving to a chapter in *Lumen Gentium* and then, not finding an appropriate home, almost falling by the wayside. But the soil had been well tilled by the American Jesuit John Courtney Murray who had been promoting a Catholic pluralist vision in talks and publications since the Second World War. His was in no way a promotion of "relativism" but an acknowledgement of religious diversity, the need for response from the Catholic Church to it, and a new and mature reflection on the role of the modern State. The influence of the Protestant observers and the important contribution of the Protestant Churches in enshrining religious freedom in the UN's Universal Declaration played a significant role. There was to be a separate and distinct document on religious freedom — the American bishops made sure of that.[34]

Murray's approach to religious freedom followed logically from the debate on Revelation. If Revelation was a free act of God, freely acknowledged and accepted in faith, freedom of conscience was a theological truth, a human necessity. But the Pope vacillated under opposing pressures. No one could easily deny that a singularly stark "development of doctrine" was being proposed. There were grounds for concern, a whiff of "modernism" and the implications of unruly intellectual freedom within the Church to worry about. In response to this inevitable reaction, almost two hundred American bishops rounded up in a remarkable show of unity, demanding the document go forward. Archbishop Hurley described how the "stentorian voice of Cardinal Richard Cushing of Boston rolled and thundered under the dome of St Peter's", while the scripture scholar, Cardinal Albert Meyer of Chicago, put enormous pressure on Pope Paul VI.[35] Finally the Pope pushed the Declaration on Religious Liberty, in modified form, through to a winning vote. He was about to make the importance of religious freedom a key component in a speech to the United Nations. In the event he could hardly contemplate the schema's failure.[36]

The final Declaration showed the impact of concerted attacks from its opponents, the curialists, Spaniards and Colombians, in changing versions of nuanced wording from its proponents. Some expressions were creative and important; juridical "immunity from coercion" replaced a positive assertion of toleration of "error". The State did not have to do something; it had to refrain from something—coercion. Religious liberty was to be derived from an objective natural law, the nature of human dignity and the social order, rather than from a more subjective and personalist championing of freedom of conscience.[37] And it was this theme of human dignity that played a central role in the fourth Constitution promulgated by the Council, *Gaudium et Spes*, for which the Decree of Religious Liberty was an essential adjunct. The Church had undergone a seismic shift since the nineteenth-century Syllabus of Errors, and this shift was to shape Catholic thought in relation to States, and participation in pluralist democracies, for the next half century.

Dialogue with the Modern World

The Second Vatican Council failed in the end to achieve the Montini-Suenens' call for overall balance between the *ad intra* and the *ad extra*. This was because to a great extent it had to rediscover its identity, or at least describe its identity, in a language that touched the heart as well as the intellect. The Council Fathers had no choice but to give priority to the theological work *ad intra*, the nature of the Church, what was meant by divine Revelation, how the Church perceived itself in relation to God's plan of salvation in history, and how this relates to what Christians ought to be doing in the liturgy. And this meant recovering confidence in a dynamic Christian humanism and a Christian understanding of human being, a Christian anthropology.

To do so required nothing less than a corporate retrieval and reinstatement of key parts of two millennia of Catholic tradition by the bishops. As the first chapters of this book illustrated, the reference point for the Council's discarded preparatory documents had been legalistic thinking that barely reached back beyond the late nineteenth century and rested on the writings of Pius XII. "Tradition had shrunk", wrote the Church historian Eamonn Duffy, "from being a cathedral of the spirit to a storeroom in the cellars of the Holy Office".[38] The two great Vatican II Constitutions, *Lumen Gentium* and *Dei Verbum* were *dogmatic* constitutions that undertook this retrieval and reinstatement, restoring tradition to its rightful place above ground in the life of the Church. *Sacrosanctum Concilium*, the Constitution on the Sacred Liturgy, set out to create the conditions in which flesh—sacramental, symbolic, and poetic—was put onto the spirit of the dogmatic texts to communicate their content and meaning to the Christian community. Through these three Constitutions, the Church began to rediscover her identity.

But, as Cardinal Montini told newly ordained priests in Milan in March 1963: "Not only is the Church in search of herself, she is also in search of the world". The fourth and final constitution of the Council, *Gaudium et Spes,* "The Church *in* the Modern World" (*in* not over and against), was—and announced itself as—a *Pastoral* Constitution; it tried to read "the signs of the times" and to argue inductively from them to theological and social insights. Pope Paul VI set the tone in his opening speech to the second session of the Council: "The world will surely realise that the Church looks upon it with profound understanding, with sincere admiration, and with the sincere intention not of mastering it but of serving it, not of despising it but of increasing its dignity, not of condemning it but of bringing it comfort and salvation". It was this emphasis that prevailed and kept out of the official documents, quite remarkably, the condemnation of Communism sought by several influential Cardinals.[39]

This proclamation of a deep solidarity was to be the inspiration and manifesto of *Gaudium et Spes*. Indeed it was finely expressed in its famous opening lines: "The joys and hopes, the grief and anguish of the people of our time, especially of those who are poor or afflicted, are the joys and hopes, the grief and anguish of the followers of Christ as well. Nothing that is genuinely human fails to find a echo in their hearts". But the theme aroused enormous—and unrealisable—expectations. After an erratic, even chaotic, history, it was finally drafted by a large, joint commission with sixty consultors and fifty advisers drawn from both the Commissions on the Lay Apostolate and the Sacred Congregation for the Doctrine of the Faith. Not surprisingly it suffered from a high degree of confusion about its content, passing through no less than eight different drafts.[40]

More importantly for the future, *Gaudium et Spes* revealed deep differences between theologians in Augustinian and Thomist traditions, in two wings of the "progressive" camp, once the common enemy of neo-scholasticism was defeated. These would become accentuated and more significant in the aftermath of the Council. The historian of the Council, Giuseppe Alberigo suggests that all the future conflicts in the Church were intimated in *Gaudium et Spes*. For example, Joseph Ratzinger was uncomfortable with what he saw as the inadequate account of human sin informing the debate, and its optimistic overemphasis on the linear progress of humanity, "an almost naïve progressivist optimism which seemed unaware of the ambivalence of all external human progress", in short a lack of clarity about nature and Grace. To a lesser degree so was Rahner. They both had the sympathies of Reformed and Lutheran Church observers. On the other hand, Cardinal Meyer of Chicago, and Archbishop Denis Hurley, supported the French theologians who wanted the Cosmic Christ theology of Teilhard de Chardin to inform the content. But this elicited even more critical opposition from the Augustinians.[41]

The lack of obvious boundaries to the theme of the Constitution meant that everyone could propose what they considered were important topics. Some of the proposals tried to fill glaring lacunae. But, had they all been incorporated, the result would have been a Noah's Ark of a document. The result was that many from the developing world felt their concerns and perspective was being left out. The Dominican, Louis-Joseph Lebret, who was later to draft Pope Paul's encyclical on development, worked through Cardinal Liénart. "It is not based enough on valid elements, in various civilisations and on non-western aspirations as they can be seen in the Far East, in the Islamic world, and in Black Africa", Lebret wrote. "I find no mention in it", said Bishop Chidimbo of Conakry, "of the difficulties of the peoples of Africa: underdevelopment, colonialism, discrimination according to race or colour; and no further description of the structures of a new society". There were passionate interventions from Archbishop Athaide from Agra in India on racial discrimination, and on tribalism from Archbishop Malula from the Congo, while Bishop Proano of Riobamba in Ecuador spoke of the country's appalling level of illiteracy and of the 15 million Ecuadorians without any schools. Pope Paul VI, under time pressure, was horrified at the "encyclopedia" which was emerging. Interventions on "socioeconomic" matters were reduced to six. "So, the impenetrable jungle of these problems was neatly bypassed", wrote Archbishop Hurley.[42]

The *aula* debate on "Promoting Solidarity of the Family of Peoples" evoked powerful contributions from the developing world. Archbishop Zougrana of Ougadougou, Upper Volta, representing seventy Brazilian and African bishops, called for the international order to be rethought in terms of the Common Good, recalling the Patristic theme that the "superfluous" belonged in justice not in charity to the poor, and lecturing the 'have' nations on their duty to the 'have nots". Patriarch Maximos IV did not mince his words; he was scandalised by " a mediocre and self-centred Christendom" that failed to "make a sustained effort at solidarity with the poor". That pretty much summed up an important element of the view from Africa, Latin America and the Near East.[43]

James Morris, President of the International Catholic Migration Council, spoke for the many laity in the developed world concerned at global poverty. Morris wanted an entire Roman general congregation dedicated to the problem of world hunger, and found support—to no avail—from several influential cardinals. With "16 per cent of the world enjoying 70 per cent of its wealth", and with the rest having an average life expectancy of only thirty-five years, he called for the creation of the machinery to mobilise Catholic efforts on a global scale. The solution was to "spread the benefits and the know-how and resources of the North Atlantic Community to the rest of the world". His vision would be realised in the late 1960s as the major Catholic development agencies got off the ground.

Cardinal Frings wanted national bishops conferences to set up "episcopal works" to alleviate poverty and hunger. Father Gerald Mahon, Superior-General of the Mill Hill Fathers, a missionary society, saw "socio-economic activity as an integral part of the missionary function of the Church". He was promoting the idea of a post-conciliar body dedicated to social justice with two of the Indian bishops, an idea that was to come to fruition in Pope Paul's Justice and Peace Commissions. During his short visit to Bombay in 1965 he called for a World Fund to tackle the problem of underdevelopment. This tantalisingly brief debate was the only public airing of what would become a global concern of the late twentieth century.[44]

At the time of the fourth session twenty women were praying and fasting for unilateral nuclear disarmament in the Cenacle Convent in the outskirts of Rome.[45] Nuclear war had nearly ended the Council in October 1962 and the Cuban missile crisis had been an important stimulus to *Pacem in Terris*. In 1964, against a background of the conflict in Vietnam, and the fall of Khrushchev, China exploded its first atomic bomb. Early in 1965 President Johnson ordered retaliatory raids on North Vietnam, and US bombs were soon raining indiscriminately down. Only nine bishops spoke out in the USA about the plight of civilians. Cardinal Ottaviani, the "conservative", called for a total condemnation of war using every possible means to eliminate it, with much the same passion as Lercaro dealt with the issue of poverty. Pope Paul VI made his famous address to the United Nations, the day before war and peace were discussed at the Council: "No more war, war never again".[46]

Archbishop Hurley "the progressive" saw no way to give up nuclear deterrence.[47] The resistance of bishops from the nuclear powers, the USA and the UK, made any clear outlawing of possession of nuclear weapons impossible. *Gaudium et Spes* left open the question of deterrence in the absence of other ways of ensuring the security of nations, but unequivocally condemned "total war"—indiscriminate destruction of whole cities—and thus any use of nuclear weapons. The arms race was "the most serious injury to humanity and an intolerable one to the poor". There was a long struggle with those who clung to the "presumption of right of lawful authority where no violation of the Law of God is manifestly clear". But the right to conscientious objection to bearing arms was clearly endorsed. Less than a decade earlier Pius XII had said it was wrong for Catholics to be pacifists and to refuse to serve in a just war. Gordon Zahn's *In Solitary Witness*, the story of the 1943 martyrdom of the Austrian Catholic conscientious objector, Franz Jaegerstetter, who repeatedly refused the military oath of unconditional obedience to the Führer, played its part. So had the lobbying of the Cenacle women among whom was a persuasive trio: Dorothy Day, Barbara Wall and Eileen Egan. As the American monk and author, Thomas Merton, wrote somewhat optimistically: "Anyone who follows the Pentagon line does so now with a bad conscience if he is a Catholic and can read".[48]

More than any other document *Gaudium et Spes* showed Catholic theology was far more complex than a simple progressive-conservative divide. It was the Council's vision, the feeling of deep solidarity with the human race and its history, far more than its analysis that marked the importance of *Gaudium et Spes*. By the end of the debates three major emphases emerged: overcoming the split between culture and the Gospel, faith and daily life; repositioning the Church in solidarity with the world; and redefining the rightful autonomy of human beings in a Christian understanding of what it means to be human—a distinctive anthropology based on the person of Christ. There was not a zero-sum game between acknowledgement of the created nature of human being and human autonomy, namely Feuerbach's dilemma that to "enrich Man, one must impoverish God".[49] Rather autonomy meant "created things and societies have their own laws and values which are gradually to be discovered, exploited and ordered by Man".[50]

Nor did Church and Society confront each other as two "perfect societies", signing solemn Concordats; they occupied instead different dimensions of the same space and reality. The real dichotomy lay between the City of God and the Earthly City and these were not coterminous respectively with the Church and the modern world. "By preaching the truth of the Gospel and by clarifying all the spheres of human activity through its teaching and the witness of the faithful, the Church respects and promotes the political freedom and responsibility of citizens", was the conclusion, carrying with it echoes of the Thomist, Jacques Maritain, a close friend of the Pope, and the ever-present French Dominican theologian, Marie-Dominique Chenu.[51]

A New Vision

A transition was taking place: a passage from mediaeval nostalgia to openness to pluralist democracy. The movement gained momentum beyond expectation during the Council. From moralising advice to greater attentiveness to needs. From rote doctrinal answers to questions people had stopped asking, to investigation and enlightened enquiry, a participation in humanity's struggle for the Truth. Not a secular humanism detached from the transcendental, a fundamentalist individualism ignoring the social, but a genuine autonomy. Test everything, hold fast to the good, even the good in the aspirations of Communists for a more just world, but not the ideology of Communism.[52] The new *Ostpolitik*, the Vatican's change in East-West policy, nonetheless came as a shock.

Gaudium et Spes was a far more fitting conclusion to the Fathers' deliberations than the dismissive condescension towards the document—not long to follow—suggested. This was heady stuff for bishops though the changes were well embedded in the calm language of a Pastoral Constitution. The document signed off by the bishops in a mighty rush on 5 December 1965 could never realistically have been a Catholic manifesto on poverty and peace, and it never pretended to be more than work in progress, a first step on a new path. Indeed the document itself provided the pre-conditions for such a path to be opened up. Sensitive topics such as clerical celibacy, birth control and the "population explosion" were kicked into touch by the Pope. Others such as the role of women in the Church were not considered despite the feminist St Joan's International Alliance holding their general assembly in Rome that September. All that had happened was that Cardinal Suenens had successfully called for some women lay auditors to be admitted in October 1963. Some hoped that markers were laid down, but in vain.[53]

The wealth of the Church, especially that concentrated in the Vatican, hovered like the ghost of Hamlet's father over the Council. Cardinal Lercaro said in one of his impassioned speeches: "The Church herself is in truth the theme of the Council, (especially insofar as) she is the Church of the Poor".[54] This was certainly the intention of *Gaudium et Spes*. But Lercaro's hope and plea went only half heard. The Pope in a symbolic gesture gave up the Papal tiara, given to him by the people of Milan. It ended up, though, in the National Shrine of the Immaculate Conception in Washington. Evangelical conviction about poverty was reflected strongly in the life of Men and Women Religious but did not get much of a hearing in the theology of the Council. It would emerge later in the theology of the Church as a consequence of liberation theology. The Church of the Poor was to be championed not in St Peter's but in the city slums and impoverished villages of Latin America.[55]

Bishop Manuel Larrain of Talpa, Chile, and President of CELAM at the time, gave notice during the Council. Latin America had to be attentive to its own "signs of the time" or "the Council will just pass us by", he said.[56] This was no less true but less insisted upon by the local Churches in other parts of the world. Larrain's thoughts were already moving in the direction of a special conference to read the signs of the times for Latin America. Before Larrain died tragically in a car crash in 1966, the seeds he had sown on rough ground in Rome were germinating in richer soil, and would bear fruit at the meeting of the Latin American bishops at the Medellín Conference in Colombia.[57]

As the bishops packed to go home on 8 December 1965, they probably reflected on how much the Council had achieved after a none too propitious start, and worried what it all meant for their own dioceses. They felt part of a confused process of change in the Church. Voting throughout the Council had shown a high degree of consensus and had been overwhelmingly in favour of change; a vote of 1,700 in favour of a text, 500 against, as occurred in the debate on nuclear disarmament was considered abnormally contested. Hearts and minds had been changed, sometimes those of quite prominent figures such as Archbishop Florit of Florence and Bishop Pietro Parente of the Holy Office, converted to episcopal collegiality, Cardinal Lercaro converted to the peace movement, and Cardinal Léger of Montreal who went off to work with lepers in Africa. This was not simply the product of the *aula* speeches, commissions and formal encounters, but the many informal meetings over coffee and meals that brought together bishops from different continents and cultures. What had not been changed were the Curia and the administrative culture of the Vatican. The consoling thought that "they'll be going soon" was a misunderstanding of the way bureaucracies work.

Charting a new course was the problem. It needed a new consensus to hold fast. Newman had written that confusion followed every great Council of the Church; there were certainly significant differences emerging among the "reform" theologians, and a disgruntled minority of the bitter-enders still in place in Rome.[58] And Newman's thought might have indirectly contributed to the Council's deepest process of renewal: "the healing, within Catholicism, of that dissociation of mind and heart, of argument and experience, of structure and feeling", the negative legacy of the Enlightenment's achievement.[59] Or to use a formula of great relevance to the twenty-first century, the refusal to allow faith and reason to be pulled apart by secularism.

Some of the bishops might have wondered if the Council had also succeeded in "bridging the gulf between ourselves and the contemporary society", one of its tasks set by Pope Paul VI.[60] But how could it when the laity were not represented, and none of the participants were women—when it was not a Council of the whole Church?

As the bishops went home, the first shoots of Catholic development agencies in Europe were emerging; lay initiatives, they were responding to "world hunger". Eventually they would grow into organisations with multi-million dollar budgets, the envy of cash-strapped bishops. A significant number of Women Religious in the USA were moving out of schools in the suburbs to work in President Johnson's anti-poverty programmes led by Sargent Shriver, a committed Catholic. Encountering the poverty of black ghettoes in 1965 and campaigning for racial justice with the National Catholic Conference for Interracial Justice (NCCIJ), they became visible in the great Selma to Montgomery protest march for voting rights in Alabama. "After Selma, Sister, you can't stay home again," wrote Sister Mary Traxler, a dynamo in the NCCIJ. Nor did they, as nuns the world over abandoned large convents and strict discipline for small houses and the discipline of working with marginalised people of all sorts. Around the world Catholics, Lay and Religious, were in search of "a new and truer Christ recognizable by identity with the poor, by compassion and a thirst for justice". For many the search took them out of the Church.[61]

How to build a bridge to the contemporary world seemed clear enough to these important networks in the Church. To Church leadership, with a few exceptions, it was unclear. What this bridge meant to the future of Catholicism and Religious life was far less obvious. It was not, as its opponents endlessly repeated, a "secularisation of the Church", rather the rediscovery of a spirituality that acknowledged God's immanence amongst the poorest and, correspondingly, the sacramental quality of the Church's presence in the world. "Bridging the gulf" was at heart a theological problem. In Alberigo's apt summary "Vatican II paid in an obvious way the price for the inertia that first the Catholic conflict with modernity and then the persistence of 'baroque' theology had inflicted on theological thought." One bridge *had* been built: between bishops and theologians from different continents.[62]

No, the Council had dealt inadequately with the critical issues faced by the contemporary world. There had been too many theological battles to be fought and won, or at least not lost. But a pre-condition for doing so, a mature active role for the laity, had been adumbrated, and the groundwork for an incarnational theology had been laid. Had it reformed *ad intra*? No, nor was that an easy matter against entrenched opposition, but structural checks and balances, collegiality, were affirmed. Now there was a firm intention of amendment that drew on the wealth of theological insights in the Council documents and on the inspiration that the Council had imparted to the wider Church. Just how firm, time would tell.

The immediate question was how would the Council be received in the different cultures and Catholic communities around the world? Who would mediate this reception? What were the different constructions put on the transition wrought by the Council to be in local Churches? And had it succeeded in opening up new networks of interaction within a world Church that would no longer be Eurocentric and did not wish to be embedded in a "European" culture? Not least how was the Church going to deal with the challenge of world poverty in future? These were questions about finding creative responses to local needs and about selection of priorities, not simply implantation of an updated universal model of institutional Catholicism put together in Rome which the following chapters will try to explore.

5

THE CHURCH OF THE POOR
IN LATIN AMERICA

At the outset of the Second Vatican Council, an intergovernmental Freedom from Hunger campaign highlighted poverty and world hunger as the moral challenge of the day. The UN declared the 1960s the first development decade and there it was hoped that self-sustaining economic growth would raise living standards for all. Here was a reality experienced directly by the Church in Latin America, Africa, Asia and Europe. Bishops in Latin America, and missionaries and lay workers in Africa and Asia, were already implementing social action programmes to improve the living conditions of their congregations.

In Europe the worker priests had responded to the relative poverty of industrial labour, and the Cardijn groups continued to encourage young Catholics to see the world as it was, not as it might be in the perspective of eternity. But whereas liturgical reform and catechetics appeared with established Catholic movements behind them, combating poverty and world hunger did not. The tangled ideas of the group that came together to discuss poverty at the Council illustrated why not. Voluntary renunciation as a virtue, underdevelopment and injustice, relative and absolute poverty, witness, mysticism, and the worker apostolate, drew them together around the undifferentiated theme of "poverty".

The Council's official message to the world on 20 October 1962 sounded clear enough; it spoke of "compassion for the crowds that suffer from hunger, misery and ignorance" and of the Church's concern that "goes out first of all to the most humble, the poorest, the weakest". But in the Council's subsequent formal documents and proceedings, the scandal of poverty amidst affluence was the dog that didn't bark.

Indications that poverty was a primary concern for the Church were confined to the margins of the main conciliar events, or formed minor interventions in the discussions of two or three Schemata. Occasional *detailed* textual signs of these interventions were only to be found in *Lumen Gentium* and *Ad Gentes*.[1]

The failure to address the problem of poverty was not for want of trying. This was the faltering beginning not the culmination of a cohesive movement. A small but dedicated group of bishops formed early in the first session of the Council to raise the issue. Their difficulty stemmed from the wide, and at times dissonant, variety of perspectives they brought to the problem. As far as influencing Council documents was concerned, two of their contending approaches had built-in limitations. On the one hand, there was the experience of the French worker-priests alert to the relative poverty and deprivation of the European working class, and its distance from the Church, but weakened by Papal condemnation and Pius XII's dissolution of their movement.[2] On the other, was the vast perspective of the "Third World" Church with its experience of the damaging consequences of what was described as "underdevelopment", a theme much referred to by the Latin Americans, and most notably by the charismatic Bishop Helder Camara from Brazil and Manuel Larrain from Chile. At a time when intercontinental travel still was not easy and Popes moved out of Rome infrequently, the Latin American experience remained distant, a viewpoint marginalised by the Eurocentric bias of the Council's preoccupations. Since 1958 there had been worker-priest movements in a number of Latin American countries, most notably in Argentina where they played an important role in the radical national Movement of Priests for the Third World. This radical strand was even more marginal.[3]

Poverty as a path to holiness did not necessarily motivate action for social justice. A third and important linking perspective was a more generalised anxiety among many of the Council Fathers about the prevalence of episcopal *luxe*, the finery of high office in the Church, viewed in the light of the Church's mission, a concern that reached all the way to the Papacy. Its corollary, a radical response of evangelical renewal through poverty and simplicity, a personal commitment to poverty of life in the light of the Gospel, associated notably with Charles de Foucauld, introduced a voice from within the Muslim world and was championed by Bishop Georges Mercier of Laghouat in Algeria.[4]

A doughty proponent of poverty as holiness was Father Paul Gauthier. In 1954 Gauthier left the Major Seminary in Dijon where he was a professor to become a worker priest, then, with Archbishop George Hakim, the Melkite Bishop of Galilee, he set up the *Fraternité des Compagnons de Jésus Charpentier* in Nazareth in 1958. This was a Christian settlement of some 100 families in a workers' co-operative. The powerful Patriarch Maximos Saigh IV supported Hakim's ideas. Gauthier's friendship with Bishop Charles-Marie Himmer of Tournai recruited to the cause another advocate of the mission to workers, along with Bishop Alfred Ancel and his Cardinal Archbishop, Pierre Gerlier, of Lyons. The Argentinian theologian, Enrique Dussel worked as a carpenter in the community from 1959-1962, seeing in it a model for the "popular" Church. It was more an association based on personal contacts than a movement.[5]

The first meeting of the soon to be called "Church of the Poor" took place on 26 October 1962 led by Cardinal Gerlier. He described the group's priority: "to act in such a way as to bring the problem of the evangelisation of the poor, of the apostolate in the worker *milieu*, to the centre of the Council's preoccupations". It was Gerlier who, after a Eucharistic Congress in Rio, had convinced Dom Helder Camara to use his considerable charisma in favour of the poor of Rio's *favelas*.[6] The underlying rationale of the Church of the Poor group was, in the words of Bishop Himmer, echoing those of Pope John, that the Church could only be true to itself by reflecting "its essence" which was "ordained by its founder for the service of the poor".[7]

Himmer, at the time, was circulating Gauthier's *Les Pauvres: Jésus et l'Eglise*, a book which dwelt on the division between workers, the poor and the Church, a growing concern also for the Latin American Church. The complex nature of the debate was indicated by Bishop Mercier's headings for topics that the group needed to consider and which included both relative and absolute poverty: "[1] development of poor countries [2] evangelisation of poor and workers [3] poor face of Church, social presence of Christian practice of poverty in the Church [4] enlightening public opinion, simple gestures and a world congress". By World Congress he meant a Christian version of the 1955 non-aligned Bandung Conference, an idea of Helder Camara's, whom one commentator called " a seeker of the impossible".[8]

A second meeting of the group in the Belgian College on 5 November drew together some fifty bishops, including Cardinal Montini from Milan and Cardinal Yago from Abidjan, Ivory Coast, though most of those present were Latin Americans—mainly from Brazil, with some from Colombia, Chile, Argentina and Uruguay. Cardinal Lercaro sent a representative to the group during the First Council Session, but unlike Mercier and to some extent Gerlier, did not become an integral member of it, nor see himself as answerable to it. Bishop Mercier was also promoting another big idea, a caucus around the Pope to advise on the problem of underdevelopment.

Montini, once elected Pope, requested in October 1963 his fellow Italian, the Bologna Cardinal Lercaro, to submit concrete proposals on the themes that the group wanted incorporated into the Council documents. Lercaro was more interested in mystical theology, centred on an evangelical Church of the Poor, rather than wanting to promote the more pastoral vision of the majority. He had some interesting ideas about cultural poverty: "renunciation of the covetous possession of a finished and closed conceptual system" being the most striking and resonant. He also suggested that Catholics should substitute giving to the poor for fasting and abstinence. But there was no clarity; the injustice of poverty as oppression sat next to poverty as a virtue and a mystical path to God. A potentially key link between the Pope and the group was turned into a bottleneck. The Bologna cardinal, President of the Liturgical Commission, and with fingers in several pies, submitted nothing for over a year.[9]

The other major difficulty was that the "Church of the Poor" bishops occupied on the whole junior episcopal offices and were under-represented on the major Commissions. Once big Bandung-style ideas, or a proposed Secretariat for Modern Issues to deal with poverty, were squashed, the Commissions were the only entry points to the Council's deliberations. Thirteen bishops from East and Central Africa wanted the introduction to *Lumen Gentium* to deal specifically with poverty.

During the highpoint of the group's activities in the Second Session, when they were meeting weekly, the Council Fathers showed a growing sensitivity to the theme of poverty in the Church, largely attributable to their action. Some references in *Ecclesiam Suam* published by Pope Paul VI in Summer 1964 reflects this mood. A few hundred bishops were willing to sign thirteen propositions that circulated committing them to "poverty of life according to the Gospel". The worker priest movement was not entirely moribund. After meetings in France on the worker priest issue that involved both Himmer and Ancel—they were still held in high regard by many—some worker priests who were toiling secretly in factories asked the Council to debate the issue.

The group's impact on Paul VI was most clearly demonstrated by his response to the Italian President on the tarmac prior to departure for the Holy Land on 4 January 1964, in what was the first foreign visit of a Roman Pontiff outside the Vatican since the beginning of the nineteenth century. Father Gauthier and Bishop Mercier had both formally invited him to Nazareth during the Second Session, though there is no evidence that this was critical in his decision to take this unprecedented step. Nonetheless his parting shot in front of the Italian press corps was to explain his visit as taking the concerns of the poor, the sick, refugees and those deprived of justice back to the "source" in Jerusalem, as if in direct response to the Church of the Poor group. The tenor of the entire visit was characterised by an evangelical simplicity—there were only twelve people in the Papal entourage—and it was evident that Paul VI was using his sense of the symbolic to effect. Likewise the gesture of giving up the Papal tiara indicated the same intention, to put his authority behind calls for evangelical poverty in the Church.[10]

But during the third session, when the poverty group met only twice, it was clear that the early promise was not going to be fulfilled. The tangled ideas were slowing them down and the group was beginning to fragment. In late 1964, the Pope had to remind Lercaro twice to return to the task he had requested a year earlier. Ancel asked eleven bishops to form a consultative body to get things moving. But Lercaro's final report appeared to ignore the preparatory work of the group entitled "La Pauvreté dans l'Eglise et dans le Monde". The report was passed to the head of the Council of Presidents, Cardinal Tisserant, and died the death. An additional pastoral enquiry on the wealth of the Council bishops irritated some of the French contingent though it may have recruited one or two others.[11]

It was soon apparent that it was Schema XVII, *Gaudium et Spes*, that held out the most promise for an elaborated treatment of the topic. Its final mixed Commission had group members on it: Ancel as a Vice-President of the central sub-commission, Camara, Larrain (Chile) and the ex-missionary bishop of Mwanza, Tanganyika, Blomjous. But Bishop Ancel who was working with Congar and Louvain theologians was thoroughly frustrated. He disagreed profoundly with what he saw as the naïve symbolic approach of Mercier and the Foucauldians whose emphasis was on "living the mystery" rather than articulating it theologically. Several felt this penchant for symbolism demonstrated "an unwillingness to come to terms with the way the Council worked".[12] Paul Gauthier got fourteen supportive bishops to sign a preface to his new book, *Consolez mon Peuple: Le Concile et l'Eglise des Pauvres* (*Console my People: the Council and the Church of the Poor*). Much to Ancel's dismay, an Italian version was launched preemptively in Rome into the midst of the controversy. To underline the symbolic link to the Early Church, the Foucauld faction led by Patriarch Maximos Saigh IV concelebrated a mass in the catacombs of Saint Domitilla with a new recruit, the Melkite bishop of Beirut. Whereupon Bishop Ancel withdrew from the group taking his political skills with him, leaving the "Church of the Poor" group with little tactical expertise and much the poorer for it.[13]

The group's fundamental problem throughout the Council was the lack of a theology that could incorporate the range of issues, doctrinal, pastoral and developmental that vied for attention under the heading of "Church of the Poor". It was difficult to bring experiences as diverse as immersion in the Muslim world, the European worker *milieu* and missionary Sisters among black Americans, the plight of the Latin American peasantry and the developing World, into a coherent story. The "Church of the Poor" group was simply too diverse to remain united. It was dealing with at least three distinct kinds of problem, and spanning several conciliar documents and decrees, in a Council that had, by 1965, an impossibly heavy schedule. In the febrile atmosphere of conciliar Rome, with bishops very tired, it remained fragmented, overwhelmed by contending priorities, needing a common context of concern and the benefit of the slow process of maturation that had already begun among Latin American theologians on their continent and would culminate at the Medellín Conference. It is to this process that we now turn, away from the European Church and into the experience of the Church of the Poor in what was then known as the "Third World".

"Catholic Action" in Brazil

The importance of the Second Vatican Council for Latin America, as for much of the rest of the world, was that the theology of the Church, contained particularly in *Lumen Gentium*, acted as enabling legislation. It affirmed a movement that saw the life of the Church in historical perspective and rooted its reflection in biblical sources. It gave a green light for the laity to take up their responsibilities in economic, social and political forms of engagement in their different countries, and to do so as leaders rather than docile followers in a hierarchical structure.

Gaudium et Spes encouraged Catholics to act after analysing the particularity of their local circumstances, rather than merely implementing directives from the centre. This put the experience of local communities at the forefront, thereby privileging those with education who were willing and able to articulate their experience in theological and political terms. Given the vast Catholic population of Latin America, its history and political context, this was inevitably where Catholicism was pre-disposed to favour change.

The founding of the Latin American Episcopal Council (CELAM), meeting in general assembly for the first time in 1955, created an official continent-wide body through which the variety of Latin American religious experience, particularly in work for social change, could be shared and sometimes coordinated. Bishop Manuel Larrain of Talca, Chile, French-trained and head of the JOC, Young Catholic Workers, in Chile, a participant in the "Church of Poor" group, was one of its enthusiastic founders. Its meetings, operational departments, and pastoral institutes drew in theologians from around the continent who began sharing new forms of pastoral experience at a continental level. They in turn were forming continent-wide alliances. Between 1964-1965 four encounters involving—mainly—Catholic theologians from around the continent, were held in Bogotá, Colombia, Cuernavaca, Mexico, Havana, Cuba, and Petropolis, Brazil. Their perspective was increasingly how the Church and the social forces at work in Latin America affected the poor and oppressed, and what this meant for the future of theology. The Centre for Intercultural Formation in Cuenavaca, Mexico, led by Ivan Illich, and the *Instituto Pastoral Latinoamerica* in Quito, Ecuador, drew in Church workers from all over the Americas, and spread new pastoral methods. Father Rutilio Grande, a Salvadorian, for example, could spend time there, or visit the Ecuadorian diocese of Bishop Leonidas Proano, Riobamba, to watch the practical training of lay Delegates of the Word in their communities. CELAM itself rapidly became *par excellence* a "site of struggle" for the heart of the Latin American Church.

What happened after the Council in Latin America took place not as a distant echo of events in Rome, a disturbance rippling outwards to the periphery. There was instead a dynamic already apparent in parts of the Latin American Church that was given unexpected momentum at a critical moment. It was not that the Latin American bishops came away from the Council in 1965 with a whole new set of ideas to implement, though some did, but that for an important minority the Council could be interpreted as a powerful affirmation of their deepest intimations and sense of their Church's direction. For other Latin Americans it confirmed their fears that the Barque of Peter was heading for the rocks.

In its North-East dioceses, the Brazilian Church was in many ways remarkably advanced in awareness of, and reaction to, poverty and injustice. Though desperately poor the region was not ecclesiastically isolated or backward. As a result, Brazil during the 1950s formed the crucible of Catholic responses to "development" in Latin America which ranged from support for neo-conservatism to Christian Democracy and revolutionary movements. The Brazilian Church supported the country's populist governments and their reformist policies. The meetings of the Bishops Conference at a national level allowed a sharing of experience and analysis in a fast changing situation. Because of his position and personality, Helder Camara's charismatic commitment to social change, formerly exercised mainly as national assistant for Catholic Action, an officially sanctioned movement for social transformation, had relatively free rein. In this he had the support of the Papal nuncio, Dom Armando Lombardi, during the critical decade 1954-1964.[14]

Brazil changed from being a predominantly rural to a predominantly urban society prior to the Council. The strains of migration and rapid economic growth, followed by rampant inflation, and then stagnation in the early 1960s, produced a growing social and political crisis in a country marked by stark disparities in wealth and divided into a socio-economic patchwork: from semi-feudal, patrimonial estates in the impoverished North-East to a modern industrialised economy—cars, washing machines, TVs—and a burgeoning middle class forming in Rio, Belo Horizone and São Paulo a triangle of wealth.

Despite the agrarian reform efforts of two governments, poverty—70 per cent illiteracy and 50 per cent infant mortality in the North
East—was increasing. Radical rural movements, the *ligas camponesas*,
flourished, led by Marxist militants pitted against the owners of the
fazendas, large estates, and adeptly mobilising semi-servile labourers
deprived of basic human rights. In 1964 the military seized power, reacting to President Goulart's left-wing rhetoric and nationalisations,
and ending a period of populist government with which the Church
had closely collaborated.[15]

Throughout the 1950s the bishops of the North-East and Minas Gerais spoke out against the inhuman conditions of the rural poor, the
scourge of unemployment and hunger, and the challenge to the Church
of the structural changes taking place.[16] In some cases it was motivated
by fear of Communism. Dom Eugênio Sales of Natal Diocese in Rio
Grande do Norte—later as Cardinal Archbishop of Rio to become an
opponent of liberation theology and the "popular Church"—made one
of the earliest practical responses to widespread injustice and impoverishment. His *Serviço de Assistência Rural* (SAR), established in 1949,
and then stimulated by the successful advance of the *ligas*, became a
vehicle for Church-led anti-Communist rural unionisation. Transplant-
ed to Pernambuco where several bishops joined with Dom Eugenio to
found in July 1961 the *Servicio de Orientação Rural de Pernambuco*
(SORPE), the movement spread to all the North-Eastern states by 1964.
Meanwhile Dom Eugenio, with government support for "educate to
transform", was pioneering Catholic radio schools and, by 1960, the
Brazilian Catholic Bishops Conference (CNBB), influenced by the bishops of the North East, had introduced radio stations into five dioceses,
and by 1963, with government funding for literacy and distance learning, they were operating in 57 dioceses with 7,500 instructors on the
ground. As far as the Council was concerned this might have been happening on the moon.[17]

The same period witnessed in the Church a conscious differentiation of the "*assistential*" approach to action—essentially traditional
forms of charitable works—from its model of rural development and
agrarian reform. This shift did not initially call radically in question
the dominant liberal capitalist model, rather bishops thought in terms
of appeals to landowners and more rapid "modernisation". But most
importantly, the CNBB broadly endorsed *conscientização*, conscienti-

sation, the awakening through literacy of the rural poor to the roots of their poverty in unjust structures. This was not a matter of either/or, of rejecting charity for political action, but both/and. Helder Camara started CARITAS Brazil in 1956 to perform traditional works of charity, such as feeding the hungry, and, representing the bishops of the region, worked with government on a regional development plan, *Operação Nordeste*. This later became SUDENE, *Superintendência do Desenvolvi do Nordeste*, the North East Regional Development Agency. CARITAS itself later supported health work in industrial areas as a basis for community organisation and conscientisation, abandoning the old distinction. [18]

The reformist and progressive bishops were strengthened in 1961 when Pope John published *Mater et Magistra* encouraging rural reform, and appealing for "structural reform and improvement for the underdeveloped masses" as an urgent task. The Chilean bishops responded in 1962 with two strong pastoral letters on these themes, *La Iglesia y el Campesinado chileno* and *El Deber social y politica en la hora presente*. "Land expropriation", declared the Brazilian CNBB in 1963, "not only does not contradict the Church's social doctrine, it is one of the means of realizing the social function of rural property".[19] Agrarian reform remained a major demand of Latin American Catholic Social Teaching expressed repeatedly in pastoral letters, and leading much later to ecological concerns.

The Brazilian Church's commitment to the *Movimento de Educação de Base* (MEB) whose President was Dom José Távora, Bishop of Aracaju, was of a different nature. Paulo Freire, whose radical methodology the MEB adopted, was director of an education extension programme run out of the University of Recife, Pernambuco, the *Serviço de Extensão Cultural* (SEC). Freire sought ways of breaking the shackles of fatalism using literacy, so restoring the individual's capacity to exert their creative powers and transform the world as part of a dynamic community. His description of Brazilian agricultural labour as "beings in the process of becoming"—not as economic units—contained a substratum of existentialism as well as elements of early Marxist thought. "Through their continuing praxis, men simultaneously create history and become historical-social beings", was Freire's *credo*. The methodology was not expressly Christian but it dovetailed with the historical theology emerging from the Vatican Council, and was absorbed into liberation theology. The groups gathered together to listen to the literacy programmes on Catholic radio schools often later turned themselves into basic Christian communities (CEBs).[20]

Freire's thought was radical and socialist but a far cry from Leninism. The capacity to transform was "not a gift bestowed by the revolutionary leadership but their own *conscientizão*". The goal was not dissimilar from forming what the Italian Marxist Antonio Gramsci called "organic intellectuals", not a vanguard Party, and required the fullest participation of the poor in decision-making. Indeed this approach created a certain ideological *basismo*, what Clodovis Boff called a "fetishism of the people", that eschewed the "manipulation" of the popular will by strong political parties directing the popular movement, and differentiated the Catholic from the secular Left.[21] Before the 1964 military coup, MEB was an important agent for the politicisation of up to a quarter million of the Brazilian rural poor. It drew in radical elements in the Church and, unlike other Church movements, was less obviously competing with Communist-led organisations, indeed could be, and was, seen by the Right as part of a common subversive preparation for revolutionary change.

The grit in the oyster of Catholic Action was the Catholic student movement organised in *Juventude Universitária Católica* (JUC), fed by the younger school-age *Juventude Estudential Católica* (JEC), and their radical chaplains. Many of these chaplains had spent study time in Europe absorbing *la nouvelle théologie*, and thanks to the Cardijn methodology of see-judge-act felt comfortable dealing in the language of class and class conflict to describe the Brazilian situation. Inspired by the Cuban Revolution, the tenth annual meeting of the JUC in 1960 was a turning point; it openly defined the movement as part of the "Brazilian revolution".[22] JUC militants fanned out, attempting to radicalise further the Church's educational and agrarian programmes, and dominated the National Union of Students.

In 1962, reacting to the brakes increasingly applied by an anxious hierarchy, a militant minority of some 3,000 formed *Ação Popular* (AP), an openly vanguard movement of students, workers and peasants committed to mobilisation "in a struggle against the double domination of capitalism (international and national) and feudalism". Bishop Helder Camara and some of the bishops from the North East tried to mediate between AP and the Bishops Conference, but alarm bells were ringing and outright opposition from the Cardinal Archbishop of Rio, Dom Jaime Câmara, was evident, before the military crushed and repressed the revolutionary group. The JOC, the Catholic worker youth movement, which boasted 23,000 members in 1961, and its adult counterpart (ACO), followed an almost identical trajectory, but one that stopped short of overt Marxism; both were savagely repressed during the later 1960s and early 1970s, and virtually wiped out.[23]

Brutal military dictatorship in Brazil between 1964-69 swung the majority in the Church into a more defensive and less radical direction. But not Bishop Helder Camara. Within three days of the launch of the 1964 military coup, he persuaded seventeen bishops to sign a protest to the army calling for release of prisoners and respect for human dignity. Troops broke into his episcopal palace in Recife the following day. A document emerging from the CNBB abjectly described the coup as the army preventing "the implantation of a Bolshevik regime" thus avoiding the possible suppression of "the most sacred freedoms and especially religious and civil freedom".

By the time the national CNBB held their annual meetings in Rome in 1964 and 1965, the springtime for the radicals was over. The bishops formulated an Emergency Pastoral Plan that called for manageable small communities within the parish. The Conference made middle-of-the-road choices for the offices of President and General-Secretary. The reformist bishops hung on to leadership of key departments—Dom Eugenio Sales, Public Opinion, and Dom Fernando Gomes of Paraiba, Special Pastoral Action, among others. Dom Helder given Social Action was reduced to working mainly in the North East around his new diocese of Olinda-Recife, and hardly at all at a national level. At the same time the Catholic Action movements were brought back under diocesan control. The changes were not a complete "counter-reformation" against the advocates of social change. But an epoch of spirited pastoral direction in the CNBB was ended. The co-ordination of radical pastoral action within the Brazilian Church was weakened, and the "moderates", in the cautious centre ground, could no longer be taken for granted to support social and economic measures promoting the poor.[24]

On the Right of the Church stood a powerful lay minority with clerical backers, most notably Archbishop Proença Sigaud of Diamantia—who later founded "Family, Tradition and Property" as a Catholic anti-Communist crusade. Military chaplains and archconservative priests formed a religious alliance with authoritarian rule, with a rump of upper middle class pious associations as its tacit supporters. During the 1968 CNBB conference, seventeen bishops representing this position wrote to President Arturo Costa da Silva pledging allegiance to the regime. But the vast majority were either conservative modernisers who believed in a well-trained and disciplined laity or reformists open to more free-wheeling lay movements and the Council's vision of the need for structural change to end poverty.

National Security ideology, devised in Brazil's National War College, spread to other Latin American countries during the late 1960s and 1970s, as oligarchies backed by the military, or outright tyrannical military rulers trained and supported by the USA, came to power. It shared similarities throughout Latin America and sparked unprecedented militancy in the Church against both the state and cautious Church leaders. In Venezuela, Guatemala, Argentina, Peru, Mexico and Chile, a period of dictatorship saw small groups of dissident clergy and students confront nuncios and Church leaders, challenging their authority and sometimes calling for elections of new bishops. Often such militant groups only succeeded in alienating sympathetic reformers and frightening the authorities in Rome. Radicalism in Church and in social matters generally, but not invariably, now went together. The Catholic Right identified this turmoil and insubordination in the Church as a sign of Communist infiltration, and a backlash was not long in coming. The Church in Brazil—and to a lesser degree later in Argentina—was characterised by clergy disenchanted with Church leadership still retaining the support of sympathetic figures among the hierarchy. Brutal repression drew different ranks in the Church together.[25]

This solidarity as a group was important. Under the National Security State, many bishops who were more than ready to condemn radical Catholics, for one reason or another, privately or publicly, rallied to call for their release from prison and, by extension, for an end to torture and repression of all opponents of the government. The arrest of the radical Dominican, Frei Betto, along with his fellow São Paulo Dominicans in 1969, was a case in point. The same reaction but with less long term solidarity in the face of revolutionary threats was shown in Central America where the language of human rights provided common ground and rallied bishops against brutal dictatorships. The National Security State, set up as a bulwark against what was called

Communism but encompassing all social change in the interests of the poor, brought together Christians to protest against torture who might otherwise have been divided on politics, strategy and theology. The experience of the Church in Chile after General Pinochet seized power with the violent overthrow of the Allende government in 1973, shared similar features with that of Brazil a decade earlier. Cardinal Raúl Silva of Santiago, who led CARITAS Chile before being made a bishop in 1959, set up organisations to defend the victims of human rights violations in the wake of the military coup. The political Right was also in evidence; Bishop Eladio Vicuna of La Serena went out of his way to praise the end of democracy in Chile.

Attitudes to revolutionary disorder and violence as a means of achieving political change were critical here, and lay behind factional divisions. Paul VI in his 1967 encyclical on development, *Populorum Progressio*, found violence admissible only in the context of longstanding tyranny and as a last resort. The decision of Father Camilo Torres to seek laicisation to join the Colombian guerrillas in 1965 had widespread reverberations. One of only a handful of examples throughout the continent, it became the—false—stereotype of radical involvement in social change by a Church that was overwhelmingly non-violent. Father Gaspar Garcia Laviana, was the other notable example in Nicaragua, a worker-priest and Sacred Heart Religious from Spain who died quickly, in 1978, once in combat. In Guatemala, Six Maryknoll missionaries, three priests and three Sisters, were about to do the same in 1967 when they were betrayed, fled to Mexico, and then to the USA. Such examples were extremely rare but enabled the Right to equate radicalism with revolutionary violence.[26]

In Nicaragua, despite united opposition to Somoza, Church involvement fragmented around identification with a political Party, support for the Sandinista cause and its armed struggle against the tyrant. What sustained unity in Brazil was that the perceived threat of revolutionary change was far weaker, so the dangers of lay radical action seemed less. Nonetheless, Catholic Action was initially outside the hands of individual local bishops. The large numbers of Church leaders and Religious, both Brazilian and foreign, who had become committed to radical social change through the influence of lay organisations, both inside and outside formal Church institutions, had a national impact.

The Vatican's support for human rights, strongly stated and legitimated in Pope John's 1963 encyclical *Pacem in Terris*, provided a timely common language for a variety of centre-left positions. The secular discourse of human rights provided an almost uncontestable currency for talking about social morality. The advocacy of non-violent action and championing of the UN Declaration, the key strategies adopted by Helder Camara and forming the basis of the movement he promoted, "Action, Justice and Peace", were difficult to counter from a Right wing Christian perspective. Some other charges had to be, and were, trumped up. Conversely the modest Communist threat could be used by radicals precisely to justify interventions by Church leaders that might otherwise have been opposed by the Right. "To persist in a purely spiritual evangelisation would soon result in giving the impression that religion is something separate from life", Dom Helder said in a speech in October 1964, opening the Regional Seminary for the North East. "It would even tend to support the view that religion is a great alienating influence, the opium of the people."[27] Given the perennial fear of Communism in the Curia in Rome, this was a potentially unifying tactic and a compelling response to the anxieties of the middle class.

The Church's responsibility to pre-empt violent revolutionary action and the encroachment of alien Communism was widely felt and shared across a spectrum of political positions. The role of the Soviet Union in post-revolutionary Cuba in 1961-1963, bringing atheistic Communism into the Caribbean, offshore from Latin America, had increased fears. Only sometimes did this result in a strong Christian Democrat Party, occasionally well funded by the CIA. National Democratic struggles against oligarchies and the military were using the Marxist analysis of home-grown intellectuals. The work of Anibel Ponce in Argentina, José Carlos Mariategui in Peru and Farabundo Marti in El Salvador were avidly studied by the student Left. In both poetry and literature Latin America was discovering a growing sense of itself as a cultural and political entity under no-one's tutelage, and with few intellectual preconceptions. Mario Vargas Llosa's *La Guerra del fin del Mundo* (The War of the End of the World), published in Spain in 1981, is a fine example of this literary imagination coming of age.[28]

Many erroneous preconceptions about Catholic Latin America have been used to further a line of theological argument. In El Salvador, in Aguilares' ten urban communities and twenty-seven rural ones, total population 30,000, just 40 kilometres from the capital, no more than 5,000 "had any inkling of the Gospel", for 2,000 it meant something, and only 400 could be said to be committed Christians. In Latin America overall mass attendance varied from 12 to 25 per cent with a vast difference between elite and masses in understanding of the content of faith. At the Catholic University in Rio almost 70 per cent of university students professed to be "atheist" in 1960s surveys. The industrial proletariat was small. And only a tiny minority of the Latin American movements of the Left were Soviet-style Communist. Rising levels of student support for the Church by the end of the decade was certainly associated with Catholic engagement with social issues and hopes that the Church might become an ally of the Left. It was easy to use misleading statistics to make it look as if political engagement by the Church was diminishing the vibrancy of a committed Catholic community. The opposite was often the case.[29]

The assertion of the continent's maturity and independence amid highly contested political visions was reflected in economic theories, some of which were adopted by liberation theologians. Latin American economists talked about "dependent capitalism" and "peripheral economies" linked to the centre, North America. On the one hand there was the work of Fernando Henrique Cardoso focussing on internal factors within the dependent countries, on the other that of André Gunder Frank, adopted by the radical Church, that saw the roots of Latin American poverty in the "underdevelopment" created by the industrialised "North Atlantic" economies, as a result of what was confusingly called J.F. Kennedy's "developmentalism", a pejorative term for his "Alliance for Progress".[30]

An influential figure in the economic debate was the Argentinean Raúl Prebisch, secretary-general of UNCTAD (United Nations Conference on Trade and Development). Prebisch later headed the UN Economic Commission for Latin America. He pointed to short term instability, fluctuating prices and long term deterioration in the terms of trade as the roots of the continent's economic problems. The niceties of these debates mainly passed the bishops by though some of the basic ideas were absorbed. In 1966 CELAM held a planning meeting in Mar del Plata, Argentina and Dom Helder Camara again pressed his call for "structural transformation" and raised the problem of "underdevelopment" in the region.[31]

The Development of Peoples. More influential for the Church's social teaching in the long run than the Latin American economists was a Breton Dominican Louis-Joseph Lebret, whose ideas rallied Catholic developmentalists on several continents. Early experiences organising local fishermen against fishing cartels off the Britanny coast introduced him to the problems of development. High office in the French navy brought him to national prominence before he joined the Dominican Order. In 1964 the United Nations Conference on Trade and Development (UNCTAD) met for the first time in Geneva. Only two men received a prolonged standing ovation from the representatives of the assembled nations; one was for Louis-Joseph Lebret, Pope Paul VI's envoy, the other was for Che Guevara, sent by Fidel Castro. Their speeches seemed to encapsulate the rival choices facing Latin America.

By 1964 Lebret had become an internationally recognised promoter of integral development having worked as a consultant for a number of "Third World" governments. He knew Latin America and had served as Helder Camara's adviser during the preparation of *Gaudium et Spes*. An early proponent of a "right to development", language that took the Church onto the terrain of the Left, he had the ear of the Pope. "In a humanity which realises solidarity", Lebret declared, "the right of all peoples to development must be recognised and respected". At the time it was a challenging application of human rights thinking.[32]

After Geneva, UNCTAD became a permanent UN institution and the Pope asked Lebret to draft an encyclical addressing its principal responsibility: world trade and development, cast in the Catholic mould of international social justice and the relationship between rich and poor nations. The resulting *Populorum Progressio* (Development of Peoples) appeared in 1967 as a development of the Church's reflection on the requirements of human dignity in the context of the contemporary world: Western-directed international development, an incipient new wave of globalisation, and the dominance of modernisation theory. The document was derided by the *Wall Street Journal* as "warmed over Marxism" and *Time* magazine detected in it " the strident tone of an early twentieth-century Marxist polemic". It was seized on by Dom Helder who immediately gave a paper at the 1967 CNBB conference on the importance of its implications for Brazil. A CELAM meeting that November discussed the encyclical and endorsed its commitment to the poor.

The second Vatican Council had acknowledged that "created things and societies themselves enjoy their own laws and values which must be gradually deciphered, put to use, and regulated by men", in other words a full acknowledgement of the rightful autonomy of science, economics, culture and politics.[33] *Populorum Progressio* draws on these disciplines to undertake just such a critical decipherment and, most notably, attempts to analyse causes before proposing preliminary solutions. Acknowledgement of the autonomy of the social sciences, as Clodovis Boff and José Miguez Bonino welcomed, allowed Marxian analysis in through the back door as a way of mediating theological understanding. As liberation theologians repeatedly explained, this did not necessarily mean adopting Marx's position on religion, or commending the domination of politics by ideology.[34]

Prominent among the causes of injustice cited are unjust structures. Pope Paul VI, making his own the radicalism shared by Camara/Lebret, demanded structural changes, "bold transformations in which the present order of things will be entirely renewed or rebuilt".[35] The rationale came from the integral humanism found in Maritain: "the economy should be at the service of Man"; the "universal social bonds of the human family" require everyone to commit themselves to the promotion of development.[36]

What made *Populorum Progressio* a seminal document for Latin America was the way it set out the responsibility of the Christian community to work for development, and critically repudiated false contemporary approaches to development, the *economism* that derogates from, or ignores, the principle that economics are at the service of Man. The encyclical is unmistakably political. There is a clear rejection of colonial and neo-colonial solutions to problems of poverty and injustice. Paul VI, using language reminiscent of Latin American theologians, asserted that all peoples and nations have the right to be "artisans of their own destiny". And there are direct quotations from Lebret: "We do not believe in separating the economic from the human, nor development from the civilisations in which its exists", thereby feeding in to the contemporary Latin American debate about culture.[37] Life itself is described as a "vocation" to development and fulfillment—but always in particular societies. In other words, "to develop" is an active verb; people develop themselves, and for this they need literacy and education. However, within nations it is governments and elites, the Pope obviously thinks, who remain the trustees of development, not a theme to find echoes amongst radicals on the continent.[38]

The Catholic understanding of "integral development", development of "the whole man and Everyman," is described as "transcendent humanism". "Less human conditions" are contrasted with "more human conditions" by way of concrete examples indicating how integral development is a journey of transformation for individuals, peoples and nations. The end and purpose of this journey is in sharp contrast to that of atheistic Communism. "By reason of his union with Christ, the source of life, man attains to a new fulfillment of himself, to a transcendent humanism which gives him his greatest possible perfection: this is the highest goal of personal development".[39]

Populorum Progressio places the language of development alongside John XIII's commitment to human rights in an authoritative account of the Church's mission in social change, and distinguishes it from the dominant US approach to development. However for many Latin American radicals the word "development" was too tainted for use; only "liberation" would do. It was the—loyal—Catholic centre that most felt the push and pull of the encyclical and adopted some of the language. A discourse of human rights, human "promotion" and development, offered an inclusive language conferring legitimacy on social action as well as on particular political projects that might otherwise have appeared suspect. The Christian Democrats in particular shared Paul VI's irenic view of the possibility of avoiding serious class conflict through a commitment to multi-class alliances, development with social harmony. But this same centre could be fickle and easily swayed one way or the other by changing political circumstances, effective theological advocacy, or the cold winds from Rome and Washington.

However much the Second Vatican Council and the Papal encyclicals of the 1960s and 1970s provided a common ground for social action, the social and political crisis in Latin America meant that, to varying degrees in different countries, the Church remained divided. A clerical Left formed their own national splinter groups, *Golconda* (named after a *hacienda* where they met originally to study *Populorum Progressio*) in Colombia, *ONIS* (National Office of Social Investigation) in Peru and the innovative *Movement of Priests for the Third World* in Argentina associated with the Peronist Left. The most important, though not the most strategic, was *Christians for Socialism* with its centre in Chile. None of these ever represented more than a small minority of socially engaged Catholics. They provided a too easy political excuse for the Right to reject what was a much wider, growing and mainstream movement soon to be characterised as the "Church of the Poor". The Catholic Left's outspokenness blocked constructive interaction between liberation theology and Catholic Social Teaching, and heightened the contradictions between them.

The training of lay agents for particular *milieux* and within movements introduced new forms of organisation that brought together socially active Sisters, clergy and lay workers in structures outside those of the conventional parish. The *milieu* movements using the Cardijn methodology of See-Judge-Act, so important in Brazil, had already created cell-like groups throughout Latin America accustomed to analyse their social context. This led in Chile, for example, to Catholic Action militants providing almost half of the Party workers for the Christian Democrat Party elected in 1964. They were led by Eduardo Frei who was himself reared in the same Cardijn Catholic tradition.

The Catholic Right saw all this activity in favour of social justice as intensely threatening, as an erosion of the spiritual mission of the Church in favour of a subversive political agenda inspired by "Communism". The term used was "watermelon": green on the outside but red inside, through and through. Such efforts to transform the world were viewed as an impious pollution of the Church's true spiritual mission, or materially as downright threatening to a status quo that benefited landowners and a privileged middle class. Most on the Right would not have understood their support, active or passive, for powerful conservative forces as "political" in any way disloyal to the Church, or indeed as political at all.

Basic Christian Communities. Latin American parishes were simply too big, too understaffed, and too anonymous to provide a firm basis for an active Catholic community. On average only 10 per cent of baptised Catholics went regularly to Sunday mass. A wide variety of lay-led organisations proliferated in the 1960s representing different Christian commitments to Gospel values. Basic Christian communities (CEBs— *communidades ecclesiales de base*) were but one element in a wider pastoral and liturgical upheaval that grew out of the Vatican Council's re-evaluation of the importance of the laity. The Brazilian bishops' 1962 Emergency Plan and particularly their 1965-1970 Comprehensive Pastoral Plan reflected some of these directions; the Pastoral plan called for the subdivision of parishes into smaller "basic communities", and for the training of lay pastoral agents to serve them. Without knowing it they had opened a Pandora's box.

As growing numbers of priests left their ministry to marry in the 1960s, more than 10 per cent of parishes in Latin America found themselves without a regular celebrant of the Eucharist. The promotion of lay leadership and Biblical literacy was a response to the growing number of urban parishes and the shortage of priests. In Brazil this had reached crisis proportions. Dom Agnelo Rossi, later to become Cardinal and with no radical intentions, adopted a strategy of training catechists as community co-ordinators while he was Bishop of Barra do Pirai in 1956. In Nizia Floresta in Rio Grande do Norte nuns and laity ran parishes in the absence of priests.

During the 1960s, more Sisters and some clergy able to free themselves from the constraints of parish structures began working with small Christian communities, *circulos biblicos*, using the Bible as a critical mirror on life in urban slums and rural parishes. Such local groups promoted a more active lay leadership with intimations of future "de-clericalisation" of ministry. They showed a variety of attitudes and concerns, an emphasis for example on marriage in the Family of God movement in San Miguelito, in Panama. Family life was more usually a theme of the middle class *cursillos* movement that nurtured a more emotional form of Catholicism. But a conservative approach could easily give way to a more radical one. Art and poetry came out of the radical Solentiname community in Nicaragua, founded in 1966 by Father Ernesto Cardenal, later Sandinista Minister for Culture, on an island in Lake Managua. In Brazil the radio schools generated groups with literacy as a focus. Some of these grew to nurture political action.[40]

The continuing shortage of local vocations—particularly in Bolivia, Cuba, Guatemala, Honduras and Dominican Republic where they made up less than 20 per cent of Men Religious—meant that in most Latin American countries missionaries still played important roles. By 1971 a little under three- quarters of Latin America's Women Religious were locally born but only a little over half of its Men Religious. New waves of missionaries such as the Maryknoll Fathers and Sisters made a considerable impact on pastoral practice. This influx was a result of Pope John XXIII's call after the Cuban revolution for the established

Churches to send 10 per cent of their personnel to Latin America. Many lay "Papal volunteers" from the USA responded to his call. According to US Church records, the number of US mission personnel in Chile doubled between 1958-1964, from 122 to 246, and throughout Latin America from 2,126 to 3,506. Money followed them, some $34 million from North American and European Catholic organisations supported by their bishops. Money and personnel went predominantly to under-staffed poor parishes that lacked priests.

Pastoral experiments in San Miguelito, on the outskirts of Panama City, begun by missionary priests from Chicago in 1963, became, like Solentiname, showcase models inspiring imitations around Central America. The movement expanded, mainly among peasants as well as into the slum areas of big cities, such as St Paul the Apostle in Mana-gua, led by dynamic young priests, some straight out of Spain like its founder, Father José de la Jara. The community's reflection on the Bible turned to questions of justice, poverty and liberation from oppressive structures. Under Latin America's military regimes, these groupings, known as CEBs, attracted new recruits from the urban poor dissatisfied with large anonymous parishes, as well as from other active lay people whose regional or national organisations were coming increasingly un-der attack and suffering severe military or paramilitary repression.[41]

The CEBs, like the radical clergy, were soon shrouded in an ideologi-cal mist reflecting divisions in the Latin American Church. They were inspired by Biblical renewal and a scriptural lay spirituality, not mo-tivated by Marxism. Adult catechesis was moving from abstract, uni-versal theological principles to an inductive, contextual, and interactive relationship with the Bible. In Juan Luis Segundo's words, their cycle of action-reflection-action, was determined by " the continuing change in our interpretation of the Bible which is dictated by the continuing changes in our present-day reality both individual and societal".[42]

A typical member of a CEB was a low income farmer or a poor urban artisan. The CEBs attracted an impoverished "aristocracy of la-bour", hard working, pious people with a small stake in society, suf-fering grinding poverty, leading honest lives, with a dogged desire for betterment. Translated into the religious ethos of Victorian England they would not have been out of place in an early Methodist meeting. Nor, as their more romantic promoters would claim, did the CEBs mo-bilise the poorest of the poor. The very poorest living in the rural areas and *barrios* were simply too hungry to sustain regular and demanding meetings for prayer and reflection; their needs were too immediate.

The CEBs formed a non-violent, structural movement that was Biblical and liturgical movement all in one. Vatican II had mandated and blessed the pilgrim "People of God" and summoned them to action. In its theology they were no longer passive sheep led by shepherds; they were called to fulfill God's plan that began in history. Whether understood according to Kant, Rahner or Freire, their coming of age was impelled by a quasi-teleological vision of history. Their "free and creative praxis" was informed by the mystical impulse of their pastors and theologians who configured it in terms of a Christian eschatology. But this meant neither autonomy nor a new paternalism. Now *they*, gathered in the CEBs, were the "artisans of a new humanity", the heart of the *igreja popular*. This was the real legacy of the Council for Latin America, a rooted version of modernity, albeit a Christian modernity, the pride of what Helder Camara called "a post-conciliar period worthy of Vatican II".[43]

Unfortunate CEBs. Never was such high-octane fuel available for such humble vehicles. They were doomed to labour under the sheer weight of the symbolism and momentous significance assigned to them by friend and foe alike. According to your perspective they could be the Promethean beginnings of a new and holy Church, or a radical contestation of episcopal authority and a new heresy; an amalgam of Protestantism and Marxism; never just groups of Christians trying to fathom the appropriate response to the mystery of God in their world.[44] The gap between their daily life and the utopian vision of liberation theology was vast. To take the first steps, to drum up a few drains and some clean water, was a triumph. A minority of a small minority, even in their heyday the CEBs added up to far less than 5 per cent of the mass-going Catholic community. They were simply mustard seeds starting to grow. But if anything expressed the sacramental imagination of the Latin American Church, they did.

Was the theological vision of the CEBs a purification of the Enlightenment project of human emancipation that had been distorted by European secularism, a quest for "intra-historical transcendence", or was it a form of political mysticism? It had elements of both. One thing was sure: the vision of the Basic Christian Communities as "collective emancipatory agents acting from below", or using Pope Paul's words "artisans of their own destiny", was a vision of theological hope. Or put in another way, by any mundane, pragmatic calculation it was implausible, even in the political turmoil of the 1960s with its heady expectations, even driven by the radical political energy unleashed in reaction to US-backed tyrannies in the 1970s. Yet for the majority of Catholics in the CEBs, this was an entirely plausible way of "being Church". In its incarnational theology, the movement spoke to their condition, and inspired them in their spirituality, struggle for justice and a better life. It formed a beacon of hope as the military and oligarchies brought the shutters down on any pro-poor policies and reform. But it was not the kind of hope that Rome wanted to endorse.[45]

The Medellín Effect. The 1968 CELAM conference at Medellín in Colombia got off to a shaky start with Paul VI, the first Pope ever to visit Latin America, speaking of the dangers of " a spirit of subversive criticism" arising from "historicism", and obviously worried about the prospects of violent revolution on the continent. But it ended with an official seal of approval for the growth of the CEBs and for a Latin American theology that took history seriously. The CEBs were described by the bishops as "the first and fundamental ecclesiastical nucleus which on its own level must make itself responsible for the richness and expansion of the faith as well as of the cult which is its expression".[46] The one hundred and fifty assembled bishops, archbishops and cardinals wanted to "encourage and favour efforts of the people to create and develop their own grass-roots organisations for the redress and consolidation of their rights and the search for true justice". Because historical conditions were "intimately linked to the history of salvation", indeed the "aspirations and clamours of Latin America are signs that reveal the direction of the divine plan", the Conference concluded. "In the search for salvation we must avoid the dualism which separates temporal tasks from the work of sanctification". In other words lay action for social justice made people holy. It followed that "historical events and authentic human striving are an indispensable part of the content of catechesis". In the economy of salvation, "the divine work is an action of integral human development and liberation which has love as its sole motive".[47]

It was only three years after the end of the Council whose full significance was only just sinking in around the world. The lay Catholics asked to implement the divine plan and championed at Medellín had barely been consulted before the deliberations began. Meetings of Catholic students and workers at the Café Castilla were broken up by the Medellín police. The bishops were guided in their deliberations by their theologians who cast themselves in the mediating role of "voice of the voiceless". José Comblin was particularly influential. Medellín was thus able to reflect the ferment in the Latin American Church in the *iglesia popular* and among the priests and Sisters whose vision of Mission had taken them close to the daily lives of the poor majority. It stimulated a radical revision of pastoral priorities from north to south, from the hills of El Quiché in Guatemala to the back streets of Santiago in Chile.

"We ought to sharpen the awareness of our duty of solidarity with the poor to which charity leads us. This solidarity means that we make ours their problems and their struggles, that we know how to speak with them", the Medellín bishops declared.[48] It would be difficult to imagine a more thoroughgoing endorsement of the CEBs' programme and methodology from a continental episcopate, or a more conscious effort to translate the vision of *Gaudium et Spes* into the Latin American context. An entire chapter in the conclusions to the CELAM Conference are dedicated to the poor in a way that clarifies the Biblical significance of poverty for the Church, a text that would have been invaluable for the *Church of the Poor* group at the Council. Medellín's conclusions continued to emphasise personal conversion in the pursuit of structural change. And they stop short of waiving priestly celibacy in order to ordain lay pastoral agents for the CEBs, though celibacy was discussed at the end of the conference. This was a radical, not a liberal vision, and the bishops, prompted by their theological advisers, had somehow corporately gone beyond the position of their individual national conferences. The text of the conclusions were quickly published and distributed to pre-empt interference from Rome and to avoid repressive regimes interdicting them.

Bishop Helder Camara, looking over his shoulder at the Catholic Right and the Curia, had tried before Medellín to rally those fearful of "Communism" to the cause of radical change. His excitement was palpable. A sense of history in the making, the realisation of political dreams, was in the air. "At this time, we Christians can offer to socialism the mystique of universal brotherhood and total hope, incomparably more vast than the narrow mystique of historical materialism."[49]

But this did not persuade the growing and organised Catholic Right for whom socialism equalled Communism. And it was this part of the Church which pulled strings in Rome, wrote letters denouncing bishops and priests whose views they did not like, and acted as whistle-blowers for the conservative Vatican.

Political dreams were in the air in Europe too but different ones, more anarchic, more anti-authoritarian, and definitely not the product of an engaged and radical Catholicism. For Rome they were nightmares of libertarian excess and flamboyance. The *annus mirabilis* of the New Left, 1968, saw Europe rocked by waves of student-led protest. The movement was complex, essentially cultural, involving a series of symbolic tantrums against any form of authority, battering the complacency and pomposity of the universities, schools and the trustees of morality, leaving much valueless political detritus and some refreshing political novelty and expectancy. It was later to have a disproportionate impact on the European Church, through one man, Professor Joseph Ratzinger, who did not take kindly to his classes in Tübingen being disrupted, nor to the university chaplaincy being taken over by the Left with the support of hostile younger lecturers. The prolonged disorderly insubordination in the hierarchical world of the Catholic university alarmed him.[50] The events of 1968 seemed to be harbingers of things falling apart in the Church. The Soviet invasion of Czechoslovakia in August 1968 was a further sign, if any were needed, that Pope John's distinction between ideologies and historical movements, as far as Communism was concerned, had its flaws.

In Latin America 1968 was no less a turning point for the Church though in a different and less neurasthenic way. Four years before the Medellín conference, a Peruvian theologian, Gustavo Gutiérrez, produced a modest working paper for a meeting of progressive theologians gathered in the fish-processing port town of Chimbote. In it he referred to a "theology of liberation", soon to have a comparable impact to Martin Luther's theses, but less of their lasting divisive consequences. This was no thanks to the Vatican. The emergence and development of liberation theology cut the umbilical cord of dependency that tied Latin America to the theology of the Europe. Despite many of its theologians having studied in Europe, it was part of a broader cultural assertion of the continent's particular genius, and, later, made a major contribution to the life of the universal Church. Its spread was an integral part of the globalisation of Catholicism though it took place before the communications revolution took effect.[51]

The Theology of Liberation and the Liberation of Theology

The richness of the Latin American Church was personified in the formation and work of its best known and most influential liberation theologian, Gustavo Gutiérrez. He studied in Rome during the 1950s and was ordained there in 1959, a priesthood virtually co-terminous with the emergent new order of the Second Vatican Council. He made lasting friendships in the Major Seminary in Santiago, notably with Sergio Torres, who was later one of the founders of Christians for Socialism. The enlightened policy of its Rector from 1950-1958, Emilio Tagle, later to become a conservative Bishop in Valparaiso, exposed students to the needs of the poor in working class areas. Gutiérrez also spent time in Louvain and Lyons—so was well versed in the undercurrents of la nouvelle théologie and the worker-priest movement, and he was much taken by Chenu's historical approach to theology.[52]

The major formative influence on Gutiérrez was his experience in Peru as spiritual adviser to UNEC, the National Union of Catholic Students, and with lay movements in Rimac, a bleak, noisy working-class Lima slum. The two were related during the 1960s as students moved into the worker milieu and joined basic Christian communities. A cross-pollination of ideas and experiences—like his own mixed Quechua ancestry—occurred: the meeting of Maritain, Lebret, and Congar with Mariategui and the nationally acclaimed Peruvian novelist José María Arguedas, germinated in the period 1968-1971. During this time, Gutiérrez's pastoral priorities were fed into CELAM, particularly at Medellín.[53] His Teologia de la Liberación was first published by the Lima Centre for Studies and Publications in 1971 and translated into English and published by Orbis, the Maryknoll Press, in 1973. There were other publications on similar themes: the Brazilian, Hugo Assman, wrote Theology for a Nomad Church which appeared in Spanish in 1971 (Opresión-liberación: Desafio a los Cristianos), and, in 1972, another Brazilian, Leonardo Boff published Jesus Christo Libertador in Portuguese in Petropolis.

Together they opened up a new theological terrain known henceforth as "liberation theology". Although only Assman, in Marxist mode, dwelt on the rupture with "North Atlantic theology", liberation theology represented an assertion of a Latin American Catholic identity, radical and rooted in solidarity with the poor, out of whose faith, struggles, sufferings and hopes, this theological reflection had arisen. It was a tangible expression of a conscious, and chosen, diversity in the Catholic Church, as well as being ecumenical. Jon Sobrino SJ in El Salvador, ordained in Frankfurt, and the Franciscan Leonardo Boff in Brazil who studied under Karl Rahner, with the Uruguyan Jesuit Juan Luis Segundo, who studied in Louvain, joined Gutiérrez as liberation theology's leading exponents in the mid-1970s.[54]

Notwithstanding the European links of its founding Fathers, liberation theology was the first locally realised product of the world Church proclaimed by Rahner during the Council. The CEBs and liberation theology represented a new pluralism in theology and ecclesiology, resented and fought over, even abhorred, but a *de facto* pluralism nevertheless. True there was a growing and significant cultural adaptation of the European model of worship, liturgy and prayer in Africa and Asia, notably in Taiwan, Vietnam, Philippines and India. But this did not have great implications outside the local Church. Latin America, though, had discovered a radical methodology for "doing" theology, an attempt to re-centre the life of the Church that put "Christology at the crossroads" not just locally but for the universal Church, and offered a profound vision of a world transformed.[55]

Why, though, call it "liberation" theology, a word inevitably associated with liberation movements, violence, and the easy target of the Colombian guerrilla ex-priest Camilo Torres, Gutiérrez's classmate in Rome? This is not simply an academic question. Frei Betto and the São Paulo Dominicans were arrested in 1969 and accused of making contact with the guerrilla force, Action for National Liberation. Put simply, the methodology of liberation theology was to seek knowledge of God through a critical reflection on praxis, understood as the action and practice of the poor in seeking their own liberation from every kind of oppression. The locus of "doing theology", the right place for theologians according to this perspective, was not the wood-panelled libraries of seminaries and Pontifical universities, but the tin roofed shacks of Latin America's burgeoning mega-cities, the police cells, and the hovels of servile agricultural labourers and impoverished farmers. It was a subversive vision of a world turned upside down.

The necessary qualification for this endeavour—which Gutiérrez insisted was primarily an *ecclesial* rather than an intellectual responsibility—was immersion in the world of material poverty and injustice, and this in turn could, and did, qualify pastoral agents, Sisters and priests for imprisonment, torture and death. The discovery and proclamation of what was called "the evangelising power of the poor", a reversal of the model of the missionary bringing the Gospel, was one challenging consequence.[56] Liberation theology was both an epistemological break with deductive, abstract academic theology and it pre-supposed the inevitability of a social break with the middle-class. But this was rooted in a radical attempt to reunite: here was an overlapping, not conflation, of salvation history and human history partially, not completely, destroying the division between the political and spiritual, the Earthly City and the Heavenly City. And this amounted to a rejection of "traditional" Catholic dualism. Rome worked on a canvas with sharp boundaries and clear divisions, between the "spiritual concerns" of the Vatican and the supposedly "this-worldly concerns" of the liberation theologians. It made condemnation easier. Just how "intra-historical or transcendent", how much "here and now" or "to come" was the Kingdom of God, varied in emphasis from theologian to theologian. Liberation theology could never *absolutise* itself because it never claimed to be more than a theological reflection on human liberation in its particular Latin American context. It would always be "work-in-progress".

Impact and Definition

Because liberation theology originated—and remains—at the intersection of contested political and religious goals, a universally accepted definition is difficult to reach. Some Catholic theologians would deny that the utterances of theology may be subject to social conditions or have political content. At most they would agree that theological truths have implications and possible consequences in the realm of the political. Anything more is denounced as the "politicisation" of theology. But liberation theologians had a strong case in claiming that to accept theology as valid only if it is "apolitical" requires self-deception, and is itself a political position amounting to covert support for the *status quo*. This was certainly true during the political conflicts of the 1970s.[57]

If the "Church of the Poor" lacked a viable theology to weave together its different strands during the Council, liberation theology might be seen as coming to the rescue. It elaborated a theological analysis of poverty in terms of structures and from the perspective of the "Third World" poor. But the zero sum theory of "underdevelopment" was an unfortunate flag of convenience to sail under, and was later thoroughly discredited by economists. Meanwhile a "Third World theology" had been born. The activism of the worker-priests and their class analysis were moved into the wider struggle for justice, absorbed and transformed by the Basic Christian Communities. Voluntary poverty could be lived out in the deprivations of life in the *barrios*, in the midst of this struggle, no less than in a monastery garden. Work for justice could be, and was, instrumental in fostering the Christian virtues and Christian spirituality.

Liberation theology deepened and transformed *présence,* the spiritual and mystical concept of followers of Charles de Foucauld. It made presence amongst the poor, their "accompaniment", into the foundation of epistemological privilege; here was where and how the mystery of God might be encountered and the possibility of human transcendence realised. This took the Church practically much further than its preoccupation with its own wealth as an impediment to its witness. It led the Medellín bishops in a final chapter of their conclusions, on poverty, to what later was called "the option for the poor". "The Lord's distinct commandment to 'evangelize the poor' ought to bring us to a distribution of resources and apostolic personnel that effectively gives preference to the poorest and most needy sectors and to those segregated for any cause whatsoever," they declared.[58]

The rediscovery of Biblical themes of justice, theology as reflection on concrete action for justice, was the unifying framework that the Church of the Poor had needed. During the 1970s, it became an important strand of thinking in Latin America, and far beyond, but more important a profoundly inspirational motivation for Christian commitment to social justice and "integral human liberation" in the universal Church. What this meant in practice is the subject of the next chapter.

6

THE CHURCH IN CONFLICT

Liberation theology grew out of a Christian reaction to poverty and oppression at a particular juncture in the life of Latin America, and in the life of its Church, as a theological reflection in the light of Biblical narratives. An important minority in the Latin American Church recognised that the political and economic circumstances of the continent demanded an "option for the poor". Liberation theology expressed the faith of millions of Latin Americans who saw in its themes a Christian meaning for their lives and a Christian hope for change—away from an "option for the rich". But in the same sense that the Jesus of the Gospels promised division as the price of fidelity, and even the breaking of ties of kinship, so too a radical and theological commitment to an option for the poor demanded taking sides and promised a divided Church. This was because the vast majority of Catholics who materially benefited from political economies creating and defending gross disparities in wealth, feared this option as a threatening apostasy, dragging the Church into a secular and political sphere away from its true spirituality of pietism and allegiance to tradition, polluting its ordered life and worship with Marxism and threatening civil disorder. Or to put it in more Biblical language, preaching Good News to the Poor was dangerous.

In less extreme circumstances of inequality and injustice than Latin America such divisions in the Church might have been described as a "creative tension" and held together in a formula to preserve unity. But as the Cold War was nearing its climax, governments invariably viewed movements for social justice through its prism and thus branded them as "Communist", with their leaders qualifying for prison, torture or assassination. By 1978, south of the Central American isthmus, which

121

had civil wars in different stages in Nicaragua, Guatemala and El Salvador, only Colombia, Venezuela and Guyana were not governed by full-blown military dictatorships, and to all, save obviously Cuba, to greater or lesser degrees the USA extended military support. Tens of thousands of Latin American military officers received US training and passed through academies such as the School of the Americas in Panama while CIA advisers proliferated throughout the continent. Between 1950-1975 the US supplied some $2.5 billion in armaments to Latin America's armed forces who deployed them on their civilian populations.[1] The denial of the social implications of fidelity to the Christian Gospels, a counsel of caution, was a political option taken by many.

In the wake of 70 per cent of the Catholic clergy fleeing or expelled from Cuba after Castro seized power in 1959, many of the new foreign missionaries coming into Latin America were American, and many like the Maryknoll Fathers and Sisters committed to the "struggle for social justice" and the defence of human rights. In Guatemala less than 20 per cent of the clergy were locally born and the Conference of Religious, CONFREGUA, was able both to denounce human rights violations and foster international solidarity. Some 40 per cent of the Confederation of Latin American Religious, CLAR's 160,000 members, were working with the poor by 1978; double the number before Medellín a decade earlier. A 1969 report by Nelson Rockefeller pointed out the alleged dangers to the security of the United States. The CIA began providing dossiers to Latin American intelligence agencies on many Church personnel, and feigned ignorance as 850 priests, Sisters and bishops, several of them US citizens, were arrested, expelled or tortured and murdered alongside thousands of Latin American lay catechists, Delegates of the Word—who led Sunday services—union leaders, and leaders of Basic Christian Communities, CEBs, or parish activists.[2]

State action against Church workers for social justice soon fell into a remarkably similar pattern in different countries. Informal co-ordination of Latin American military intelligence agencies sponsored by the CIA began under the auspices of the Bolivian Ministry of the Interior, dubbed in 1975 "the Banzer plan" after the country's military dictator Colonel Hugo Banzer who portrayed himself as a defender of "Western Christian civilisation". The strategy aimed at sharpening internal divisions in the Church by smearing "progressive Church leaders" and creating alarm among "centrist bishops" who might otherwise have supported them. The arrest and deportation of foreign missionaries on trumped-up charges of subversion was a key plank in the programme. After the March 1976 military coup in Argentina, clergy were selectively assassinated; the only outspoken critic of the military regime in the Conference, the Bishop of La Rioja, Enrique Angelelli, was forced off the road by two cars and killed in an "accident". He was returning from a mass during which he had denounced the military and was carrying papers incriminating them in the killing of two of his priests; the papers disappeared.

The Banzer plan's attempt to divide and rule found witting and unwitting allies at all levels *within* the Church leadership just as in Eastern Europe a different form of oppression generated Catholic collaborators, doubtless no less able to justify their conduct as a defence of a beleaguered Church or a quest to retain privileges hard won from the state in adverse circumstances. Most notable for Latin America was Alfonso López Trujillo, a very young and very ambitious Colombian auxiliary bishop of Bogotá, later protégé of Cardinal Sebastiano Baggio, president of the Pontifical Commission for Latin America and a previous nuncio to Brazil. He became a pugnacious opponent of liberation theology and the "Church of the Poor", *iglesia popular*, and of the principal conclusions and spirit of the Medellín Conference. An adept student of ecclesiastical preferment, he was made secretary-general of CELAM in 1973, Archbishop of Medellín in 1979 and, pushed all the way by Baggio, three years later a Cardinal. Transferred to Rome in 1990, in the teeth of repeated warnings from Latin American prelates about his unrepresentative views, he became a powerful and manipulative head of the Pontifical Council for the Family. As politics polarised during the short-lived Allende government in Chile, 1970-73, Lopez Trujillo organised swift reaction against liberation theology. This reaction was soon international in form and gained powerful allies.[3]

The Chilean Crisis

Christians for Socialism, Christianos por el Socialismo (CpS) was founded in Chile in November 1971 by a group of some eighty Latin American priests working among the poor. Typical of the Latin American Church in the 1970s, about half of them were foreign-born. Their position was clear: socialism was the only legitimate Christian option;

"the liberative power of God's love" could be found within "revolutionary praxis"; and it was essential to take sides. In the words of the Chilean theologian, Pablo Richard, soon to be exiled, "the Chilean revolution does not admit spectators and arbitrators".

The Christian Socialist option in Chile demanded committed support for Allende's Popular Unity coalition and "revolutionary projects", and was condemned by the Chilean bishops for its "partisan political attitude"; they exerted "undue influence in the temporal and political realm". CpS drew to an international meeting in Santiago in 1972 some 200 priests and Sisters, 160 lay Catholics and 40 Protestants. It counted, at the very most, on the sympathies of 10 per cent of the clergy in Chile. Sergio Torres, vicar-general of the diocese of Talca was a leading promoter. Gonzalo Arroyo, director of the Jesuit Latin American Institute for Doctrine and Social Studies (ILADES) in the late 1960s wrote prolifically for the movement. Cardinal Silva refused to attend and made his disapproval public.[4]

The Cardinal's position was not one of knee-jerk anti-Communism, nor did it lack a willingness to see the best in the newly elected Government. He wrote: "I believe that socialism contains important Christian values, and in many respects is very superior to capitalism—the value it places on work, and the primacy of the person over against capital … its break with the necessity and tyranny of the pursuit of profit and its ability to co-ordinate all levels of production". The socialist vision was in short "very close to the Church's preferred goals in the organisation of society". Moreover he backed Salvador Allende's contentious nationalisation of the copper industry without compensation for the controlling US companies—a red rag to any imperial power as Egypt and Iran had found to their cost in the 1950s—and he lobbied hard internationally to avoid its deleterious effects on World Bank relations with Chile. It was the strident tone, advocacy of violence, and proposals for Church life of the CpS that he found objectionable.[5]

The CpS wanted a worker priest dispensation with the possibility of optional celibacy and re-integration of married priests into ministry. Invited by Castro to Havana in March 1972, twelve of the CpS leaders endorsed resort to revolutionary violence in response to "reactionary violence" and spoke of the Church's "great historical sin of backing the rich".[6] Their attitude to bishops who criticised them was sometimes patronising and often devoid of respect: the bishops, they said, suffered from the ideological defects of the *"pequeña burguesia"* most notably trying to sustain an unreal unity in the face of class conflict. This theme of unity was to re-appear again and again in Vatican attacks on the wider liberation theology movement.[7]

President Allende himself urged CpS to moderate their language, knuckle under and improve their relationship with the hierarchy. But it was too late. During April to September 1973 the Bishops Conference began preparing to denounce and ban the movement. But although they prudently decided to shelve the document, "Christian Faith and Political Activity" after the Pinochet coup it was unilaterally and maliciously published by Bishop Carolos Oviedo in October. The Chilean bishops, it read, did not believe that humanity "can arrive at the reign of liberty by exacerbating conflict to the utmost", nor that class struggle is "the specific means which Christ gave to his Church to contribute to the ultimate triumph of justice in the world". "Christian liberation", they concluded, "stems from Christ's resurrection, and not from social processes or struggle". This was the "dualism" that liberation theologians were consciously trying to counter. The bishops had been driven into presenting an opposition between the founding event of Christian faith and action for social justice, a defensive juxtaposition that inevitably grew out of the polarisation of the Chilean political experience. The CpS had as intended "sharpened the contradictions" but damaged support for "the Church of the Poor".[8]

The fall of Allende proved to be the formative experience for radical Christians in the early 1970s. *Christians for Socialism* only found supporters among a very small minority in a number of different countries, but the tragic events in Chile touched the political marrow of both Left and Right in the Latin American Church, leaving unhealed emotional wounds. Shock waves reached Bogotá, Buenos Aires, Lima and all capitals to the north. Things would never be the same again. The Chilean experience defined the division in the Church less as two sides of a theological conversation, more as a political fight to the finish between the "Medellín men" and the conservatives, who quietly supported the Pinochet coup as inevitable and who at heart rejected and resisted Medellín. The view of the coup from the camp of the "Medellín men" was bleak; they were dismayed at the violence that followed in its wake. They were not necessarily doctrinally liberal, nor in practice outspoken critics of oppressive governments, nor keen on political engagement, rather promoters of a particular pastoral vision that placed the poor at the heart of evangelisation.

It was under these circumstances that the conservatives in the Church identified the capture of CELAM, based in Bogotá, as pivotal in curbing the spread of the theological ideas and pastoral practices redolent of the turmoil, insubordination and disorder that they deplored. As a corollary, they prioritised the creation of contestational forms of literature and material promoting their vision of Church order and theology. For one of the things the *igregia popular* or *la iglesia que nace del pueblo* was particularly good at, thanks to Paulo Freire, was the cheap publication of popular booklets for promoters of the option for the poor. Through complaints to Rome, the conflict quickly involved key Cardinals in the Vatican who lent their weight to the conservative ranks and their strategy.

The dynamic moving centre of this "counter-reformation" strategy was the Belgian Jesuit Roger Vekemans, a multi-talented sociologist and linguist, founder of the Centro Bellarmino in Santiago and confidant of the Chilean Christian Democrat leader, Eduardo Frei, who suffered electoral defeat at the hands of Salvador Allende. In Chile Vekemans wielded the clerical power found in "big operators" in the USA, a man with access to the Kennedys, an ideological crusader who would "take money from the devil himself if it were necessary to stop the Communists", cutting financial corners and shaking down indiscriminately USAID, ADVENIAT, the pastoral arm of the West German bishops' Conference, and CIA money, for his social projects. His Chilean experience in agrarian reform and the trades union movement from 1957 until the time of Allende's take-over in 1970 led him to see Communists behind activist bushes. He left for Bogotá and the arms of López Trujillo in 1970, having been dumped by the Chilean Christian Democrats. A disappointed man wedded to a "theology of conspiracy", he championed a new crusade against an imagined "fifth column" in the wider Latin American Church.[9]

In Bogotá Vekemans set up CEDIAL, a Research Centre for the Development and Integration of Latin America, modelled on Centro Bellarmino lines, and began publishing *Tierra Nueva*. The periodical provided an outlet for López Trujillo and other conservative thinkers to attack liberation theology and set out their "New Christendom" ecclesiology that justified retaining the support of the civil power for the

Church's mission. CEDIAL allowed co-ordination of the conservative political and intellectual counter-attack. The conflation of *Christians for Socialism* and liberation theology in *Tierra Nueva* was particularly damaging and disingenuous—by this time the CpS movement was in reality insignificant, a straw man by 1975. The attack was widened to CELAM's Department of Social Action, presented as an egregious example of the "political instrumentalisation of the Church in Latin America". ADVENIAT, influenced by the strong anti-Communism of the German bishops, provided money to monitor developments in liberation theology. Most of the Colombian but also the Argentine bishops found solace in these developments, and there were episcopal supporters elsewhere.[10]

Thus the stage was set for a major ambush of the *iglesia popular* at the November 1972 meeting of CELAM in Sucre, Bolivia. The agenda included re-structuring and replacement of secretariat personnel, the future and financing of CELAM institutes, and the formulation of guidelines governing pastoral work. Bishop López Trujillo was elected to the key position of CELAM secretary-general and a conservative ally, the Brazilian Bishop Luciano Duarte, to the Presidency of the Social Action Department. The radical work of the Latin American Pastoral Institute (IPLA) was condemned. CELAM training institutes that had given priests and Sisters formation in pastoral and catechetical methods, and produced hundreds of committed lay workers, were reduced to a single centre in Colombia, subject to López Trujillo's vigilance. The Sucre assault was a great setback for the "Medellín men", a turning point after which liberation theology, the CEBs and the *iglesia popular*, were obliged to watch their backs, organise more effectively, and develop subtle strategies to deal with the internal politics of the Church. This was not, for the most part, a matter of adopting a form of ecclesial identity politics based on a traditionalist-progressive dichotomy, but a far deeper commitment to keeping faith with a liberating God "who heeds the cries of his people".[11]

The momentum of work for social justice was far from fully checked by this backlash. From 1969, the plight of indigenous Indian peoples of the Amazon region was increasingly taken up by the local bishops. The Amazon and North East bishops of Brazil synchronised different pastoral letters to celebrate the 25th anniversary of the UN Declaration of Human Rights on 6 May 1973. Their pastoral letter "*I have heard the Cry of My People"* championed peasant rights and spoke of "official terrorism", while *"Marginalisation of a People"* denounced the invasion and violence of the agribusinesses and settler invasion of territory occupied by the Amazon Indian, roundly denounced capitalism and called for "socialised use of land". The respected Franciscan Cardinals, Paolo Arns, appointed to the key archdiocese of São Paulo in 1970, and Aloisio Lorschieder, elected as President of CELAM, gave weight to the Brazilian Conference. The brutal authoritarian policies of the military dictatorship were confronted and condemned. Government bans on working with the Indians were simply ignored. This led nationally and locally to open conflict. The price was high. In Bishop Pedro Casaldáliga's prelature of São Felix do Araguaia in the Matto Grosso, priests were jailed and tortured for organising resistance to "development" companies and large landowners, *latifundia*. He and Bishop Tomás Balduino, president of the Brazilian Indian Mission Council (CIMI), became targets of harassment: right-wing denunciation, death threats and house arrest. Meanwhile the Church institutionalised resistance and support for the popular movements in its Pastoral Land Commission (CPT) and Workers Pastoral Commission. The problem for the conservatives was that Latin America's biggest Church was also its most radical.[12]

Repression in Central America

The total population of the five Central American countries in the 1970s was only three-quarters that of Colombia, a mid-ranking Latin American state. Their small size made national level organisation achievable out of local networks. So popular mobilisation and organisation against militarised, repressive regimes was easier. But the ferocity and impact of repression was correspondingly greater. As elsewhere in Latin America, the sheer magnitude of human rights violations pushed segments of the Church into open rebellion. In El Salvador and Nicaragua, and to a lesser degree in Guatemala where brutal repression was both indiscriminate and unpredictable, with systematic massacres of indigenous peoples, the national army and irregular death squads undertook the repression. Costa Rica, without an army as such, and Honduras which did later suffer from small-scale and intermittent death-squad activity, were mainly spared.[13]

Priests, Sisters and lay workers throughout Central America had intimate knowledge of their parishes and were able to compile detailed lists of those killed by army, National Guard forces and death-squads. This information passed up the hierarchy, bringing bishops continually into contact with reality on the ground. The language of human rights enabled the Church to engage politically with tyrannical governments whilst keeping their distance from political parties. There was a constant translation going on within the Church, from the Biblical language of the *iglesia popular* to the human rights language of church-state relations, both of course part of the repertoire of mainstream Catholicism.[14] Archbishop Miguel Obando y Bravo in Nicaragua was an adroit exponent of government relations and symbolic gestures. On his installation as Archbishop of Managua, he accepted a Mercedes from the Somoza regime, then sold it giving the money to charities for the poor.

The Nicaraguan bishops produced a number of pastoral letters in the 1970s which attempted to clarify the why and the how of their political interventions: they recognised the "irrepressible cry of a people" seeking " a whole new order", that obliged them in faith to struggle "for a more just order", but yet as pastors to "refrain from entering into partisan struggles".[15] The inherent tensions of this position were self-evident. The *Frente Sandinista* were fighting the National Guard using guerrilla tactics in a campaign that increasingly drew in Nicaraguan peasants, many of whom were devout Catholics, plus some priests and Sisters particularly those working in parishes and hospitals. The radical Jesuit Father Alvaro Arguello complained that the bishops were "delegitimising Somoza but at the same time de-legitimising the only group which was the historical alternative to the dictatorship". The non-violent solution promoted by the bishops seemed sadly improbable and its practicality in the face of brutal repression, dubious in the extreme.[16]

By January 1978, the Nicaraguan Bishops Conference was denouncing the economic, social and political conditions of the people in forthright language abandoning its usual abstract style that required careful interpretation and confined itself to expressing anxiety about deplorable situations.[17] A month later, Obando y Bravo, while commending his own non-violent stance, was elucidating the conditions in which some Catholic moralists permitted armed struggle as a just war against tyranny. By then Father Miguel d'Escoto and Father Ernesto Cardenal together with his Jesuit brother Fernando Cardenal, were politically aligned with the *Frente*. The Jesuit Centre for Education and Agricultural Promotion (EAPA) was supportive. Meanwhile, the Spanish Sacred Heart priest Father Gaspar Garcia Laviana had joined the guerrilla forces, following several Delegates of the Word, trained by the Capuchins in Zelaya, and members of the Solentiname community. In August 1978, Obando signed a document from the Managua Priests' Council that proposed Somoza should step down and make way for a government of national unity.[18]

The tide seemed to be turning. The incoming Carter administration in the USA was concerned about human rights and was, at times, lukewarm in its support of Somoza, and the bishops were well aware of the overwhelming support given the *Frente* by their peasant parishoners. But it would be wrong to dismiss the growing anti-Somoza bias of official Church pronouncements as an opportunist desire to build up good relations with what seemed increasingly to be a government in waiting. The future political configuration of the state was uncertain, and the strong Catholic presence in the revolution meant that the Church needed to be neither ingratiating nor accommodating. The Church leadership slid easily into an accustomed role: trying to mediate a peaceful transition to an uncertain new order.

The growing mobilisation and military success of the Central American liberation struggle during the 1970s coincided in the Church with a move away from the use of cautious and convoluted Vaticanese. They no longer spoke as if only to a small educated Catholic bourgeoisie, essentially middle way supporters and readers of *La Prensa*, mouthpiece for an umbrella political coalition opposing Somoza. Yet celebrations of the *Frente*'s victory were barely underway before the bishops were fretting in public about future religious freedom, materialistic and atheistic ideologies and other spectres of Communism that did not, or could not, immediately speak their name. This was hardly ingratiating, rather profoundly annoying to the revolutionary leadership who were ushering Catholic priests into government ministries, in the heady atmosphere of the *Frente*'s first year in power.[19]

The official Church position on the transition aimed at avoiding some form of moral dissolution amid the revolutionary fervour, with parts of the faithful becoming a mere religious arm of the *Frente*.[20] It dealt with the overlap between *Frente* cadres and the occupants of the pews, between Delegates of the Word and foot-soldiers and supporters of the revolution. The conscience of the Catholic guerrilla was torn. He (and she) felt the ambiguity of their loyalty to the armed struggle, for example confessing the deaths for which they were responsible during fighting with the National Guard, and seeking absolution in the confessional. High enemy casualties were a revolutionary victory but at the same time a personal sin. They did not expect the bishops to advocate guerrilla war, merely to understand that there was no alternative.[21]

The bishops' fear of "revolutionary Christians" becoming a sect outside their jurisdiction, and concern to re-establish unity within the Church, resulted most immediately in public opposition to the Marxist language of the Sandinistas, especially the emphasis on class conflict— less often its practice—through a constantly reiterated recommendation of the language and thought of Catholic social teaching. The problem for the bishops was not so much what the Sandinistas were doing but the way they were talking about what they were doing. Perhaps if the revolutionaries had found a way of describing things in the language of Catholic social teaching all might have been well in the eyes of the hierarchy. The shadow of Cold War ideologies, bearers of threatening stereotypes, hovered over Central America.[22]

There was nothing particularly sinister about the "revolutionary Christians". Many lay Catholics had roles both in Church organisations and "popular" peasant organisations and could often see very little difference between their immediate goals. The utopianism of the bishops' non-violence—that never resulted in the withdrawal of military chaplains and was thus suspect—was matched by the utopianism of the *Sandino* priests who could err on the side of romanticism about the poor. Belief in the primary task of building the Kingdom of God could easily become overconfidence in human social perfectibility. They had become involved in the revolution by taking the Medellín pastoral theme of "accompanying the poor" to its logical conclusion, a party political conclusion. For priests and Sisters, Rome could not tolerate such a form of dual allegiance; it was incompatible with Church order. Nonetheless, a solid body of Church leaders across Central America, priests, Sisters, catechists, Delegates of the Word, who accompanied the poor, did not share Rome's conclusion. In El Salvador and Guatemala, it was their fate to suffer the severest repression before a negotiated settlement of the liberation struggle could be achieved by outside intervention.[23]

The parish of Aguilares and El Paisnal some 27 miles north of San Salvador offers a glimpse into the pastoral practice of many of those "accompanying the poor". Huge sugar cane plantations left the peasants with only the poorest of soils and a wretched life. The Jesuit parish team would choose the "natural leaders", who would emerge during intense two week missions, from groups of about sixty parishioners gathered for training as Delegates of the Word. In a second phase those selected were given short courses over a three year period preparing them to administer the sacraments of baptism and marriage, using the preparation as a vehicle for evangelisation; they would go on to undertake youth work, and lead worship based on communal prayer, reading and reflection on the Bible as well as presiding at meetings dealing with local issues.

Father Rutilio Grande, the parish team leader, preached that injustices were always to be denounced but that the Church could not cross the line into party political involvement. Parish workers were committed to "building a new world" not to putting the Church behind any political grouping, though leaders studied the Salvadorian Constitution and were made aware of the tricks of politicians to gain electoral support. An innovative form of local harvest festival celebrated the end of the training period.[24]

The second half of the 1970s brought El Salvador into economic and political crisis. As poverty grew the popular movements rapidly gained recruits. Though the guerrilla war was yet to break out fully, the reaction from landowners and government was violent repression coupled with minor agrarian reform concessions. After the killing of a landowner during a peasant demonstration in Aguilares, a quite unprecedented wave of reprisals from government and Right-wing groups hit the Church, culminating around the February 1977 elections. Several foreign priests were deported and a Salvadorean, Father Rafael Barahona was arrested and tortured. Crowds in the central Plaza Libertad in San Salvador holding a vigil to protest the massive rigging of the elections in favour of government Party candidates were massacred by the National Guard in the early hours of 28 February. By the time the retiring Archbishop, Luis Chavez, was able to intervene with the authorities, it was too late. The death toll was close to 100 with some 200 wounded and 500 arrested.[25]

Archbishop Oscar Romero had taken over from Chavez only six days earlier. This was a shocking introduction to the realities of San Salvador. Appointed as a safe pair of hands after showing himself uncomfortable with the new pastoral methods, he was known as a timid man not much given to public denunciations of government. He had once reacted to the murder of five peasants in his diocese of Santiago de Maria; while others had cold feet, he wrote to the President. But this atrocity was on altogether a different scale. This time he and all the bishops were decisive: the Church had to open its doors to those in danger, the clergy were told. In a hard-hitting pastoral on 5 March the Salvadorean Bishops Conference committed the Church to being with the dispossessed. "This will produce, as in the case of Jesus, persecution, and lack of understanding from the powerful, surprised perhaps that the church should become involved in the things of this world, and annoyed, seeing this mission as a threat."[26] Prophetic words indeed. A week later Father Rutilio Grande was in his car travelling through the cane fields when it was raked by gunfire, killing him and two other occupants of the vehicle.

This was a Gethsemane moment of anguish for Romero. He had become increasingly aware that the "Communist" label, with which those working for social justice were branded, was a calumny designed to smear the evangelical work of the Jesuits and the *iglesia popular*. The assassination of Rutilio Grande, a friend with outstanding evangelical commitment whose fidelity to Church discipline was unquestionable, left Romero in no doubt that he must now go on a collision course with the Salvadorian regime. It was outrageous to present Rutilio as a Communist infiltrator in the Church. The prevailing "theology of conspiracy" promoted by conservatives to taint and curb the "Church of the Poor" was a shabby façade for a theology of collaboration with the National Security State.[27] The military oligarchies of Latin America did not find the difference between revolutionary Christians and workers for social justice pertinent. They all qualified for sudden death if they threatened the system.

Catholic schools in the Archdiocese of San Salvador were shut for three days' mourning. The following week, all masses were cancelled save the single mass in the cathedral led by Romero; meanwhile YSAX, the official archdiocesan radio station, began broadcasting protest songs, hymns and prayers typical of the *iglesia popular*. The government-imposed state of siege was ignored. Romero left for Rome three days later to talk to Pope Paul VI about the deteriorating situation. Among Salvador's oligarch families, this was not what was meant by a safe pair of hands. On his return, Romero refused to attend the official inauguration of the new President, General Carlos Humberto Romero.[28]

Rutilio Grande's funeral mass produced a brief show of unity born of shock and mourning, with the Maltese nuncio and four bishops joining the new Archbishop, alongside hundreds of Aguilares Catholics. Not long after the fundamental fault lines in the Latin American Church opened up again. On the one hand there were Archbishop Romero and Bishop Rivera Damas, sharing the conciliar vision of the Holy Spirit at work in the world, animating the peasant movements such as FECCAS, the Christian Federation of Salvadorean Peasants; on the other was the fear and foreboding of their lacklustre and sometimes incoherent fellow bishops who probably imagined the Faith was being undermined as the virus of Communism infiltrated and contaminated the Church.

The nuncio, sharing a common right wing perception in Latin America, believed that "politics" was "manipulating" the Church and that this required a spiritualisation and institutionalisation of the Gospel. Material poverty was not the issue; the rich shared an equality with the poor in "spiritual poverty", and the Church was the rock on which a new Christendom would be built. For others the way forward required a "third way", between capitalism and Communism, that recognised the authority of legitimate government. Romero believed the Holy Spirit was turning passive victims into artisans of a new humanity through social and political change. And that this demanded a loving reaching out, an "accompaniment" of the poor, albeit a prudent and prayerful accompaniment, seeking justice, but with a courageous willingness to face a backlash of violent denigration and even martyrdom out of obedience to the Gospel.

The Puebla Conference

It was against this background of mounting violence in Central America and government change in the USA that CELAM began to prepare for the third General Conference of Latin American Bishops scheduled for October 1978 in the historic Mexican city of Puebla. It was to prove a critical moment in the life of the Latin American and wider Church. The

CELAM secretariat, made up largely of sociologists, canon lawyers and theologians sympathetic to Bishop López Trujillo's point of view, drew up what was to become known as the "Green Book", a 214 page preparatory document entitled *Present and Future Evangelisation in Latin America*. Those reading the document as it circulated between 1977-78 might have been forgiven for believing that the persecution of the *iglesia popular* in National Security states was not taking place, Medellín was a distant memory, and Latin America's fundamental problem was the social consequences of a necessary transition from an agrarian to an urban and industrial economy. The enemies of evangelisation were secularism and Communism rather than poverty. An intense and widespread reaction followed; some Catholics wondered whether they were preparing for a European rather than a Latin American conference.[29]

The "Green Book" was a blessing in disguise. Such was the rising protest, with even the "traditionalist" Colombian bishops reacting against the neglect of Medellín's conclusions, that it set off throughout the Latin American countries a rolling seminar on the post-conciliar mission of the Church, its pastoral priorities and its analysis of the contemporary economic and political situation. CEBs, Justice and Peace groups, sectoral Catholic organisations such as Young Christian Students and Young Christian Workers, councils of priests, and the Religious Orders, were given a foil that enabled them to challenge the thinking of the conservative cabal controlling CELAM. By July 1978, the CELAM President, Brazil's Cardinal Aloísio Lorscheider, riding the wave of opposition to the Green Book, convened a group of bishops in Bogota to produce a shorter and more acceptable working document retaining the "Third Way" emphasis of the original on culture as the focus of evangelisation, but breathing into it the spirit of Medellín and its option for the poor. The compromise document, making good use of appendices, forced the Medellín-resisters to talk about Medellín even if only in terms of its "false interpretations".[30]

Skirmishing continued. Papers from Vekemans' CEDIAL and other right-wing sources landed periodically on the bishops' desks courtesy of CELAM. A common theme was the threat posed by liberation theology at a time of Marxist influence within the Church, most notably that attributed to the Latin American Confederation of Religious (CLAR). CLAR, founded in Lima in 1960, was both well established and well respected; many of its members worked with the poor. But it was with

CLAR in mind that the label "parallel magisterium", an alternative source of authority to the bishops, first emerged in conservative circles. Invitations to the conference were a major bone of contention. Only threats of resignation from Cardinal Lorscheider got a ban by López Trujillo on attendance by CLAR at Puebla revoked; given the vital role of Women and Men Religious in the Latin American Church the ban was seen as particularly outrageous.[31]

In the event, 350 official participants were invited to the conference; only a little more than half were allowed to vote. In addition to the 140 voting delegates elected by the Latin American bishops, there were nineteen bishops from the CELAM secretariat and sixteen Presidents of national bishops' conferences. The secretary-general persuaded the Curia to improve the odds and twelve additional delegates were appointed; these were to a man under-enthusiastic about Medellín, or downright hostile, such as Cardinal Munoz Duque who held the rank of brigadier-general in the Colombian army. The final weighting of the voting delegates was 20-25 committed to a Medellín vision, 35-40 Medellín resisters with the remainder forming a cautious, amorphous and largely "traditionalist" centre. The National Conferences were limited to one elected bishop per five episcopal members of the Conference up to the first hundred, then one per ten members. This had the effect of depressing the total representation of the large Medellín-oriented Brazilian Conference with its over 300 members.[32]

In case Cardinal Lorscheider's office of CELAM President accrued too much power, the Conference presidency was expanded to include Rome's men: Cardinal Baggio, now in addition to his Latin American hat also Prefect of the Congregation of Bishops in Rome, plus the "traditionalist" Archbishop of Mexico City, Ernesto Corripio. Given the vital role of theologians at Medellín, there was a major effort to control the influence of theological advisers, the *periti*. The new Pope, John Paul II, selected *periti* both from nominees of the Bishops' Conferences and from the Curia; only three months into his job, with negligible knowledge of Latin America, he was presumably largely in the hands of Baggio, though a number of "progressives" managed to see him. Just one of those invited to Puebla as a *peritus*, Father Lucio Gera from Argentina, might be described as positively influenced by liberation theology. One *peritus*, a layman who had taught in a Guatemalan military academy was a local representative of a transnational corporation. Those excluded or missing, bishops and priests alike, added up to a roll-call of what was widely called the "progressive Latin American Church".[33]

The delay in staging the conference, resulting from John Paul I's sudden death, was as short as López Trujillo could decently make it. Cardinal Lorscheider had wanted at least a year. He got barely three months, until January 1979. But the Medellín men had a little extra time to marshal their forces and try to develop a concerted strategy. Most important, the CELAM secretariat's ploy of curtailing consultation and prior discussion of the Working Document, by sending it out only three weeks before the original scheduled opening session in named and numbered copies, was now destined to fail. The document was disseminated outside the circle of participants and some considered theological reactions were collected from theological advisers. But their reaction was hardly a coordinated strategy.[34]

The Puebla Conference was held on the outskirts of a conservative colonial city in the vast echoing Palafoxiano seminary, more open prison than sanctuary for seminarians, set in eighty acres behind a ten-foot high fence. There had even been anti-liberation theology demonstrations by business organisations and students in the town before the bishops arrived. Bishops could escape into the many local Churches to say their Sunday mass but, like modern celebrities, they were subject to rigorous security precautions put in place to "protect" them. López Trujillo had all the participants, and the visiting new Polish Pope, John Paul II, with his entourage, nicely contained.[35] The human geography provided a visual aid for pre-Tridentine theology. In all senses the goal was to keep the *iglesia popular* on the other side of the wall.

Life was difficult for all but the CELAM *apparatchiki*. The theologians pitched camp in town in convents, priories and hotels, met with "escapee" bishops, and gave talks, seminars and press conferences, giving a platform to prominent figures from the conference. Thanks to an alternative information and news centre, they were able to run a proxy campaign to keep the spirit of Medellín alive from outside the walls, with figures such as Helder Camara and Oscar Romero as major attractions. Against them was the traditionalist ambience of the city, with a hostile Right-wing Press that lost no opportunity to make it clear that they—particularly women's lobby groups—were unwelcome. There were one or two invited ecumenical observers but these could not play the kind of indirect role afforded them by the second Vatican Council.[36]

Quite different was the reception of the new Polish Pope. His arrival in Mexico was, in the words of Moises Sandoval, the editor of the *Maryknoll Magazine* "as if the legendary divinity Quetzalcoatl had returned".[37] There was no holding back in the face of Mexican anticlerical laws: posters of Our Lady of Guadeloupe much venerated in Latin America, photographs of the Pope, the characteristic white and yellow plastic flags of the Vatican fluttering everywhere in the capital, clerical garb to the left and the right in exuberant defiance of the liberal, secular government. It served as a dress rehearsal for an even more emotional visit to the no less secular regime in Poland a few months later. Some 20 million people came out to see the Pope during the five day visit and lined the streets, even the 100 miles of road from Mexico City to Puebla along which he drove on an open bus. A "plebiscite of popularity", one observer called it. But how would this popularity be deployed? What was he going to say? How was he going to handle CELAM ecclesiastical politics? Already a few words to journalists on his flight, referring to, though not naming, the problem of the Marxist sociological analysis used as a tool by some theologians, were being spun into a comprehensive condemnation of liberation theology in the mass media.

But no such sweeping condemnation featured on John Paul II's immediate agenda. His early reflections on Marxism had been scholarly and nuanced, though he had become increasingly worried and irritated by the way liberation theology approaches were setting the agenda at the bishops' synods in Rome, undermining, as he saw it the struggle against Communism, and ignoring the experience of the "Church of silence". Perhaps the most notable feature of the Pope's attempt to steer the Puebla conference was a steely determination to chart a course between extremes and thus avoid increasing the polarisation of the pastoral debate. It was the "whole Gospel" that set people free and liberated them, not different parts selected by partisan groups. Only this gave "integral liberation". His keynote address, "Unity in Truth", opening the conference, indicated an intention to divert argument from the narrowly political to the more philosophical and theological roots of salvation.[38]

John Paul II's opening speech was in two parts, the first a reaffirmation of traditional christology and rejection of any reduction of Christ to a "merely" political figure, a position inevitably used against liberation theologians yet one with which they would concur, the second a reflection on the Church as a defender and promoter of human dignity, revealing a deep Christian humanism. This second theme soon had him wading out from the shallows of democratic freedoms and the "liberation of the whole man" into the deeps of collective violence, human rights, torture and the Church's teaching on private property which— redolent of calls for agrarian reform and expropriation—he insisted was always limited by what he called a "social mortgage", the demands of the Common Good. In the affluence of the few and the poverty of the many, in the suffering of peasants and workers, and indifference to the Common Good, this mortgage was potentially in default. Christ did not "remain indifferent to this vast and demanding imperative of social morality. Neither could the Church." The conservatives, with some gritting their teeth, could just concur with the language of this section too, with its traditional references to the Church Fathers and Aquinas. No direct mention of liberation theology, the elephant in the seminary; only oblique references were evident: "the idea of Christ as a political figure, a revolutionary, as the subversive man from Nazareth, does not tally with the Church's catechesis", he declared. "Man is not a being subordinated to economic and political processes; these very processes are ordered by man and subordinate to him". But referring to work for justice there was a direct call to action: "let us get back to work in this field": in all a balanced performance on ground to which he was not accustomed.[39]

The second feature of the Papal tour which touched the conference was his evident sympathy with the Mexican poor—to the point of choosing "to be your voice" as he told the crowds. In a powerful speech to Indians and peasants at Oaxaca, he rooted the option for the poor firmly in Christian tradition, echoing some of the great Fathers of the Church—and Pope Paul VI's *Populorum Progressio* which he had cited frequently at Puebla: the rich who deprived the poor of their due were involved in "bare-faced robbery", to bring about change required "bold and thoroughly innovative transformations", not "alms nor a few crumbs of justice". These strictures seemed—perhaps deliberately—modelled on Friar Montesinos' passionate sermon against the *conquistadores* in the early sixteenth century. The Pope was deeply moved by the response from the crowd. His commitment to the worker movement and appeals for the rights of migrant labour—he had been a worker in Cracow himself and his second encyclical was a theology of work—were recurrent themes in his speeches. John Paul's use of the term "structures of sin" must have been music to the ears of the Medellín men—and women. Likewise a talk given when he returned to Rome indicates how little the newspaper reports reflected his thinking at the time. "The theology of liberation insists that human beings should not only be instructed in the word of God, but also speaks of their social, political and economic rights," he said approvingly. He would return to all of these themes in encyclicals.[40]

But there was also a clear indication that Pope John Paul's experience of bureaucratic state Communism and its economism had inoculated him against some of the language of liberation theologians. His corrective talks often seemed to take the form of a re-articulation of what he understood to be the problematic of liberation theology in the traditional language of the Church Fathers, Thomism and Catholic Social Teaching. Moreover, his past "inoculations" against Soviet Communism and National Socialism made him particularly sensitive to anything that smacked of a breakdown in the orderly hierarchy of Church life, a breach in the Church's defences that might be manipulated by its detractors. For in truth, unity, love and discipline he found the only strength available to Christians against totalitarianism. Thus repeated references were made to a somewhat mysterious entity, a "parallel magisterium", perhaps derived from the problem of collaborationist "patriotic" associations under Communism.[41]

"Parallel Magisterium" was a term beloved by the Latin American conservatives and they doubtless highlighted it for the Vatican. Their attempts at magisterial control of all pastoral practice, even that of their fellow bishops—and a desire for a trouble-free relationship with government—was shorn up by rhetoric about "ideology". They saw the *iglesia popular* as a "parallel" Church, not as the liberation theologians seemed to see it, the Sacred Heart of the One Church. All of the Pope's corrective talks could sound to radical Catholics like an attempt to pull the Latin American Church into an alignment with the preoccupations of Rome and Europe, a denial of truth, of collegiality and pluralism, and of the sheer diversity of the universal Church.

In something of a replay of the first session of second Vatican Council, once assembled, the bishops began to break out from the pre-ordained constraints imposed upon them. Cardinal Lorscheider spoke to the assembly of the Church of enacting, celebrating and preaching the Gospel with poverty, justice and love, in the face of injustice and domination on the continent. The CEBs were an example of the creative pastoral practice of which a dynamic Church was capable, he said. A compromise Working Document was being presented not to dictate a circumscribed discussion but to spark further creativity.[42]

The bishops voted that the conference would begin with the contemporary analysis of Latin America not doctrinal discussion, and they, not the Presidents, would elect the coordinating committee in charge of the final document—and thus ensure that it was not stuffed with Medellín resisters. Just as with the Council, a new spirit was kindled. A final draft document safeguarding the trajectory of Medellín emerged. Thanks to concrete discussions about the role of indigenous people, Afro-Americans and marginalised women in evangelisation, this deepened and differentiated the idea of the poor. To quote the Jesuit liberation theologian, Jon Sobrino, the Church would indeed try to be not only "the People of God but the People of God's Poor", in all their particularity.[43]

Liberation theologians insisted that Salvation History was to be discovered in the midst of the struggle for justice. But for the bishops this insight required the addition of a caveat. In their final message to the peoples of Latin America, they warned of a "disintegration of the language of faith into that of the social sciences, the draining away of the transcendental dimension of Christian salvation". The problem of parallelism in the Church was not the mythical "parallel magisterium" but the disjuncture between pastoral theology and doctrine, a problem not solved at Puebla because so much of the doctrinal content of the final document had to be conceded to the "traditionalists" to safeguard the pastoral dynamism of the Latin American Church.

Ministers and Martyrs

One of the great stars of Puebla—outside the walls—was Archbishop Oscar Romero who drew large crowds to hear his reflections on El Salvador. He was the personification of the Church that the conservatives wanted to forget or muzzle. "My job seems to be," he said after reclaiming his sacked church in Aguilares from the military, "to go

141

around picking up insults and corpses."[44] His pastoral letters situated the Salvadorean Church within the violent history of his country not in a transcendent realm outside. His sermons and his broadcasts on the Catholic radio station, YSAX, were specific about the growing number of human rights violations, the supine judiciary, the arrests, torture, disappearances and murders. In 1978 he abandoned striving at all costs for unity in the El Salvador Bishops' Conference and published with Bishop Rivera Damas alone *The Church and Popular Political Organisations*, a reflection on how in El Salvador they might play a role in the Church's vision of an "option for the poor", and on what the demands of political life meant for the Church and people.[45] The other bishops produced a vacuous and negative pastoral statement later that week on much the same topic.

The victory of the Nicaraguan Revolution in 1979 was viewed as a second Cuba by the Latin American oligarchs and military. The political Right in Central America turned more intensely to naked terror. During 1980 the level of repression in the Guatemalan diocese of El Quiché, with assassinations of catechists and clergy and the expulsion of Bishop Juan Gerardi, resulted in the unprecedented step of the diocese being temporarily closed. In El Salvador thousands died, many hideously tortured and mutilated. The Carter government in the USA, beset by the Iranian hostage crisis, was fast losing all control of the Central American situation, stumbling from one military coup to the next as revolutionary forces gained in co-ordination and boldness. Between January 1981 and March 1982, Guatemalan Indian villages came under routine attack by the Guatemalan army supported by civil patrols. Whole communities were massacred. Meanwhile President Reagan, elected in 1980, had begun supporting a covert war against Nicaragua led mainly by ex-Somoza guardsmen, with Honduras increasingly the bridgehead.[46]

In the USA, neo-conservative intellectuals formulated a new hard-line foreign policy around national security that sidelined Carter's attempts to promote human rights. During 1980, as détente collapsed after the Soviet invasion of Afghanistan, the more extreme wing of this movement, with religious affiliations to the Unification Church (Moonies) and its mass media outlets, formed a self-styled *Committee of Santa Fé* in preparation for a Reagan Presidency. Their 1982 policy document, *A New Inter-American Policy for the Eighties* described promotion of human rights as a "culturally and politically relative concept" and they pointed their finger particularly at the perceived menace of liberation theology. "U.S. foreign policy must begin to counter" read their third proposal, "(not react against) liberation theology as it is utilized in Latin America by the 'liberation theology' clergy". One suggested tactic was the promotion of Protestant groups to weaken the hold of radical Catholicism. Apart from that, it resembled a passably good imitation of the attitude to state-sponsored terror and to the radical clergy and Sisters within some segments of the Latin American Church. And it was to be the local blueprint for part of the Reagan administration's proxy "Second Cold War" during the 1980s, with one whole session of the Senate Security and Terrorism sub-committee, in October 1983, dedicated to liberation theology.[47]

The murder of Archbishop Romero on 24 March 1980, organised by a Salvadorian military officer, Major Roberto d'Aubuisson and ordered by the military high command, must be seen in the context of these unfolding events. Its proximate cause was self-evident. Romero in his advocacy of justice for the poor and of peaceful democratic ways forward for El Salvador had challenged the military both nationally and internationally. His effective use of the mass media available to the Archdiocese of San Salvador had been spreading his message around the country. His understanding of preaching "good news to the poor" included real news in his Sunday sermon in the cathedral, notably about the human rights violations by the army that were censored in the Press.

On the Fourth Sunday of Lent, the day before he was killed, and a week after writing to President Carter asking him to end financial aid to the Salvadorian military because of the repressive role of the army, Romero preached for an hour and a half to a packed cathedral congregation. As always he discussed with a team of priests and Sisters what he would say; agreement was reached that silence was not an option. The level of killing by the military had become intolerable. His sermon ended with a passionate and direct appeal to the Salvadorian army who were, in the main, at least nominally Catholic. "You are killing your own brothers and sisters among the peasants. God's law, which says 'Thou shalt not kill' should prevail over any order given by a man. No soldier is obliged to obey an order against God's law. No one has to carry out an immoral law. It is time to recover your conscience and

143

obey it rather than orders given in sin". This part of his sermon was interrupted by repeated spontaneous applause from the congregation.[48]

Romero's last dramatic appeal almost certainly sealed his fate. "In the name of God, and in the name of this long suffering people whose cries rise ever more thunderously to heaven, I beg you, I implore you, I order you, in the name of God: stop the repression." The length of the applause that greeted this direct appeal over the heads of the military junta would certainly have been registered by informers in the congregation, and its significance by those who monitored their reports. Romero was using the Gospel to challenge the mystique, cohesion and tactics of the military, a triple blow aimed at the martial heart of the nation. His words went out live on the Catholic radio station only just back on the air after being bombed by the military.[49]

The next day, 24 March, Archbishop Romero celebrated an evening mass in the chapel of the Divine Providence Cancer Hospital. The reading for the day was John 12: 23-26: "Unless the grain of wheat falls to the earth and dies, it remains only a grain. But if it dies it bears much fruit." His homily ended with a prayer that the Eucharist "nourish us so that we may offer up our body and our blood to suffering and pain, as Christ did, not for himself but to bring about justice and peace for our people".[50] A car drew up outside, a gunman got out and, it seems almost casually, came into the church. Romero saw him, flinched but continued. As he reached for the bread and wine and began the offertory prayers, the gunman shot him through the heart from the door of the chapel. Romero slumped dead under the large crucifix.

His murder during the mass ended the diary of a death foretold. But in the sacramental imagination of the Church of the Poor, it was an icon of the sacrificial love of Christ for the world, a true martyrdom, the seed of a faithful Church, the profoundest expression of liturgy imaginable. For the Salvadorian military it was an exemplary punishment for treachery against the nation. It was some measure of the contemporary divisions in the Church that whilst the last act of this modern Passion was being enacted, three of the most important Curial Cardinals, heading the Congregations of Bishops, the Doctrine of the Faith and Clergy, were trying to rid his Archdiocese of Romero.[51]

To underline their message, a few days later the army set off bombs and opened fire on the quarter million strong crowd gathered for Romero's funeral in and leading into the Plaza Libertad. They came from all the parishes together with contingents from the popular organisations, and had assembled in large numbers in and around the cathedral; the funeral oration was to have been preached outside in the Plaza by the Mexican Cardinal Corripio, one of the Presidents of the Puebla Conference. In the rush to escape from the Plaza caused by the explosions, and in the crush as people sought sanctuary inside the cathedral, twenty-six people died. It added a vicious footnote to Romero's assassination. All this happened under the eyes of the many foreign dignitaries attending the funeral. The Salvadorean military did not care a fig for international opinion.

Archbishop Romero's death was quickly and very naturally viewed as "martyrdom" by the Church of the Poor in Latin America. This setting of his death within the tradition of the Church of the first centuries contested the entire theological vision of the conservatives. It trumped arguments about the "Social Gospel", or at least trapped those who denied that Romero was defending the Faith within a palpably mean account of his life: misguided recklessness and cavalier disregard for prudence in high Church office. Moreover, this argument against him lacked consistency: only three years earlier an audible sigh of relief had gone up from the political Right when it seemed that one of "their" bishops had been appointed to the leading Archdiocese of San Salvador. Alternatively, only pure pedantic archaism justified denying that Romero was a Christian martyr. Martyrdom soon became an inspiring and motivating theme in the theology of the *iglesia popular*, an exemplar and proof of the authenticity of their practice and its spiritual ancestry in the early Church.

The assassination of Archbishop Romero was the tip of a very large iceberg. It is estimated that 2,780 civilians were murdered in El Salvador in the period June to August 1980. Latin America's killing fields were filled with the graves of Church workers and "ordinary" Christians whose fate, alongside that of more secular colleagues, had been the direct result of fidelity to their understanding of the Gospel message. The Jesuit theologian Jon Sobrino wrote of "crucified peoples" and, given that most were brutally tortured, this was no pious exaggeration of the reality.[52]

Given the international outcry at the murder of missionaries, and the impact on Catholics around the world, it was remarkable how little the US government was deflected from its Santa Fé strategy by adverse publicity beyond trying to find more acceptable faces to front the continuing repression. Or, perhaps more realistically, how little the USA was willing, or able, to curb the paroxysm of violence from its proxy-forces in Latin America. Non-Salvadorian Religious such as two Maryknoll Sisters, Ita Ford and Maura Clarke, and an Ursuline, Sister Dorothy Kazel with an American lay worker, Jean Donovan, raped and murdered on the airport road from San Salvador in December 1980, and, nine years later the massacre of six Jesuits, their housekeeper and her daughter, in their community at the University of Central America, (UCA), continued to provide names to mourn and celebrate. During the week the Jesuits were murdered there were 28 other killings: among them the head of a university women's organisation, a union leader, ten university students, and nine members of an indigenous farming cooperative. The renown of priests and Sisters served almost as a substitute for the thousands of unnamed victims of repression.[53]

In neighbouring Nicaragua the Bishops Conference had begun early in the 1980s to fear that the Sandinista revolution would be another Cuba. Given the close relationship immediately forged by the Sandinistas with Castro this was not altogether surprising. Led by Archbishop Obando y Bravo whose credibility stemmed from his past sustained public criticism of Somoza's tyranny, the bishops saw their duty as forming a critical opposition; in this sense, Obando y Bravo was following the political sentiment of the middle class. But he also faced the uniquely ecclesiastical problems of having priest-ministers in the Sandinista government, and clergy and Sisters in the pro-revolutionary Catholic bodies, from the mavericks of the informal middle-class *Christians for the Revolution* to a solidly pro-Sandinista Jesuit pastoral institute. The position of Ernesto Cardenal as Minister of Culture, Fernando Cardenal, head of the Sandinista youth movement, Alvaro Arguello, on the state advisory council, Edgar Parrales, ambassador to the Organisation of American States and Miguel d'Escoto as Foreign Minister remained unresolved despite high-level consultation with the Vatican. Several leading Sandinista figures not unreasonably began to interpret the Church's position as hostility, and a few as downright ideological warfare. Meanwhile Archbishop López Trujillo and CELAM began an international campaign of prayers for Nicaragua.[54]

It may well have been the sense, communicated by some of its bishops, that Central America was going to hell in a handcart, or at least wrapped in a revolutionary flag, that brought Pope John Paul II for ten days in March 1983 to Central America and Panama, Belize and Venezuela. A few weeks before his departure in a letter to the Nicaraguan bishops, he had described the *iglesia popular* as "born from the supposed values of a particular stratum of society", not from "God's initiative" and easily infiltrated with ideas about revolutionary violence and class struggle. In Nicaragua he was entering a political arena that had already been structured in people's minds around an opposition between a Catholic hierarchy backed by the middle-class versus a popular Church and a Marxist Sandinista government which had suffered from four years of civil war with 35,000 dead. But, unlike Puebla, where inexperience had dictated a consultative style for the Pope, after four years in Papal office his was now a more authoritarian presence in Nicaragua. After patiently listening to a denunciation of US intervention in Nicaragua from Daniel Ortega, John Paul II's theatrical finger-wagging at the Minister for Culture, Father Ernesto Cardenal, kneeling respectfully at the airport to kiss the Papal ring indicated to the watching world that his retention of political office, and disobedience, was unacceptable to Rome. On 3 March the Pope's cries of "*silenzio*" during a vast open-air mass in the July 19th Plaza reverberated around the congregation of half a million people, but no less around Latin America and the world.

The Pope's attempt to silence the congregation came in response to provocative Sandinista chanting of "we want peace" and "power to the people" against a background of banners and portraits of Sandino, Marx and Lenin, the Plaza bedecked with black and red flags of Sandinismo fluttering alongside the Papal flags. The largely pro-Sandinista congregation, or at least its sharp Sandinista activists, may itself have been provoked by the Papal homily. Condemnatory reference to "the conception of a Church which replaces the true one", after a pointed reference to "unacceptable ideological commitments", was heard as accusations against the revolutionary Christians and the *iglesia popula*. His obvious irritation caused consternation. The congregation included in the front rows, within easy access of the microphones, "mothers of the fallen" in the Contra war, carrying pictures of their dead sons; seventeen young men had been buried the day before after a funeral service in the Plaza. So John Paul II's anger at the interruptions seemed lacking both in compassion for the bereaved and, more generally, in

147

understanding of the plight of Nicaraguan citizens suffering under Contra attacks.[55]

His mishandling of the crowd may have been the result of poor briefing from the Nicaraguan bishops who had refrained from any serious or direct denunciation of what amounted in many instances to US-sponsored terrorism. They had clearly not stressed enough the sense of threat and crisis under which the Sandinista government was operating during the Contra war. But it also reflected a mindset that saw the Sandinistas as a typical Communist regime playing familiar propaganda tricks, an organised symbolic confrontation, enough to put iron into the soul of a Polish Pope. The Sandinistas had already stopped in June 1982 the national *La Prensa* from publishing—ludicrously under state of emergency censorship—a letter from John Paul II criticising the popular Church, only to repent and reverse the decision in August.

The image of an angry Pope before hundreds of thousands of loyal Catholics with no word of understanding, condemnation or consolation for the suffering caused by the Contra war was a low point of a Papacy that had once struggled to catch the harmonies rather than accentuating the dissonances of the Latin American Church. It was moreover a propaganda gift for the Reagan administration who could and did portray the congregation's vocal shock and disappointment as the baying of a Communist rent-a-mob sent to insult the Pope, and confirmation for the Marxist secular left among the Sandinistas that chasubles and mitres indeed hid powerful enemies of the revolution. Moreover, the Pope did little to disguise his belief that what Central America needed politically was social democracy

The Vatican Intervention

During the late 1970s and early 1980s the proponents of liberation theology, and pastoral workers influenced by it, were forced onto the defensive both inside the Church and under the wave of repression by militarised Latin American States supported by the Carter and Reagan administrations in the USA. A Vatican International Theological Commission, a consultative body for the Congregation for the Doctrine of the Faith (CDF) set up by Pope Paul VI, produced a study on "Human Development and Christian Salvation" in 1977. It raised some pertinent worries: about baptising Marxism, conflation of secular and salvation history, advocacy of violence and class struggle. But it was broadly sympathetic to liberation theology's commitment to the poor and acknowledged the necessary role of politics in work for social justice. The Pope's anxieties about liberation theology, gently expressed at Puebla and dramatically illustrated in his visit to Nicaragua, were shared *a fortiori* by the CDF. From 1981 under the direction of Cardinal Joseph Ratzinger, later Benedict XVI, a war of attrition began in earnest. The writings of Gustavo Gutiérrez and Leonardo Boff came under intense scrutiny. After the radical -elected- Superior-General of the Jesuits, Father Pedro Arrupe, suffered a debilitating stroke, a temporary replacement was imposed on them by Pope John Paul and their General Congregation delayed for two years.

In March 1983 the CDF sent ten criticisms of Gutiérrez's work to the Peruvian bishops, to which he replied at length. There was little outcome because the Cardinal Archbishop of Lima, Landazuri, would not budge. Then attempts, blocked by some of the Latin American bishops, were made to get CELAM to move against key liberation theologians. More threatening, Rome inspected the seminaries in Cardinal Arns' archdiocese of São Paulo in Brazil, where the seminarians lived in small groups, had jobs and participated in basic christian communities.

At the end of August 1984 the CDF issued an *Instruction on Certain Aspects of 'Liberation Theology'*. It bore all the hallmarks of Ratzinger's forensic intellectual style, a certain refined theological condescension born out of wood-lined libraries and dim Vatican offices, starkly at odds with the earthy Jesus in the clamour of the shanty towns and *favelas* from which liberation theology grew. It was indisputably a document that reflected and elaborated on the Pope's thinking, pre-occupied with the alleged impossibility of using Marxian analysis without buying into its entire epistemology and its ethical consequences. Fearful of class conflict and its apparent incompatibility with non-violence and the unity of the Church, but radical in its expressed commitment to place the problem of poverty at the heart of the Church's life, it was not a rejection of all forms of a theology of liberation but of deviations "which seriously depart(s) from the faith of the Church and, in fact, actually constitute(s) a practical negation". Phrases such as "perversion of the Christian message" describing aberrant tendencies rather than substance were typical of Cardinal Ratzinger's style of argument. By the end of the year Rome brought the time of the priest-ministers in Nicaragua to an end by having their different congregations suspend them from the priesthood. This was the preferred way, a word in the ear of a Superior-General.[56]

The CDF *Instruction* did not sound like the diatribes that had confronted "modernism" early in the century but showed the same tendency to evoke and then demolish a generic monster that simply did not exist. Some criticisms of one or two theologians were fully justified. Unbalanced formulations in others, *taken to their logical conclusion* and set up for condemnation in irresolvable manufactured dualisms, as Ratzinger did, might even take their authors outside mainstream Catholicism. But that which was criticised was not what a "generic" liberation theology was proposing or articulating. Gustavo Gutiérrez, a founding Father, was far too orthodox to fall victim to such intellectual *force majeure*. Despite a pressing summons to the Peruvian Bishops to come to Rome in September 1984 to condemn Gutiérrez's work, they held firm and were not bullied.

There had been moves against Leonardo Boff since 1982 and he was more vulnerable as a result of his book of essays *Church: Charisma and Power* which attacked the idea of hierarchy in the Church, questioned whether Jesus intended to found a Church, and fed into fears about a "parallel magisterium". He was accompanied to Rome for a "colloquium" on 7 September 1984, to defend his writings, by two of his fellow Franciscans, Cardinals Arns and Lorscheider, and by the President of the Brazilian Bishops Conference, Ivo Lorscheiter. This impressive team, at first excluded from Boff's examination, managed to attend the second half of the meeting. Arns had studied at the Sorbonne, served as a professor at the Catholic University in Petropolis, and could hold his own intellectually. The Brazilians painstakingly explained their understanding of the roots of the option for the poor in the Bible and Catholic Social Teaching and warded off condemnation of Boff's foundational *Jesus Christo: Libertador*.

Boff's opposition between Church and Kingdom of God, discipleship and hierarchy, cost him an imposed disciplinary silence beginning in April 1985 —no teaching except to Franciscans—and a ban on publishing. After their spirited defense, the Brazilian Cardinals saw this as an attack on them as well. Boff obeyed but repeated harassment took its toll. He finally left the priesthood in 1992. Gutiérrez moved more into the rich spirituality of the option for the poor and ensured there were no grounds for further misunderstandings. He later became a Dominican—firmly placing himself in the great tradition of sixteenth-century champions of the rights of Latin America's indigenous peoples, making himself less dependent on the —changing—Archbishops of Lima.

The second plank in the Vatican intervention came in a subsequent Congregation for the Doctrine of the Faith (CDF) document, *Christian Freedom and Liberation*, published in March 1986. Cardinal Agostino Casaroli, the Vatican Secretary of State, had not liked the negative tone of the first. The logic of his criticism was that the former instruction had said what was wrong with the prevailing theology of liberation, and this now required supplementing with some positive general principles about the shape of a "correct" theology of liberation, a task the Pope set himself. The short CDF document was overshadowed by his personal struggle with Marxism and contained a sustained critique of a linear vision of the secular Enlightenment, the movement inexorably towards a humanity "totally free at last". "Freedom is not the liberty to do anything whatsoever. It is the freedom to do good, and in this alone happiness is to be found," he pronounced. For this reason the Church's chosen means of seeking liberation for the poor was *virtuous* acts: to be precise, charity.[57] This position seemed inconsistent with his own highly political promotion of what amounted to a Catholic liberation struggle in Poland.

The overall tone of *Christian Freedom and Liberation* was less censorious and the product of the respected Marseilles head of the Pontifical Justice and Peace Commission, Cardinal Roger Etchegaray. The CEBs were described as a "source of great hope for the Church". The Church's social teaching was not a closed system but "remains constantly open to the new questions which constantly arise; it requires the contribution of all charisms, experiences and skills". Provided they were interpreted within the tradition of the universal Church—read in accordance with the contemporary views of the Magisterium—these "particular experiences can constitute a very positive contribution ... highlighting the work of God, the richness of which had not yet been fully grasped".

What this meant in Latin America was spelt out in a letter from the Pope dated 9 April 1986 to the Brazilian bishops gathered on retreat and delivered by an African Cardinal, Bernardin Gantin. Liberation theology was "not only timely but useful and necessary", it said. It "must constitute a new stage—intimately connected with those that

151

have gone before—of theological reflection". There was great rejoic-ing.[58] This was far more positive than the tone of the first Instruction and was reminiscent of John Paul II's 1980 speeches in Brazil when he acknowledged that the Church wanted to be "the Church of the Poor". "Only a society which attempts to become ever more just has a reason for existing," he had said then. Yet he had not been happy with Cardinal Arns' support for the 1980 auto-workers strike in São Paulo. Consensus existed on the ends but not on the means employed to achieve them.[59]

The 1986 Instruction drew a line under the official theological de-bate about liberation in the Church but did not end the conflict. Rome through its nuncios and apostolic delegates made sure that suspect pro-liberation theology clergy were not appointed bishops. CELAM kept a tight rein on who was elected to high office and key departments, and what was sponsored at a continent-wide level. Notable radicals and revolutionaries—Franciscan Biblical scholar Father Uriel Molina in Santa Maria de Los Angeles, Managua, the Salesian Father Jean-Bertrand-Aristide, later elected President of Haiti—were expelled from their Orders. Bishop Pedro Casaldáliga of São Felix in Brazil was si-lenced and told not to leave his diocese. Cardinal Arns' huge archdio-cese was split into four, destroying an integrated pastoral plan for the megacity. The champion of the urban poor was left presiding over the middle-class section of São Paulo.

Before the doctrinal commission of CELAM in Mexico in 1999, Cardinal Ratzinger wrote his epitaph to liberation theology. The sud-den collapse of Communism, he said, "turned out to be a kind of twi-light of the gods for that theology of redeeming political praxis".[60] That particular dragon was slain. And yet it was a strange victory speech from an admitted admirer of Greek culture, cradle of Man the political animal, though the future Pope was more a Platonist than an Aristote-lian, an Augustinian rather than a Thomist. He was already moving on to the oriental dragon of "relativism", snorting offstage in Asia.[61]

News of the death of liberation theology was greatly exaggerated. Liberation theology was disposable, not an end in itself. The prefer-ential option for the poor and its—redeeming—pastoral practice were not. These had long since entered the bloodstream of the Church and migrated around the world. Or, to join in the "mission-creep" beset-ting infallibility in the Church, championed by Cardinal Ratzinger at the CDF, the option for the poor had become part of the Church's "definitive teaching" deriving from Revelation. The life of the Church in Latin America, and arguably the universal Church, had been irrevocably changed.

7

RADICALS AND LIBERALS IN THE PHILIPPINES AND SOUTH AFRICA

The Catholic Church re-discovered in the 1970s that it believed the poor came first. The migration around the world of ideas and practices deriving from Latin American liberation theology, and their entry into the bloodstream of the universal Church, is one of the most remarkable stories of pre-Internet communication. Did the development and spread of a local liberation theology indicate that a genuinely pluralist "world Church", in the form of a new networked global community, had grown out of the Eurocentric, Rome-centred pre-conciliar Church? Were Catholics in the Church in South Africa, Philippines, and Peru talking to each other directly at all levels, sharing ideas across continents? Were they henceforth able to mould the thinking and language of the universal Church? Or was the rediscovery of the option for the poor a unique event, something deep in the Church's gene-pool easily triggered under the right circumstances, redolent of no major change in the dynamics of Church organization.

A bishop is not, to quote Cardinal Lorscheider, "the local branch manager of the International Spiritual Bank Inc."[1] The minimum requirement for a Church to merit the title "world Church" is that ideas and practices flow globally throughout its component structures and institutions. For it to be described in addition as pluralist in internal structure and interaction with the modern world, these flows must be without let or hindrance, encouraged and free. Moreover, the fundamental principle of Church unity must be balanced by a cherishing, nurturing and celebration of local diversity.

A fully global and pluralist Church is by nature collegiate, a community of communities, rather than a rigid hierarchical structure with its satellites controlled and ruled from a dominant centre. Or in the words of the then Cardinal Ratzinger, a definition given in July 1965: "the concept of collegiality, besides the office of unity which pertains to the Pope, signifies an element of variety and adaptability that basically belongs to the structures of the Church but may be activated in many ways...an ordered plurality".[2] It was a view that he appeared to abandon as head of the Church's doctrinal congregation, the CDF.

The groundwork for extending pluralism in the Catholic Church was put in place during the Second Vatican Council. National bishops' conferences such as the Southern African Bishops' Conference and the National Conference of the Bishops of the Philippines, inaugurated during Pope Pius XII's pontificate, and the synods of bishops that began after the Council, were acknowledged as having legitimacy. *Lumen Gentium* provided a doctrinal endorsement of episcopal collegiality that bore the supreme authority of Pope and Council, the *suprema potestas in universam ecclesiam*. A number of regions, nodes and networks, sharing a common culture and intellectual heritage, emerged more clearly within the Catholic Church in its wake. It now became meaningful to talk of the African, Asian, Latin American, West and East European, and North American Churches, though the influence of national and ethnic identities remained strong and significant.

The generic name for these fruits of enhanced adaptability was "inculturation". Both a process and state of affairs, the term captured the key role of cultural diversity in mission and evangelisation, and its significance is explored more fully in a later chapter. An element of intellectual particularity, most notably in the form of different theologies, generated both by context and by concern for safeguarding "Catholic Truth", is an important aspect of genuine inculturation. And the weight afforded theological articulation of the faith varied from continent to continent. The theologians of the Latin American Church—most notably the Brazilian Church—provided an outstanding example of theological development building on the past. The African and Asian Churches created a "popular Christian culture and spirituality". The sense of local Catholic Christians, at ease with hybrid religious symbols and multiple identities, and responding to their spiritual needs, is striking. Reflecting on Christology after the Council, Walter Kaspar wrote:

"It is now a matter of talking about Christ in such a way that human beings feel they themselves and their problems are being discussed".[3]

Catholicism has traditionally contained the emergence of such differentiation and interactions in the Church. The collegial concept of the Petrine office understood as *primus inter pares*, or as "the servant of the servants", the still centre of the Papacy, did not demote the Pope's primacy. Nor, as it turned out, was the Vatican bureaucracy bound and restrained after the Council, despite Paul VI's intentions to bring about reform. There was to be no post-conciliar fragmentation of the universal Church either in doctrine or worship. Pope Paul VI made sure of that. Ideas still had to be funnelled through Rome. He maintained control, endorsing or gently offering a limiting critique of the theological currents coming from the "Third World" via—primarily but not exclusively—the newly formed synods of bishops and most notably from Latin America. If "Catholic Truth" was the ball, Rome very definitely kept possession.

A new perspective, generating through its networks new life in the Church, that of the Pontifical Commission for Justice and Peace, led by the Quebec Cardinal Maurice Roy, was another significant innovation introduced by Paul VI. Established in 1967 it comprised influential lay experts and development thinkers such as the environmentalist Barbara Ward.[4] Local Justice and Peace Commissions soon proliferated in response to the many different forms of injustice and conflict in the world, and soon communicated with each other. Justice and peace workers were invariably most in jeopardy when governments turned to frontal attacks on the Church. In the Communist world any organised opposition to the Party was hazardous and likely to result in counter measures; commissions were almost never allowed to operate freely, and mostly not at all. In Latin America and white-ruled Africa, alongside Christians in leadership roles in the worker movement and human rights campaigners, Justice and Peace groups were frequently targets for surveillance and repression.

However repressive a government, however many Churches were shut, and priests imprisoned, deported or killed, in the face of the programmatic atheism of eastern Europe and the Soviet Union, or China's repression during the Korean war and the vicious Cultural Revolution, the Papacy remained, at least in theory, the symbolic guarantor that the catholicity and integrity of the Church would endure. The pull of the Papacy touched even the Chinese Catholic Patriotic Association, set up by the Chinese Communist Party as a national Church yet, by the 1980s, praying for the Pope during the mass in some of its churches. Even when ties were broken and contact hazardous, Rome retained symbolic potency.

Paul VI's powerful Secretariat of State, headed by Cardinal Agostino Casaroli, pursued a policy of *Ostpolitik*, an "opening" to Eastern Europe much at odds with the climate of the Cold War. To bishops fettered but unbowed by Communist rule, and worried that agreements and diplomatic handshakes would safeguard neither the integrity nor the catholicity of the Church, Rome's diplomats at times seemed naïve and wrongheaded. In order to ensure the survival of the Church, or so they believed, on occasion Eastern European bishops dared quietly defy the strategy promoted by Rome. The confused signals could work to the Church's advantage. As the archives of the Communist parties, opened after the fall of the Berlin Wall testified, the respective *nomenklatura* were often at a loss to chart the crosscurrents between Vatican and local bishops, and nonplussed by the tenacity of the Catholic Church.[5]

Indirect endorsement of a new pluralism—or at least the relative autonomy of action in local Churches—came in Paul VI's 1971 letter to Cardinal Roy, *Octogesima Adveniens*, celebrating the eightieth anniversary of the first major social encyclical. In it the Pope acknowledged the "widely varying situations" in which the Church found itself and the need in each situation to discern "the signs of the times". Political engagement and democratic participation, "shared responsibility", not of course armed struggle, was one of the few general prescriptions offered as the Catholic antidote to economic injustice and authoritarian rule.[6]

Rome was contributing to a variety of information flows within the global Church, controlling them, yet recognising that the Vatican was no longer their sole *fons et origo*. Local Churches provided a remarkably effective global communications network. They not only passed on liturgical, catechetical and theological ideas arising in their pastoral centres, but also collected, reported and transmitted information about human rights violations around the world through their Justice and Peace Commissions and diocesan human rights organisations. Bishops were able to, and did, influence their governments on human rights violations. The tribal trust lands of Ian Smith's Rhodesia, the hills of the Asian island of Timor, and the depths of the Amazon forest, were off the beaten track for most journalists, but they were served by an international Catholic justice network that could bring details of human rights violations to the Western mass media within hours.[7]

The second Rome Synod of Bishops held in 1971 shortly after the publication of *Octogesima Adveniens* resulted in another influential, and contentious, document entitled *Justice in the World*. It showed clear indications of Latin American influence. God was "liberator of the oppressed"; the way out of structural injustices in the post-colonial world was "liberation through development". This was a confusing and probably negotiated compromise between radical and reformist approaches; the bishops criticised unsustainable modes of contemporary development with their failure to alleviate poverty and their heavy environmental costs. The policies of the rich nations risked "irreparable damage...to the essential elements of life-on-earth, such as air and water, if their high rates of consumption and pollution, which are constantly on the increase were extended to the whole of humankind." Prophetic words.

Justice in the World endorsed a vision of evangelisation comparable to that promoted by liberation theology: "Action on behalf of justice and participation in the transformation of the world fully appear to us as a constitutive dimension (*ratio constitutiva*) of the preaching of the Gospel, or, in other words, of the Church's mission for the redemption of the human race and its liberation from every oppressive situation." Justice as a *"ratio constitutiva"* lay at the heart of the Church's mission—as Aquinas had proclaimed seven hundred years before. There were to be many subsequent skirmishes between Left and Right about what the Latin phrase meant. But in countries such as South Africa, Philippines and Korea, *Octogesima Adveniens* and *Justice in the World* mandated local bishops to act against grave injustice and endorsed a new language and theology with which to do it.

The Split Church

The Cold War and its proxy "hot" wars divided ideologically the Church no less than the secular world; the most important barriers to the migration of ideas were the geo-political contours of the time. The post-war division between capitalist and Communist blocs defined by the disposition of great armies and *Realpolitik* statesmen, set in stone

159

at Yalta despite Pius XII's protests, made all interaction between West and East difficult and fraught. The rival ideologies clashed in the "Third World" and in "hot wars", perpetuating oligarchies and tyrannies of different kinds but similar brutality, opposed by national democratic movements. This unique conjuncture generated a new group of religious intellectuals working with the poor, soon dubbed Third World theologians, attracted to the core ideas of liberation theology.

The Church in the Communist bloc and its Third World satellites kindled the hope of liberation no less than the Church in Latin America and Philippines. It had been, and still was, a persecuted Church which suffered death, imprisonment, torture, banishment—and the debilitating effect of collaborators—even more than Churches suffering under military dictatorships and Right-wing death squads. Despite the beginnings of a thaw at the end of the 1960s, the Church lived mainly underground, or, visible, suffered severe harassment; in Poland the sheer numerical strength of Catholicism, and the skillful manoeuvring of Cardinal Stefan Wyszynski, forced some grudging accommodation by the state. Lublin was home to the only Catholic University in the Communist world with students. At the end of the Council in 1965, the Polish Church counted 60 bishops in 17 dioceses with 18,000 priests, 28,000 nuns and 4,000 students in 70 seminaries. Neither the Polish government nor the Vatican found them easy to handle. Where the Orthodox Church had been dominant the Catholic Church, even more a minority, was in a far worse situation.

Khrushchev's reforms in the 1960s had not amounted to much as far as the Church was concerned. Since the Bolshevik Revolution, one thousand Catholic churches, and nearly as many clergy, had already disappeared under Lenin and Stalin in the Soviet Union. In Soviet-annexed Ukraine a collaborationist group simply dissolved the link formed with Rome in the sixteenth century by the Greek Catholic Rite with its four million Christians, the "Uniate Church". In Albania Christianity was systematically destroyed. Enver Hoxha murdered seven bishops and 115 of the country's 160 priests. All manifestations of religion were banned in 1967 and the Catholic cathedral in the capital was turned into a dance-hall.[8]

In China the situation was repressive but complex. All links with the Pope had been forbidden in 1951. Both the underground Church and state-sanctioned Catholic Patriotic Association suffered intense persecution during the 1966-1976 Cultural Revolution. But the under-ground Church suffered longest and worst. Bishop James Shiguang of Mingdong, for example, ordained as the Communists came to power, was first imprisoned in 1955 and spent almost half of the rest of his long life, twenty-eight years, in jails and re-education camps. It was only in 1978 as Deng Xiaoping began major reforms that some space was made for registered Churches in China. North Korea's hundred or so priests disappeared into Kim Il-Sung's prison camps. It was a far cry from Communist Poland.[9]

The Catholic publishing house *Znak* in Cracow produced political theology and *Tygodnik Powszechny* brought together Catholic intel-lectuals who would seed the KOR, the Workers' Defence Committee, in 1976, a group in which some of Brazil's radical Dominicans might have felt at home—had they ever connected. But joint reflection with Latin American Christians on such experience came there none, nor a shared theology of oppression, rather a deep mutual suspicion based on ignorance, language difficulties, distance and government imposed travel restrictions. At General Chapters and international meetings of Religious Orders perennial misunderstanding, rather than any meeting of minds, blocked debate on the different experiences of persecution. So the ferment of liberation theology reached the captive Church of the eastern bloc and Soviet Union as a threat, and a betrayal, not eased by a few Latin American liberation theologians', often clumsy, attempts at dialogue with Marxists and Communist governments.[10] Their ideas barely reached Catholics in China at all. Even the defining terms, "pro-gressive" and "reactionary"—notably when applied to collaboration by clergy with their repressive governments—signified contrasting and opposite clusters of political views when comparing Latin America, Philippines and South Africa with Eastern Europe. Even the common-est of words could be misconstrued.

The backwash from the two opposing geo-political perspectives was felt in the 1971 and 1974 synods of bishops in Rome. Disagreement about the meaning of evangelisation emerged during the 1974 synod. So it fell to the Pope to draft its final document, *Evangelii Nuntiandi*, an ominous precedent for the assembled bishops. The term "liberation" was affirmed with his authority as the goal of evangelisation. Witness, life and action, rather than simply verbal preaching of the Good News was the keynote. The goal of evangelisation was wide and comprehensive: liberation from "everything that oppresses people, particularly from sin and the Evil One". At stake—an emerging theme—was the transformation of *cultures*. The document had less to say about economic, social and political structures, or about the poor.

Pope Paul VI, never the most decisive figure, seems to have deliberately used the 1974 synod to counter-balance the previous synod on justice, responding to conservative pressures from Latin America against liberation theology. On his eastern flank were bishops who felt strongly that the 1971 synod had not adequately reflected the injustice of Communist regimes nor proclaimed what might be meant by liberation from them. The phrase "transformation of culture" served as a catch-all, a portmanteau phrase encompassing both structural and personal transformation. The tension between personal and structural was to tax a Polish Pope in the 1980s, and was resolved in favour of the personal.

Commenting on the 1974 synod Archbishop Karol Wojtyla of Krakow registered "definite progress" as far as its reflecting the concerns of Eastern Europe and notably Poland. The Soviet Union was now an undoubted superpower rivalling the USA, or so the CIA claimed. The last helicopter took off from the American embassy roof in Saigon the following year. Angola and Mozambique were threatened by Communist-supported "liberation" movements. Wojtyla identified "fatalism" as the enemy: the belief that Communism would inevitably sweep all before. Before its undeniable power, any suggestion of supine immobility in the Church had to be resisted.

Resistance for a philosopher Pope implied the need to engage intellectually as well as tactically. The false idea that Marxism offered the only positive programme of personal liberation from unjust structures had to be decisively confronted. On the contrary, Communism offered a "new form of human captivity" as the everyday experience of Eastern Europe revealed, much deeper than that of liberalism and "savage" capitalism. It "deprives people of their freedom of spirit", he wrote.[11]

Wojtyla had watched a million pilgrims descend on the Polish national shrine of Jasna Gora in 1956 and the impact of a nine year Great Novena. As a copy of its icon, the Black Madonna of Czestochowa, toured the country over a period of twenty-three years, its travels defined the cultural contours of Polish nationalism. To preach of the death of the Bishop of Cracow, St Stanislaw's martyrdom at the hands of the King in

1079, as Archbishop Wyszynski did, was to denounce the persecution of the Communist authorities. It was not, in Stalin's simplistic phrase, Rome's non-existent divisions that had to be weighed in the balance, but the spiritual power of a traditional popular Catholicism and its cultural symbols supported by a fervent nationalism. This was the new Catholic Action; this was what the Communists had to fear. And the Polish Communist Party knew it. "Come down, Holy Spirit come down and renew the face of the land, *this* land," he emphasised to vast rapturous crowds in Warsaw's Victory Square on his first return to Poland as Pope. And *they* knew what he meant. No wonder at Puebla in 1979, John Paul II engaged with the themes of liberation theology from a different perspective from Paul VI a decade before at Medellín.

Human Rights Discourse

The one overarching concern that might have acted as a bridge between the Church under Communism and under the Latin American national security states of the 1980s was a common concern for human rights. During the Cold War the language of human rights allowed Church leaders to finesse, the more difficult—and many would say inappropriate—demand to take sides politically, and to support particular lines of political action. Human Rights dealt primarily with claims on the state, to life and liberty, or freedom *from* a coercive diminution of human dignity by a variety of means. The Church's politics were expressed by working for particular economic, social as well as civil rights to be realised. Freedom *for* a specific political project or programme went too close to trespassing onto the terrain of Party politics, although in Pope John Paul II's support for Solidarity in Poland the distinction was blurred. By the 1980s Rome was keeping its distance from Christian Democracy, as were most of the bishops.

The Church had an established tradition of asserting workers' rights whether in South Africa, Philippines, Brazil, Poland or Argentina. There was an organic tradition of social justice rooted in the experience of industrialisation in Britain and Germany dating from the nineteenth century. The Church fully entered "the human rights community" during the Second Vatican Council. In Chile the Committee for Cooperation and Peace and its successor, the Vicariate of Solidarity, in Bolivia and Argentina, the Permanent Assemblies of Human Rights, in Brazil, the Land Commission and the Justice and Peace Commissions, in Philippines, Task Force Detainees, all began with, or gained, episcopal support.[12] Church-sponsored human rights organisations elicited Catholic international financial support, particularly from Germany, and, unlike the CEBs, liberation theology, and other pastoral expressions of the "Catholic Left", did not incur intense surveillance from the Vatican. Support was readily forthcoming after state attacks on priests and nuns. Bishops suffered humiliation, forced into uncomfortable positions as petitioners before state and military officials who openly showed their contempt for them. Human rights NGOs could not be exported to Eastern Europe because of the level of repression, nor easily to Africa. Their motivations and language, the rights of the person, were everywhere readily understood as being central to the Catholic conception of human dignity with its social and civil implications.

But of women's rights, and the special plight of women living in poverty, there was no mention. Medellín had ignored the question. Latin American liberation theology never entirely escaped the *macho* culture around it, or the male domination of clerical culture in which it was embedded. Effective and organised feminist advocacy, rather than feminist theology, emerged first in the Church among Women Religious in the USA in the 1970s, but it was over thirty years after the Council before the Church produced a pastoral letter that spoke out clearly on women's rights.

Women Religious worked predominantly in education in the early twentieth century. After Medellín, several Religious Orders in Latin America and Philippines shut their elite schools and, adopting its priorities, sent Sisters into marginal areas, slums or poor villages, in groups of three or four. They lacked income, episcopal support, or even the modest interest of the majority of bishops. There were no immediate ways of communicating their pastoral experience to the rest of the Church. Their prayer-life was deepened and changed and, in the main, enriched by their experience. Sister Katherine Anne Gilfeather described the spirituality of small communities in Santiago's slums as "affective, evangelical, down to earth, communal, intimate, interiorised and based on life".[13] The scale of this move away from institutions and education was at first modest but grew during the 1980s.

Radical spirituality in a world of poverty coexisted with a set of more "liberal" demands *ad intra* in the Church. A significant number of such women, many but not exclusively North American missionaries, were acutely frustrated by their predicament, the way their responsibilities were not matched with positions of authority, and Rome's "illogical and inadmissable" position on women's ordination to the priesthood.[14] "*Women's lib*"—as it was then called—like black theology demanded both psychological liberation from submissive behaviour and increased power in the Church. In October 1979, in a large public meeting, Sister Teresa Kane greeted the new Pope, John Paul II, on his first visit to the USA and asked him to make all ministries in the Church open to women. He ignored her. The Cardinal whom he appointed two years later to the Sacred Congregation for the Doctrine of the Faith, his successor as Pope, went on to declare that it was a logical necessity for priests to be men; that women priests were prohibited by the Church was allegedly no less authoritative than the prohibition on abortion. It was beyond discussion for Catholics. Though one or two women had been ordained clandestinely in Eastern Europe under Communism.

The Flow of Ideas

One natural bridge for ideas and people linked South with North America. The United States Bishops' Conference had developed strong links with Latin America in the 1960s through its Latin America Bureau (LAB) and mission programmes. A new Catholic Inter-American Cooperation Program (CICOP) led by an Iowa priest working for LAB, Father Louis Colonnese, began holding high-level conferences in 1964 to analyse the situation in Latin America. A second conference in 1965 brought together several of the radical Latin American bishops with a diverse audience of US bishops, diplomats and journalists who heard from François Houtart, a *marxisant* exponent of socio-economic and political analysis from Louvain, and Helder Camara's adviser at the Council. The US State Department tried to shut the conferences down but to no avail. The annual meetings provided a conduit for radical analysis and contact with emerging Latin American ideas about the "Church of the Poor". The US bishops eventually took fright and issued a warning about Mission being reduced to a merely socio-economic enterprise in 1971. Colonnese was sacked, the CICOP shut down, and henceforth the US bishops limited themselves to expressing solidarity on the safer terrain of the struggle for human rights in Latin America.

Beyond the Americas, the methodology and central themes of liberation theology, migrated with remarkable speed to theologians in

165

"Third World" countries—such as South Africa and Philippines—sharing similar political experiences. The methodology found a receptive audience. Books and articles from Latin American theologians in Spanish, Portuguese and then, from the mid-1970s, in translation, carried the ideas. From 1973 the Maryknoll Mission Society's new publishing house, Orbis, promoted the translation into English and publication of liberation theology, and other radical theologies. These soon found their way around the Anglophone world. During international gatherings and General Chapters, face-to-face links within Religious and Mission Orders enhanced transmission. A 1972 meeting of the Jesuit Institute of Faith and Secularity brought a number of Latin American liberation theologians to the surprising venue of the Escorial palace in Spain. Another important network for the global spread of ideas was the Ecumenical Association of Third World Theologians (EATWOT) that came together in 1976 in Dar-es-Salaam, Tanzania.

While liberation theology harmonised with the pastoral experience of Women Religious as much as with their male colleagues, their own spirituality and theological reflection was barely evident in the main body of published work in Latin America. It took three years, until 1979, at EATWOT's meeting in Tepeyac in Mexico, for women's theology to come onto its agenda. Only during the 1980s did the particular experience of poor marginalised women in the Third World begin to inform the evolution of liberation theology. This differentiation of "the poor" challenged the implicit—gendered—assumption that *the* subject of history was male. As the Sandinistas assumed power, and later, as negotiated settlements brought predominantly male "freedom fighters" into government in Central America, the problem of how little liberation movements did in practice to liberate poor women, *qua* women, became pressing.

Gender differentiation within liberation theology emerged as one of several theological accounts of the ways in which people were poor and experienced their poverty; notably through their ethnicity, status as indigenous, or being black. After Rosa Parks declined to give up her seat on an Alabama bus in 1956, the US civil rights movement developed fast and, a decade later, in its wake followed radical black theology. The question of gender was in a different category, overarching and hardly particular in the same way as all other contextual aspects of power and dominance. The phrase "contextual theology", used later in South Africa, included feminist and woman's theology.

This elaboration, sometimes unravelling, of "the poor" as the subject of history, followed the migration of liberation theology around the world.[15] When the Church professed a preferential option for the poor, the rich and middle class were potentially in the unusual position of being sidelined. The *angst* of the middle-class was like that of the rich young man of the Gospel, who turned away from Jesus' tough demands of justice. Those who were alienated by surrender to materialism and individualism, and in psychological distress as a result, were now sometimes described as suffering from "spiritual poverty". It was real enough. But the re-branding of the rich as "spiritually poor", rather than confused, frightened, hedonist or plain greedy, provided a means of emptying the preferential option for the poor of serious meaning. "Spiritualisation" of poverty left Catholic radicals open to a classic ambush: to counter this binary opposition between material and spiritual they risked relegating the spiritual and replacing it with the material, a theological own-goal.

For contextual theology, the contexts that counted were those that specified the diversity of the poor in terms of marginalisation, oppression, material hardship and want, the conditions that Gustavo Gutiérrez described as the denial of the love of God and of the Gospel message. The most similar to these contexts, and the most immediately threatening for the unity and integrity of the Church under the Latin American National Security State, was the Philippines under martial law. Another was the unique experience of oppression under apartheid in South Africa.

The Philippines Experience

The dictatorship of President Ferdinand Marcos in the Philippines between 1971-1986 had features in common with those of Latin America: government by a landowning elite for a landowning elite, a rural insurgency fed by the failure of land reform, dominance of the military, the rise of a National Security State initially with IMF and World Bank support, the political role of the USA in influencing and sustaining a repressive regime, and, outside of the island of Mindanao with its large Muslim population, a dominant Catholic culture.

The response of the Church to "authoritarian modernisation" was also broadly similar: a period of critical collaboration giving way to critical opposition, illustrating four main responses from Catholic Christians on the basis of theology, class loyalties and political preferences: rightist, conservative/traditionalist, reformist and revolutionary. The bishops created a National Secretariat for Social Action (NASSA) in 1966 and the Association of Major Religious Superiors (AMRSP) formed Task Force Detainees (TFD) in 1974. These were the two main expressions of Church concern for human rights. The Bishops Conference promoted credit unions, housing and rural resettlement programmes, agricultural projects, and seminars through NASSA. Programmes begun in the 1950s, mainly Jesuit and Maryknoll run, were aimed at countering Communist influence. National peasant organisations, notably the Federation of Free Farmers (FFF) founded in 1953, moved into pressing for social reform in the face of the nascent Maoist, *Huk*, movement in rural areas. There were also significant differences from Latin America; until the late 1960s the question of inculturation and the role of "colonial" missionaries were dominant themes among radicals, in quest of a "Filipino theology". And this bore strong nationalist convictions.[16]

Religious Orders were the main vehicle mediating the reformist impact of the Vatican Council. From October 1968 to February 1969 the Maryknolls held a Special—international—Chapter of Affairs which began a reform process. They chose " to identify with the Church of the Poor...the poor in the true gospel sense: the spiritually dehumanised, socially oppressed, culturally marginated, or economically deprived".[17] Sisters in the Philippines were already living in small houses and working among the poor supported by income from teaching at the Quezon City Maryknoll College. Students at the College edited the Federation of Free Farmers newspaper under the direction of Sister Pauline Linehan. Others joined this apostolate; for example Sister Mary Grenough left work in a private hospital in 1969 to join the Social Action Committee of the Diocese of Bacolod under the direction of the dynamic Bishop Antonio Fortich. Bishop Fortich, son of wealthy sugar cane planters, suffered for his pro-worker convictions; the worst of several incidents were a hand-grenade attack and the burning of his house to the ground. The Maryknoll stance was endorsed during Pope Paul VI's 1970 visit to Manila when he spoke of the Church's "determination to eradicate entrenched injustice and replace oppressive structures". The National Association of Major Religious Superiors (AMRSP), representing 7,000 Sisters and 3,000 priests and Brothers, was to play a major role in pushing for social reform and working for human rights through specialist task forces set up in 1974.

By the mid-1970s ideas from Latin America and European radical theology were circulating in the Philippines. For a Divine Word priest such as Father Ed de la Torre, newly ordained in 1969, the message of the social encyclicals was deepened and challenged by reading Helder Camara and the revolutionary Camilo Torres, as well as Metz's political theology. Informed by insights gained from immersion in an organised peasant milieu as a chaplain to the Federation of Free Farmers Movement, his thinking was moving on towards a local variant of liberation theology.[18] It was a highly politicised environment. The student-led uprising in Metro-Manila, dubbed the "First Quarter Storm", and Marcos' declaration of martial law on 21 September 1972, found the Student Christian Movement studying Mao's *Five Golden Rays* part of a vibrant coalition, the Movement for a Democratic Philippines. A concerted Maoist take-over of the far Left of the radical political terrain drew several Church activists into the Communist Party of the Philippines and into its armed wing, the New People's Army (NPA).[19]

What distinguished the Philippines' from Latin American experience was both the crude Maoist political analysis highlighting landlordism, feudalism and "service to the people", and the remembered history of Church resistance to invaders and colonisers, Spanish, American and Japanese, promoted by nationalist clergy. Three cultural priest martyrs, Burgos, Gomez, and Zamora, the Gomburza martyrs, who died during Spanish colonial times in the cause of the rights of secular Filipino priests—against colonial friars—were eponymous ancestors to the modern "national democratic" revolution. The first assembly of the revolutionary Christians for National Liberation (CNL) on 12 February 1972 celebrated their centenary. CNL, initially some 72 members, declared in their *Gomburza Declaration* the end of "our separate search for authentic service to our people". The centenary "starts our organized struggle along the narrow path to national liberation and democracy".[20]

CNL tried to offer a "more organized and disciplined participation in the struggle".[21] At first a legal organisation reminiscent of contemporary radical groups forming in Latin America, CNL was outlawed under martial law and obliged to operate clandestinely both within the Church, which became its special "site of struggle", and outside. It later joined the Communist Party umbrella organisation, the National Democratic Front (NDF). The indiscriminate implementation of martial law, the detention and radicalisation of social democrats alongside Communists and Communist sympathisers, drove a group of bishops, with particularly the Jesuits, to form the nucleus of a "reformist centre". Marcos' brand of counter-insurgency was perennially adept at creating a multi-class alliance against himself despite his efforts to fragment it.[22]

Much of the innovative theology emanating from the Philippines came from Ed de la Torre who retained a remarkable degree of personal independence within the NDF. The seminarian Ed Garcia who was later to champion the concept of "peace zones" and pioneer work in conflict resolution was another independent-minded founder. The theology of Father Karl Gaspar related "people's struggles" to Religious Life and the role of basic christian communities with an emphasis on spirituality, liturgy and prayer. He became the executive secretary of the Mindanao-Sulu Pastoral Conference. In contrast CNL documents lacked theological depth and were full of jargon and sonorous Maoist phrases.[23]

The Communist Party of the Philippines was far from being an enlightened coalition partner. It decreed policy to coalition members from the hills leaving little leeway for a semi-autonomous civil society movement to develop its own—adaptive—strategies. Unlike the creative de la Torre, who was a founder member, some CNL members brought a mixed Catholic-Maoist brand of authoritarianism to their dealings. Although Gutiérrez's "Notes for a theology of Liberation" were widely circulated in CNL circles in the early 1980s, there was little sign that his methodology was absorbed and effectively applied. Instead CNL produced a hybrid ideology in which Maoist political analysis, reminiscent of a Marxist penny catechism in its rote learning, lack of sophistication and absence of empirical purchase on contemporary society, dominated a few crudely presented liberation theology themes. The secrecy and tactics of the CNL aroused suspicion and disqualified it from the role of an effective ginger group in the Church. Rather it was seen by many politically active Catholics as an entryist group, a nominally Christian section of the Revolution. On the other hand, the corporate involvement of Christians in a revolutionary process introduced more strategy and planning to Catholic attempts to bring about radical change, and an almost obsessive passion for social and political analysis. But, to work undercover in a Christian ambiance inevitably produced disquiet, mistrust and fears that the Church was being instrumentalised and infiltrated by Maoists. CNL qualified for the conservatives' dismissive claim that liberation theology was politics dressed up as religion.

The existence of an underground movement in the Church put in jeopardy NASSA's efforts at conscientisation through basic christian communities, strongly supported by the radical Bishop Julio Labayen. The BCC-Community movement drew on both the Latin American experience and that of community organising in the USA, the Alinsky method from Chicago, and by 1981 had created a national network with over forty centres. But conscientisation could easily turn into indoctrination along the lines set down by the Communist Party. Though the programmes sponsored an important new generation of Catholic lay leaders, instances of conscientisation that amounted to a Maoist analysis undermined the position of the fifteen or so radical bishops among the 95-strong Bishops' Conference, leaving them open to accusations of being dupes to Communist infiltration.[24]

Just as in Latin America, the Church was soon targeted by the military and feeling the impact of the Sante Fé document and the Banzer plan strategy of divide and rule.[25] Contacts between security services and international Right wing groups, often US-mediated, followed hard on the heels of liberation theology. During the martial law decade, 1972-1982, several Church personnel were arrested and detained, and a number of lay workers killed; some foreign missionaries were deported. Two Catholic radio stations were shut down and the AMRSP's publication *Signs of the Times* closed. Marcos' Decree PDA 823, banning strikes, and outlawing all foreign mission personnel from participating in union activities, brought a remarkable 3,000 priests and nuns to the Santa Cruz Church in Manila for a protest mass in early 1976. The Gdansk shipyard workers in Poland could scarcely have asked for more. Major Religious Superiors, "friends of the workers", continued to join marches by strikers and to challenge multinational companies. Four priests went underground to join the NPA in 1979 and more were certainly sympathetic.

Until the early 1980s, much repression was the consequence of supporting peasants and workers against the power of multinationals and rapacious landlords, rather than of direct Church confrontation with government. Despite his family background of plantation owners, Bishop Fortich in Negros became the champion of the sugar workers and their union. Strikes in the textile industry resulted in whole convents, motivated by Catholic Social Teaching, being mobilised to carry out tasks in support of those on the picket lines. The motivation for such solidarity was a long way from the anti-Communist rivalry behind Church promotion of the Federation of Free Workers and Farmers in the 1950s. A similar though less widespread support for radical trades unions by Religious was evident in South Africa, also backed up by the new Pope's, John Paul II's, commitment to worker rights.[26]

There were plenty of Religious and secular priests who frowned on this kind of social activism. Marcos' Intelligence apparatus appeared on the whole complacent—probably correctly—about being able to contain the Catholic radicals, and the likelihood of them swinging the Church behind their subversive agenda. A solid body of Opus Dei members and some influential Jesuits supported the technocratic modernisation of the state used to justify Marcos' authoritarianism. However one Intelligence assessment warned that because the Basic Christian Communities were creating a political infrastructure, they needed careful watching—a conclusion drawn after interviews with conservative priests. After 1982 the Church was targeted in a stepped-up counter-insurgency drive with a surge in arrests of Church workers. In response the bishops, fearing CNL manipulation and loss of control, refused to recognise the NASSA Board precipitating a crisis and an exodus of radical staff.[27]

But the Catholic centre held. The middle class was smaller than in several of the Latin American countries that had spawned military oligarchies and identified less with the rich and corrupt elite around Marcos who were in power. The Philippines was a deeply Catholic culture, and the elite around Marcos were flamboyantly greedy and privileged. Though they did not always do so, the Catholic middle class could find reasons from the Church's teaching to approve of Task Force Detainees, led by a Sister who might have taught them at school, Mariani Dimaranam. "We cannot jail a man indefinitely and still call ourselves Christians," declared Cardinal Jaime Sin of Manila, as if that was common sense. Though the velvet glove came off in 1982, the military could not revert to the iron fist without strengthening the reformist Church and pushing the Catholic centre into the arms of the radicals.[28]

The state's murder on 21 August 1983 of Senator Benigno "Ninoy" Aquino at Manila airport killed the hero of the country's reformist centre. It was the last straw. The Filipino middle class, most notably the influential Makati Business club, rallied against Marcos. Church radicals followed the lead of a blundering Communist Party that had lost touch with reality, boycotting National Assembly elections. The AMRSP adopted the same policy and published a call to boycott in letter form. Cardinal Sin and several of the leading bishops threw their weight behind NAMFREL, the National Citizen's Movement for Free Elections, headed by a prominent Catholic layman Jose Concepcion, and called on Catholics to vote.

By the 7 February 1986 elections, the Church's support for Corazon Aquino, Ninoy's wife, was barely disguised. Jesuit priests, Jaime Ongpin, Opus Dei, and Joaquin Bernas, President of the Atheneo University in Manila, were helping her prepare for office. Cardinal Sin was brokering an alliance with opposition leader Salvador "Doy" Laurel. Marcos rigged the election. The fraudulent presidential poll left him with no moral basis with which to govern. Radio Veritas, the Catholic station, spread the message that the time had come for him to go. For four days, the Epifanio de los Santos Avenue (EDSA) filled to bursting with mainly middle class protestors, nuns in full Religious dress clasping rosaries and confronting soldiers. Cardinal Jaime Sin called on the two million strong crowds to surround central Manila's two military camps, Crame and Aquinaldo. The airforce went over to Corazon Aquino. In the end air power provided the key element of iron in the EDSA glove, alongside pressure from the US embassy, convincing Marcos his time was up. But the reformist Church—as would soon prove to be the case in Poland—had been decisive. Marcos was bundled out. The mighty had been pulled down from their thrones by a mass movement in the first of the "velvet revolutions". The reformists and the middle class had gained a great victory from which the radicals had stood aside and gained nothing.

The World Council of Churches (WCC) fully backed the "people's power" revolution.[29] The ecumenical links of the reformist and radical Church in the Philippines consolidated opposition to Marcos and removed any recourse to a Protestant counter-weight such as the Indonesians had tried to create in East Timor. But Marcos maintained support to the end on the political Right of the Catholic Church: among charismatic Christians, with some of the influential international *Opus Dei*, and among the local, ultraconservative *Ecclesia in Christo*.

In South Africa with its large Dutch Reformed Church, the ecumenical picture was different. The nature of the tyranny and its relationship to one important strand of Christian theology was unique, as was the radical theological response to it. But the profile of the fissure lines running through the Church, and the political differences on each side of them, reformist versus radical, human rights focus versus partisan political focus, radical theology versus "Church theology", were similar.[30]

South Africa and the Apartheid Heresy

The Second Vatican Council said very little about racism. Apartheid was not mentioned. Its agenda drew on questions of longstanding significance for the Church, brought forward by Catholic movements gaining momentum and commending themselves for attention. Yet the defeat of apartheid was becoming one of the outstanding moral and political struggles of the second half of the twentieth century. The bishops gathered at the Council missed a great international ethical challenge. No one describing the forces that brought down the mighty Afrikaner military state would place the Vatican high on the list. But the local Church was another matter. Unlike the Philippines, liberals and radicals for the most part complemented each other.

Even during the decade following the Second World War the "South African Church" was still best described as the "Church in South Africa". It was not only internally divided by race but remarkably out of touch with the rest of Africa even compared to the Church in southern Africa's other settler societies. The clergy followed one of two different ministries and assumed distinct roles: serving the settler white—and Coloured and Indian—Catholic communities of the country, or continuing to build up the nineteenth-century African mission Church with its network of schools. Many priests were drawn from Religious Orders, and had trained overseas, particularly in France or Ireland. All the bishops were white. African and Coloured vocations to the priesthood came slower than in the rest of Africa. It took until the 1970s before they represented more than 10 per cent of the country's clergy.[31]

Denis Eugene Hurley, born of Irish immigrant parents, after studying in Rome was made bishop of the English-speaking stronghold, Durban, in 1947, at the remarkably early age of thirty-one, the same year as the foundation of the Bishops Conference, the South African Catholic Bishops Conference, SACBC, in which he was to play such a prominent role. The establishment of the South African hierarchy followed in 1951. In thinking and practice Eurocentric, yet white African, the bishops had little corporate understanding of the political ferment on their doorstep. Despite having been through a traditional seminary training, Hurley was a fervent liberal, outspoken on contraception and a married priesthood, and, even more worrying for Rome, a devotee of Teilhard de Chardin's mystical cosmic theology.[32] More important he was willing, and able, to provide courageous leadership of his cautious fellow bishops, and a succession of Apostolic Delegates, in resisting apartheid. Disregarding some opposition, the SACBC acknowledged his youthful leadership, voting him its chairman, and subsequently looked to him during times of crisis.

The National Party victory in the 1948 elections came as an unpleasant surprise for the Catholic Church. Dutch Reformed theology, developed in the dominant *Nederduitse Gereformeerde Kerk* (NGK), underpinned the "Christian Nationalism" of apartheid. Sharing the same Protestant anxieties and misgivings about Catholic patriotism found in the USA, Dutch Reformed mistrust and fear of *Die Roomse gevaar*, the Roman threat, were more intensely visceral, xenophobic, and expressed politically. When it came to patriotism, in the eyes of Afrikaners Catholics in South Africa were doubly suspect: wrong religion, wrong language. There had been virtually no Afrikaner converts to Catholicism; the first South African born bishop, Daniel O'Leary, had only been consecrated in 1925.

The leaders of the African National Congress (ANC), Albert Luthuli, James Calata, Oliver Tambo, and Professor Z.K. Matthews were Protestants, and mainly from the Anglican Church. Their political vision largely escaped the attention of the Catholic bishops, or was distorted through the prism of anti-Communism. The Anglican Church provided the sympathetic white visionaries, most notably Archbishop Geoffrey Clayton of Cape Town whose pastoral letter "Church and the Nation" recognised the African Mineworkers' Union and called for an extension of the franchise to blacks. Then there were the indomitable

175

Anglican priests, Trevor Huddleston and Michael Scott, the latter jailed for three months for his Campaign for Right and Justice. But ecumenical contacts were virtually non-existent. The Catholic bishops were not talking to the right people. They were thus ill-prepared for what was to come. Beyond deploring segregation, there was little reflection on social and racial issues.

Bishop Francis Henneman of Cape Town responded to the National Party victory with a pastoral letter appropriately entitled "Crisis in the Life of the Nation" describing apartheid as a "mischievous, unchristian and a destructive policy". Pursued to its logical consequence, it would open the doors to the "world's most formidable enemy today—Communism".[33] A familiar Catholic trope but true enough. In the form of the underground South African Communist Party (SACP), it had already begun to make minor inroads among both whites and blacks, indelibly stamping the future Congress Alliance with its non-racial thinking.

For the Church there were more immediate and no less ideological threats. The Eiselen Report on education, commissioned by the government and prepared between 1949-1951, made government control of Church schools the price for continuing state subsidies. Its author, Dr Werner Eiselen from the University of Pretoria, tellingly a social *anthropologist* rather than an educationalist, reflected National Party thinking on the role of the different races. And education was the soft under-belly of Catholicism.[34]

The SACBC issued its first critical "Statement on Race Relations" in 1952. Drafted by Archbishop Hurley, it reflected liberal Progressive Party opinion as much as Catholic social teaching. Discrimination and segregation were both contrary to human dignity; "natural rights" were seriously impaired by discriminatory legislation, and by "social conventions and inefficient administration". So far the traditional Catholic approach. But there was to be no promotion of an unqualified franchise for blacks; political rights were contingent on education, property and European cultural norms. It was the bishops' first major intervention against apartheid, and showed no signs of being influenced by African Nationalist opinion.

The schools threat heralded by the Eiselen report materialised in the 1953 Bantu Education Act which gave the Church the choice to hand over its schools to the Afrikaner state or lose state funding for them. Subsidies would be run down to zero over a three year period.

Archbishop Hurley, now chairman of the SACBC, chose to struggle on. This entailed a massive fundraising drive. But the mission schools' days were clearly numbered. Further apartheid legislation designed to enshrine white supremacy and guarantee a docile black labour reserve continued to implement the apartheid vision of the National Party. The 1956 Native Laws Amendment Act legislated for government control of African attendance in Church institutions by requiring express permission of the Minister of Native Affairs. This was a step too far for the Church which refused compliance. The church clause in the Act was never enforced.[35]

It was after the Church had successfully fought off this direct attack on its core prerogatives, education and control of its places of worship, and after the 1956 Congress of the People, the Freedom Charter, and the opening of the great South African Treason Trial, that the SACBC stiffened its resolve. In a pastoral letter sent to churches in 1957 it called for blacks to have "full participation in the political, economic and cultural life of the country" and spoke of the "fundamental evil of apartheid" defined as "when the practice of discrimination is enthroned as the supreme principle of the welfare of the state". Political gradualism, though, was still seen as necessary to preserve good order.

The Church recognised that it had to put its own house in order if it were not to be accused of hypocrisy—and it was no shining light on the hill of equal opportunities and non-racialism. When the new rector at the Catholic Major Seminary in Hammanskraal, an English Dominican, Oswin McGrath, told his assembled black seminarians in September 1957 that some of them would one day be bishops, his remarks sparked protests in Church circles. Contemporary prejudices and fears lurked in the presbyteries. The Church remained to all intents and purposes divided along racial lines.[36]

The Council and Apartheid

It might be imagined that the Catholic account of apartheid as "intrinsically evil", conveyed in the 1957 pastoral, would, like the later World Reformed Alliance declaration of apartheid as a heresy, have settled once and for all the Church's moral position. The logic of the bishops' position was that apartheid now had to go; the argument was whether gradually or promptly. But for some of them it was not that simple, far less so for their white laity and clergy.

The advent of Henrik Verwoerd as leader of the National Party and his canny presentation of apartheid as "separate development" based on Dutch Reformed doctrines of "Christian Nationalism" complicated matters. For Archbishop Patrick Whelan of Bloemfontein, whose mother was one of the few Afrikaner converts and who was inclined to be jealous of Hurley's preeminence, apartheid understood as "separate development" was not necessarily morally repugnant. How this concept was implemented was what mattered, and Whelan had already roundly condemned how it was being implemented.[37]

The unanimity of the 1957 bishops' conference had been something of an illusion. Not all concluded that apartheid should simply, and immediately, enter the dustbin of history. What they had been thinking now seems unclear. Though thanks to the enormous stimulus of the Vatican Council, Archbishop Hurley himself had no doubts. The continuation of apartheid represented a crisis for the Christian conscience. After he returned from the second session, his condemnations became more robust and politically focussed. Fired up by *Pacem in Terris* and the Pope's endorsement of human rights language, Hurley shifted easily into a more resonant secular discourse, describing apartheid as a fundamental infringement of human rights. In his Hoernle Memorial Lecture of January 1964 in Cape Town, Hurley delivered a powerful denunciation of apartheid to the South African Institute of Race Relations. It left no doubt about the unacceptability of "separate development". "Every test of human charity devised by Christ demands that we meet the evil of apartheid not merely by not adding to it but by going forward courageously to replace it by what is positive and constructive and redemptive." The illusion that his might be a consensus position of the bishops was soon shattered by a public dispute between Whelan and Hurley featured in both the national and religious press.[38]

Apartheid: A Crisis of the Christian Conscience tackled the subterfuge of "Christian nationalism" and touched a raw nerve in Whelan. A fellow Oblate and an archbishop, he seems to have grown irritated by Hurley's youthful ascendancy in the hierarchy. In his speech Hurley attacked the National Party head on, setting out the pre-conditions for "separate development" to be acceptable to the Christian conscience. And none of the pre-conditions, notably the assent of the participants, he demonstrated in detail were fulfilled. This shot Whelan's fox. Whelan was the SACBC Director of the Department of Press, Radio and

Cinema and knew how to place a good story. He made public his dissent from Hurley's unequivocal condemnation of apartheid.[39]

The politically resonant public dispute over whether separate development was bad because it was badly implemented, or because it was intrinsically evil, damaged the Church's credibility. It discredited the bishops among African political activists both Christian and secular, and gave credence to Verwoerd's dismissal of Catholic opposition to his legislation as unrepresentative. It may have incidentally stopped the South African bishops making any public input at the Council into the brief condemnation of racism in *Gaudium et Spes* for fear of the dispute irrupting again in the heart of Rome. Despite some African bishops condemning racism in the aula speeches, and a few American bishops with the civil rights movement in mind, apartheid proved to be another dog that didn't bark.

Archbishop Hurley was genuinely shocked and surprised by Whelan's reaction and confined himself to writing to the Vatican Secretariat of State explaining his own position. The Apostolic Delegate's anxiety that the Church was being discredited by disunity while alienating the South African government weighed on him. He promoted his cause only behind the scenes. But, given the growing international concern about apartheid, its failure to feature in the deliberations and documents of the Council stood out as a strange omission particularly given the prominent conciliar role played by Hurley on a range of topics from English in the liturgy to seminary training.[40]

The South African bishops must have glimpsed their vulnerability. A day before Harold Macmillan delivered his celebrated "wind of change" speech to the South African parliament in Cape Town on 3 February 1960, they issued a pastoral letter which showed their awareness that pressure was building and African nationalism on the move, that "the wind of change is blowing through this continent", as Macmillan memorably put it.[41] After the pictures of the Sharpeville massacre flashed around the world a few weeks later, "separate development" became synonymous with racism, brutal state repression and the refusal of democratic rights. The South Africans bishops seemed to have little idea what to do about it.

Repudiation of apartheid was obviously a suitable topic for inclusion in Catholic Social Teaching. Essentially a self-consciously evolving body of ideas, forming an organic tradition dating from the nineteenth century, social teaching was studied by seminarians as social doctrine, an abstract corpus, and applied as a series of deductions from first principles and the Christian virtues: love, charity, human dignity, subsidiarity and solidarity. Virtues and principles informed the set of human values that should be enshrined in social structures, in relations between nations, in war and peace, and in the conduct of individual states. The bishops' role was to apply these principles and virtues and denounce aberrations from normative conduct. The core values of social teaching could be, and were, expressed in secular language, as a checklist of human rights, and enshrined in international law. Whelan's way of arguing had not been unusual—though his conclusions were tendentious, and to those not trained in the tradition, beside the point. Scholastic abstractions did not lend themselves to passionate anger at injustice. As Hurley wrily admitted in his Hoernle lecture, in comparison to the South African Communists, Christians already looked "like flabby and ineffectual windbags if not downright supporters of an evil system".[42]

The Catholic tradition described the conditions and practices under which states could claim legitimacy. The state had authority provided it served the Common Good and promoted the welfare of the whole community. The interests of "national" groups could not take precedence over the Common Good. All this had an impeccable ancestry and the inheritance of Thomas Aquinas' thought. The Mixed Marriages Act contravened Catholic teaching on the right to choose a marriage partner freely and without coercion. Africans were being thrown off their land to which they had traditional title. So the Group Areas Act contravened Catholic understanding of the right to private property.

But when you were dumped in the bush amidst rows of pit latrines with no running water or electricity, and a family to feed, contravention of Catholic Social Teaching was not the immediate problem. What the Catholic tradition could not do was to prescribe practical means to deal with such unjust laws and their consequences. Violence and armed struggle were condemned except in situations of extreme tyranny. Church leaders in the Roman Catholic tradition did not easily break the law, and also looked over their shoulder at the spectre of Communism gaining ground around the world. Civil disobedience, boycotts and strike action were therefore dubious as means to bring about change, but Church leaders such as Archbishop Hurley were, like some of their Anglican counterparts, increasingly willing to contemplate, countenance and sometimes support them. There remained the persistent fantasy in Church circles that polite talks behind closed doors, local and Vatican diplomacy, might entice the Afrikaner wagons away from the ruthless implementation of apartheid onto a more humane and non-racial course. But the Church was facing a juggernaut.

From Black Consciousness to Non-Racialism

By the end of the 1960s as the wave of successful independence movements swept over the European colonies in Africa, a black movement drawing inspiration from the growth of Black Power groupings in the USA became popular among the African clergy of all the mainstream Churches. The Black Consciousness Movement (BCM), born out of the University Christian Movement, retained strong Christian roots: it sought a form of psychological liberation, the dignity and independence of blacks—and this included "Coloureds" and "Indians"—in the face of white liberal paternalism. Between 1968 and 1971 black students withdrew from NUSAS, the non-racial but white dominated national students union, and formed their own black consciousness groups in centres of higher education. SASO, the South African Students' Organisation, led by Steve Biko from 1969 until his murder by security police, was at the cutting edge. It was soon banned.[43]

By now ecumenical contacts pioneered by Archbishop Hurley had grown. He went onto the board of the radical ecumenical Christian Institute, set up by Dr Beyers Naude in 1963 in the aftermath of the World Council of Churches' Cottesloe Consultation. Cottesloe aimed to discuss the Churches' response to the Sharpeville massacre, but had sparked off an important theological debate about the BCM. Beyers Naude courageously renounced the theology of his own Church, the *Nederduitse Gereformeerde Kerk*, and it in turn had withdrawn from the WCC.[44] The BCM, welcomed and supported in the Christian Institute, was a symptom of a widespread theological ferment in South African Christianity which was now spreading to the Catholic Church.

By 1971 the one million strong black Catholic community could count only one African bishop, Peter Buthelezi of Umtata. There were 144 African plus 28 "Coloured" and "Indian" priests. On the other hand, the 170,000 white Catholics could count 1,380 white priests and 25 bishops. Things had not really changed greatly for black Catholics and the frustration of black priests was reaching breaking point. While the Christian origins of the BCM made it appealing to some of the more farsighted bishops, its implications in the face of such an imbalance were threatening. The South African bishops were inevitably going to find it difficult to accommodate the BCM particularly after the creation of a Black Priests Solidarity Group out of the black alumni association of St Peter's Seminary, Hammanskraal.

The initial aim of the BCM in the Catholic Church was "reconditioning (sic)" the mentality of black Catholics, but the ultimate goal was to rectify the scandalous power imbalance.[45] Calls came for a black bishop for the vast African townships of Soweto, and for a black Cardinal—Cardinal McCann had blotted his copybook by advocating a limited black franchise. There was also forthright denunciation of the way black priests were treated as "glorified altar boys", an allegation that had some truth in it. Things came to a head at a plenary session of the SACBC in 1971 with protestors bussed in to the Hammanskraal Seminary as a lively background to a demonstration by black clergy during the bishops' meeting. A number of the Hammanskraal staff suggested the appointment of a black Rector, but the bishops panicked and appointed the white Father Dominic Scholten, SACBC secretary, sparking resignations from the staff.[46]

In tandem with a quest for Black ecclesiastical power came the promotion of Black theology. Inspired partly by the work of the Black American James Cone, and partly home-grown, it attracted seminarians and clergy alike. South African black Christians began to focus on their unique "context" and to develop their own Biblical hermeneutic.[47] In some ways, black theology came more naturally to the Protestant tradition, and particularly to blacks suffering under the deformation of Afrikaaner Reformed theology. "We had to choose between rejecting it (the Bible) because it was misused, or otherwise taking responsibility, re-appropriating the Bible, putting it in its rightful place, and reinterpreting it" wrote Frank Chikane, later general secretary of the SACC, who was active in the Student Christian Movement in 1971. The slogan was therefore: "Re-read the Bible and reinterpret it in the light of the truth and turn it against the oppressor."[48] That, of course, was a workable description of liberation theology. Such a powerful set of ideas easily crossed permeable denominational boundaries.

As a contextual theology, black theology was open to further elaboration as major political events occurred in South Africa. After the

Soweto uprising, the Reformed theologian Allan Boesak in his 1977 *Farewell to Innocence* explicitly made the connection between black power and the biblical imperative of human liberation.[49] The question of apartheid was decisively moving out of the framework proposed by manuals of moral theology with their abstract deductive logic. The message conveyed to the Churches was that change must now come not from pious appeals to the privileged but from protest action by the oppressed: trades union action, community organising and boycotts, and student political activity, all within increasingly integrated strategies to confront the apartheid state.

What did these trends mean for the lives of radical black clergy? During the decade 1966-76, for a 27-year-old priest like Smangaliso Mkhatshwa, ordained in 1965 after an education with the Brothers of Charity and five years at St Peter's Seminary, the contrast between the moral theology of the manuals and the pastoral decisions required to confront the grinding poverty, economic exploitation and political oppression around him, appeared stark and immediate. Four years of pastoral ministry at the Sacred Heart Mission in Witbank, starting in 1966, working with migrant labourers, youth, students and urbanised township dwellers, would have increased the number of unanswered questions. His other main network was SPOBA, the alumni association of St Peter's Seminary, a ginger group set up by black clergy to desegregate the Church and press for Vatican Council changes to be fully implemented.[50]

The passage from deductive logic to Biblical hermeneutics, and from verbal condemnation to active resistance, which several priests such as Mkhatshwa negotiated, was not followed by all the bishops. Archbishop Hurley was an exception, actively resisting forced removals in his archdiocese and participating prominently in opposition to forced removals from the Durban Limehill area that turned into an epic campaign. True, combating forced removals fitted easily into a white paternalist paradigm of action on behalf of black victims dumped in a wasteland to make way for whites. It was in Hurley's active support for the 1972 dock workers' strike and, mediated through the Young Christian Workers office in Durban, for the wider worker movement, that a different model of action was glimpsed. He responded decisively and positively to the South African Council of Churches (SACC) 1974 resolution on selective conscientious objection. He did not believe the defence of apartheid could possibly be just, so conscientious objection to it was by definition desirable. His subsequent unequivocal support for Christian draft resisters, in and out of court from 1977 onwards, showed that this was not just a nice piece of Catholic reasoning. His stand rattled a government aware of the growing number of whites not turning up for active service. But, behind the scenes, Hurley, yet again, did not have the full backing of the Conference.[51]

The Decade of Growing Crisis: 1976-86

The brutal repression of demonstrations by 20,000 schoolchildren in Soweto on 16 June 1976 was a turning point for South Africa and for the Church. Reprisal killings of 146 young black people by police on the rampage shocked the world. The student uprising was aimed at "Bantu education" and enforced teaching in Afrikaans, but amounted to a long overdue youth revolt.

In 1973 the SACBC had finally swallowed the bitter pill and handed over black Catholic schools to government; the low salaries being paid because of lack of funds risked turning Church schools into a counter-witness to the Church's opposition to apartheid. Many good teachers left. In consequence most of the bishops, Sisters and clergy felt great sympathy for the young protestors, and outrage once the extent of the killing became known. Convents, priories and presbyteries sheltered student activists on the run, and, as during the Durban strikes, the Church was drawn into a more intimate relationship with militant Africans.[52]

Echoes of the national crisis reached the Hammanskraal seminary where, reminiscent of prison riots, bad food emerged as the pretext for mass protest. The bishops reacted by appointing as rector Father Lebamang Sebidi, a promoter of the new black theology. But the situation was irrevocably polarised. Many white staff opposed the appointment. The fifty strong Black Priests Solidarity Group waded in with a blistering letter about paternalism and racism. The seminary had to be closed after Sebidi and most of the white staff resigned.[53]

Yet out of this debacle came the SACBC's *Declaration of Commitment on Social Justice and Race Relations within the Church*, a 21- point plan to eradicate what would today be called "institutional racism" in the Church. After government bannings of the BCM's constituent organisations, the bishops' declaration that they were "on the side of Black Consciousness in regard both to those who promote it and those who suffer for it" was a clear and courageous statement of solidarity. The tragic Soweto uprising, and the seminary closure, had been a salutary shock to gradualist complacency. Nonetheless it was only in the late 1980s that racially integrated seminary formation became possible.

The thinking behind evangelisation in the 1975 papal encyclical *Evangelii Nuntiandi* and, through it, Latin American liberation theology, were beginning to make an impact in South Africa, reinforced by the language of black theology. In their February 1977 *Statement on the Current Situation and Citizen Rights of Blacks* the bishops called for the political system to be radically revised; "in this we are on the side of the oppressed and, as we have committed ourselves to working within our Church for a clearer expression of solidarity with the poor and deprived, so we commit ourselves to working for peace through justice". The Declaration of Commitment contained the phrase "work for complete human liberation". The bishops believed that "evangelization includes transforming the concrete structures that oppress people". They wanted "to be seen in solidarity with the legitimate aspirations of oppressed people".[54]

Many of these lofty aspirations were beginning to be realised in practical ways through the Justice and Peace commissions in the major towns, Johannesburg, Durban and Cape Town, through campaigns and compassion funds for political prisoners and victims of detention and banning orders. In addition the Association of Women Religious called for the "quiet infiltration" of white schools by selected blacks. Springfield Convent in Cape Province admitted the first eight "Coloured" pupils in early 1976, a clear act of civil disobedience. Moreover, the admissions were without prior permission from the bishops. But the Cabra Dominican Sisters, led by Sister Genevieve Hickey, pressed on.[55]

In a far more provocative action Holy Rosary Convent in Port Elizabeth admitted thirty-three African pupils in January 1977. Having requested a number of white convent schools to take the children of black foreign diplomats and leaders of homeland administrations, the government was on the back foot. The confrontational position of these Women Religious was not to prevail. The comparatively liberal government minister Piet Koornhof got into prolonged and complex negotiations with the SACBC, settling finally for an agreed quota system; if exceeded, it triggered a loss of government subsidies. As the formidable Irish Bishop of Umtali, Donal Lamont, declared to the north against similar pressures of the Smith regime in Rhodesia, you could not have "a percentage of a moral principle". In South Africa the bishops managed to settle for that. Half a loaf was better than no bread at all when it came to desegregation.[56]

And yet, compared with the white Sisters, the world of a radical black Sister such as Sister Bernard Ncube who belonged to the ANC-linked Women's League, or a radical black priest such as Mkhatshwa, had a discrete dimension that changed perspectives and priorities dramatically. Influential in the St Peter's Seminary alumni association, Mkhatshwa had been attracted to black theology and was one of the leaders of the 1971 protest in the Bishops' Conference meeting. Quickly dispatched for philosophical and theological study to the University of Louvain for two years, a pleasant exile where he absorbed the post-conciliar changes, he was back in 1974 to become secretary for Justice and Peace, Development and Ecumenism at the SACBC in Pretoria, in time for the Portuguese collapse in Mozambique and Angola that was soon exciting black nationalism in South Africa. Arrested and detained for five months in the sweep after the Soweto uprising, he was served with a five-year banning order in the BCM purge of 1977 and detained without trial for five months again until March 1978.

Such stretches in prison acted as a finishing school for detainees' political education, and, a forcing house for the theological development of black Christians, especially black priests. Prison discussion and debate among inmates provided an intense introduction to the world of the South African struggle. Who you were detained with and in which prison became a political pedigree, with Robben Island as the prestige university for political science. Making sense of this experience later, in the rigorous clerical life of the Catholic Church, was demanding. It created at best a certain intellectual and cultural hybridity, or at worst a priest could feel torn apart by conflicting pressures.

Things Fall Apart

The demise of Portuguese fascism dramatically and suddenly changed the political contours of southern Africa when in 1976 the new government pulled out its troops and granted independence to its African colonies. The ANC in exile, now with easier direct access from Mozambique and Swaziland and with guerrilla bases in Angola and Zambia, began to wage a high profile campaign of "armed propaganda", the sabotage of prestige targets inside South Africa, to accompany its internal organising in trades unions, student and women's organisations and civic associations. This limited military activity was to create endless inconclusive debate within the Churches about violence, and arouse opposition to the World Council of Churches' Programme against Racism. After 1976, the ANC's military wing, *Umkhonto we Sizwe*, was reinforced by waves of student recruits who, although suffering severe attrition owing to informers, were infiltrating across South Africa's borders. The numbers were small and the military impact not even remotely comparable to that of the Patriotic Front guerrillas to the north in rural Rhodesia. But for every prestige target bombed or targeted by ANC rockets, such as Sasolburg or Vortrekkerhoogte army barracks, the appeal of the movement grew in the eyes of the black majority, especially black youth.

Universal conscription for whites into the apartheid army was in place from 1967 onwards, and, from 1977, this meant an initial two years of unbroken military service. Latin American style National Security ideology became official state policy with the appointment of the Defence Minister, P.W. Botha, as Prime Minister in October 1978, and his replacement by General Magnus Malan. South African-occupied Namibia, with its own independence struggle led by SWAPO was fast becoming Pretoria's Achilles heel. Pretoria put itself on full counter-insurgency footing and waged a protracted clandestine war inside Angola from Namibian bases. The Angolan-Namibian frontier existed only in name. This intensified military activity opened a vulnerable new front for South Africa.[57]

Steve Biko's life and death became a dramatic symbol of South African repression. Biko was murdered on 12 September 1977 by security police principally because he was on the point of bringing the BCM lock, stock and barrel into the fold of the African National Congress (ANC). But his intentions were not widely known. In prisons black theology and politics evolved towards a non-racial class analysis of South African society, along Marxist lines; heated political debate among black Christian activists passed away the long hours. Both Mkhatshwa and the talented black theologian Buti Tlhagale went down that road, though with different emphases. Others no less talented did not. This

187

difference in political analysis was a perennial cause of friction until elections in 1994.[58]

The South African Council of Churches (SACC), under the leadership of the indomitable Anglican Archbishop Desmond Tutu, declared apartheid a heresy in a 1982 conference resolution. Botha pushed through a new reformist constitution that split off "Coloureds and Indians"—given parliamentary seats in separate Chambers—from other blacks who were relegated to a township level of representation as councillors or to "representation" in the Bantustan crony governments. In 1983 the ANC supported the creation of the semi-autonomous United Democratic Front (UDF), an internal coalition movement to fight for the principles of the Freedom Charter and democracy in a unitary South Africa. The Catholic bishops opposed the new South African constitution in a pastoral letter read in parishes in September 1983.

The bishops broadly agreed with the UDF's goals. It was a civil society coalition with some two million members at its peak and not a banned terrorist organisation. This made open support easier—as it was intended to do. The Johannesburg Justice and Peace Commission, and the Witwatersrand branch of the South African Council of Churches, both joined. Mkhatshwa was made a UDF patron alongside the black theologian Allan Boesak and Beyers Naude. When it came to resistance, the question of denominational affiliation was now entirely secondary. The generally Protestant leadership of the ANC was of no great relevance. Communist leadership more so. The question was "what side you are on?" not "what Church are you in?"[59]

Led by Archbishop Hurley a series of secret meetings with the ANC took place, at first informally and one-to-one with Oliver Tambo in London in April 1983, and then more formally between Thabo Mbeki and the SACBC in Harare, Zimbabwe. The Church's primary goal in these encounters was to clarify their understanding of the ANC. The discussions shed light on the restraints imposed by the ANC leadership on *Umkhonto we Sizwe*, their narrow target selection for guerrilla attack, but the bishops remained unhappy about an armed struggle which could not always avoid civilian casualties. Security and arrangements for meetings were in the hands of the tightly knit South African Communist Party, a necessary precaution in view of informers in the wider ANC at the time. The first meeting was warm and congenial—Hurley and Tambo had affection and respect for each other—an early herald of the wider process of South African civil society coming to terms with the ANC. But such contact was outside the comfort zone of several of the bishops. One or two began focussing their anxieties about political partisanship on the SACBC's general secretary, Mkhatshwa; they wanted contacts with other political parties such as the Zulu-based Inkatha, and felt swept along by events. They were more at home with promoting international opposition to the apartheid policy of forced removals, a campaign they shared with the SACC and took to the United Nations in 1983.[60]

Even as the SACBC were taking the case against forced relocations overseas, events were outstripping them. The bishops were being pressed to take up more overtly political positions and faced splits in their dioceses along racial and ideological lines, while confronting more classic human rights violations and the impunity of the security forces. South Africa had become increasingly a militarised society led by the State Security Council with an inflated defence budget and draconian security legislation—a state of affairs instantly recognisable to Latin Americans and likewise the context for the development of South Africa's own version of liberation theology.

Contextual Theology

To describe the emerging South African theology of the 1980s as "liberation theology" would have been to link it inextricably, and inadvisably, with the liberation movement and armed struggle. Another word was required. The Institute for *Contextual* Theology (ICT) originated in the University of Cape Town in 1981. The subsequent opening of an ICT office in Johannesburg, led by the radical theologian Frank Chikane reared in the Apostolic Faith Mission, spread the word "contextual" far and wide. The ICT soon attracted a valuable asset: the South African Dominican Albert Nolan, author of *Jesus before Christianity* who, like Gustavo Gutiérrez, had been a chaplain to university students.[61] The ICT became the hub of a network developing what they called *Kairos* theology, South Africa's contribution to liberation theology. Contextual theology had found a home in Africa.

The Institute had a number of black consciousness theologians associated with it. It also provided a centre for those, like Albert Nolan, Beyers Naude and Frank Chikane, for whom doing theology "from within the context of real life in the world" meant in practice coming

189

to terms with the ANC and its non-racial internal movement, the UDF. Human liberation was for them an integral part of evangelisation. "Building the Kingdom of God" and political change were not two separate processes occurring in two different realms. Rather evangelisation expressed the quest for the totality and completeness of liberation. Thus its realisation, the hoped-for coming of the Kingdom of God, necessarily transcended—though included—all other partial forms of human liberation.

In the context of apartheid it was assumed that those "doing" theology would have to carry the cross, possibly to the point of martyrdom. Detention and imprisonment were commonplace. Practice of the Christian virtues was found to be just as important for Catholics participating in the different forms of national democratic resistance, than in a more traditional form of Christian spirituality. In short there was a "spirituality of struggle" that drew on and reformulated traditional forms of spirituality. It was rooted in the same biblical themes that underpinned liberation theology. Gustavo Gutiérrez was reaching the same conclusions in Peru; Ed de la Torre much the same in the Philippines.[62]

There was little enthusiasm for contextual theology in the SACBC even though it was led from 1981-87 by Archbishop Denis Hurley as President. The Institute for Contextual Theology, in its radicalism and practical ecumenism, remained more marginal to the mainstream Churches than its theological predecessor, the Christian Institute. Some Catholic bishops found themselves on much the same ground as the ICT by following the logic of their seminary courses and the Vatican Council, notably themes of justice and workers' rights. They were being brought into the broader political struggle in South Africa through a range of organisations over which they presided or held a watching brief: Justice and Reconciliation commissions, Young Christian Workers and Students, the Grail, and by the advice of a handful of key individuals, many of them Religious women, who bridged the clerical and black activist world in their ministry. These confidants of the bishops served as a new kind of diaconate, unofficial, *ad hoc* go-betweens, bridging cultural divides, invaluable in guiding the SACBC pastorally and politically.

The meetings of the SACBC were, by contemporary episcopal standards, remarkably open. The bishops invited and listened attentively to black miners and trades union officials, black activists, and university sociologists during study days. Some of their visitors' experience and analysis left its mark. The SACBC sponsored St Joseph the Worker Fund supported the burgeoning activism of the black trades union movement and the bishops opened their churches to union meetings, much to the chagrin of more conservative clergy.[63]

Among White Catholics, the most significant—and contentious—role of Archbishop Hurley was in championing—and through the SACBC legitimating—conscientious objection and in denouncing the war against SWAPO in Namibia and Angola. The Evangelical Lutheran and Anglican Churches in Namibia led Christian opposition to the South African occupation. The SACBC entered the field in May 1982 with a *Report on Namibia*, the product of lobbying by their Justice and Peace Commission that had resulted in a full Church delegation being sent in September 1981. The visiting Church leaders linked up with the Namibian Justice and Reconciliation Commission led by the German Oblate missionary, Heinz Steegman, who organised extensive interview sessions across the country. The Report contained a litany of human rights violations by South African special police forces, *koevoet*. An abbreviated popular press summary of the report was banned.[64]

Archbishop Hurley was committed for trial three years later under a section of the Police Act on the grounds of making allegedly "without reasonable grounds for believing them to be true" statements against the *koevoet* "police", after a SACBC plenary conference in 1983. A number of concerned callers were informed by Hurley on a tapped telephone that he had been given his episcopal ring in Rome by Cardinal Mindszenty—the scourge of Hungary's Communist government even whilst suffering imprisonment and persecution—a nice detail for the notebooks of the listening security police. Pressure on the South African ambassador to the USA from the US Church was more direct and less subtle: strong protests and warnings. Hurley was now a star in the wider Catholic firmament. The case attracted a large number of overseas observers, including Vatican officials, and was dropped three days before a dramatic opening session at which the state capitulated ignominiously. However hard it might have been for the Church to get defence witnesses to testify, the state did not relish the dossier of atrocities held by defence counsel being broadcast day after day in court. Hurley's civil claim for damages, a second attempt to use the judicial process to publicise the plight of Namibians, was settled out of court.[65]

Far from being intimidated, the Oblates sent a chaplain to the Namibian refugees in the SWAPO run camps in Angola and Zambia.[66] In order to lobby the Western Contact Group mandated by the UN to resolve the illegal occupation, the SACBC joined further delegations to support the Namibian bishops.

The South African National Security State showed its full colours in July 1985 when it began detaining some 33,000 activists and leaders, killing within the year 1,200, many in police custody, under a partial state of emergency. Pursuing a classic human rights approach, the bishops used their Namibian experience to extensively document police violence in Sebokeng during "Operation Palmiet" in the Vaal Triangle. Their report on Police Conduct in the Vaal used sworn affidavits and appeared in the national and international media. It provided a devastating indictment of three months' state terror in which 150 died and thousands were injured, shredding any vestiges of legitimacy accruing from the regime's reforms. Rent boycotts against collaborationist town councils were the main weapon for the black majority—nobody wanted to pay rent anyway. But in response to police spies and state terror "peoples courts" began dispensing summary justice and arbitrary punishments, and youth groups rampaged through townships "necklacing" suspected collaborators with burning tyres. As the townships became lawless under the impact of extra-judicial killings and criminal gangs, the leadership vacuum, particularly among youth, generated a justified fear of anarchy among the Churches, and drew them into new engagements, public positions and national prominence. It also put pressure on the Churches to take sides more clearly and to define their relationship to the liberation movement.[67]

The crisis was systemic and events could have moved in any direction. ICT brought together in workshops over a hundred theologians to analyse the situation, and reflect on its as Christians. The product of this extensive consultation was *Challenge to the Church: a Theological Comment on the Political Crisis in South Africa, The Kairos Document*, published in pamphlet form in September 1985. *Kairos*, a New Testament term describing a moment of grace and an opportunity for repentance, yet redolent of catastrophic danger, seemed to best describe the historical moment. It reflected the immediacy of the political crisis. The theologians were not mistaken. A full State of Emergency was imposed in July 1986 netting 22,000 political detainees, 25 per cent of them adolescents, mostly boys.

The *Kairos Document* castigated the Church leadership for promoting "Church Theology" based on a principle of reconciliation that was inapplicable. "If we call for reconciliation and negotiations now before repentance and equality have been established, we will be calling for reconciliation between good and evil". The Church leaders' mistake was addressing their statements to whites and hoping that an appeal to conscience would bring about change. "True justice, God's justice, demands a radical change of structures. This can only come from below, from the oppressed themselves. God will bring about change through the oppressed as he did through the oppressed Hebrew slaves in Egypt. God does not bring his justice through reforms introduced by the Pharoahs of this world." It followed that the violence of the oppressor and the oppressed, the latter in self-defence, had to be distinguished and was not morally equivalent. This amounted to a call for revolution in South Africa and a repudiation of reformist ideas.[68]

The *Kairos Document* contained theological emphases found in the writing of Frank Chikane and Albert Nolan, and, from the South African Council of Churches, showed the influence of Beyers Naude and the Lutheran Wolfram Kirstner. These were the principal draftsmen. It could not have been more ecumenical. Choice of content and drafting amendments were "work-shopped", a cooperative effort in consultation with 152 different theologians who each signed off the text. Presented as a people's document in the preface, the *Kairos Document* inevitably contained disparate strands of theology. On the one hand, there was an apocalyptic contestation of what was called "State Theology" appealing to a more evangelical or pentecostal form of African Christianity: "The god of the South African State is not merely an idol or false god, it is the devil disguised as Almighty God—the antichrist." On the other, there was a careful, reasoned account of why the apartheid state fell under the heading of tyranny; it was an enemy of the people, *hostis boni communis*, and irreformable, so devoid of moral legitimacy. This was a classic Thomist argument. The option for a prophetic theology, Biblically rooted, had strong resonances with Latin American thinking, and was denounced by P.W. Botha as "so-called liberation theology".

The pamphlet was printed and distributed in great secrecy and great numbers. A potent form of South African *samizdat*, it took the government and security forces completely unawares, a remarkable achievement in itself. For a short piece of theology, its impact was extraordinary. Christian congregations in the black townships read it and, with delight, saw in it an expression of their own sentiments and contemporary faith. The bishops of the mainstream Churches had not been asked to sign and some, such as Denis Hurley and Desmond Tutu, took its challenge to heart, hurt by its attack on "Church theology" which seemed to them unfair in the light of their commitment to the anti-apartheid struggle. The state produced its own propaganda response for South African state television: a snake coiling around the map of Africa and *Kairos* theology presented as the fruits of Communist infiltration of the Churches.[69]

The *Kairos* message was clear: the South African state was illegitimate and could be overthrown. Under the leadership of Frank Chikane the SACC reached the same conclusion in less striking language. This position was strongly discouraged by the Vatican and never taken up publicly by the SACBC; nor did the Catholic bishops ever wholeheartedly support economic sanctions. They treated the latter reluctantly as the lesser of two evils: resistance *could*—not should—include "economic pressure—the pressure of divestment, disinvestments, sanctions". The bishops' consent to sanctions was conditional on their not destroying the economy, on minimising job losses, and support being provided to those affected. "We dread what this may mean for many people", they said. They had no choice but to consent. The alternative was escalating violence. The SACBC did with great humility admit that it needed to "spell out the justice of the cause in the struggle for liberation", and admitted that it had not fully understood the role of blacks in their own liberation.[70]

Thanks largely to Smangaliso Mkhatshwa, acting general secretary from 1980 and confirmed in the job a year later, the SACBC as an institution acted as a clearing house for funding from overseas to a wide variety of internal organisations, many of which clandestinely supported the ANC. He was detained and tortured in a thirty hour interrogation during the 1986 State of Emergency. By then there were clandestine channels to the SACBC from the Swedish government, and later an open budget line from the European Community (EC). Both European bodies accepted direction from key Churchmen on what would be suitable recipient organisations, the EC after formal negotiations in Brussels by representatives of the Protestant and Catholic Churches.[71] This external support encouraged the Conference to take the unprecedented step of legally owning and publishing an independent newspaper *The New Nation*, funded by European Catholic agencies and edited by a UDF star, Zwelakhe Sisulu, son of the Robben Island prisoner and ANC general secretary, Walter Sisulu. Launched in January 1986 as a fortnightly, the paper could scarcely have been more political and less like a normal Church paper. It rapidly became a much-read weekly. Zwelakhe Sisulu was detained under the December 1986 emergency legislation.[72]

Archbishop Hurley spoke of the need to relate formally to the ANC, which he saw as having overwhelming support in the country, during the January 1986 plenary session of the SACBC. Later in the year he told P.W. Botha the same in a fraught meeting. On 14 April, he led Bishop Wilfrid Napier who was SACBC Vice-President, Bishop Mansuet Biyase, from the critical Kwazulu-Natal region where he had to deal with Inkatha, and Father Smangaliso Mkhatshwa, to the ANC Lusaka headquarters, for eight hours of formal talks. This was largely an exercise in convincing his colleagues of the need for an ongoing relationship, and he acted as the devil's advocate in touching on most of the sensitive issues for the SACBC: armed struggle, the future role of the South African Communist Party, possible imposition of a socialist economy, and the Church's future. This was his last year as President. There was a sense of urgency now. But nagging doubts remained among his colleagues as did pressure to relate to Chief Mangosutu Buthelezi, the leader of the Zulu Inkatha movement, increasingly being promoted from overseas as a bulwark against the ANC with its ties to the South African Communist Party.[73]

Repression in South Africa removed layer after layer of black leadership, leaving Church leaders acutely exposed as the few remaining spokesmen for the black majority. Sisters such as Sr Bernard Ncube, prominent in the ANC-aligned Women's Movement, were particularly visible and vulnerable. *Toyi-toyi* marches, processions through township streets to Mass, symbolic liturgical protests, civil disobedience and non-violent action increased Church leaders' exposure as did their role in presiding at the funeral of prominent ANC activists where the

Communist Party's red flag would be unfurled behind the celebrant.[74] Alongside the popularity of the *Kairos Document*, this reinforced the state's perception of the Churches as a forcing ground for ideological opposition to their "reform" agenda.

Church workers increasingly shared the fate of other radical activists, were detained and tortured. Father Mkhatswha was told by members of his Shoshanguve parish that government agents had offered more than a year's salary to inform on him. Frank Chikane was a prime target for assassination; he was poisoned but, remarkably, survived.[75] White Christian detainees found themselves confronted by evangelical Christian interrogators, or subject to attempts at "honey-trap" entrapments by attractive female security agents. Khotso House, the headquarters of the SACC was stormed by security forces. Khanya House, the Catholic Secretariat in Pretoria, suffered an incendiary attack. Two of the people sleeping in its residential accommodation narrowly missed being burnt to death.[76]

This intense and partisan political role for Church leaders did not go down well in Pope John Paul II's Vatican. The apostolic delegate the Belgian Archbishop Joseph Mees, gave a pointed reminder to the 1987 SACBC plenary session; the Church "wisely" banned priests from involvement in politics, he said, arousing the wrath of the bishops. He even intimated that there was a request from the Pope for the bishops to dialogue with the South African government. Archbishop Hurley called his bluff and enquired from the Pope what was meant by "involvement in politics" in his admonition. The subsequent sudden withdrawal and replacement of the apostolic delegate was viewed as a triumph for the SACBC; they had got rid of Mees.[77] Nonetheless the Pope's unfortunate "diversion" to a South African airport during his 1988 southern Africa visit and his subsequent meeting with P.W. Botha—he had already received him at the Vatican—was seen as something of a betrayal by many black clergy.

How much did liberation theology guide and motivate Christian participation in the struggle against apartheid? For radical Catholics, a great deal. But not at all for the bishops. Their position and pastoral engagement, as in the Philippines, grew directly out of Catholic Social Teaching. Among a small and dispersed group of white and black activists who gravitated to the Dominican Priory in Mayfair where Albert Nolan lived, it was particularly influential.[78] They had a considerable interest in the Sandinista movement of Nicaragua because of its Christian links. Frank Chikane had been at the 1986 conference of EATWOT theologians in Mexico. But *Kairos* theology was largely home-grown. The methodology was the same as in Latin America; the resulting product different.

Kairos theology travelled fast through international Church networks. Ecumenical groups in the north of Ireland were interested in its application to their situation. Theologians from the Philippines, Korea, Nicaragua, South Africa, Guatemala and El Salvador began meeting to consider what might be said about the international context of Christians' work for justice at the height of the Cold War. The resulting document *Road to Damascus*, published in July 1989, called for repentance from those persecuting Christians working for social justice around the world. It was launched simultaneously in the different contributing countries. The theological offspring of radical Christians during the Cold War, with the Berlin Wall unexpectedly about to come down, it was quickly overtaken by events. " We are all in continuous need of self-criticism and conversion. But now the time has come for a decisive turnabout on the part of those groups and individuals who have consciously and unconsciously compromised their Christian faith for political, economic and selfish reasons", it declared, a truth neither contingent nor easily denied. But such was the isolation and uniqueness of South Africa that *Kairos* theology did not spread to the rest of the African continent, nor did it find many proponents there.[79]

The struggles against apartheid and Marcos' authoritarian rule brought liberal and radical Christians onto the same perilous terrain. Seen as a simple story of white oppression of black people, apartheid transcended what was commonly understood as politics. It entered directly into a moral and theological realm of "structures of sin", and, as Christian Nationalism, heresy. Christian resistance, the SACC, and the SACBC opposition to the Afrikaaner state, was ideologically more significant and effective than in other revolutionary contexts. And such was the prodigious uniqueness of apartheid that it elicited in opposition a unique—*Kairos*—theology.

The Church's contribution was less public and flamboyant than its role in Marcos' downfall in the Philippines but it came from the same convictions about justice and human rights. It was overshadowed by the towering figures of Nelson Mandela and Desmond Tutu. Yet, neither the fall of the apartheid regime nor of Ferdinand Marcos ushered in an epoch of unmitigated good news for the poor. There were improvements in their lot. Important freedoms opened up, freedoms that people ardently desired. The case studies of the Church's pursuit of justice in the next chapter illustrate how the long walk to freedom is full of pitfalls and may end not in the Promised Land, but in tragedy.

8

DEMOCRACY AND NATIONALISM IN AFRICA

For many centuries the Roman Catholic Church has presented its core structures as divinely ordained. Its interpretation of the Petrine Office, what it might mean for St Peter to be "the rock" on which the Church is built, has been influenced, one way or another, by models of authority found outside the Church, notably kingship and the administration of the Roman Empire. Democracy for several centuries played a negative role, defining what the Catholic Church was not. Irrespective of their theology and practice, Basic Christian Communities were perceived as a threat, a congregationalist movement within a hierarchical Church.

The Second Vatican Council encouraged widespread hopes for a more participatory and consultative Church life. In several African countries before the Council was announced, the rigid disciplinary order of seminaries run by missionaries was coming under attack from seminarians. This was partly a muted expression of growing anti-colonialism and cultural nationalism. Expectations varied according to the strength of democracy in different political cultures, or according to the relative importance of urban elites and the rural poor.

Post-colonial elites spun stories about a mythical past. Africa had wise chiefs, consensual politics in timeless African villages, harmonious organic societies, even if in reality there had been chief-centred authoritarianism, coerced conformity based on fear of exclusion or other social penalties, and conflict. An imagined past for a hoped for future. Notwithstanding turbulent transitional periods, the religious power of the missionary, partly a byproduct of the dominance of colonial authorities, but drawing on aspects of chiefly authority and traditional religion, transferred easily to the African priest or bishop. Indeed nationalist leaders often treated Church leadership much as they did traditional chiefs: significant potential allies, or enemies, who needed to be taken seriously and kept under control. On the other hand, Biblical renewal, blessed by the Council, had disturbing consequences that cut across the seamless "inculturation" of Catholicism in post-colonial societies, as it had done in the European late Middle Ages.

The Philippines and South Africa both offered dramatic examples of this interplay. They were part of a wider experience of Catholics drawing on Biblical insights and historical parallels to construct an ethical critique of prevailing social, economic and political conditions. The rejection of cultural impositions, the quest for an authentic local expression of Christianity, the denunciation of racialist relationships in Church and society—typical of some major seminaries during the 1950s—were the first fruits of taking the Gospels seriously as an ethical yardstick for Christian social conduct. Their legitimacy, and thus their danger, was rooted in a rediscovery of the scandalous reversals proclaimed by the Gospel Jesus, his "turning the world upside down", so that the poor came first, and the realisation of the subversive potential in such a radical shift.

These small-scale religious awakenings from the 1950s to the 1980s were linked to the burst of expectations associated with the growth of African nationalism. Nationalist leaders often adopted a religious aura as Saviours of the Nation. The tidal force of anti-colonial sentiment swept in on a Church whose young clergy and Religious contained a small but important minority excited by Biblical and catechetical renewal, and the promise of inculturation. As the tide ebbed, leaving behind disappointment at the failure of African political leadership in one-party states, a second wave began to build. Now the resentment was of corrupt, authoritarian African governments, not colonialism, and the call was for greater democracy.

After the political kingdom had been sought according to Kwame Nkrumah's injunction, the persistence of hunger, destitution and injustice required further explanation and response. One way was to understand it all, lumped together, as the presence of "Evil", or "sin made visible", in a Christian theophany. In the face of popular beliefs about witches, demons and evil spirits, this was in some ways a modernising concept. The 1985 South African *Kairos* document—(see above)—proposed a concept of evil in which the "Satanic" was symbolically located not in witches but in tyranny or kleptocratic government, and this gained acceptance. The pre-condition for deliverance from evil, Salvation, thus became effective participation in national decision-making, *demokrasi*, or so it seemed to many at all levels in the Church. As long, of course, as this did not apply to appointment of bishops.

In a number of instances, the post-conciliar Roman Catholic Church in Africa came to see the promotion and building of democracy as an expression of the "Good News", part of the radical content of the Gospel message in its encounter with the world. But in the years before the Council the standard seminary manuals, with their account of Social Ethics, provided the model. For missionary clergy in Africa this provided a critique of colonial rule or European Trusteeship of African societies, but almost never gender relationships of women and nuns. After the experience of Italian fascism, German National Socialism and Communist rule, missionaries did not easily translate Catholic teaching into enthusiasm for political ideologies, nationalism, whether African, socialist or otherwise. But they did, in their growing attentiveness to the plight of Africans, discern some of the pre-conditions for building a democratic multi-ethnic or multiracial society.

This was an indirect conclusion drawn from the meaning of human dignity rather than the core of a theology with democratic participation as a basic element. The growth of African theology after the Council did not help matters. Its primary focus was inculturation with a strong emphasis on the importance of ancestral spirits to an African spirituality (see Chapter nine, below). As Leopold Senghor underlined in his theory of *négritude*, cultural liberation was for Africa a constitutive element of political liberation. But theologically the two were rarely elaborated in an integrated way. African Catholic promotion of social justice and democracy—outside South Africa—remained essentially rooted in ethics rather than in an inculturated political theology. In Latin America, it was the other way round with liberation theologians coming late to integrate culture into their political theology.

Promoting social justice and democracy within an African nationalist project—not often in the 1950s directly by name but by advocating necessary features—had strikingly varied consequences according to political context. In Rwanda the outcome was catastrophic. In Zimbabwe, likewise, though it was difficult for nationalist politicians to blame the Church. In Malawi, after initial blunders, more of a success though a long way from living up to expectations. The importance of the Church's role, as the following illustrations show, varied considerably. After the totalitarian tragedies of Europe, in no case was the Church unambiguous about the growth of African nationalism. And in no case was it able to counter the power of ethnicity or regionalism. But by the end of the 1990s it could without pretension, despite terrible setbacks, claim to be a friend of democracy in Africa.

Rwanda

In Rwanda work for justice was stimulated, endorsed and encouraged, rather than jump-started by the Council. During the 1950s African Catholics would travel to anniversaries of mission settlements, ordinations, and for the major feasts in the Catholic calendar, providing opportunities to discuss grievances and talk politics. The Church provided both a network and forum. At the same time, for the elite, Catholic Social Teaching provided an analytical model to frame debate.

An African theology, drawing on themes from Rwandan history and culture, entrenched ethnic differences, indeed became part of the ideological repertoire of the country's minority ruling class.

The Catholic understanding of Justice, one of the largest sections in the treatment of virtues in the *Summa Theologiae*, was taught in major seminaries. Aquinas had little to say about the state, nothing about nationalism, but a great deal about the right ordering of an organic society. Seminarians got a condensed exposure to the Thomist account of "social justice" as the core of political virtue. The Swiss White Father Monsignor André Perraudin, later Vicar-Apostolic of Kabgayi Diocese, for example, taught the *"traité de justice"* from 1950-56 in Rwanda's Nyakibanda Major Seminary. He wanted his new priests to emphasise the Catholic obligation to pursue "social justice" whether in the pulpit or in the confessional".[1]

Seminarians would have instantly recognised the origins of the challenge to Belgian Trusteeship made by Bishops of the Belgian Congo and Rwanda-Burundi after they met together in Leopoldville (Kinshasa) on 21 June 1956: "All the inhabitants of a country have the duty of actively working together in the common good. They therefore have the right to take part in the conduct of public affairs". African "political emancipation" required Belgium to take the appropriate steps. Before the year was out Abbé Joseph Malula, with the Catholic intellectuals Joseph Ngalula and Joseph Ileo, was demanding the future independence of the Congo from Belgium in a political manifesto. Catholic cross-border networks were expanding.[2]

The task of "political emancipation" was daunting. Rwanda functioned under indirect rule with a king, the *mwami*, and court, drawn from two noble Tutsi lineages; only in 1952 had an executive *Conseil Supérieur* been set up. The transformation of complex "feudal" relationships into a bureaucratic state, hardened social and economic differences. Social mobility between peasantry and aristocracy, cattle owners and agriculturalists, occurred but was modest. The words "Tutsi" (c.15 per cent of the population) and "Hutu"(c. 80 per cent) changed from describing class divisions to take on a fully "tribal-racial" character. The system of classification on identity cards, defining Tutsi as "Banyarwanda with more than ten cows" remained as testimony to the transition.[3]

The gulf between a rich and well educated Tutsi elite and the Hutu peasant masses was brought home to Church leaders daily. Its injustice increasingly featured in the regional Francophone press. After a massive wave of Tutsi conversions in the 1930s, Rwanda was dedicated to Christ the King in 1947 by the *mwami*, Rudahigwa—emphasising the importance of the—supposedly racially distinct—"Hamitic" kingship and ruling clans. The ideology of Christian kingship served to prop up Tutsi rule with the dynastic history held by court historians *abiru* viewed as an indigenous Old Testament and preparation for the Church, notably in the writing of the distinguished noble Abbé Alexis Kagame. Between 1950-56, in the major seminary of Nyakibanda 45 out of 59 priests ordained were of Tutsi origin. The percentage of Hutu proceeding from primary to secondary education revealed a similar skewed ratio.[4]

The clergy were divided by this stratified society. For those emerging from, or teaching in, the seminaries during the 1950s, what had become an ethnic "Hutu problem" was readily expressed in the categories of Catholic Social Teaching as unjust discrimination and inequality in society. But individual and collective differences, could and did, strongly influence perceptions: French-speaking Walloons against Flemish Belgians, or Tutsi Catholics reared on a diet of "the Christian

Kingdom of Rwanda", against Hutu *"évolués de campagne"*, educated Francophone Hutu, suffering Tutsi control and condescension.[5]

The future Archbishop, André Perraudin, from a poor Swiss family, had a commitment to social justice and an instinctive sympathy for the struggles of farmers—he had minded the family's cows in his canton as a boy. On becoming Vicar-Apostolic in 1956 he immediately threw his weight behind the foundation of the farmers' co-operative, TRAFIPRO (Travail, Fidelité, Progrès), catering at first for poor Tutsi—there were many *"petits Tutsis"*—and for Hutu alike, and later a national institution funded by Swiss Development Cooperation.

Evolués de campagne increasingly described their difficulties in terms of ethnic discrimination, and anger was growing. Far more Hutu young men took advantage of seminary education than ever became priests. Three Hutu ex-seminarians, Joseph Gitera Habyarimana, Grégoire Kayibanda and Aloys Munyangaju, both of the latter trained as journalists, made sure that their feudal analysis of Rwandan society was widely broadcast. Meanwhile the establishment of Rwandan-only portfolios in the *Conseil Supérieur* indicated the first steps towards independence under Tutsi rule. The Tutsi elite had used the Church educationally, institutionally and ideologically as a springboard to more modern forms of political power required by Belgian Trusteeship. Grégoire Kayibanda saw that the Hutu counter-elite now had the same opportunity and needed to act quickly.[6]

Kayibanda was lay editor of the influential fortnightly Church periodical *Kinyamateka*. By 1956 some 25,000 copies of the vernacular 12-page weekly were reaching the Rwandan public promoting democracy and Catholic Social Teaching while disseminating his brand of social analysis and non-violent contestation of Tutsi rule. The Francophone *L'Ami*, later *Temps Nouveaux d'Afrique,* and the vernacular *Kurerera Imana* for Catholic teachers, also provided an outlet for articles. On 24 March 1957, following Abbé Malula in the Congo, Kayibanda and eight other Catholic Hutu *évolués* founded the *Mouvement Social Muhutu* (MSM). Its Manifesto, *Note sur l'aspect social du problème racial indigène au Rwanda,* was sent to the Vice-Governor General of the Belgian Congo and Ruanda-Urundi, Jean-Paul Harroy.[7]

The Bahutu Manifesto, as it was soon known, outlined and defined Tutsi hegemony as *racial* and rejected any moves towards independence that consolidated Tutsi control. The bishops of Ruanda-Urundi in their Easter pastoral also entered the fray but limited themselves to calling on the political authorities to work for the Common Good, while deploring specific instances of bad governance. In September 1957 Kayibanda was sent for a year to Belgium for journalist training in Namur.[8]

Formal debates on the Bahutu Manifesto in a special committee of the *Conseil Supérieur* reached deadlock in 1958. This was due to the Hutu personalities involved apart from the intransigence of the key Tutsi participants. For example, the flamboyant Joseph Gitera Habyarimana, a pious Hutu Catholic, often sounded like an Old Testament prophet when denouncing Tutsi rule.[9] Gitera's public diatribes about the "idolatry" of *kalinga*, the royal drum at Nyanza which was the *mwami*'s symbol of office, or if you preferred the "national emblem", reached such a pitch that Perraudin remonstrated with him after an inflammatory piece written in the name of *"Jeunesse Chrétienne"*.[10] He formed a radical *Association pour la promotion de la masse*, APROSOMA with a Hutu Catholic colleague, Aloys Munyangaju.

Future accusations by Tutsi leaders to the contrary, there was no concerted political campaign by the missionaries. One or two Belgian priests lobbied behind the scenes in the Ministry for the Colonies in Brussels for more rapid reform, or at least argued for their analysis of the problem and how it might be dealt with speedily. Perraudin produced a pastoral letter on charity on 11 February 1959 setting out a Catholic account of the practice of "social charity" in government and society, what today would be called "good governance". While written in general terms, the pastoral clearly targeted the failings of Tutsi rule in Rwanda; "the monopoly of power in the hands of one group" was challenged, the economic and social privileges that devolved from this monopoly no less. The failure to assure fundamental rights and political participation for everyone was noted. Perraudin acknowledged the right of groups to defend their interests collectively by forming "associations", but not to use violence to achieve them. He denounced "race" hatred and "class conflict" and made an appeal to forget differences in the unity of the one Church.[11]

The conclusion to be drawn was that wealth and poverty depended in large measure on racial affiliation. The letter said as much. Such open criticism came as a shock to king and court. The Brothers of Charity believed their *Groupe Scolaire*, for training—largely Tutsi—

205

government officials was dealing with the problem, and the intervention ill-judged. The pastoral was quite enough for the *mwami* and Tutsi nobles at the Nyanza court to identify the Church as a dangerous new enemy, and for them to foster anti-clericalism. Some voted with their feet and moved off into the Anglican fold.[12]

Political developments moved fast. The Vicar-Apostolic was now one step behind the events. On 15 February 1959 Gitera and Munyangaju transformed APROSOMA into a *"Parti Politique Hutu"*. The horse was bolting and it was not clear who was in the saddle.[13] The traditionalist discourse of court Catholicism in the ruling circles at Nyanza that glorified a stratified society where all knew their place under the beneficent *mwami*, was abruptly abandoned. Now themes of national unity came to the fore. The court wanted the words *Hutu* and *Tutsi* banned from public discourse. The blame for all social ills was projected back onto the Belgian "colonialist". The Vicar-Apostolic of Nyundo, a Tutsi bishop, Aloys Bigirumwami, broke ranks with Perraudin and began describing the growing crisis in the same vein as interlocutors around the *mwami*. Perraudin called on all his clergy to abstain from partisan politics, and for schools to give courses on Catholic Social Teaching to older pupils. Meanwhile after official business at Church meetings, Kayibanda, returned from Namur, was able to organise political support. Church networks, his leadership of the Legion of Mary—6,000 members—TRAFIPRO, and the Catholic Teachers' Association, afforded him regular opportunities to promote his cause.[14] The Church was splitting apart around irresolvable antinomies and an ethnic power struggle.

The sudden death of the *mwami* after a stroke in Bujumbura and the formation of the UNAR, *Union Nationale Rwandaise*, in August 1959 representing conservative Tutsi interests underpinned by nationalist anti-colonialism, heralded the descent of Rwanda into bloodshed. Pamphlets appeared around Nyanza linking Perraudin with the *mwami*'s death and calling him, alongside reformist nobles, a traitor. In September Kayibanda revamped his political movement, the MSM into the *Mouvement Démocratique Rwandais/Parti du Mouvement de l'Emancipation Hutu*, MDR-PARMEHUTU. One or two of the White Fathers had been openly in favour of the formation of PARMEHUTU. Its programme amounted to majority rule, rejection of racial domination and hatred, and a gradual movement towards independence—after five to seven years.[15] With independence imminent, there were now two competing visions of Rwandan nationalism.

By late 1959, violent incidents suggested that Tutsi militia were starting to target their political opponents. Communal conflict then broke out with activist groups killing their opponents, even the Hutu gangs often claiming and believing that they were acting on the *mwami*'s orders. In the north-west, away from the Tutsi heartland, the Tutsi minority were hunted down and chased out. The two Vicars-Apostolic issued warnings: about the exclusive claims to patriotism of the UNAR, which they said were reminiscent of National Socialism, and the racial hatred promoted by APROSOMA.[16] But, given the uncertainty and pressure for self-determination, they kept silent about PARMEHUTU, the apparently gentler option.

The Rwandan Catholic press made much pointed reference to the French Revolution and, to some degree, the violence and disorder that broke out in early November 1959 was a rural *jacquerie*. There were poignant reports of solitary Tutsi nobles defying Hutu mobs as they plucked up enough courage to throw the first spear or strike the first *panga* blow. But it was the Belgian decision to move rapidly towards self-determination and majority rule, rather than the insurrection, that played the greater role in power changing hands. The Belgians replaced Tutsi chiefs and sub-chiefs with Hutu mayors, *bourgmestres*, and the process was consolidated in June-July 1960 communal elections when PARMEHUTU swept the board, leaving only 19 Tutsis among the 229 *bourgmestres*.

On 28 January 1961, to avoid further intervention from the United Nations which was chafing at the transition from one "racial dictatorship" to another, the Belgians declared the first democratic Republic of Rwanda, in a "legal coup", with Grégoire Kayibanda as Prime Minister. Some eighteen months later, after PARMEHUTU overwhelmingly won legislative elections, he became President. Tutsi counter-attacks from across the Burundi and Uganda borders resulted in brutal retaliation, most of it spontaneous, and intensified the persecution of local Tutsi families, rich and poor alike. The exodus to Uganda gained momentum as Tutsi politicians and leaders were summarily executed.[17]

Between 1959 to 1964, 10,000 people died, many more were displaced to camps or fled the country. There was also a crisis in the Church. Pamphlets circulated linking Kayibanda and Perraudin and calling for them to be eliminated. The Party was well organised across the hills with a cell structure copied by Kayibanda from the Legion of Mary groups. But the Tutsi dominated UNAR also had clerical backers despite becoming increasingly and stridently anti-clerical and threatening to take control of all Catholic schools. Leading UNAR officials, one a brother of a bishop, wrote to the Propaganda Fide in an attempt to get Perraudin removed.[18]

Rwandan clergy were divided. Some left with the refugees. Archbishop Birigumwami called for respect for the *mwami* and obedience to the traditional chiefs. He was reprimanded by the Belgians for holding a partisan position, contrary to their policy.[19] From 1959-63, he, Perraudin and the new bishop of Ruhengeri, Joseph Sibomana, pleaded repeatedly for calm, an end to violence and restoration of public order. The bishops of Ruanda-Urundi called for national authorities and the Belgians to work for a resolution of the political crisis and the refugee problem, and *Secours Catholique*, later CARITAS Rwanda, was set up to provide help. Private letters from Archbishop Perraudin to Rome show that he was heartbroken at the bloodletting and what would today be called ethnic cleansing.[20]

To a great extent Church leadership emerged into the First Republic unscathed. A disproportionately large number of Tutsi clergy still occupied key positions such as seminary professor, vicar-general and bishop. But from February to July 1973 a second wave of ethnic cleansing swept the country, this time not sparing the Church, its seminaries and schools. Students tested ethnic affiliation by checking physical features, fingers and noses, before chasing out suspected Tutsis.[21] Some Tutsi priests and Sisters fled. Nyundo seminary was taken over by Major Alexis Kanyarengwe. On 5 July Major-General Juvénal Habyarimana put his armoured cars into Kigali, staging a military coup on the grounds of restoring order. A northern clique of Hutu leaders, who had fared badly under Kayibanda whose support base was central Rwanda, took power, inaugurating the Second Republic and forming a new ruling party, the MRND (*Mouvement Révolutionnaire National pour le Développement*).[22]

Every Rwandan was deemed to be a member of the Party. Parish priests automatically became members of the *conseils techniques* (development and educational councils) of the *communes* and as such of the *commune* committees of the MRND. Many did not attend. A major problem was Monsignor Vincent Nsengiyumva. He had grown up in the MRND heartland of Ruhengeri Diocese and, after first replacing the retired Archbishop Bigirumwami at Nyundo, became Archbishop of Kigali and confessor to the President's wife. As chairman of the National Social Commission he attended the Central Committee of the MRND and drove around in a government car. There was disquiet among clergy, but Nsengiyumva appeared not to see what they were worried about.[23]

In April 1985 Pope John Paul II, a stickler for priests staying out of political office, made it clear that he would not go ahead with a Papal visit to Rwanda unless the Archbishop of Kigali resigned from the Central Committee. Eight months later, when it was obvious the Pope meant what he said, Nsengiyumva obeyed. In the Catholic media, *Kinyamateka* and the Francophone *Dialogue*, presenting a range of critical views was keeping the candle of social and political criticism burning... but only just.[24] In February 1990 the bishops responded and drew on criticisms in the press—the rich-poor divide, nepotism, regionalism and ethnic conflict—in a moderately worded pastoral letter. But opinion in the country was generally hardening for and against government.

By the end of the 1980s Habyarimana was coming under pressure both internally and from France to end corruption and introduce a multiparty system. At the same time Tutsi exile groups in Uganda, trained in the Ugandan army and with access to its weaponry, finally decided on war to regain power. The *Rwanda Patriotic Army* (RPA) invaded Rwanda in October 1990. Although Tutsi Church personnel were imprisoned, there was no public challenge to Habyarimana from the predominantly Hutu bishops. The massacres of Hutu in neighbouring Burundi, the creation of the Hutu extremist *Coalition pour la Défense de la République* (CDR), the mustering and training of Hutu militias, *interhamwe*, together cranked up the tension. The perception of Hutu power under immediate threat created by the Arusha Accords between the parties to the armed conflict—an externally imposed solution—heralded the descent of Rwanda into the MRND's final solution: genocide.[25]

From 1990 to 1994 sporadic minor attacks on local Tutsi grew into major organised massacres. The Apostolic Delegate who had formerly served at the UN in Geneva, Monsignor Giuseppe Bertello, supported the growth of human rights organisations, and kept the Vatican informed about the increasing gravity of the situation. Despite the compromised position of the Archbishop of Kigali, his namesake Monsignor Thaddée Nsengiyumva, consecrated as Perraudin's replacement on his retirement, acted as a counterweight from Kabgayi Diocese. Finally he spoke out on the precarious situation facing the Church. "Submission to temporal power" meant the Church was living "a continual lie". In a forty-page pamphlet published in December 1991 in consultation with his clergy, he wrote that Catholics needed to be converted to Christianity if they were ever to live together in peace. He pointed out that the roots of the country's social and economic crisis were ignored: lack of action to remedy the poverty of the peasantry, discrimination in education, and a politics where "assassination is now commonplace".[26] But though President of the Bishops Conference, he could count on very little active support from his fellow bishops, apart from the Apostolic Delegate and some of the clergy, for further outspoken analysis either of the "sick Church" that failed to speak out on human rights or the "sick society".[27]

A missile shot down and killed President Habyarimana alongside the President of Burundi when their plane was coming in to land at Kigali airport at about 8.30 pm on 6 April 1994.[28] The assassination triggered a well-prepared genocide of the Tutsi and the elimination of all Hutu opponents of the regime. Among the approximately 800,000 victims of the genocide, between a quarter and a third of Church leadership, Sisters, priests, Brothers, bishops were killed in the following three months, some 320 priests, nuns and seminarians. On the first day of the genocide, the Apostolic Delegate narrowly escaped with his life over the back wall of the Delegation. Archbishops Vincent and Thaddée Nsengiyumva along with Bishop Joseph Ruzindana of Byumba were later targeted and murdered by Tutsi RPA forces in June near Kabgayi. Opening the African Synod in Rome on 10 April 1994, after just four days of killings, the Pope did not mince his words: "I raise my voice to tell you. Stop these acts of violence. Stop these tragedies. Stop these fratricidal massacres."[29]

What the Pope described as this "overwhelming tragedy" was a particular catastrophe for the Church. In one way or another Catholics who had received leadership training or formation in the Church, catechists, Church elders and some Sisters and priests, were complicit in the genocide, mostly but not always, in situations in which refusal to aid the killers would result in death. Over twenty secular priests and Men and Women Religious are awaiting or have stood trial. With at least 70 per cent of the population Catholic, Church-goers were inevitably involved in the genocide doing the killing, and being killed. A commitment to social justice, democracy, and majority rule in the 1950s ended in churches filled with butchered and burnt corpses in 1994. The bloody bonds of ethnicity and imagined solidarity, coupled with naked fear and hatred, were stronger than the water of baptism.[30]

Post-war trained young priests had in the main been sympathetic to democracy and majority rule. But Rwandan politics had little to do with the Common Good. The Church's promotion of human rights in Papal encyclicals might just as well not have existed. Nationalist politics amounted to nothing more than a brutal violent struggle between an elite and counter-elite, both instrumentalising the Church and the peasantry for the achievement of personal power and gain. Church leaders had been right in their wariness of nationalist rhetoric. In Rwanda democracy was a winner-takes-all, zero sum game. Losers were executed, murdered or fled. The genocide was the ultimate expression of an underlying political reality.

And yet Monsignor Thaddée Nsengiyumva had only been partly right: not all the body was sick. There were Tutsi hidden and sheltered at great personal risk, genuine martyrs who died because they refused to betray Tutsi friends to the mob, or refused to use their Hutu origins to escape when the *interahamwe* came killing their doomed Tutsi colleagues. Cyprien and Daphrose Mugamba of the multi-ethnic Emmanuel community died in this way. Felicitas Niyitegeka died in Gisenyi, despite the pleading of her brother to leave the Tutsi Sisters in her community to their fate. Father Boniface Senyenzi, a Hutu priest, refused to desert his congregation and died with 11,400 parishioners inside the town church of Kibuye. This was small consolation as priests and Sisters were brought to trial for complicity under the new government, led by men who had fought their way into Kigali and ended the genocide by force of arms. It did not avert ongoing hostility from the incoming government to the once powerful Catholic Church.

Rhodesia/Zimbabwe

If Rwanda found the Church exposed to the betrayal of an African people by their nationalist elites, and the promotion of social justice and democracy treated with lethal contempt, Rhodesia furnished a

211

further Hobbesian nightmare. Here contending nationalist groups also emerged, though in this instance indubitably racial in their organisation. Here also a significant part of the Church identified with an oppressed majority only later to suffer violence and tragic disillusionment. Here also a Leviathan ate its own children.

From 1890 Rhodesia was an English colonial state that looked over its shoulder to the Afrikaner apartheid regime. After 1953, locked into a Central African Federation intended for white-ruled Dominion status with Northern Rhodesia and Nyasaland, it became a settler state. In the 1970s, right-wing White nationalism confronted African nationalism in a conflict between the Rhodesian Front of Ian Smith and Joshua Nkomo's Ndebele-dominated ZAPU and the Shona-dominated ZANU (PF) of Robert Mugabe. The dynamics were different from Rwanda though there were many commonalities as far as the role of the Church was concerned. This was also a predominantly rural Church with the slogan of the Catholic Association Congresses, "better hearts, better harvests, better homes", capturing the dual purpose of missionary activity and its fears of urbanisation. Again the nationality of the missionaries was important, and there were many nationalities after the influx of mission societies after the Second World War.

For many years the English province of the Society of Jesus dominated the local Church in Southern Rhodesia, from 1953, sustaining a cosy relationship in the early years of Federation with the British Governor-General, Governor, Prime Minister and Cabinet. In the eyes of many educated Africans, the Church appeared as the religious arm of colonialism. Again, as the nationalist movements developed, a dynamic missionary bishop appeared on the scene to upset the apple-cart with calls for social justice. In 1957 Donal Raymond Lamont was made bishop of Umtali on the Mozambique border. An Irish Carmelite, he combined the driving force of Terenure College First XV with a Master's degree in English metaphysical poetry, the inbred triumphalism of the Irish clergy with a sympathy for the downtrodden. He shared the latter with Bishop Aloysius Haene of Gwelo Diocese, not unlike Perraudin in Rwanda, a Swiss bishop from a poor family. Together they bypassed the Jesuit Archbishop of Salisbury, Francis Markall to denounce the injustices of colonial rule.[31]

Lamont's seminary years in Rome before the Second World War had been formative. He harboured no doubt that during the "tragedy

of Europe" the "supreme authority of the Church" had defended freedom of conscience and the natural rights of man against Communism,
Mussolini and the Nazis, not to mention the Mexican regime. "About
that time the powerful arm of Fascism reached right into the College...
and deported our Professor of Theology. Later on in Holland another
Carmelite, the Rector of the Catholic University of Nijmegen, would
be punished for his loyalty to principle... He was dragged to Dachau
and died there rather than betray his conscience and serve the state. He
has been my hero."[32] As an Irish Churchman, his inclination was to see
government as redolent of moral disorder. As an Irishman, the English
colonial state was not given the benefit of the doubt.

The All-African Peoples Conference in Accra, Ghana, in December
1958 brought the "Central Africans" into contact with Nkrumah and
put wind in the sails of the African National Congress throughout the
Federation. The declaration of a State of Emergency in February 1959
came in response to widespread pressure and protest by the Congress
at the consolidation of the Central African Federation. It highlighted
for Lamont the pressing need for a pastoral letter on race relations and
civil rights. Compared to South Africa, the Catholic Church in Rhodesia believed it retained some leverage with the state and maintained a
clubby civility. The Archbishop of Salisbury, Francis Markall, and his
advisers in the Society of Jesus did not want to lose influence by signing a joint pastoral letter that was "arrogant" and "biased against the
European". Nor did Rome. In June 1959, Lamont defied the Apostolic
Delegate and published *Purchased People*, as an "instruction" from
Umtali Diocese on the contemporary crisis.[33]

Purchased People opened with a bombastic assertion of the rights
of the Church: "her divine indefectibility" and "her imprescriptable
right to intervene in temporal matters". In response to his Jesuit critics
Lamont explained why he intervened: "the ideal of social order based
on Christian principles of justice and charity may be abandoned as
unrealistic, impractical, and visionary illusion". An acceptable form
of nationalism was "the desire of the people to participate fully in
the life of their country", being equal not second class citizens, holding on to things of traditional and cultural value "not contrary to the
Moral Law", so that they were not "de-characterised and presented to
the world as *ersatz* Europeans". Nationalism that fed on race hatred,
xenophobia and Pan-Africanism, detected in the demands of the Afri-

can National Congress, was inadmissable. But Africans could not be blamed for being swayed by "subversive propaganda" if, while eking out a tenuous living, they saw acres of better unused land owned by absentee landlords. Even more undermining of white settlers was his condemnation as "without moral justification" of "violent seizure of a territory which was at the time inhabited and cultivated by a native tribe", exploitation of the country "as would destroy or impoverish it or lead to the establishment of exclusive privileges for the newcomer to the detriment of the indigenous people".[34]

The theoretical core of Lamont's attack was standard fare derived from a 1952 translation of a German treatise on Catholic social, political and economic ethics by Messner, probably the same text on which Perraudin's courses were based in Rwanda. The echoes of the triumphalist Constantinian Church came from Pope Pius XI: the Church as an alternative society, a *societas perfecta*, had a right to all that it needed to fulfil its divine mandate.[35] But the text also reflected insights and passion from Irish history, and life in fascist-ruled Rome, that gave it a distinctive edge.

From 1959 the planned slow and sedate growth of a multiracial middle class, engineered during the 1950s by the reformist Prime Minister, Garfield Todd, foundered on settler intransigence and racism. Todd paid the price for pushing modest multiracialism and gradualism, but had given Church leaders a vision of a possible future, something to hold on to. With Todd gone, the situation was deteriorating and there were warnings from educated African Catholics of defections from the Church if it continued to be seen as the enemy of African nationalism in the pocket of the state. Bishop Lamont gained a Spanish ally in Bishop Ignatius Prieto of the new Wankie Diocese. *Peace through Justice*, signed by all bishops in 1961, declared: "the doctrine of racial superiority as taught and practised by many in this country, differs little in essence from that of the Nazis whom Pope Pius XI sternly rebuked". The Nazi comparison did not go down well in the *Rhodesia Herald*. But the principal idiom remained an appeal to "natural rights" with a call for radical change and "thorough land reform".[36]

New political parties were forming. Robert Mugabe, a Catholic teacher educated by the Jesuits at Kutama, became publicity secretary for the multiracial National Democratic Party (NDP). He could attract 2,000 people in the Monomotapa Hall in Gwelo. Within a few years Mugabe had become the general-secretary of Ndabaningi Sithole's ZANU Party. "Democracy" in Church statements still could not quite speak its name; "full participation in society which justice demands" had to make do. The Church in official pronouncements was still talking to the Whites, though just beginning to listen seriously to the Blacks. Bishop Haene was a regular visitor to one of the founding fathers of ZAPU in detention, an ex-seminarian, Leopold Takawira. Simon Muzenda, later President of Zimbabwe, was active in his diocese in the lay apostolate.[37]

Just as in Rwanda, the Catholic Press was gearing up to play a pivotal role. The main influence here was also Swiss, the Bethlehem Fathers of Immensee, a practical, twentieth-century missionary order who put their imprint on the Rhodesian heartland of Gwelo Diocese. Three Sisters of St Peter Canisius set up a Mission Press in 1958, and a year later a semi-vernacular monthly aimed at an African readership was launched. In May 1960 this was transformed into what was soon to become a national monthly newspaper, *Moto*. Mambo Press printed the paper and published and disseminated the bishops' pastoral letters widely. It also printed the Party cards and posters funded without fanfare by Bishop Haene for the first ZANU Party Conference.[38] With Paul Chidyausiku as editor-in-chief and a radical Zurich journalist, Father Mike Traber, as director, *Moto* reflected African Christian opinion, growing in circulation from its original run of 3,000 in 1960 to 18,000 in 1964 and 34,000 in 1969. Traber trained a number of journalists destined to become key figures in ZANU: Dzingai Mutumbuka, Stan Mudenge and Simbi Mubako, as well as the later BBC correspondent, Justin Nyoka.[39]

The white extremist Rhodesian Front was swept to power in—white only—elections on 14 December 1962 to pre-empt the rise of African nationalism. African political emancipation, proceeding at a snail's pace, came to an abrupt end. Ian Smith, "a farm boy from Selukwe, devious, parochial and suspicious", took over the Rhodesian Front (RF) in 1964.[40] The era of private chats between missionaries and government ministers over a cup of tea had finally come to a shuddering halt. Mambo press was bombed in 1979, a token of the esteem in which it was held by the Smith regime.

The Rhodesian Front's victory while the Rhodesian bishops were at the Vatican Council, galvanised the Church. In the long periods back in

Rhodesia between sessions Lamont ran ecumenical meetings on *Pacem in Terris*. He was not unaware that it was an authoritative vindication of his 1959 statement.[41] In Salisbury the Jesuits gave courses on social ethics in African townships, while middle-class African Catholics were brought together to discuss what kind of nationalism the Church could promote. In December 1964 Father John Dove SJ took over the Jesuit noviciate, Silveira House, and transformed it into a leadership training centre. Close to Salisbury, it became a major Catholic meeting place promoting credit unions, and sustainable agricultural development. Father Ted Rogers, a late vocation after years as a sailor, then a worker priest in Le Havre, developed a new School for Social Work with trades union training weeks. The vision and energy from the Council were reaching Rhodesia.[42]

Smith's Unilateral Declaration of Independence (UDI) on 11 November 1965 provided a further spur to British Jesuit opposition. It added rebellion to the Crown, and thus illegitimacy, to the Rhodesian Front's profile as a government. The bishops now had to submit their pastorals to censors who cut two passages from the Shona and Ndebele versions of the bishops' *Plea for Peace* in response to UDI. As a result the bishops issued only an—uncensored—English version. The bishops had been particularly incensed by the claim that UDI was designed to preserve "Christian civilisation". Their thoughts on this travesty formed one of the pastoral's sections deemed by censors unsuitable for African eyes.[43]

As in the first years of the National Party in South Africa, the RF rapidly passed legislation that would ensure racial segregation and a supply of cheap black labour. This was done through Education, Residential Property and, most importantly, Land Tenure Acts.[44] Had the Church complied fully with the new bills, Church life would have become totally segregated by race—admittedly in a Catholic community already *de facto* partially segregated. In 1969 a new Constitution excluding black majority rule in perpetuity—designed according to the RF to "ensure that government will be retained in responsible hands"—created the necessary constitutional basis for white minority rule. A joint ecumenical letter of protest and public demonstrations followed. The Bethlehem Father, Mike Traber, was the first priest to be deported after including a cartoon in a special June edition of *Moto* showing white "responsible hands" squeezing the lifeblood out of Africans.[45] "The real terrorists in this country," fulminated Lamont, "are the people who framed the new constitution; they have already subjugated nearly 5 million people."[46]

Seen from the perspective of infringement of the Church's rights, the RF legislation and Land Tenure Act brought on much, initially united, protest. But this was a prelude to compromise. Rome became involved. The Propaganda Fide favoured negotiation over confrontation to save the schools in "the Africans' interest". The Church knuckled under, accepted a 6 per cent quota limit on Africans in its white schools though ignored some of the limitations on African clergy and Sisters serving in "white areas". State registration amounted to collaboration with an *apartheid* education system and the Notre Dame Sisters' Superior, Sr Mary McLeish, refused to compromise. She held that shutting Church schools was now a matter of principle, and was reprimanded by the bishops, then shunted off to Botswana by her Superiors after pressure from conservative Marianhill clergy in her diocese. The editors of the Catholic English-language magazine, *The Shield*, tried to rescue the integrity of the Church: the bishops had "betrayed both her nature and the members of her body", they wrote. They then resigned. Bishop Lamont did not. "What," he nonetheless wanted to know, "was 6 per cent of a principle?"[47]

Pope Paul VI's promotion of Justice and Peace strengthened Lamont's hand. The embattled Lamont went to the 1971 Synod of Bishops in Rome, and, much encouraged, began to extend internationally his campaign for social justice against the Smith regime.[48] With a new Apostolic Delegate, Archbishop Alfredo Poledrini, and support from the Secretariat of State in Rome, the Rhodesian bishops took the step of ending their "temporary working arrangement" with the state. They could scarcely have done otherwise; 1,000 Africans had just been evicted from the Chishawasha Mission land under the Land Tenure Act.[49]

In a major meeting at Chishawasha chaired by Bishop Haene in November 1971, an interim committee was formed to set up a Rhodesian Justice and Peace Commission (RJPC). For whites and talking to whites, and at first far from radical, with members who went off and joined the RF, the Commission worked on sermon outlines on justice; fewer than 5 per cent of clergy used them, most white Catholics were indifferent and some were outraged. It was a faltering beginning but the Commission was soon to come to prominence.[50]

Guerrilla attacks were now beginning in the north-east of the country and repression was rapidly intensified. "Dogs and guns and internment and restriction are all that the Rhodesian Front Government has to keep it in power" Lamont wrote in *Moto*, nearly getting its new director, Father Albert Plangger, deported.[51] Others were radicalised. New Spanish Mission Institute priests in Wankie decided to abandon formal education altogether to concentrate on "conscientisation". They brought with them theology from the Council and Latin America. "If the people suffer", wrote Father Xavier Lopez, "the Church must suffer too. For there can be no Church without the people". Their goal was the "integral liberation of man".[52] In January 1972 the country finally got its first African bishop for Salisbury, Patrick Chakaipa, a gentle and scholarly authority on the Shona language and author of three novels. His writing reflected his profound dislike for what he saw as westernised town life that destroyed traditional values of solidarity. His consecration was an important if late development in the life of the Church.[53]

Guerrilla incursions from Zambia and Mozambique, foreshadowing full scale rural insurgency under the banner of the Patriotic Front, and civil war, shifted the focus of social justice for the Church away from principles, multiculturalism and constitutions to human rights, taking sides, and survival. As the personnel of the Justice and Peace Commission changed to make it more of a likeminded group, white liberals with one or two black participants, and, for a brief while, a radical Maryknoll Sister, so did its focus. One of its most clear-sighted members was a young East German Jesuit, Dieter Scholz, who had become aware of the extent of security forces' violation of human rights around the Jesuit-run St Albert's Mission in the north. Lamont now held the formal episcopal oversight of the Commission, a mixed blessing.[54]

The RJPC's programmes were shifting their emphasis to surveying social and economic conditions, and publication of findings on human rights violations and injustices. A formidable Dominican sociologist at the university, Sister Aquina Weinrich, lent her expertise. Legal advice to detainees and victims of Security Force brutality took up a great deal of staff time; they were voluntary and unpaid with the exception of a taciturn Canadian Brother, Arthur Dupuis.[55] Church mission personnel in rural areas were also drawn into defending Zimbabweans against state repression, and by default or intention supporting the *vakomana* (guerrilla forces); a minority strongly opposed the guerrillas. African Church personnel, catechists, Sisters and several priests increasingly chose to aid the incoming guerrillas with shelter, food and medicines, and some left for Mozambique to join them.

Despite Rhodesia's isolation, Church thinking was developing, slowly absorbing ideas from abroad. The Bishops' Holy Year Message for 1974 showed signs of Dieter Scholz's influence: "we are convinced that the problem of Rhodesia is not so much that of colour but of power—of political and of economic power—which those who have it are unwilling to share and which they claim as their almost exclusive right".[56] These intimations of a move away from moral appeals about race, and the attendant failure of multiracialism, towards analysis of the structures of social, economic and political power found parallels in the evolution of Church thinking revealed in the Rome synods.

Juan Luis Segundo's *The Liberation of Theology* was circulating among younger Rhodesian Jesuits.[57] This contact with Latin American liberation theology was notable only in the sense that there had previously been so few signs of a shift from pre-conciliar to post-conciliar ways of thinking and acting—a reference or two to *Populorum Progressio* and *Octagesima Adveniens*. The Jesuits in their General Chapter in Rome were on the point of declaring the Society's "option for the poor". Locally the Bethlehem Fathers—they also had missions in Latin America—were at the forefront of promoting post-conciliar themes, "reading the signs of the times", and applying them in practical guidelines for their missionaries' actions.

But formal statements from the Bishops Conference had become almost irrelevant. Church policy was being formulated in prudential judgements at the level of rural mission stations. In a rapid reversal of normal power relations, black Zimbabwean catechists, seminarians—who met nationalist leaders during their holidays—and priests, held the fortunes of the Catholic Church, at least in the rural mission stations, in their hands. There were still only fifty-one African priests (c.f. 329 missionary priests), and twenty African Brothers (133 Missionary Brothers) though the number of Zimbabwean Women Religious, 435, was nearing the 564 from abroad. Another sign of the times was a boycott of classes by seminarians at Chishawasha Major Seminary over the expulsion of a student; he was later ordained and offered to act as a chaplain to guerrilla forces. Tellingly, the boycott led to the appointment of a new Zimbabwean Rector, Father Tobias Chiginya, soon to become bishop of Gwelo and President of the Bishops' Conference. Political forces from outside the Church were now driving changes within it.[58]

Mission stations along the country's borders had been the first to be affected by ZANLA's arrival (ZANU's military wing), but by the end of the 1970s the country was awash with guerrillas. The April 1974 military coup in Portugal followed by the rapid move to independence in Mozambique under FRELIMO, transformed the military balance of power by providing a long permeable border and a friendly host government. Towards the end of 1974, Smith, under pressure from the USA and South Africa, released Joshua Nkomo and Robert Mugabe. In prison Mugabe had gained a reputation as a pious Catholic. He was given a telephone and office at Silveira House where two of his sisters worked in women's development programmes. The prison chaplain Father Emmanuel Ribeiro organised his escape across the Mozambique border in two cars containing elderly Dominican Sisters with Sr Aquina as lead driver to distract police at road blocks.[59]

It was not so much that the Catholic Church had got into bed with ZANU—some Church personnel had—but that a significant number of ZANU's nationalist leadership had developed their skills in a Church context, then taken them into the liberation struggle, bringing with them a great deal of mutual respect and goodwill. To take one example, Peter Masanu from St Albert's Mission, prevented from becoming a priest by his father, worked as a catechist from 1969-72. He was approached by FRELIMO to look after Mozambican refugees. These contacts led to meetings with ZANLA—who were training with FRELIMO forces—then to imminent arrest and flight into Mozambique where he and his wife joined ZANLA under the name of George Rutanhire. He was back home in April 1973, working as a political commissar involved in political education, conducting *pungwes*, night meetings around the mission to mobilise the local community. Songs with political messages were his stock-in-trade—he had a fine singing voice—and he used the same melodies he had learnt from his Catholic hymnal. The Shona Church hymn tunes were used remarkably widely in political education—a spontaneous strategy as adaptive as making sandals out of bald tyres.[60]

Some women fought in ZANLA but, for most, supporting the guerrillas was an extension in wartime of their normal gender roles. Zimba-

bwean Women Religious, for example the Little Children of Our Blessed Lady, and the Diocesan Congregation of the Infant Jesus in Gwelo,
were active in medical work and teaching. In many instances they provided invaluable assistance to ZANLA forces—who were sometimes
relatives—with medical supplies, food and drink, and often acted as
liaison with the priests. What to do when ZANLA forces turned up
at the convent was potentially a life and death decision; "aiding and
abetting" was punishable by death, and a false move in front of guerrillas, some of whose groups were anti-Church after political indoctrination, could have dire consequences.[61] On some occasions Zimbabwean
Sisters were left with little alternative but to cross into Mozambique
either to Catholic mission stations or into ZANLA camps. After being
threatened by Security Forces, Sister Helen Nyakupinda, the Carmelite
Superior at Avila Mission, was taken across the border by ZANLA
forces and delivered safely to a Mozambican mission station.[62]

One bishop, twenty-three foreign missionaries, and a Zimbabwean
priest died during the war. Sometimes it was as a result of a teenager
with a grudge and a weapon. Seven missionaries including the only four
Women Religious to die were killed in unsolved massacres at the Jesuit
mission of Musami. Black Catholics tried to protect Church personnel
from mines laid by ZANLA and ZIPRA, the armed forces of the umbrella Patriotic Front, and from their wayward guerrilla commanders,
generally charting with skill and perseverance a difficult course between
their sympathy for the *vakomana* and their loyalty to the Church.

The behaviour of the security forces now became a major focus of
Church concern. A system of "protected villages" learnt from counter-insurgency tactics in Malaysia and elsewhere, uprooted countless
Zimbabweans leaving them destitute and hungry in settlements akin
to open prisons. Reprisals against civilian populations, burning down
of houses, arbitrary brutality, torture of detainees, became commonplace. The RJPC's human rights documents were sent to prominent
Rhodesians and there was an ecumenical call for a judicial enquiry.
These bulging dossiers formed the substance of a number of publications based on the RJPC's work: *The Man in the Middle, Civil War
in Rhodesia* and *Rhodesia the Propaganda War*, co-published with
the Catholic Institute for International Relations in London. By highlighting the human rights situation in a war supposedly for "Christian
civilisation", from 1975 they opened up a propaganda front during the

critical period of the "Internal Settlement" when Smith was seeking legitimacy through a political front with the African United Methodist, Bishop Abel Muzorewa. The government's main response was to rush through an Indemnity and Compensation Act to allow the torture and brutality to continue with impunity. The RJPC, now under intense security police surveillance, were not always able to take what had to be rapid decisions up the hierarchy for approval, and this was causing friction with the Bishops Conference.[63]

Lamont's temperament did not make things easier. Yet again having failed to get the bishops to sign a letter declaring the state illegitimate, he wrote his own open letter to government, concluding: "You may rule with the consent of a small and selfish electorate, but you rule without the consent of the nation, which is the test of all legitimacy".[64] That was a step too far. He was charged on four counts relating to failure to report the presence of terrorists, pleaded guilty, and was deported. His 1976 *Speech from the Dock* provided the platform he relished, one never afforded a South African bishop under apartheid. His clergy paid a heavier price. Father Patrick Mutume was arrested and for five days tortured by simulated drowning, dragging by a jeep and electric shocks. He later replaced Lamont as bishop. Father Ignatius Mhonda, taken with him, was severely beaten and suffered a perforated ear-drum. Shortly afterwards Bishop Haene retired. He privately admitted that, though a man of peace himself, he supported the liberation struggle. Lamont had instructed his diocese not to report the presence of *vakomana*. *Moto* was banned.[65] The Bishops' Conference was now virtually rudderless.

In September 1977, the RJPC suffered a major crisis when the CID arrested and charged four of the staff. One was Sister Janice McClaughlin, a Maryknoll who had been seconded from Kenya. While her house was being searched, a politically compromising diary was found. In court she admitted to supporting the liberation struggle.[66] She was imprisoned and deported, followed by Fr Dieter Scholz SJ a year later. He had been arrested along with Brother Arthur Dupuis and a courageous Catholic liberal, John Deary, on charges of causing alarm and despondency. The CID net had failed to snare Brother Fidelis Mukonori, a Jesuit, who was to play an extraordinary role moving around quietly in guerrilla zones, collecting evidence for RCJP to be published in London, liaising with ZANLA commanders, and trying to moderate the violence of the civil war. He reported directly to the ZANLA commander-in-chief, Josiah Tongogara.[67]

The RJPC on several occasions, some successfully, pressed for the removal of undisciplined and brutal guerrilla commanders by alerting the ZANU/ZAPU leadership to atrocities. Some of the military leaders had Catholic connections: Josiah Tungamirai for example, who ranked third in the ZANLA military hierarchy, was from the Bethlehem Fathers' Mutero Mission. He had spent time training for the priesthood before leaving and later joining the guerrillas. Similar interventions to moderate the violence were going on at the level of local mission superiors and ZANLA platoon leaders. But appeals to the leaders of the Patriotic Front gathered in Geneva during the 1976 Conference, to modify a guerrilla ban on executed "sell-outs" being buried, backfired; the bearer of the appeal from the RJPC, Joseph Mugore, was suspected of being a government spy.[68]

It would be easy to see the actions of this engaged minority, the stories of Zimbabwean Sisters disguised in rough clothes slipping off with medical equipment to wounded guerrillas, the guidelines on relationships with guerrillas drawn up in Switzerland for Gwelo Diocese by Father Joseph Amstutz with Dzingai Mutumbuka's help, the chaplains and support for Zimbabwean refugees in Zambia and Mozambique, the high cost of "accompanying the people", as a new post-conciliar Church being born.[69] But the rump of White Catholics remained what they saw as "apolitical". There was the diligent, clever and distinctly upper-class English Churchman, who served as general-secretary of the Bishops' Conference in its worst hours, Father Richard Randolph SJ.[70] He would have fared well in Eastern Europe parrying an intransigent Communist regime. Then there was the Roman perspective, the Apostolic Delegates whose first preoccupation often seemed avoiding the confiscation of Church property, but who were great promoters of an indigenous clergy. And there were the missionary Sisters and priests who castigated their colleagues for consorting with guerrillas. These were no less "the Church".

Fathers Patrick Mutume and Ignatius Mhonda were brought, after torture and beating, barefoot and handcuffed before a Catholic magistrate, a man to whom, on a following Sunday, Mhonda would be giving communion. In what then exactly lay the unity of "the Church"?[71]

Conflicts of nationalism, as much as race, were the anvil on which the Church was hammered to the point of disintegration.

The guerrilla war ended when the different nationalists, confined to Lancaster House in London in one hundred days of negotiations, under overwhelming pressure, called a ceasefire and produced a new constitution. The *vakomana* came out of the bush. The Church rejoiced. ZANU won the February 1980 elections convincingly. So when on 17 April 1980 Archbishop Patrick Chakaipa, standing alongside the elected Prime Minister, Robert Mugabe, and a Protestant President, Canaan Banana, blessed the new nation, there were great expectations of a new chapter for Church and Zimbabwean people alike. It was not to be; the euphoria was short-lived. Respite from the near anarchy of the rural insurgency was used by the Bishops' Conference to restore hierarchical control over a "Rhodesian" Justice and Peace Commission that in the worst of times had been making its own history. After heated arguments about its future, key players, including Br Fidelis Mukonori resigned, to adopt the approach of private dialogue with government that had characterised their opponents in the past, the conservative English Jesuits. It was renamed the Catholic Commission for Justice and Peace in Zimbabwe and, led by Mike Auret from 1981-1990, tried to defend human rights and build up local diocesan commissions.[72]

In the last years of the war ZIPRA and ZANLA had been in open armed conflict leading to serious casualties on both sides.[73] The Patriotic Front had only ever existed on paper at a leadership level, despite the best efforts of many to forge a multiethnic guerrilla force. It was put together by outside forces. In 1982 the "coalition" government fell apart and guerrilla attacks began again in Matabeleland. Government repression in the area was fierce and the suffering was compounded by a catastrophic crop failure. In January 1983, Mugabe unleashed his notorious North Korean trained Fifth Brigade, the military wing of ZANU (PF), to crush 400 armed dissidents and destroy ZAPU political strongholds in Matabeleland. The newly constituted Commission collected information on military action and human rights violations against the Ndebele-speaking population from courageous Church personnel in the Bulawayo Diocese. It painted a sorry story: a systematic policy of rape, torture and indiscriminate killing of some 20,000 civilians. The Bishops Conference denounced the "maiming and death of hundreds and hundreds of innocents" in an 1983 Easter pastoral *Reconciliation is Still Possible* but declined to publish the detailed report.

In response, the Minister of Justice denied all accusations. Nothing untoward had occurred in Matabeleland. Mugabe was furious with the bishops for going public without consultation. The government's response to the Commission's full report, "The Situation in south-western areas of Zimbabwe", finalised in July 1983, but not published until the 1990s, dispelled the thought that Zimbabwe might develop into a Nicaraguan-style blend of Catholicism and Socialism, despite the Catholic roots of its President. Henceforth the Commission brought dossiers of human rights violations to government, issued press releases, and from 1986 onwards took several cases to court. The arrest and brief detention that year of its director and acting chairman, Mike Auret and Nicolas Ndebele, brought the Church back full circle to the days of Ian Smith.[74] The most that could be achieved by this kind of pressure was minor temporary respites until Unity Accords signed between the two political Parties on 22 December 1987. But by now the Church was confronting a vicious Shona nationalism spiced intermittently with Marxist rhetoric about scientific socialism.

By the turn of the twenty-first century ZANU had created a corrupt, brutal and dishonest regime enjoying much the same rich pickings for a small clique as had occurred under Habyarimana in Rwanda. In addition it had created an economic catastrophe out of one of the more viable economies in Africa. Mugabe had become a tyrant clinging to power and, in perennial denial, destroying his country. Archbishop Pius Ncube in Bulawayo Diocese followed the same outspoken path as Donal Lamont, even calling for foreign armed intervention, but was discredited on grounds of sexual misconduct and obliged to resign. Against all odds, Catholics courageously persisted with others in working for human rights, development and social justice. In a 2007 Easter pastoral *God hears the Cries of the Poor*, the bishops protested at the worst injustices and against the consequences and causes of the country's economic collapse. In it Mugabe was warned that either he went or the country would go into open revolt. They briefly got the attention of the battered Zimbabwean people. Finally in April 2008, after rigged elections and political stalemate, with the leaders of other Christian Churches they called for external help because "we shall soon be witnessing genocide similar to that in Kenya and Rwanda". But

Mugabe, who had lost the election to the Movement for Democratic Change (MDC), was beyond such warnings; no intervention came and no revolt took place. Instead there ensued a period of "power-sharing", brokered by South Africa with the MDC, leaving Mugabe weakened but still in control.

The horror of Zimbabwe was not deaths by *panga* and gun as in Rwanda, and to a far lesser degree in Kenya—there were those too—but deaths by neglect, illness, hunger and malnutrition, and wealth for the Party hacks and ZANU clique around Mugabe. Genocide in Rwanda had appalled the world. But this betrayal was no less total and its death toll, spread over the long term, no less monstrous.

Malawi

The slings and arrows of colonial fortune resulted in Nyasaland becoming a British ruled backwater blessed with a strong Scottish Presbyterian presence, the Church of Central Africa Presbyterian (CCAP). "Foreign" Catholic missionaries, in the nineteenth and early twentieth centuries, mainly French and Dutch and then many nationalities, had to work hard for acceptance. As Malawi, Nyasaland's post-colonial history had a dark theatrical quality: the story of young nationalist intellectuals crushed after their imported figurehead, the *Ngwazi*, Dr Hastings Kamuzu Banda, an elder of the Church of Scotland, returned home after forty years away, to lead the independence movement. Banda eliminated most of those who had brought him to power with ruthlessness and cunning. His one man, one-party rule became one of the longest and most bizarre periods of tyranny and greed experienced in Africa.

Anti-colonialism in Nyasaland emerged initially as part of the story of the British-brokered Central African Federation and its discontents. The early rise of African nationalism in the early 1950s, in the form of the Nyasaland African Congress, did not much trouble the Missionaries of Our Lady of Africa, the White Fathers of the Nyasa Vicariate—in the centre and north of the country—led by their Vicar-Apostolic from Alsace, Joseph Fady. The Apostolic Delegate to East Africa, David Mathew, had improbably warned the missionaries in 1953 to avoid "all differences of opinion with their flock on purely political matters."[75]

True, there were fears of "Communists" at work particularly among the African elite, and anxieties about the way old theology pupils, or a

Brother, or ex-teacher after years in a Catholic school, sometimes led Africans astray into *soulèvements de mécontents*, "uprisings of malcontents". What was particularly needed was a solid and enlightened formation for the African elite so that they could play an influential role in the African Congress. Indeed Fady's directive was that "Catholics must not stay aloof from this (political) grouping, even as sympathetic observers". Otherwise the Catholic viewpoint would be lost by default. And, worse, the Protestants would have a field day.[76]

Fady's policy was not adopted in the colonial trading centre of Blantyre and southern part of the country where the Dutch Vicar-Apostolic—made Archbishop in 1959—Dr Johannes B. Theunissen presided over the Apostolic Vicariate of Shire staffed by Montfort missionaries. Blantyre Diocese was almost entirely Dutch after Montfort Fathers of other nationalities had separated to staff a new diocese based on Zomba in 1953. The experience of the Catholic Church in the Netherlands was that Protestant domination could best be countered by forming powerful Catholic groupings in civil society topped by a strong Catholic political party. They encouraged such developments in Nyasaland. A Catholic Teachers' Association, for example, broke away from the Nyasaland Teachers' Association in 1956.[77]

By July 1958 when Dr Banda returned to adoring crowds, the Dutch Montforts were probably neither less nor more enthusiastic about a gradualist form of African nationalism than the White Fathers. But there was nothing gradual about the pace of change at the turn of the decade. In September, the African Congress began exploring radical alternatives and contingencies: civil disobedience—and violence if it did not produce results. The resulting February 1959 State of Emergency resulted in forty-seven deaths and put almost 1,500 behind bars including Dr. Banda.[78]

As the detainees were released seven months later, the ANC turned itself into the Malawi Congress Party (MCP) and, after Dr. Banda came out of prison in April 1960, adopted a one-Party state policy and increasingly promoted the *Ngwazi*, in the idiom adopted by Nkrumah in Ghana, as Saviour of the Nation. Aleke Banda, a fiery young acolyte, created a Party propaganda sheet, the *Malawi News*; in it statements were made about nationalising schools and hospitals, and the creation of a national Church. What made matters worse for the Montforts was

227

that over two thirds of the MCP's core membership belonged to the CCAP. This did not look or sound good to them.[79]

The Federation bishops gave limited support to African opposition, saying on 14 October 1959 that it was " a great injustice to impose upon them a form of government unacceptable to them", and condemning "statutory law based on race distinction".[80] But Archbishop Theunissen was convinced that what he saw as the Communist leanings of the MCP required action from the Church not words. He had brought a new Dutch Montfortian to Malawi to develop Catholic Action programmes to combat "Communism", and recruited four more Religious Orders, including the highly effective international Medical Mission Sisters.[81] That was not the half of it. When Fady met Theunissen in early 1960 there were already rumours that he was exploring the potential for a new Catholic Democratic Party. Fady asked him directly, but he was evasive, and then marshalled a number of arguments against such a demarche, but in vain. When a prominent Catholic, John Msonthi, later MCP Minister of Education, organised a visit in June 1960 for Banda and the MCP leadership to meet Fady in Lilongwe, the new Catholic Party was the main contentious point. "Certain Churchmen are seeking to introduce into Malawi the politics of their Mother-Country" Banda asserted perceptively to cap a litany of complaints about the Church's lack of support for him. Fady, with considerable diplomatic skill, replied that the Pope had said the Church rejoiced at the independence of new nations. The bishop declared his confidence in "God-fearing men" and, he believed, "Banda was such a man". He had no difficulty with Catholics joining political parties "provided that their doctrines (sic) and goals do not contradict the Christian ideal".[82]

The rumours about a Christian Democratic Party had substance. John Chester Katsonga was the ex-seminarian son of a catechist, a businessman with a grandiose construction plans for a hotel in Blantyre's Soche township. He had been the African Congress' Blantyre district chairman and a substantial donor to Banda's reception committee. For his pains, he spent most of 1959 in detention and was subsequently marginalised in the new MCP. Sickened by the growing personality cult, not to mention the hole in his pocket, he left the Party. Gilbert Pondeponde, a Lever Brothers' book-keeper, had a similar political trajectory. He left the MCP in August 1960 when Banda made himself President-for-Life. A man of principle, he refused to knuckle under;

Banda only finally eliminated him politically by having him murdered. Just as in Rwanda, the African Catholic Teachers' Association was a forum for political discussion and provided participants for an August meeting on Katsonga's home ground in Soche township. Negotiations at Lancaster House from 25 July to 4 August 1960 had ended with a commitment to Africanise the Executive and Legislative branches of the Nyasaland Government— independence was obviously fast approaching. The Christian Democrat Party was hastily launched with Katsonga as leader and Pondeponde as general-secretary on 14 October 1960.[83]

Theunissen had "given advice" to the new Party and appointed a priest to serve as "spiritual adviser". He supported its launch—though a typewriter from the diocese was the only proven material aid. No matter, it was a spectacular political blunder, "an unfortunate provocation", Fady called it. Banda was already being treated by much of the population as a national leader and British rule was visibly waning. Rosaries and Holy Medals were taken off and destroyed by scared Catholics. Fady had to write to the Governor Sir John Armitage and his wife not to honour earlier commitments to visit his mission stations as news of their imminent arrival had resulted in a near MCP siege of Guillemè Mission. The nationalist movement was in full flood; *"ali oyera achoka"*, all whites must go. The international community of the White Fathers had considerable experience in Africa and knew what nationalism in full flood could mean. A Catholic Democrat finger in the dyke would inevitably be chopped off and washed away.[84]

MCP reaction was indeed swift, an eleven-page attack on the Christian Democrat Party filling the *Malawi News*. It was not simply *ad hominem* but drew on P. Blanshard's infamous anti-Catholic diatribe *Freedom and Catholic Power*, which J.F. Kennedy had to circumnavigate in his Presidential campaign, and on a sinister interpretation of the Catholic Action manual. The Catholic Church was presented as attempting to divide the country, and use Catholic Action as a third column to thwart the legitimate aspirations of the people. People had to be Malawians first and Catholics—a bad—second. The new enemy was "Vatican Imperialism" and its agent Theunissen. Either he "went down" or Dr Banda. The argument was rather undermined by the additional claim that no other bishop supported Theunissen and that the "bishop of Lilongwe is a good friend of our leader Dr Banda".[85]

Banda made haste to meet with Fady. On 31 October, the bishops issued a statement encouraging the desire for Independence and expressing a willingness to work with any government "provided it adhered to
the principles of charity and justice". Katsonga prophetically wrote that
if the MCP came to power one form of oppression would be substituted for another. The African Teachers' Association distanced themselves
from Theunissen while defending the Church. The Apostolic Delegate
in Nairobi was perturbed. On 20 March 1961 the bishops issued an
irenic letter *How to Build a Happy Nation* welcoming forthcoming
elections as " a great step forward towards independence". They insisted that the laity could weigh up and join political parties which
were not anti-Christian but the Church itself, in a time honoured form
of theological levitation, was above politics.[86] The doomed CDP joined
up with another splinter Party to form the Christian Liberation Party
and was trounced at the polls. Members of all opposition Parties were
liable to physical attack. Katsonga's house was burnt to the ground. He
later apologised to Banda. Pondeponde did not and was murdered on
Christmas Eve three years later.[87]

Malawi became independent on 6 July 1964. Theunissen, having
decreed parishes should have either Montforts or Malawian clergy but,
to preserve community life of the Order, no mixing of secular with Religious clergy, opened a racial hornets' nest, and he resigned three years
later. He was succeeded as Archbishop in 1968 by his auxiliary bishop, James Chiona. He joined the only other African bishop, Cornelius
Chitsulo, appointed to a newly formed "African" vicariate of Dedza in
1956, at a time when such arrangements were less sensitive.

The Christian Democrat affair had the long term effect of placing
most of the leadership of the Catholic Church in Malawi on the back
foot, for thirty long years almost mesmerised by the apparent invul-
nerability and power of the *mwini mbumba*, President-for-Life, Dr
Banda with his Homburg hat, fly-whisk, and female dancers.[88] The
Episcopal Conference of Malawi, slow to respond to the direction
given by the Vatican Council, and the social encyclicals of the Popes,
did not agree to Justice and Peace Commissions until 1992, and was
wary of any confrontation with the MCP. Setting up Small Christian
Communities was interpreted as the creation of subversive cells. Dr
Banda's rule encouraged sycophancy, tolerated no opposition, and
was draconian in its punishments for dissidents. Fear prevailed, jus-

tified but corrosive; informers were everywhere. The bishops kept their heads down as did most.

As in the Philippines and Guatemala, the Associations of Men and Women Religious, ARIMA and AMRIM, took a hesitant lead. "We notice a trend towards something like the South American situation of a rich dominant minority in possession of the land, and a majority of poor tenants. We fear this will lead to violence as this cycle of poverty cannot be broken in any other way", they warned in 1983.[89] Fine words were spoken at regional meetings of episcopal conferences but they seemed a substitute for rather than a spur to action. Only a handful of priests, mostly expatriate, took risks, visited detainees, worked for their release and usually were rewarded with deportation.[90] There was a reason for keeping a low profile, important work for the people of Malawi, clinics, education, not endangering colleagues, but the excuses were wearing thin.

Pope John Paul II visited Malawi in May 1989 and spoke privately to the bishops about the need to promote human rights, though he refrained from mentioning the flagrant violations in the country in public. It may have been this private challenge that tipped the scales. Malawi's membership of AMECEA (the Association of Member Episcopal Conferences of East Africa) kept the bishops aware of what their colleagues elsewhere were thinking and doing, and brought them into contact with Justice and Peace Commissions from other countries with their more radical lay agendas. Multi-party elections in Zambia were an encouraging sign, and a team from Zambia had begun Training for Transformation workshops in the White Fathers' dioceses using the radical Paulo Freire methodology. However the disenchantment of the Protestant CCAP at the impoverishment of the country and violation of human rights was being detected in ecumenical encounters. Banda's Central Chewa regionalism was stopping better educated teachers from the North teaching outside their home region, causing staff problems and shortages for all Churches. As in Rwanda, power in the regime had been reduced to a small regional clique around the President.[91]

More likely the Kenyan bishops' courageous condemnation of Arap Moi's regime in Kenya, *On the Present Situation in Kenya*, published on 20 June 1990, and read shortly afterwards by the cautious Archbishop James Chiona, pushed the Malawian bishops finally to act. The Kenyan bishops' letter described a state of affairs that sounded like a carbon copy of that in Malawi. It warned that "the philosophy of National Security" condemned by the Pope at Puebla "may become installed in our country". Chiona was strongly influenced by it. The experience of Latin America was stimulating the thinking of African bishops. Monsignor Tarcisius Ziyaye, soon to be bishop-elect of Lilongwe, had been profoundly moved and influenced by a video about Archbishop Romero of San Salvador. Romero's martyrdom had made him realise how central being a "witness for justice" ought to be for a bishop. In December 1990 he abandoned hope of progress and said "enough". The other bishops drew their understanding of the prevailing dire conditions of poverty from the extensive Catholic participation in the education and health systems of the country.[92]

It was only after 27 January 1992, after Bishop Chimole was challenged by the CCAP on why the Catholic Church was so acquiescent, that the bishops implemented a plan to write a pastoral similar to the Kenyan bishops. They produced it with great dispatch and secrecy in one month with a team of six drafters working in a standing committee. Because he was Irish, Bishop John Roche who had left Nigeria after the Biafran Civil War, and had been superior of the Kiltegan Fathers, was suspected by the MCP of being the *éminence grise* behind it. He had played an important role "topping and tailing" the text and working for a long weekend on the third and final draft, but was not "the author". He was singled out for special denunciation by the MCP, arrested on Good Friday and deported. The British High Commissioner sent a car to accompany him to the border to be on the safe side.[93]

The letter, *Living Our Faith*, which resulted from an unusual degree of cooperation between the different dioceses and missionary orders, was read at mass on 8 March 1992, sometimes to the astonishment and spontaneous applause of the congregation, and reached tens of thousands of people. "These are our brothers and sisters who are in prison without knowing what they are charged with, or when their case will be heard," they wrote. The story of the bishops' "scathing attack" on Banda's destruction of civil liberties was covered on the BBC World Service the next day.

The pastoral, when contrasted with Bishop Lamont at his scabrous best, or worst, was an essay in diplomacy: the opening sally, "we joyfully acclaim the progress which has taken place in our country, which we attribute to the climate of peace and stability" might have come as a surprise to a population suffering a severe drought and widespread hunger. In the core of the text there was much "this is most regrettable", "we would like to draw your attention to", and "we can only regret". But there was plain speaking about rights and poverty in Malawi. As the BBC rightly highlighted, the strongest passages focussed on freedom of expression and association, with implicit accusations that the judiciary was in the pocket of the executive, that citizens were coerced into buying Party cards, and so on. The total effect in a country in which fear and compliance ruled supreme, and from a Bishops Conference assumed until then to be incapable of offering resistance, was remarkably damning.[94]

The government response was to require the bishops to appear at the Police Training Centre in Blantyre where they spent eight hours with the Catholic Inspector-General of Police, Lunguzi, accompanied by senior officers from the military, police and security services. A line-by-line "refutation" of the pastoral from Lunguzi followed. At the same time what amounted to a national convention of the MCP led by the Minister of State in the Office of the President, John Tembo, took place in the headquarters of the MCP in Lilongwe. The proceedings, as was normal, were recorded by the Malawi Broadcasting Corporation for future editing. The delegates, shocked and frightened, outdid each other in denunciations, threats, calumny and obscene abuse of the bishops, particularly of Chimole and Chiona. Tembo spoke as if the Christian Democrat affair was about to be revived. Banda later repeated the line on "historically treacherous Catholics" but gave the Malawian bishops a way out by blaming a foreigner, an Irish Catholic, Monsignor John Roche, for the pastoral.[95]

That was the response of the delegates in their more serene moments. The secretary of the Lilongwe's Women's League suggested that "to make things easier we just have to kill these bishops". The refrain was taken up by others at the meeting, to hysterical applause. Someone reported the death threats to an embassy in Lilongwe and they rapidly reached London. Foreign media got hold of the story, and some of the bishops briefly went into hiding. They had been in real danger. Diplomatic pressure on Banda, notably threats to cut off aid, was immediately and effectively exerted. There was in addition an international demand for detainees to be released, Red Cross visits, and freedom of speech. Banda realised that Tembo had started a firestorm and hastily backed off.[96]

This was a long way from being a replay of the Christian Democrat affair. The vast majority of the population and certainly the Catholics, though frightened, supported the bishops. The pastoral, although declared seditious and effectively banned, was avidly read and actually sold by entrepreneurial Catholics in markets. Rosaries were also selling like hot cakes as a symbol of resistance. Churches were packed. Despite police intimidation, the Catholic students at the university marched to the cathedral and issued a letter of support. Theirs was one among many that were flooding in from governments and Church leaders abroad.[97]

It was at this point, one month after the pastoral had sparked the equivalent of a velvet revolution, that the Vatican intervened. Archbishop Giovanni de Andrea was sent as a special envoy from Pope John Paul II, and conferred with the nuncio Archbishop Guiseppe Lanza. They proceeded to draft an episcopal memorandum for the bishops to be presented as a peace offering to Dr Banda. Tembo wanted an apology. The bishops refused. The final miserable document showing Vatican influence ended with "there is no way the Bishops could want to be disrespectful to His Excellency the Life President of the Republic, whom they hold in high esteem". It would have been even worse if the Papal representatives had had their way.[98]

The Vatican may have thought its representatives were saving the Church from destruction at the hands of the MCP. On the basis of the leaked transcripts of the infamous MCP Lilongwe meeting, the MCP must have seemed like an African branch of the Mafia. But the danger was past. The support from parishioners against attacks on "their bishops" and international pressure had seen to that. The two Vatican diplomats left without even reporting back to the bishops of Malawi on their meeting with Banda, leaving them with several disconsolate priests who felt the bishops had indeed apologised. The future looked turbulent and uncertain.[99]

By the end of 1992, the world's, and Africa's, geo-political contours had changed dramatically. The collapse of Communist governments in Eastern Europe and the implosion of the Soviet Union from 1989-1992 gave hope that a glad new dawn for democracy would also break over Africa. The image of the time was not only the Berlin Wall coming down but Nelson Mandela walking out from house-arrest in Cape Town, a symbol of new hope. Like some bright beacon South Africa had broken through to multiparty democracy. So why not Malawi? Banda was now eminently dispensable and isolated. Barely one year after the Bishops' pastoral letter, Malawi rejected the one-party state in a referendum. As the results were announced rejoicing crowds flocked to celebrate around their local bishop's house. One year later the MCP were finally defeated in national elections after a successful campaign by a diverse ecumenical coalition.[100]

Malawians were rid of Kamuzu. At a ripe old age, he soon went to an unpretentious grave by one of Lilongwe's highways, leaving behind the $320 million he had amassed. In a land where the path of nationalism was never straight, a velvet Christian revolution brought to power a new Party, the United Democratic Front, and a new State President, a Muslim who had held high rank in the MCP, Bakili Muluzi.

The changed context and sense of expectation of the early 1990s was caught by the bishops in *Choosing Our Future*, their pastoral issued before the 1993 Malawi referendum. "The new Spirit is now sweeping through all of Africa. Some have even spoken of a new independence comparable to the liberation from colonial domination...Citizens of one country after another have demanded that political power be restored to the people and that elected representatives become more accountable to the electorate. What people are seeking is genuine democracy in which the leaders are servants of the people...not government by or for the privileged few." The mood did not last long. But, at the least, even in the face of dire poverty and a devastating HIV/AIDS epidemic, the defeat and passing of Dr Banda, had made a space for democracy and renewed hope.

Midwife and Mediator

The Malawian bishops were not alone in tapping into a sense of short-lived political euphoria. Something akin to the "Second Liberation" of Africa was being talked about. So was there, at last, something new coming out of Africa? In Ghana and Uganda it looked that way. There was a general acceptance, stemming from chronic problems in post-Communist Russia, that a vibrant civil society was vital for democracy and good governance. Likewise it was acknowledged that the Church, when seen as emblematic of civil society, could be a key contributor to democratisation through education and training, or by mediating difficult transitions. This was as true of Gabon as of Guatemala. In failed, and in failing states where nationalism was exhausted and decayed, there was simply no other alternative source of legitimacy. Mainstream Church leaders were the last vestiges of moral authority and the only—fragile—vessels for public confidence.

Pope John Paul II's dance on the grave of the Communist system, in his 1991 pastoral letter *Centesimus Annus*, gave democracy Rome's official *nihil obstat* and blessing. "The church values the democratic system inasmuch as it ensures the participation of citizens in making political choices, guarantees to the governed the possibility of both electing and holding accountable those who govern them, and of replacing them through peaceful means when appropriate." Democracy had dared to speak its name as the unequivocal choice of the Vatican.

So in Africa as in Latin America from 1990-94, Church leaders, particularly the Francophone bishops, were in demand as mediators and midwives of democratisation. By popular demand, they assumed chairmanship of politically charged secular National Conferences. These were either aimed at stopping a descent into anarchy, or moving dictatorships to multiparty elections. Bishop Laurent Monsengwo Pasinya of Kisangani, later a prominent member of the Pontifical Council for Justice and Peace, was elected to chair Zaire's National Conference in 1991. In Gabon and Togo local bishops also presided. After chairing the National Conference, Monsignor Isidore de Souza, the Archbishop of Cotonou, was surprisingly given permission by Rome to become—temporarily—President of the Haut Conseil de la République in Benin during the transition phase to democracy. Monsignor Ernest Kombo received the same dispensation in the Congo alongside Sister Brigitte Yengo. The question was, after piloting the process through the political rapids to successful national elections, what was going to be the Church leaders' contribution to consolidating democracy? Sadly not a great deal. It was usually back to their daily job.[101]

9
INCULTURATION AND DIALOGUE
WITH ISLAM

During the 1990s five continent-wide synods were held to reflect on and celebrate the coming of the third Christian Millennium. It was a new internal Church dialogue of sorts. These consultative synods indicated a recognition of a degree of pluralism in the Church, as well as an attempt to keep it under firm central control. Rome prepared the *lineamenta*, preparatory documents, and orchestrated the summary document published afterwards. But the local Church sometimes had the last word. After the African synod, *Ecclesia in Africa* was simplified and published in Tanzania as a booklet, *Cooked in an African Pot*, designed to nourish African Catholics in ways that the African bishops wanted.

Ecclesia in Asia, an "Apostolic Exhortation" produced with due delay after the 1998 Asian Synod, was presented in New Delhi by Pope John Paul II on 6 November 1999. It diluted and diverted the thrust of local bishops' concerns in order to reflect the views of the Pope. Nothing very new in that—local Churches proposed and Rome disposed. Usually post-synodal documents, prepared under the steely control of the synods' general-secretary, the Belgian Cardinal Jan Schotte, eliminated what the Vatican did not want to hear or have broadcast. This did not stop the Asian synod highlighting a fundamental challenge for Catholicism that would not diminish in the twenty-first century: the relationship between Christianity and culture in an age of globalisation.

The Asian continent held half the number of Catholics in Africa, and half the Asian Catholics lived in one country, Philippines.[1] But there were more Asian dioceses, bishops and priests, their communities had greater historical depth, and they were in a better position to stand up to Rome when necessary. They lived as a tiny minority—107 million among Asia's 3.65 billion at the time of *Ecclesia in Asia*—in Hindu,

Buddhist, Confucian and Islamic societies, and had to co-exist with and make sense of the religions around them. The Federation of Asian Bishops' Conferences (FABC), set up in 1972, was a comparatively cohesive grouping whose radical theology came to rest on a challenging trinity of dialogue, inculturation, and liberation. Building the Kingdom of God was understood by many as the sole purpose of the Church. These neuralgic themes and views guaranteed that Rome would be pained.

The Japanese bishops dismissed sections of the 1998 synod's preparatory documents as "offensive". That was not the only complaint. Most participants felt that "the official liturgy is often experienced as alien and does not touch their hearts". The Indians saw the Church called to "ecclesial conversion", to become a Church of the Poor. The dragon of liberation theology was alive and well. The Pope, unabashed by the rejection of the *lineamenta* and the emphases of the bishops, was gently corrected after his exhortation in New Delhi. "Yes, it is true there is no authentic evangelisation without announcing Jesus Christ Saviour of the whole human race," replied Cardinal J. Darmaatmadja. "But for Asia, there will be no complete evangelisation unless there is dialogue with other religions and cultures."[2]

Controversies over culture have persisted since the great century-long clash, 1645-1744, between the Jesuit and other missions in India and China over the Chinese and Malabar rites. Or, come to that, since the first dispute within the Church, recorded in the *Acts of the Apostles*, about circumcision and Jewish identity. Ricci and da Nobili promoted rites adapted to Chinese and Indian spirituality and Rome finally ruled against them. Some three hundred years later, Jesuit theologians, the Sri Lankan Aloysius Pieris and the Indian, Michael Amaladoss, were fighting their corner in the same fray, following the lead of their Master General, Pedro Arrupe, a missionary to Japan.

How much real dialogue was there about culture in the Church that reflected its global nature? The high level exchange in New Delhi encapsulated the growing tension in a World Church between universality and particularity in the new context of globalisation. During the synod, the Indonesian Carmelite Bishop of Manikwari, Francis Hadisumarta, openly called for radical decentralisation with, as in the Middle East, new Patriarchates and local Asian rites. But the synod also showed Rome in its dominant mode of policing, attempting to shut down debate, in this instance unsuccessfully.

Holy Hybrids or Wholly Syncretist?

During its long history, Indian Catholicism lived out in villages in Tamil Nadu, Kerala and along the coast of South India had taken root in the structures of Hindu religion and caste society where, filtered through bishops, priests, Religious and catechists, it met and interacted with the "global Catholicism" of Rome. This produced remarkable expressions of the contemplative life such as the Saccidananda Ashram at Shanti-vanam, otherwise known as the Hermitage of the Most Holy Trinity, founded in 1950 by two French priests, Jules Monchanin, and the Benedictine, Henri le Saux. The name came from the triple attributes of Brahman, Being, Awareness and Bliss, *sat, cit, ananda* resonating with the Trinitarian being of the One God. Only after the Carmelite, Bede Griffiths, took over the community were Indian monks attracted. In their struggles to bridge the divide between Christian and Hindu mysticism, are to be found many insights relevant to debates about religious diversity after the Council.[3] The cultural history of Asian Catholicism still takes place at this dynamic intersection of global and local, mystical and theological, elite and popular.

Africa and parts of Latin America present a similar spectrum of interactions within village Catholicism, both dysfunctional and creative. The errant Archbishop Emmanuel Milingo of Lusaka, faith healer to Zambians and Italians alike, manipulative thorn in the side of the Vatican, a "Moonie" now married and excommunicated, shows what can happen when things go wrong.[4] The elegant reverence, spirituality and evocative symbolism of the danced mass of the Malawian Poor Clare Sisters in their beautiful African-styled Church in Lilongwe shows what can go right.

In a world of truncated space-time created by extraordinary advances in communications technology, the global Church has to deal synchronously with a vast cultural array: Buddhism, Hinduism, Islam, euthanasia, stem cell research, spirit possession and ritual healing are only a small sample. Small wonder that a desire for uniformity undermines a quest for universality sensitive to diversity, and the perspective of eternity obscures the urgency for change. Rome remains in favour of what became known in the 1970s as "inculturation", defined carefully though elusively as "the insertion of Christianity in the various human cultures" and "the intimate transformation of authentic cultural values through their integration in Christianity".[5] Yet, the Vatican has been unable to acknowledge that its own Christianity is also "inculturated", that in all its works and pomp, doctrinal preoccupations and dislikes, Rome occupies its own particular faith-culture. A significant group of African theologians has no such illusions. Father Laurenti Magesa, a Ugandan missiologist, tellingly defines inculturation as "the process whereby the faith already embodied in one culture encounters another culture".[6]

Europe and North America at the turn of the millennium represented only a shrinking 40 per cent of the world's Catholic community—though still provided probably 75 per cent of its cross-border missionaries. So Church leaders in Latin America, Asia, Africa and Oceania (the Pacific) had numbers on their side, a reason for finding Rome's perennial policing, and the cavalier treatment of their concerns, unjustified.[7] This partial blindness at the directive heart of Catholicism might have been easier to accept in New Delhi if Rome had not appeared to believe that it was the custodian of something generically labelled "Christian culture"—readily interpreted as an export item—constructed with attentive quality control, a gift to be imported gratefully by the world's cultures.[8] This promotion of Christian culture, or rather Catholic culture, was the source of considerable confusion and attendant consternation.

In March 1993, Cardinal Joseph Ratzinger delivered a paper in Hong Kong to a meeting convoked by his Sacred Congregation for the Doctrine of the Faith, before the doctrinal commissions of the Asian Episcopal Conferences, and the Presidents of their Bishops' Conferences. In it he presented the concept of "interculturality". He implied that Christianity was itself a culture and that "other cultures" contained both spirituality and religion. The assembled theologians construed the lecture as an authoritative presentation of the state of play doctrinally on the phenomenon of "inculturation". In short it was a misnomer; a different term was needed. The talk, designed to clip the wings of Asian theologians, aroused little press interest. In 1994 Cardinal Ratzinger gave another talk on the topic, a bland, uncontentious presentation to the African Synod.[9] Suddenly in April 1995, the Hong Kong lecture emerged from obscurity, filling three pages of the official *L'Osservatore Romano*, and was distributed around the world to Catholic documentation centres. This showcase treatment did not look like a minor essay for academics, rather the official position.[10]

Ratzinger's intervention started from the reasonable premise that the Faith could not be identified with any particular local or national culture. But the idea behind amounted to an uneasy "two cultures" theory: local and national cultures against a universal "Catholic culture" to which every Catholic in the world belonged. Though he apparently considered this universal culture historically grounded, and open to anthropological description, there was no direct indication as to where it might reside at any particular moment, except in the history of *the* Church, God's chosen history, nor what qualified anyone to belong to it, beyond baptism. He seemed to conflate this "Christian culture" in a confusing fashion with both the Incarnation and Truth. He had publicly stated that European culture had been touched by Christianity in an "indelible and irrevocable way". So, notwithstanding the hybrid Jewish culture of Jesus' world—Hellenised to different degrees—"Christian culture" for Ratzinger referred to a Hellenic Christian heritage safeguarded in good times and bad by European Catholicism.[11] The bearer of this culture was the Church itself rather than "the Kingdom of God", the building of which was emphasised strongly by Asian theologians and many of their bishops. With Benedict's Papacy Christianity became indissolubly, and thus normatively, linked in Rome with Hellenist thought patterns and categories. This was not music to the ears of most Church leaders in Asia, Africa and Latin America.

Joseph Ratzinger's understanding of Catholicism and culture, then and as Pope, seemed a long way from Pope Paul VI's famous injunction to African Catholics in Kampala in 1968: "You may and you must have an African Christianity". True, it was improbable that his audience heard Paul in the way that he intended. It is hard to know exactly what he did intend. Permission to press on was heard. Where did it stop? Did Pope Paul mean that Catholics proclaimed Jesus victorious amid a plethora of benign, malign and ancestral spirits, demons and angels, guardians of the land and disrupters of social harmony, Hindu Gods and local saints? Or did it just mean having drums at mass, perhaps even some dancing and ululating, adapted mortuary rites and birth ceremonies; otherwise nothing more nor less by way of belief than the content of the catechism?

During his visit to Africa in May 1980, Pope John Paul II let the bishops know in private that he was not happy with the way "pagan" practices were mixed up with the faith. "The mistake we make," the Episcopal Conference of Malawi answered Rome in 1992 in reply to the *lineamenta* questions for the African synod, "is to see inculturation as consisting in the efforts we make to insert African cultural elements into some 'Christian' thing e.g. the liturgy which reduces the task of inculturation to a very cosmetic exercise". The Propaganda Fide repeatedly enjoined Catholics to "preserve culture" and to reject what was "religiously erroneous", but this did not *solve* the question, merely restated it.[12] Thirteen years passed before the Zairean rite mass, put forward for Rome's *imprimatur*, and opening with prayers to the ancestors, was granted approval. Liturgy and hierarchically led worship was rightly seen as the contested intersection of the universal and particular, the heart of Christian life. If its form and content could change, then almost anything could change.

The lived Catholicism of countless Christians around the world was embedded, not in Greek thought but in a changing and dynamic religious practice that drew on enduring parts of diverse cultures. Religious structures and symbols were "remoulded, dismantled and recombined, or rejected" in interaction with the wider Church. The interpretation of Christianity using an "indigenous symbolic logic" was, and remains, a process of constant active synthesis. The how, what and where of this synthesis depends on varied social relations and on different expressions of political power.[13] The result of these interactions taking place "at the grassroots" could be, and was, described in a variety of ways. And these ways, " hybrid", "syncretistic", "animist" or "popular", carried a variety of implicit value-judgements that educated Catholics could, and did, resent, while uneducated Catholics found them alien and incomprehensible. Put in another way, a Catholic identity was claimed by, and attributed to, countless people whose religious conduct reflected a rich combination of beliefs, cosmologies and rituals. These bore features that Rome, even in its more liberal or browbeaten moments, found difficult to recognise as Roman Catholic or even Christian. And this was made more problematic by the fact that many of these practices were similar or identical to those against which a reforming Church had struggled for centuries in Europe.[14]

The Post-Tridentine Church had promoted a reforming Counter-Reformation Catholicism whose patrimony and core impulses survived until, and after, the Second Vatican Council. In Africa, most preconciliar trained missionaries working in rural areas therefore saw themselves as evangelisers first—in competition particularly with Protestantism and Islam—then as border guards protecting against, "superstition" and "paganism", constant marauders across the permeable frontiers of African Catholicism. The Sword of *the* Spirit cut through the tangle of taboo and pollution. The missionaries were not opposed to their converts seeking protection in the spirit world, but sacred power had to be sought exclusively from within the Christian framework of salvation, in practice through Mary and the Saints. Who the convert prayed to was what mattered. How could it have been otherwise? A missiology concerned with conversion of peoples and cultures, followed by "planting the Church", was by definition about establishing and sustaining difference—or what was conversion to and from—and what was so distinctive about the new Church institutions, schools, parishes, and the Gospel message they imparted? But this routine of planting often produced a potted plant struggling in a lump of foreign soil, swiftly buffeted by strong political winds. More than anything else, the fine-tuned translation of the Gospel message by generations of indigenous lay catechists, adapting the missionaries' message often literally on the hoof, or the bicycle, allowed African Christians to make it their own.[15]

Anthropological insights seeped into missiology, either from practical experience—Cardinal Lavigerie instructed the early White Fathers for example to learn the language immediately and observe and record local cultures—or from university courses. Indigenous clergy and new Catholic elites did not sail under the flag of a homogeneous religious identity. In consequence, the contradictions of official inculturation could not be ignored and bishops were obliged to respond. Debates on *Ad Gentes* at the Second Vatican Council, the schema on the missions, allowed the thinking of bishops from diverse cultures, insistent on their own interpretation of inculturation, to be widely heard.[16] The expansion of regional and continental conferences of bishops was an opportunity for discussion and sharing, reinforcing the significance of cultural particularism in the problems of evangelisation rehearsed at the Council.

The Council created new difficulties but not always in obvious ways. Whilst the mindset of the pre-conciliar Church continued, comfortable both culturally and theologically with a discourse of spiritual power and protection, sacrifice and libations, the prevailing wind was not necessarily set against creative adaptation. No harm in statues, novenas, processions of Our Lady, petitions prayerfully made to saints, and guardian angels. So, whether in the highlands of Bolivia or in South India, Catholics had a number of ways they could interpret and handle misfortune and suffering, appealing to a variety of Christian saints and/or to other denizens of another realm who might bridge the gap between a helpless humanity and heavenly powers. Thus at the most critical moment in Bishop Belo's struggle against the Indonesian occupation of East Timor, taking a statue of Our Lady to join the pantheon of the Timorese ancestral spirits on Mount Ramelau, he led a large pilgrimage high into the central mountain range of the island.[17]

The leaders of the post-conciliar Church sought pre-eminently, almost exclusively, to be "exemplars" of Christ in a witness of love and service and to be dispensers of moral education.[18] The business of explaining evil and controlling it—though not predicting it—was marginal to their thinking. "The Social Gospel" and credit unions were not meant to deal with misfortunes thought to be caused by evil spirits and demons. Neither sadly could they deliver the benefits—the "Goods"—spiritual or material, fast enough for many poor people in the "Third World". In South India, the poor turned to a variety of intercessors: Saint Alphonsa, a nun who died in 1946, to the divine power, *shakti*, believed to reside in Mary, to St Anthony the Hermit or the sea-God Kadalamma. Their role was to protect, to console, and to order the acute vulnerability of the poor in a dangerous world. Each required appropriate religious behaviour to gain their attention, and there was nothing said or done in Rome would stop Catholics appealing to them. And the Asian bishops knew it. The gap between the faith of popular Catholicism and that of Catholic leaders and elite seemed daunting. Village Christians had "constantly to reconcile the demands of a universal catholic faith with those of caste, kinship and the management of impurity or misfortune".[19]

Popular Catholicism

Those searching for some way to describe the vast and rich texture of religious expression found around the World Church, opted readily for the label "popular Catholicism", *religiosidad popular* found in CELAM publications and at Puebla. The term comes from the period when radical theology from Latin America was gaining a wide audience. Its positive ring derived from a disposition to acknowledge the spiritual wisdom found in "the people". But it also reflected a methodological refusal to adopt essentialist and intellectualist accounts of Catholicism in favour of simple description. In the language of the Latin American bishops at Santo Domingo in 1991, popular Catholicism was a "privileged expression of the inculturation of the faith".[20] So the heart of the matter was discovering the positive spiritual significance of how most people experienced their Catholicism, not how, in a normative sense, they ought to be Catholics.

Valuing and respecting popular Catholicism was not the first impulse of eager European reformers after the Council, some of whom removed the array of statues that stood guard over the pre-conciliar church, and discouraged popular devotions that had proliferated around the celebration of the Eucharist. Nor were Latin American liberation theologians much attracted by a popular prayer life revolving around healing of sickness, or avoidance of barrenness and misfortune, along with offerings to saints. So they were not at first much inclined to favour promotion of Quechua and Aymara Indian theology.[21] There was enough of the Enlightenment project in some post-conciliar thinking, particularly liberation theology, for popular Catholicism to seem like a—minor—impediment to "building the kingdom". Drains got dug by communitarian action not by interventions from the spirit world, just as meteorology best explained rainfall rather than the efficacy of sacrifices at rain shrines. Popular religion looked, for better or for worse, like a counter-culture to modernity.

And yet an option for the poor surely meant that, as the bishops at Santo Domingo intimated, the particular piety of the poor had to be valued and cherished. The Pentecostal Churches that burgeoned in Latin America, and sucked in Catholics in the millions from the 1960s onwards, showed that the Church neglected popular religious consciousness at its peril. The attempt to transform or co-opt the content of popular devotions to a more radical religious agenda and strategies against poverty never satisfied the desperate, immediate, personal and spiritual neediness of the poor. Even in Sandinista Nicaragua, militants on both sides of the civil war maintained a devotion to St Dominic and Mary Most Pure.[22] For every woman who could identify with the revolutionaries' Mary who prayed for the mighty to be pulled down from their thrones there were ten who saw themselves in the Mary who stood at the foot of the Cross, or met her son on the way to Calvary. The beloved Virgin of Guadeloupe heard their prayers, and it did not matter if in 1531 a young Christianised Indian sharecropper's vision of the Blessed Virgin doubled as that of the Aztec Goddess of land and fertility, Tonantzin. Mary or Tonantzin, she would "hear their lamentations and remedy all their miseries, sufferings and sorrows". Nor, were Quechua or Aymara Catholics concerned that *Pachamama*, their traditional Earth Mother, was the other face the Virgin Mother of Christ.[23]

Yet it took liberation theology a decade before the core issues of indigenous religion and spirituality came strongly to the foreground of its concerns. The real clash with local cultures came in the realm of spirituality. Not just liberation theologians were affected. The failure to handle underlying questions of inculturation left virtually no part of the global Church untouched. Put simply it became apparent that neither liberation theology nor hierarchical authoritarianism and proclamation, nor Nationalism and Communism, would dislodge the millions claiming a Catholic identity from their own—changing—spiritual and cultural anchorage. This spirituality included a sense of the self as inhabiting a textured world of spirits and spiritual forces that accommodated the Christian symbols and the content of the Catholic catechism and sermons. And this other world often subjected the Catholic symbols and story to unexpected modifications and developments. Any incompatibility was in the eye of the beholder, with their disenchanted and rational Catholic identity, worried about boundaries and limits, yet often reared on the internalised *succubi* of modernity, Freud's mental forces.

"The content of the faith," declared Pope Paul VI closing the 1974 Rome synod of evangelisation, "is either Catholic or it is not".[24] Pure wishful thinking. It was not that simple. And, to repeat the obvious, under the impact of globalisation there is now a growing choice of religious identities for the burgeoning elites of Asia in India and China who are breaking free from their "basic iconic anchorages" in the major religions, particularly, and for those in Europe, a market in religiosity in reaction to "disenchantment" and growing secularisation.[25]

Ancestors and Angels

Pope Paul VI's endorsement of an African Christianity allowed local Church leaders and missionaries to implement a programme of approved inculturation from above. The Catholic Faculty of Theology in Kinshasa immediately took up this theme with a colloquium on African theology.

The Vatican Secretariat for Non-Christians even initiated a dialogue with African religions staged at the Gaba Pastoral Institute in Uganda. As in Asia, where the Vietnamese bishops gave permission for offerings to ancestors to be placed under the altar, the question of ancestral spirits was crucial. Cardinal Yo Ping of Nanjing had been an early advocate of inculturation and the Chinese bishops in Taiwan and Hong Kong began to incorporate Confucian and ancestor elements into the liturgy after *Evangelii Nuntiandi* in 1974. Their influence in the Federation of Asian Bishops Conferences was significant. One of the most important African theological contributions on ancestors came from Professor Benezet Bujo in Kinshasa whose Christology of Jesus as the "Proto-Ancestor" gives unprecedented importance to ancestral veneration for an African theology. This followed on the Anglophone work of Edward Fashole-Luke in the 1970s that set the ancestral world in the context of the Catholic understanding of the Communion of Saints.[26]

Perhaps because Rome was not entirely sure what it thought about its inherited mediaeval accounts of the afterlife, limbo and purgatory, adaptation of mortuary rites became a fruitful domain for experiment. But the many different beliefs about what rituals were necessary for the wellbeing of both the living community and the departed human spirit were not easily negotiable at a village level because they dealt with "the last things", literally life and death decisions. The Shona rites of *Kurova Guva* in Zimbabwe, for example, involve *kusuma*, the living ritually handing over the spirit of the deceased to the spirit world, an event that takes place a year or more after burial. There is a ritual beer drink and sacrifice of a "goat of grief"; the occasion is as important, if not more important, than burial. In the interim period the spirit, *muzimu* is believed to be in a liminal "black" (*mutema*) state, angrily wandering in the bush. Through *kurova guva*, literally the "beating" of the grave, the deceased is brought back into harmony with the living and with the ancestral members of the family. Beginning in 1977, *Musande* or *Bavadeyi,* an official Christian version involving the priest

247

sprinkling grain fermented for the beer drink with Holy Water, prayers and hymns, was introduced by the Church in recognition that the early missionaries' condemnation of the practice could not be sustained, and that, for Zimbabweans, Christian burial was far from the last word. The new rite was revised in 1982 to bring it closer to the original in form. The key differences were symbolic and narrative: the goat sacrifice now represented Christ's sacrifice, Holy Water replaced "medicine", prayers were addressed to God on behalf of the deceased, and the spirit was admitted to heaven rather than to a more terrestrial spirit realm.[27]

The Church had more difficulty with spiritual forces that could not be confined to the circumscribed familial role of ancestral spirits and which were clearly making more sweeping and competitive claims on believers. Adaptations in such instances were often the result of creative responses at a more grassroots level of leadership, and unofficial. In the Malawian rain cult for example, *tunga*, a snake spirit, an emanation or messenger of the Chewa High God *Chisumphi*, traditionally visits and possesses one important shrine priestess. By the late 1960s, though, the now male shrine priest, a catechist, explained that it was *mzimu woyera*, the Holy Spirit who visited the shrine.[28] At the distinctly non-Christian end of the cultural spectrum were Malawi's ancient all-male *nyau* masked dancers.

The *nyau* had many facets. It re-enacted in the Chewa creation myth, the reestablishment of the harmony lost between animals, human beings, and spirits. The pre-war missionaries were strongly opposed, the *gule* dance was associated with highly sexual female initiation rites, obscene ribaldry towards women, and intense drumming. A Christianised initiation rite was introduced. However, the associations of drumming with the *nyau* cult meant for many years that drums were banned in church by missionary and Malawian bishops alike, and only much later reluctantly accepted.[29] The *nyau* "cult" also practised inculturation, which included a great variety of masks and structures; one incorporated an imitation of a Portuguese colonialist from the sixteenth century, another Pope John Paul II celebrating his 1989 visit to Malawi. The dancer in the Pope mask, known as Yohane (John) carrying a fly whisk—a badge of office also carried by the President—performed with energy and dignity, sometimes kneeling and blessing people. He wore a red cross on his back. The crowd chanted "welcome, welcome, the Pope is really coming". "Yohane has caused great turmoil to those who like crooked things and like to hide the truth. Everything is in the open now because of Yohane." Originating in a hunter-gatherer ritual several millennia old, this was an extraordinary expression of popular hope rather than reality—the Malawi bishops' famous pastoral letter came only three years later, in 1992.[30]

The *nyau* pulled into their religious repertoire the contestational, prophetic, indeed political dimension of Catholicism. Nonetheless the Church justifiably saw itself in opposition to the cult. It was a rival religion with a rival cosmology even if Chewa Christians simply enjoyed the spectacle. As in all genuine inculturation, the Pope mask was a sign of respect. It illustrated how religious boundaries between old and new were highly permeable in both directions.

Healing and Evil

The official Church has no fundamental objection to individuals participating in faith-healing despite its propensity for evolving into a rival religious cult. The shrine at Lourdes annually draws popular pilgrimages led by bishops. Not only is healing undeniably a practice derived from Biblical and apostolic times, but exorcism is part of the orthodox European repertoire of Catholic approaches to possession, even if used as a last resort and treated with the greatest caution. A burgeoning Catholic charismatic movement around the world encourages ecstatic states and believes firmly in the healing power of the Spirit. Problems occurred when a bishop, priest, and to a lesser degree, a women, discovers that "God had given them the power of healing", and goes on to use this power to the exclusion of their normal duties, subverting ecclesiastical administration.

Archbishop Milingo of Lusaka, for example, acted as a Christian healer from 1973 until 1983, when he was forced to resign by the Vatican. By this time he was inducing states of spirit possession among women in his congregations—by an extended elevation of the host and repetitive chanting—and writing extensively about witches and the power of the Devil working through them, while drawing on themes of healing as liberation. As a priest he had set up the Zambia Helpers' Society to provide health care in the Lusaka townships, and founded a "pious association" intended to become a religious congregation, the "Daughters of the Redeemer". Before submitting in 1979 to demands from fellow African bishops to end public healing sessions, he was drawing crowds of up to 4,000, largely urban-based and predominantly women. After a Vatican investigation he was finally summoned to Rome in April 1982.[31]

Father Felician Nkwera and his Marian Faith Healing Ministry in Tanzania followed a similar path to suspension and excommunication. He brought the added dimension of revelations, which he claimed to have been given him by the Virgin Mary, coupled with a religious appeal to Tanzanian nationalism as the "Chosen Nation". The creation of a structured organisation, the *wanamaombi*, suggested the birth of a new sect. Both Nkwera and Milingo provided an explanation of and response to human distress. Both saw themselves as chosen to serve in a contest between Good and Evil in which they were gifted by God to be major combatants. Both drew on a spectrum of symbols from modern Christian to pre-Christian and non-Christian. In Nkwera's case there was an attempt to transform a secular national identity. Neither could be fitted into elite ecclesiastical structures. Both created a cult following. They illustrated an inexorable drift beyond the limits of Christian practice and belief perceived as acceptable; for the Church they moved away from Christian healing into spiritual warfare. If "modernity", the secular worldview, cluster of beliefs and practices that claims to be creator of material wealth through economic growth, is taken as the yardstick, then the Vatican was on the side of the Moderns in Africa rather than the Angels.[32]

Emergent African theology, at its weakest, kept a narrow focus on culture, promoting anti-Western, anti-missionary, essentialist and uncritical accounts of African culture and worldview. This was a theology that neglected to explore the full implications of making the African spirit world, one of its major themes, more important than poverty alleviation and health care.[33] Down-to-earth questions were not often seen as problematic. It was rather the condescension of the West. The primary question for African theologians was existential and about identity; in the words of Cardinal Paul Zougrana of Burkina Faso, "our very being must not be conferred on us from outside".[34] At a more affective level, as Cardinal Maurice Otunga of Kenya said after baptising his polygamous father on his deathbed, who could be expected to condemn polygamy as bad and immoral when they had grown up in a polygamous family? The Vatican Council aroused new expectations.

Young Zambian and Malawian seminarians at Kachebere were excited at the arrival of the first black staff member in 1964 and asked if he would support their new "African Way of Life club". Courses on African affairs and Africanisation were put on for seminarians. The old, lapidary seminary manuals suddenly appeared less like tablets of stone from Mount Sinai.[35]

Outside South Africa, liberation theology seemed to appeal, at most, to only one or two of the leading theologians in each African country. Then, in contrast to the African poor, most theologians formed a relatively privileged clerical elite, protected by a higher standard of living from the worst ravages of the four horsemen of the Apocalypse who stalked the continent. And by the end of the century learned tomes such as *Un Humanisme Africain* were becoming tragically distant from the reality of Zaire, Rwanda and Burundi, Liberia and Sierra Leone suffering under brutal forms of warlordism and dealing with the consequences of catastrophic social disintegration. In this context a preoccupation with identity and missionary failings could seem problematic.[36]

There were outstanding exceptions to this quest for identity. Fashole-Luke, perhaps because of his social vision based on the harmony of the living and ancestral world, saw the importance of not opening up a gap between work for social justice and cultural theology, as later did Bujo. By 1980, the Cameroonian theologian Father Jean-Marc Ela was incorporating a cultural dimension into an African liberation theology.[37] The saintly Bishop Jakob Komba of Songea, Tanzania, tending his garden with evangelical simplicity and his diocese with wisdom, promoted a thoroughly balanced view of African culture and social priorities for African Christians, as did Bishop Mandlenkhosi Zwane of Swaziland before his death in a car accident, and likewise Bishop Peter Sarpong of Kumasi.[38] The influence of such men touched whole bishops' conferences to greater or lesser degrees. The Bishops Conference of Ghana played, and still plays, an important, "modernising" and progressive role in national and international life.

The 1990s saw a more intense dialogue within the Church on culture, an indication of a more polycentric structure struggling to emerge. At the turn of the millennium, the question remained, how enduring and reciprocal was this dialogue?[39] Pope John Paul II was a strict disciplinarian who drew clear lines, but he was also a Polish cultural nationalist at heart and, in his early days, rehearsed the intellectual and affective arguments made for inculturation. "The Synthesis between a culture and faith", he wrote in 1982, " is not just a demand of culture, but also of faith. A faith which does not become a culture is a faith which has not been fully lived out."[40] Cardinal Joseph Ratzinger, though, policed doctrine, seeing in attitudes to inculturation particularly among the Asian and African Bishops, a potential tolerance of "relativism", and, in their theologians, an inadequate concern for Gospel proclamation and the reiteration of central Catholic doctrines. A "theology of religious pluralism" was his new dragon to be slain.

Dialogue with Islam

The Second Vatican Council set out a nuanced theological framework for relations with other religions. It reframed selected parts of earlier thinking in such a way as to represent a definitive break with the past. The aphorism "*extra ecclesia nulla salus*", outside the Church there is no salvation, was finally deleted. In the second chapter of *Lumen Gentium*, the Dogmatic Constitution on the Church, in the section on "The People of God", other religions appeared in a positive light. The Jews were elected by God, and "God never regrets his gifts or his call". More striking was the consideration given Islam. "But the plan of salvation also includes those who acknowledge the Creator. In the first place among these are the Moslems; *they profess* to hold the faith of Abraham, and together with us adore the one and merciful God, who will judge humanity on the last day (emphasis added)".[41] In short the Church saw itself as a universal means of salvation but not an exclusive one.

Other passages of *Lumen Gentium* ended the assumption of guilt for all those outside the Church. An acknowledgement of innocence, painfully built up over the centuries, based on certain preconditions and assumptions, replaced it. The key phrases now describing and explaining the spirituality of non-Christians were: "through no fault of their own", a sincere heart, striving to do God's will as dictated by conscience, and most notably "moved by Grace". The idea was that since "the Saviour wills everyone to be saved", the Church was already in relationship with Jews and Moslems as co-recipients of God's offer of saving Grace. In other words, the Holy Spirit in a manner known only to God, offers to everyone the possibility of being associated with the paschal mystery of Christ and thus with the Church as a sacrament of salvation. And this divine action is at work not only in "hearts and minds", but in the worship and rites of other religions, in visible, tangible "mediations" of God's love.[42]

The Council's Declaration on the Relation of the Church to Non-Christian Religions, *Nostra Aetate,* makes explicit, and takes forward, what follows from this vision. On the one hand Christ is proclaimed as the "way, the truth and the life", in whom may be found the fullness of life. On the other, while recognising differences from Christian faith, the Church "regards with sincere reverence" those ways of living, precepts and teachings, and ethical conduct found in each religion that reflect "a ray of that Truth that enlightens all people". The document makes a new start, officially affirming that Muslims "worship the one God living and subsistent, merciful and almighty, creator of heaven and earth".[43] This common ground of belief was again highlighted by Pope John Paul II in a moving encounter with 80,000 Muslim youth in Casablanca, Morocco, on 19 August 1985. No less striking was his apology during his millennium visit to Yad Vashem in Jerusalem, and his placing of a prayer of penitence in a crack in the Wailing Wall to atone for the sins of Christians against Jews down the ages.

The Council Declaration dwells at some length on the commonalities between the "Abrahamic faiths" and speaks of its esteem for Muslims because of their "wholehearted" submission to God's "inscrutable decrees", prayer, almsgiving and fasting. Judaism is dealt with most expressively in the metaphor of the roots of an olive tree onto which have been grafted "the wild shoots, the Gentiles", and in the bond that "ties the people of the New Covenant to Abraham's stock". All this gives Catholics a positive task in relation to other faiths. "The Church, therefore, exhorts her sons and daughters, that through dialogue and collaboration with the followers of other religions, carried out with prudence and love and in witness to Christian faith and life, they *recognise, preserve and promote* the good things, spiritual and moral, as well as socio-cultural values found among these men and women."[44]

Thus while retaining its universalist claim, understanding of religious diversity in the post-conciliar Church took a major step forward. Other religions were preparations for the Gospel. They contained "seeds of the Word", "rays of Truth", and provided an inculturated "pedagogy" leading towards the true God, or, inversely, they represented an initial, though incomplete, approach by God to humanity. This advance was welcomed around the world. In July 1969 at their regional meeting in Bobo-Dioulasso, the bishops of Francophone West Africa made dialogue with Islam one of their top priorities. A "Guideline for Dialogue between Christians and Muslims", published by the Secretariat for Non-Believers in Rome, was praised by Muslims, and provided a framework for new encounters. But for Cardinal Jean Daniélou, the influential French theologian and expert on early Jewish thought, any acknowledgement that "organised mediations", the communities, narratives, ritual and symbols of other religions, contained salvific content, was a step too far. His "Religion does not save. Jesus Christ grants salvation", encapsulated the hard line position.[45] And such opposition certainly influenced Pope Paul VI who, pulling back from 1968 until his death, increasingly spoke merely of the "aspirations" and "attempts" of other religions to find God.

In short, especially after the strong reiteration of the presence and power of the Holy Spirit in John Paul II's Christian humanism—"in every place, in every time and in every individual"—the Church was left with an uncomfortable ambiguity. Yes, the Spirit of Truth was working outside the confines of the Church, blowing where it willed, directing individuals towards God. "The various religions arose precisely from this primordial human openness to God," the Pope told a General Audience on 9 September 1999. But this profound affirmation of the ubiquity of Grace—what the Belgian Jesuit theologian Jacques Dupuis called "the travels of the Holy Spirit"—seemed now to stop short of taking divine mediation beyond the level of the individual to the corporate, organised reality of other religious *systems and structures*. Pope John Paul II phrased it carefully in his 1990 encyclical on missions, *Redemptoris Missio*, that through interfaith dialogue the Church encountered the spiritual riches of different cultures of which their organised religions were the principal and essential expression—even when they contained "gaps, insufficiencies and errors". But, as Dupuis pointed out—making himself unpopular—neither did the Catholic Church possess the fullness of truth, God's final revelation; that would only be given at the Second Coming of Christ in glory.[46]

What was uncontested was that dialogue is an integral part of the mission of the Church. "By dialogue," Pope John Paul II said in February 1986 to an Asian audience in Madras, "we let God be present in our midst; for as we open ourselves to dialogue to one another, we also open ourselves to God." John Paul gathered leaders of the world's religions together later that year for prayer at Assisi. His doctrinal watchdog, Cardinal Joseph Ratzinger, saw the event as potentially sending the wrong message, encouraging religious relativism. He did not attend. Clarifications were necessary. While other forms of mediation from that of Christ were not entirely excluded, they acquired meaning and value only from Christ's own mediation on the Cross and must not be considered as complementary or parallel, or so the Pope felt obliged to elaborate in the context of the Assisi meeting. "Every authentic prayer is evoked by the Holy Spirit mysteriously present in the heart of every person", he explained to the Curia.[47]

This increasingly nuanced official position raised serious issues about what the missionary mandate of the Church meant in practice, and the uniqueness of the Christian message. Yet, the faint affirmations and cautious acknowledgements of other faiths, their setting within an alien salvation history and discourse, risked sounding offensive even when the intention was the opposite. Rome was certainly taking a step back from the position of the Asian bishops who tended to see the Church as the expression of a privileged, distinctive and, of course, paradigmatic revelation of God, but not an exclusive one, and who showed an openness towards a more hybrid religious consciousness as a channel for Grace.[48] For this reason, after the dragon of liberation theology was declared dead by the Vatican, "relativism" and religious diversity took its place. Relations with other faiths took on a particular sensitivity.

The Vatican's structure of inter-religious dialogue, the Secretariat for Non-Christians, set up in 1964 and renamed the Pontifical Council for Inter-religious dialogue (PCID) ten years later, was required to operate within this complex theological framework. In this sense the PCID was perennially conducting a double dialogue: with people of other faiths and, behind the scenes, or implicitly, with the doctrinal police in the Vatican ever watchful lest the proclamation of the Gospel be subverted by dialogue.[49] *Dialogue and Proclamation*, published jointly in 1991 by the PCID and the Congregation for the Evangelisation of Peoples, reflected the desire to resolve the tension between mission and dialogue. But few were satisfied and the tension persisted.

In 1998 Cardinal Ratzinger made a critical intervention in the drafting of a document from the PCID on prayer in different faith traditions, and instigated an investigation into the writing of the Gregorian

Professor, Jacques Dupuis who had spent twenty years in the Jesuits' Indian province. Two years later the Congregation for the Doctrine of the Faith issued a missive whose triumphalism alone was going to put a brake on ecumenism and interfaith dialogue. *Dominus Iesu* returned to the fundamentalism of Daniélou's position and, with its emphasis on "error" and "deficiencies", was offensive not only to other faiths but to other Christians.

Quite soon after Cardinal Ratzinger became Pope further decisive action was taken. In 2005 there was a temporary folding of the inter-religious Council into the Vatican's Council for Culture, a serious downgrading of its status. This was accompanied by the removal of its guiding light, an English White Father, the Arabic and Islamic scholar, Archbishop Michael Fitzgerald, who was made nuncio to Egypt and the Vatican representative to the Arab League. As secretary to the PCID from 1986 under Cardinal Francis Arinze who had considerable experience of Islam in Nigeria, and then as PCID President himself, he ensured that intermittent dialogue sessions with Islamic bodies created permanent relationships with Sunni and Shi'a scholars. One of the PCID's longest standing partners, not without its early problems, was with WICS, the World Islamic Call Society, based in Tripoli.[50] Fitzgerald had been responsible for piloting through the Vatican *Dialogue and Proclamation*, originally inspired by Dupuis' thinking. In it, other religious traditions—not *faiths*—were acknowledged in their own right as social realities in which personal faith commitments were embodied. It introduced the idea of four dialogues: a dialogue of life, of action, theological exchange and religious experience. All this had made him suspect in parts of the Curia.[51]

Benedict XVI wished to place relations with Islam in the context of a shared quest for peace, common values, mutual understanding, tolerance and, especially, religious freedom.[52] Placing the PCID within a cultural setting therefore made some sense. He saw interfaith dialogue against the horizon of what one Dominican theologian called "an ultimate medium of human communication which is beyond humanity and which we call divinity", and towards which humanity was divinely ordained to proceed on its historical pilgrimage.[53] But behind this philosophical and theological vision of religious freedom as a constitutive dimension of human dignity, there lurked the reality of the immediate plight of the Church, the harassment and limitations that it encountered in several Islamic states and most Muslim societies. The code word was "reciprocity". For Vatican theologians this was full of theological resonance. For others it might sound like an inappropriate element of negotiation creeping into dialogue.[54]

The Pope's lecture, *Faith, Reason and the University*, delivered in Bavaria at Regensburg University on 12 September 2006, has to be understood in this setting. It expanded his former arguments about the indissolubility of Hellenist thought and Christianity—and the dangers of de-Hellenisation in pursuit of inculturation—into a more general re-assertion of the vital importance of the role of human reason in the quest for God. To this end Benedict used the report of a formal inter-religious dialogue between a fourteenth-century Byzantine Emperor and a Persian Muslim to argue for reason against coercion and violence. He quoted the Emperor's words, only dissociating himself from them later: "Show me just what Muhammad brought that was new and you will only find evil and inhuman things such as his command to spread the faith with the sword".[55]

The resulting furore among Muslims was unsurprising and led to the Pope explaining that the Emperor's words did not "in any way express my personal view of the Qur'an". He might have added that the Emperor was effectively an Ottoman hostage at the time, and Europe had been at almost continuous war with Muslim forces for nearly three hundred years. Meanwhile there were violent demonstrations around the world and the Pope's effigy was burnt in several countries. Benedict misdated citations from the Qu'ran, left out others that expressed precisely his own commitment to dialogue by reasoned argument, brought in the irrelevant views of an eleventh-century Andalusian scholar, Ibn Hamza, and completely ignored the rational philosophical tradition from which the Emperor's opponent actually came. Finally, he made no mention of the Crusades.[56]

In the event some good came even from such a stumble. The Pontifical Council for inter-religious dialogue was returned to independent status. Muslim scholars agreed and sent a major dialogue document, *A Common Word Between You and Us*, to the world's Christian leaders. It was an unprecedented initiative. The document was signed by 138 leading Muslim scholars from around the world, and in preliminary meetings a Catholic-Muslim Forum was set up in Rome in March 2008 to organise a formal dialogue that November. Led by the

Cambridge Professor, Sheikh Abdul Hakim Murad and the new PCID President, Cardinal Jean-Louis Tauran, the dialogue proposed was on the theme "Love of God, Love of Neighbour". The baptism by the Pope at the 2008 Easter Vigil in Rome of an anti-Islamic convert from Islam indicated that the question of proclamation and reciprocity had not receded.[57]

Grassroots Realities

The PCID was always clear that its high-level dialogue only took on full meaning if it was translated into the life of the Church in local dialogue and joint action. The refinements of the theological disputes between interfaith theologians such as Father Jacques Dupuis SJ, and the Vatican's Sacred Congregation for the Doctrine of the Faith, took place against a background of hybrid religious beliefs and practices around the world. Local bishops were left with the unenviable task of working between parallel cultural universes, which they had to make sense of, and respond to, on a regular basis. Dupuis' 1997 book, *Toward a Christian Theology of Religious Pluralism*, which tries to resolve these dilemmas, drew criticism from the CDF at Cardinal Ratzinger's instigation.

Local context is everything and the variety of situations confronting Catholics in their relations with other religions remains extraordinarily diverse. In failed and failing states, and under the impact of the communications revolution and globalisation, religious identities, particularly among political elites, grew in importance from the 1980s onwards. The US-led second invasion and occupation of Iraq, the flagrantly biased Middle East policy of the Bush administration towards Palestine/Israel, and the "war on terror" after 9/11, have together put in jeopardy the future of Christianity in the Middle East. The Latin Patriarchate of Jerusalem, the Maronite, Syrian, Chaldean and Armenian Churches in communion with Rome, all have seen emigration rapidly accelerate among their youth in recent years. Since the formation of the State of Israel in 1948, some 250,000 Christians have left the Holy Land, and similar numbers have fled Iraq to Syria and Jordan since the US occupation. In one way or another, ordinary Christians in the Middle East and North Africa are increasingly seen by Muslim extremists as proxies for all that is anti-Islamic, or, in Lebanon, for rival political factions in a fractured state, and suffer from the consequences.

The martyrdom in 1996 of the Cistercian prior of the Atlas-Tibhirine, Abbé Christian de Chérge, in Algeria, and the murder of Paulos Faraj Rahho, the Chaldean Archbishop of Mosul in Iraq in 2008, are emblematic of the general vulnerability of Christian communities in the Middle East.[58]

In sub-Saharan Africa conflicts between Muslims and Christians are often accidental symptoms of inter-ethnic struggles for land, resources and political office. Catholic attacks on Sufi Muslims in the Casamance region of Senegal in the 1990s were part ethnic, part product of cultural nationalism and separatism.[59] Nigeria, with its near 50/50 split between the two world religions, saw in 2000 the most potentially dangerous civil disorder since the Biafran secession of the 1960s as Christian demonstrators against the introduction of *shari'a* criminal law, the *huddud* provisions, clashed with Muslims in Kaduna. Scores of churches and mosques were destroyed and hundreds died in inter-communal violence. The town then spontaneously sorted itself into Christian and Muslim zones after years of peaceful cohabitation.[60]

In emerging conflict situations, Catholic Church leadership normally tries to establish channels of dialogue and put flesh on the bones of *Nostra Aetate*. The Nigerian Catholic Bishops' Conference and its secretary-general, Father Matthew Hassan Kukah, has persistently tried to adopt a more constructive and less confrontational style than the national Christian Association of Nigeria (CAN) and particularly than its increasing number of Pentecostal member Churches.[61] In the less charged context of Indonesia, Catholics have played prominent roles in creating conflict resolution centres and defusing situations that might transform themselves into Muslim-Christian violence.[62] The condoning by states of significant levels of local harassment of Catholics and other Christians, in for example Pakistan, Iran, Egypt and Saudi Arabia is condemned by local Vicars-Apostolic and Bishops either *sotto voce* or more openly in moderate diplomatic language. Here the question of religious freedom is far from academic. Local interpretation of Islamic apostasy provisions as a criminal and treacherous act means that converts from Islam often find it advisable to leave the country, and the threat of trumped up charges under blasphemy laws face Christians involved in civil disputes or what elsewhere would be called vexatious litigation.

In other contexts, most notably where there are Muslim minorities as in Europe, North America, and Philippines, the Catholic Church has locally been active and has sometimes undertaken innovative action against poverty and to promote interfaith dialogue. This has involved the appointment of voluntary interfaith workers in dioceses, bishops given a special portfolio in their Conference as head of Episcopal Commissions for Interfaith Dialogue, dialogue in a variety of bishops-ulama meetings nationally and regionally, and creative work by Sisters and individual parish priests in towns characterised by outstanding religious diversity. The Philippines Bishops-Ulama Forum (BUF), for example, gave valuable support to peace zones on the conflict-ridden Muslim island of Mindanao.[63] However, stereotyping, lack of knowledge of Islam, and longstanding or recent, repressed or open, hostility to Muslims are all found in Catholic parishes around the world, particularly in post-Soviet eastern Europe and in parts of Africa where ethnic identities clothe themselves in a religious garb. This is only partly explained by knowledge of human rights violations against Christians and lack of religious freedom in authoritarian Islamic states, or in some predominantly Muslim societies, in certain instances amounting to persecution.

That the Catholic Church has persevered in its relations with other faiths, and particularly Islam, with its large global following of one billion, is in some ways attributable to the fear of a resurgent and aggressive secularism. Islamic states have proved important allies for the Vatican when it operates as a member state in the United Nations and in international fora on issues of reproductive health and sexuality. In a world hungry for spirituality, and in a Europe suffering a *recul du sens*, a diminishing sense of meaning in life, despite the demands of reciprocity, there is what amounts to a shared interest in moral "metapolitics". But whether it is dialogue of this kind about shared values, or a dialogue of life and action in all its ambiguities and asymmetry, it has been in the domain of inculturation and relations with other faiths that the post-conciliar Church looks and feels, from top to bottom, significantly different from its pre-conciliar past.

10

A GLOBAL CHURCH IN THE TWENTY-FIRST CENTURY

There is an insidious refrain heard in some parts of the Church that the Second Vatican Council undermined the firm edifice of Roman Catholicism and began the unravelling of Religious life in favour of secular pursuits. The counter-chant goes that the Council saved a moribund Church isolated and irrelevant in the modern world, and re-invigorated Religious life. Neither bears too close an inspection. The Council did not represent a hiatus, a total break between the old Catholicism, before 1962, and the new, after 1965. New things were already happening before, and old things continued afterwards. Old ways withered and died and new ones were given permission to grow and flourished. The Church was the crucible; the Council was the catalyst. It conducted Catholics into generous initiatives and engagements with the modern world, into deeper insights and changes in worship and spirituality. It brought together several slowly growing movements and gave them momentum and traction. Yet it failed to stop incipient declines in vocations to the Religious life, in the number of priests, in mass attendance and formal observance.

Secularisation in Europe

The reception of the Council, how Catholics responded to it, the beginning of its implementation, and dissemination and translation of documents, coincided in 1968 with a youthful paroxysm of revolt, first against the Vietnam war, then as an expression of flamboyant secularity in Europe and North America. Anything seemed possible. The rebellion surfed the sea changes in family life, in expressions of sexuality, in the role of women in society and in the economy, and in attitudes to all forms of authority. As the Church opened its doors, it encountered a youth revolt associated with something more subversive than anti-clericalism or persecution, a mocking indifference.

The imperative of the age had become personal self-fulfillment, youth philosophy at best a vague form of libertarian personalism, at worst a hedonist individualism. The "Death of God" was preached in many universities as the birth of liberty, individual wellbeing and happiness, stage two of the Enlightenment. In a culture that rejected formal religious institutions and their asceticism, there were plenty of converts to the new world view. Post-modernism was fast outlawing or abolishing all meta-narratives not simply the Christian one of Salvation History. The European Church went into culture shock.

The disruptive outcomes of renewal combined with culture shock, loss of direction, confusion, numerical decline, and loss of authority, were easily interpreted by fearful Church leaders as the product of erroneous interpretations of the Council's declarations, "the Council's fault". Fears were realised as disorientation and loss of clear purpose took their toll on the priesthood. As they tried to implement the Council's decree on renewal of Religious Life, *Perfectae Caritatis*, Religious soon ran into trouble: the meaning of obedience challenged, divided convents, many leaving and marrying.[1]

The Vatican and fearful bishops acted to contain new forms of pastoral action and organisation. A doctrinaire attitude returned to all aspects of sexual ethics, most calamitously to contraception. The flight from the institutional Church was hastened while widespread rejection of teaching on sexuality undermined authority irrevocably. The excitement of Pastoral Congresses where bishops, priests and laity retrieved a sense of themselves as the People of God quickly gave way to disillusion. It was to be business as usual. Authority had to be re-established. The absence of healthy dialogue within the Church, the attempt at shutting down of informed debate, and the endless policing of it by Rome, pushed out frustrated Catholics in search of pastures green where their spirituality might be lived out unfettered by authoritarian structures.

The disintegration of the Soviet Union after 1989 revealed the significance of what was soon labelled civil society institutions for capitalist development. Two qualities of associational life, the building of trust and the creation of social capital, along with the institutions depending on them, were missing from Soviet society. After the Iranian revolution, the rise of the Moral Majority and aggressive forms of evangelical Christianity in the USA, and *a fortiori* after 9/11, the liberal hope that religion could be contained in a private sphere was dashed. A de-privatisation of religion was underway. A trap was then set for the Church in pluralist democracies: to become another interest group within the thick texture of civil society over which the state presided as arbiter. The Church was now conceded a public place as an FBO, a faith-based organisation, but not one with which it was comfortable.[2]

A secularist mode of governance is facilitated when Catholic interventions in the public domain can be marginalised as special interests, rather than listened to—not necessarily heeded—as the expression of a wider claim to be a universal religion and a moral teacher. When politicians are condemned by some bishops on grounds of their voting record on single issues such as abortion, interventions *a fortiori* can be dismissed as narrowly sectarian. The practice of advocacy, refined in the 1980s by Catholic lobbyists "on the Hill", or in London and Brussels, can easily contribute to this impression. Interventions on single issues such as Catholic schools, homosexual partnerships, and stem cell research, matters over which there is a growing secular social consensus, but on which there are cogent arguments on all sides, can easily be presented as interference from special interest groups. Fighting for "Catholic" issues with the fervour of a shop steward in a 1960s car factory adds to the problem. Bishops as the shop stewards of Catholicism are doomed to lose their moral authority and become one more negotiator with government.

This dilemma remains acute for Catholics at home with pluralism and wishing to engage in public conversation about society. The hope for dialogue, a "double learning process" in which public reason and religion interact in a serious discussion is dashed when secular language is taken to be neutral, while only religious language is assumed to disclose an eccentric worldview. The Church ideally wants to be in discussion at the level of metapolitics and ethics. With societies that are suffering a loss of existential meaning, a drastic *recul du sens,* this is not an unreasonable nor disruptive desire.[3] After wide consultation on issues such as nuclear warfare, ecology and climate change, economic justice, migration and the Common Good, the Catholic Church has often used thoughtful pastoral letters to initiate such conversations. Yet it still has to find the right way to respond to detailed legislation in the political forum.

The challenge is translation from the register and sense of Christian discourse into the idiom of secular political debate without losing meaning and identity. Language and style are all important. Assertion and exhortation by bishops, rather than carefully reasoned argument, risk closing down public space hard won in societies where Catholics are minorities, or simply entrenching opposition, turning Catholic concerns into secular issues that secular governments feel obliged to win. On the other hand, bringing Church resources and personnel behind shared contemporary moral challenges, such as the millennium development goals, opens up public space in a dialogue of life and action.

As the European Court of Human Rights declared in 1994, in a ruling on an Austrian case, Europe lacks "a uniform conception of the significance of religion in society". As new states with strong secular, or religious, identities join the European Union, the politics of the European Parliament begin to fracture around fault lines based on "Catholic issues", more than over classic socio-economic themes. Assertive Catholicism plays into the extreme secular identity of states such as France, Belgium and Netherlands. Since the arguments of the secular state—by its own lights—are by definition rational and universal, those of the Church are irrational and sectarian. In some instances attitudes to Catholicism are informed by wider fears about the divisive impact of single faith-based identities on social cohesion, with aberrant forms of Islam as the primary model of religion. In others, like Republican France, the nation itself is the "community of destiny" and brooks no rivals. Europe as an entity has surprisingly few settled convictions.

In contrast, Catholics in the developing world have been largely spared the disenchantment and secularisation of Europe and its attendant problems. Only a broad-brush comparison can be made, but the developing world shows less commitment to secularism, has a shared spirituality that is neither individualist, self-reflexive nor anti-authoritarian. The bio-ethics that matter are not stem-cell research but whether governments will find enough money to put in their health budgets for mothers to survive childbirth and their children to reach the age of five years old. Preoccupations are more mundane: clinics too far away and with no drugs, police and officials who are crooks, land reform, drought, dirty water and crop failure.

The antics of Paris 1968, Catholic agonies over condoms whose use was forbidden by Pope Paul VI in *Humanae Vitae*—despite 65 out of 72 members of the Study Commission opposing the Papal position—were, and are, as alien and distant to those living in villages in the developing world as the contemporary landing of the first men on the moon. Although the threat of Pentecostalism was on the horizon in the late 1960s, the Church in Africa was vibrant and growing fast. Catholic liturgy was full of life. The fires of the Easter Vigil burnt bright in the African night sky. *Alpha* and *Omega*, *Lumen Christi*, dark empty churches lit up by candles brighter than kerosene lamps, huge crowds of worshippers, clouds of incense stronger than wood smoke, baptismal water in a land waiting for rain. Loss of meaning in the Church's life, symbols and mission after the Council? Not a bit of it. Not in Africa. Except perhaps for priestly celibacy.

The Universal Crisis of the Celibate Priesthood

The crisis in the celibate priesthood is widespread and of long standing. In July 1968 the Zambian Bishops Conference expressed formally to Archbishop Sergio Pignedoli, Secretary of the Congregation for the Evangelisation of Peoples, what many Catholics were saying under their breath, that "in view of the critical shortage of clergy in Zambia, and the lack of vocations to the celibate clergy, and the extreme need for Zambianization of the Church, it was necessary to explore possibilities of instituting a supplementary, and even married, priesthood". In neighbouring Malawi the Montfort Fathers were training married couples so that, come the day, the husband might be ordained with his wife in a supportive pastoral role. Over three-quarters of the clergy in Zaire said in a survey that they wanted to de-link celibacy and the secular priesthood. In 1970 the bishops of Cameroon, Chad, Central African Republic, Congo-Brazzaville and Gabon asked for permission to ordain married men.[4]

The Vatican reacted strongly to this pressure and tried to close down all discussion of celibacy, removing all mentions from synod documents. Rome was supported by many of the African bishops, not all of whom had an immediate crisis of vocations. In Tanzania and Nigeria seminaries were full; Zaire and Uganda had almost doubled the numbers of their seminarians since the beginning of the Council. Elsewhere there were fears that the missionaries sought a second class married African clergy. This was based on sensitivities that African priests might in future receive less formal training in theology and philosophy than their missionary counterparts. African voices in favour of retaining obligatory celibacy, as well as opposed to it, were heard at the 1970s synods of bishops in Rome, ensuring that public debate about the matter was muted.[5]

In many parts of the world clergy were leaving the priesthood in significant numbers. The status and meaning of priesthood suddenly seemed in question. Someone who had once enacted the divine mystery of Christ's sacrifice at the altar felt as if they were relegated to presiding at a ritual communal meal. The man set apart, treated with deference and called "Father", wondered if he had become merely a team leader for the People of God. Pope John Paul II did not wonder. Nor was he liberal in granting dispensations to clergy leaving the priesthood, reducing many to the unwanted and distressing status of canonical irregularity. From the time of the Council until the 1990s, approximately 100,000 left the priesthood world-wide, and double that number— though a lower percentage—of Religious Sisters left their Orders. Despite sympathetic discussions among progressive cardinals and bishops, the requirement of priestly celibacy remained the disciplinary rule for all priests ordained in the Latin Rite, not just for the Religious life. This regulation was once nothing more than a reform provision to deal with problems encountered in the early modern European Church. Its purely disciplinary nature was underlined when married Anglican priests were received into the Church in Britain and permitted to continue in the practice of their priesthood. Nonetheless clerical celibacy remains the clearest red line drawn by Rome, one that has caused tension in the Church everywhere.

In the context of kinship cultures in the developing world, the severance of the new priest from bonds and obligations of family, lineage and village life is particularly demanding. Women and Men Religious unavoidably are made aware of their relative prosperity in contrast to their village-based kin, and by the—gendered—demands of solidarity and sharing. Expectations arising in a cultural milieu that gives priority to values of obligation to the extended family, and to particular attitudes to sexual identity and fertility, are powerfully opposed to the demands of official Church teaching. The outcome of polygamous marriage, as with remarriage of divorcees, is large numbers of Catholics deprived of the sacraments. Church personnel are thus continually acting against their inclinations and childhood socialisation, and are sometimes overwhelmed by the conflicting demands made on them.

This is the background in many parts of the world to the growing crisis of the celibate priesthood. The number of Catholic priests worldwide in clandestine, and often exploitative, multiple sexual relationships of different duration and kind has undermined the exemplary witness of those freed by celibacy for a lifetime of service. Promiscuous—and paedophile—clergy have been a disaster for the post-conciliar Church, not to speak of their victims' suffering. Clerical sexual conduct has given rise in many parishes worldwide to a myriad of intractable problems. So the moral issue for many lay Catholics in some countries became not whether the priest was failing to keep his vow of celibacy—failure was increasingly taken for granted—but whether he was sleeping with a married woman, failing to care for children brought into the world, or indeed, had more than one sexual partner, in short the degree to which the relationship was socially damaging and individually abusive. In many countries an official blind eye was turned—not only to occasional lapses—though when known to Rome sexual transgression blocked preferment to higher office.

While bishops tried to hush up scandal, the Vatican remained in a state of denial and repressed anxiety about the magnitude of the problem. The advent of the HIV/AIDS pandemic brought sexual issues to the surface in an acute form. By 1987 Catholic development agencies in Europe and North America, led by CAFOD, were pioneering faith-based preventive work, advocacy against stigma, and giving palliative care. Figures from India in 2005, showed Catholics, representing 2 per cent only of the population, as the second largest provider of health care for those with HIV/AIDS after the government itself. It is now widely recognised that from palliative care to reduction of stigma and care for orphans, Catholic institutions have played an extraordinary role in response to the disease around the world. This has invigorated the Church with a renewed sense of compassionate purpose and a spirituality of life and suffering, and brought it to reach out to the many other dedicated Christian and non-Christian health and care workers in national networks.

But it soon emerged that one consequence of the pandemic was that promiscuous priests, for fear of infection, were shifting their attentions to local nuns on the assumption that they would be free of the virus. In several African countries in the early 1990s, courageous Provincial Superiors of Women Religious were challenging their bishops, with little success, to act firmly to protect vulnerable members of their congregations from clerical sexual predators. One common outcome was that the priest was moved to another parish but the nun was considered to have broken her vows, and under canon law, usually had to leave her convent.

Cardinal Basil Hume of Westminster, in February 1995, sent a CAFOD dossier describing in general terms the gravity of the situation in twenty-six countries to Cardinal Eduardo Martinez, Prefect of the Vatican Congregation for Religious Life. It had been compiled in 1994 by an experienced Medical Missionary of Mary, Sister Maura O'Donohue, with extensive knowledge of the African Church and six years' background as CAFOD's HIV/AIDS co-ordinator. It raised profound concerns and set out facts from dioceses across the continents of sexual harassment and rape of nuns by priests. It was supported by evidence in a CARITAS report from Father Robert Vitillo, a trusted priest in good standing with the US Bishops Conference who worked for the official Catholic CARITAS network whose centre was in Rome. A second report on sexual abuse of African Religious from the Missionary Sisters of Our Lady of Africa was made available to Religious Superiors in Rome in November 1998. Nothing was said in public until the dossiers were leaked to the *National Catholic Reporter*, and published in Kansas City on 16 March 2001. The long and deafening silence was a symptom of a deeper, and perverse, patriarchal domination that resulted in closing of ranks and cover-up, causing a systemic betrayal of women—and children—in the Church. The official response from Rome four days after the leak did not give grounds for hope that much would be done: it was, the Vatican spokesman explained, a geographically localised problem that was being dealt with. The question was how?[6]

The creation of a married priesthood is not, of course, a universal panacea for lust and human frailty. If the financial implications of permitting such a change were paramount, it would mean in most instances a return to the model of worker priests. Single priests live on very low incomes. Nonetheless one inadvertent consequence of Rome's blocking the formation of married priests on disciplinary grounds has been a damaging erosion of respect for the priesthood. Added to this, public litigation of child abuse cases since 2002, mainly but not exclusively in the developed world, has discredited the priesthood, with a resultant loss of trust. Allegations were made against some 4 per cent of Catholic clergy in the USA between 1950 and 2002, over three-quarters of these between 1960 and 1984; 80 per cent of the alleged cases involved boys between 11-14. Five dioceses have been bankrupted; Boston made an $85 million settlement in 2003. The total financial cost to the Church is estimated as more than £2 billion.[7] The past conduct of the bishops responsible, when faced with alleged criminal abuse among their clergy, fell below normative standards of child protection found in secular social services. This heightened the sense of disillusionment. During his visit to the USA in April 2008, Pope Benedict XVI was remarkably frank in his criticism of the US bishops' handling of the crisis, and his meeting with abuse victims was an important symbolic action.

This serial public shaming of the Church came at an extraordinary moment in the development of the Papacy. It took place after Pope John Paul II raised the profile of Catholicism as a global religious force in an unprecedented way. His visit to Warsaw in 1979 was a highlight. It drained power from the Polish Communist Party, lighting up huge Catholic crowds with an enthusiasm that turned the *Ave Maria* into an anti-Communist chant.[8] His skilful diplomacy outwitted Gierek and Jaruzelski, kept the Soviet tanks at bay, and kept open enough space for the nationalist movement to flourish. Gorbachev gave him credit for starting the sequence of events that brought down Communism, though there were many other more tangible and proximate causes for the collapse of the Soviet Union. Wherever John Paul II went, he carved out a public space for the Catholic voice in the powerful tones of both *Mater* and *Magistra*, capturing the secular language of human rights and with simple appeals for peace, upstaging leaders of even authoritarian and secular states. In his tireless travels John Paul II gave a human face to the globalisation of the Church.

Responding to Globalisation

The Catholic Church arguably fared better in the twentieth-century world of nation-states than Islam. Both developed global networks while reacting against excessive nationalism. From the late 1960s onwards North American and European Catholic development agencies intervened against poverty and injustice in the "South" with money, people and ideas, and brought back a global perspective, ideas and people from Latin America, Asia and Africa to influence their home Churches and governments. Asian missionaries now go to Africa in significant numbers, African priests to Europe. As the Religious Orders seek new recruits in Africa, Nairobi vies with Rome for the number of Religious houses and headquarters.[9] The Church has created structures with which to respond to the pressures of globalisation and regionalisation. Information flows around the Church and into mass media are fast, even if often poorly managed. Bishops Conferences, lay movements, Justice and Peace Commissions, Religious Orders, meet together globally and regionally. Yet in the future in a globally networked society with an information economy, Catholicism may be at a disadvantage. The flatter, more democratic structures of Islam—and evangelical Christianity—may carry an advantage in broadcasting their message and increasing their membership.

COMECE, the Episcopal Conferences of the European Union, with a Brussels secretariat staffed by young professionals, brings bishops together from twenty-seven European Union member states. The Federation of Asian Bishops Conferences and Latin America's CELAM have an established track-record of sharing ideas, good advocacy and joint action; SECAM (Symposium of Episcopal Conferences of Africa and Madagascar), based in Accra, has been slower to develop.[10] *CARITAS Internationalis* in Rome co-ordinates relief and development efforts, and grassroots peace-making, through national CARITAS networks. Based in Brussels, European Catholic development agencies—plus the Canadians—form an advocacy consortium, CIDSE, as do Justice and Peace commissions. Representatives from regional bodies hold thematic meetings on aspects of globalisation: migration and sexual trafficking in women and children—see below—being a major concern.

The European Church is facing pastoral challenges created by the movement of migrant labour from east to west in the European Union. Whether as a result of the influx of Polish Catholics into the UK, or African migrants crossing from the North African coast to Malta, southern Italy and Spain, many parishes illustrate the original Greek meaning of "parochial", a community in a foreign land. Some, such as the Catholic Cathedral parish in Tripoli, Libya, function pastorally as transit centres. Others, inner city parishes in London, as home for settled ethnic groups. The response of host Catholic communities, spontaneous local initiatives sheltering and helping undocumented migrants, or asylum seekers, harshly treated by governments and exploited by employers, has been generous and widespread. Apart from thousands of local small-scale projects and support groups at a parish level, European Bishops Conferences have been both outspoken and engaged in high-level advocacy on behalf both of migrants and asylum-seekers. Migration South to North in the Americas has altered the Catholic demographics of the USA—where Catholics make up 23 per cent of the population—with half of Catholic youth now of Hispanic origin.

Catholics in the USA responded in a similar spontaneous way. A radical Sanctuary movement for migrants without documents and permission to work, evading border authorities, risked the sanction of the law.

The response of Women Religious to sexual trafficking in the last decade is an unsung story of globalisation, building on earlier changes in the Religious Orders. By the 1990s in North America and Europe the crisis in Religious life that struck after the Council had abated. Changes since pre-conciliar days were dramatic as a result of a wider interpretation of the "charism" of each Society's founder: from a pervasive subordination to authority in the convent and work circumscribed by bishops, to a spiritual life in small communities employed in innovative forms of catechetical, social or medical work. The degree of control exerted within, by Mothers-Superior, and from without by local bishops and Rome, had once been extraordinary. Dr Anna Dengel, founder of the Medical Mission Sisters in 1925, had to wait over a decade for the Vatican to lift a mediaeval ban on Women Religious performing obstetric work or surgery. Nuns seeking any change from prescribed convent routines had to perform abject rituals of submission to authority to gain permission.[11]

By the 1990s the majority of nuns dressed differently, thought differently, lived differently; growing numbers were professionally trained in ethics and theology, some shared in the insecurity of life in slums, housing estates and poor *barrios*. Some were ready to challenge the Pope face-to-face on the ordination of women. No wonder Pope John Paul II let twenty years pass before formally meeting the Conference of Women and Men Major Religious Superiors who lived around the corner from him in Rome. Their horizontal networking threatened the hierarchical structures that his experience in Poland told him were so vital for the Church's survival. His virtual boycott of Major Religious Superiors' organisations—the celebrity traditionalist, Mother Teresa of Kolkata a telling exception—did not result in defections. Those who were going to leave had already left. Those remaining in the developed world were predominantly ageing. Of those who stayed active—some well into their 80s—a significant minority were engaged in pioneering work of which anti-trafficking is an example. This was not enough to revitalise Religious life in Europe. Only in the developing world did the numbers hold up or continue to rise.

Religious Orders were often most effective at linking up at a global level. One example of the response by Women Religious to poverty in major European cities was social work typically based on the establishment of drop-in centres which provided different services and opportunities for contact with refugees, homeless people sleeping rough, and prostitutes. In the Netherlands, Sister Michel Keesan set up *Religious against the Trafficking in* Women (WRTV) in 1991. Returned Women Religious missionaries were able to use their contacts in the countries where they had worked for networking; in September 1997 in Amersfoort, a WRTV international conference on trafficking brought together participants from Ghana, the Philippines, Thailand and the Czech Republic. The refocusing of Sisters' pastoral work on the diaspora from their former host country was a natural transition, sometimes the resolution of a deep sense of loss and dislocation. For example in some London parishes there are over seventy different nationalities attending mass.[12]

Eugenia Bonetti, a Consolata Sister, was one such returnee resentful at being ordered back to Italy in her 60s after twenty-four years in Kenya. In 1993 she began working in a CARITAS drop-in centre for refugees in Turin. A turning point in her life came one evening hurrying to mass when she was approached by a Nigerian prostitute seeking help. "In the church Maria knelt in the last pew and sobbed. I went to the front but was unable to pray." Later she heard the Nigerian woman's story. Like that of many others it was heartbreaking: children left in Nigeria, herself tricked, trapped and enslaved by traffickers. "She became my catechist and teacher, introducing me to the complex phenomenon of this new sex slavery of immigrant women." Sister Bonetti began travelling around northern Italy talking to Women Religious to see what could be done.[13]

In 1995 *CARITAS ITALIANA* set up a Catholic umbrella body bringing together organisations dealing with migrants, the Superiors-General of international Religious Orders—plus the *Unione Superiore Maggiore D'Italia* (USMI) and the Bishops Conference. By this time Sisters had set up urban programmes with protected houses for rehabilitation and employment training. Contacts were made with the Nigerian Conference of Women Religious (NCWR) which set up a Committee on Trafficking in Edo State, the principal recruitment area for traffickers in 1997. The Committee for the Support of the Dignity of Women aimed to alert young women to the dangers of tempting offers of overseas employment, to protect families whose daughters had denounced their madams or pimps, and to provide training for new employment. Some of its members were lawyers qualified to deal with complex immigration issues. When, in September 2000 *CARITAS ITALIANA* hosted Mrs Stella Obasanjo, wife of the Nigerian President, she was addressed by former trafficked Nigerian women from the Ruth Community in Caserta. The Edo State Assembly introduced a new law on sexual trafficking later that year, and began arrests of leaders of criminal gangs a year later.[14]

The ecumenical Millennium Jubilee Campaign, which celebrated and drew on Old Testament Biblical themes of restoring land, forgiving debt and freeing slaves, was also bringing sexual slavery to the fore. It was already playing a substantial role in convincing governments to reduce the debt burden of the most indebted nations. NCWR invited the Edo Committee to Italy and a delegation led by Sister Patricia Ebegbulem, National President of the NCWR, was acquainted with the problems of work in Italy. "We exchanged ideas and discussed possible ways of collaborating and co-operating realising that there is a terribly strong criminal network behind the whole business of trafficking and it is only by forming a strong network that we can challenge or fight against them", wrote Sister Ebegbulem of the Sisters of St Louis.[15]

At a Plenary Meeting of the Nigerian Bishops Conference in March 2001, the bishops pledged to address the trafficking problem. A year later they issued *Restoring the Dignity of the Nigerian Woman*, a hard-hitting document on Nigerian trafficking. "The government should take steps to sanitise the immigration department," said the bishops.

"The place seems to be riddled with corrupt elements, who are prepared to collaborate with criminals for a fee. They are only too willing to issue fake travel documents for prospective victims of women trafficking, just as long as the traffickers pay them well." The Bishops Conference called on the Confraternity of Christian Mothers and the Nigerian Catholic Women's Organisation to become fully involved. "It is noteworthy that although this pastoral letter has been published under the authority of the Bishops' conference," the bishops openly admitted, "it has been put together largely through the efforts of those directly involved in the question, especially our Women Religious." No less unusual for an episcopal document was its simple and down-to-earth tone.[16]

By 2006, Sisters working with trafficked women were attending training sessions in Albania, Nigeria and Romania. Contact had been established with the President of the Polish Religious Conference and with other eastern European countries, and Sisters were participating in Europe-wide secular networks. Contemplative cloistered nuns in Milan gave money from a benefactor to set up a rehabilitation centre in the Ukraine. "We are poor and want to remain poor, therefore this money is not ours. It is for those who are poorer than ourselves, because they have lost everything, even their human dignity," they wrote. Meanwhile Nigerian Sisters, alerted by Sister Bonetti's Counter-Trafficking Office in Rome, were meeting deported women at Lagos airport and attempting to facilitate their re-entry, while Italian Sisters were putting pressure on the Nigerian embassy to lower the cost of visas. Plans and fundraising for a reception centre in Benin City were being made. "We've a more powerful network than Al-Qaeda", Sister Bonetti claimed, a novel variant of faith moving mountains.[17]

Such novel pioneering work found bishops being led by women. Though appreciated by the Vatican and by the Nigerian bishops, it has not substantially altered the subordinate position of Women Religious in the Church. Women, with one or two exceptions, do not occupy top Curial positions or exert power in Vatican consistories. A combination of Secular Feminism, Catholic Feminist theology, Anglican ordination of women in 1976, UN Conferences and American nuns, has evoked occasional pronouncements on the role of women from Rome. In Pope John Paul's 1995 *Letter to Women*, on the occasion of the fourth UN Conference on Women, the process of women's liberation was described as "substantially positive", but it was "difficult" and "complicated". There was as usual the seeking of common ground within human rights language. Praise was given for those working for "equal pay for equal work, protection of working mothers, fairness in career advancement" and "equality of spouses with regard to family rights". But new Women's Religious Orders, under the vagaries of diocesan bishops' control, have particularly suffered from intellectual and, in the developing world, economic impoverishment and exploitation. In contrast to the impact of feminism in the secular world, Rome has still to show a comprehensive understanding of the issue of gender relations.

The refusal even to discuss the ordination of women was based on Christ's selection of apostles and the claim that only a male priest could represent the male Christ in the sacrifice of the mass. That women were the first witnesses to the Resurrection and bearers of the Good News, that Jesus of Nazareth had revolutionary counter-cultural attitudes to women—for which he was strongly criticised at the time—and that the all-male image of those attending the Last Supper, down to the numbers of women portrayed on the canvas, derive almost entirely from paintings made more than fourteen centuries later, was deemed irrelevant. Any priest who suggested otherwise was bidding farewell to his chance of being appointed a bishop. The divide created in Catholicism by the Iron Curtain was gone. But what might be called the "Gender Curtain" is still in place.[18]

Non-Violence and Peace

Shortly before he died in 1978, as if summing up his concerns, Pope Paul VI insisted that the Church had to proclaim: "at the top of our voice the absurdity of modern war and the absolute necessity of Peace".[19] Yet, despite the ability of parts of the Church to leap nation-state boundaries in pursuit of the Common Good, the Church has rarely transcended ethnic and national identities in times of war. Globalisation means that nation states today vie with global markets and transnational corporations for control over their economies and destinies, but it evidently does not mean an end to war. The communications revolution breaks down cultural barriers but defensive and threatening new identities emerge in reaction. A propensity for violent conflict conducted both by sub-state entities and by states themselves remains a troubling feature of international relations.

Through vigorous diplomacy Rome has practised what it preaches and championed the cause of peace and non-violence. A virtually unbroken tradition runs from Benedict XV's peace-making to end the First World War to Benedict XVI's reflection on the invasion of Iraq, whether "it is still licit to admit the very existence of a 'just war'", and his description of non-violence, "responding to evil with good...not mere tactical behaviour but a person's way of being, the attitude of one who is convinced of God's love and power".[20] Pope Paul VI's "No More War" speech to the United Nations during the Council highlighted the Holy See's desire to see an international organisation embodying principles of global governance flourish in pursuit of peace. The introduction of a World Day of Peace in 1968, with its annual papal peace message on 1 January, was a further indication of the Vatican's international priorities. The Holy See dismissed violence as worse than useless as a means of solving problems. It generated more violence. It was "not in accord with the Gospel", "not Christian". The lay Sant' Egidio community based in Trastevere, Rome, made a major contribution to ending Mozambique's civil war, and is supported by the Vatican. It remains a unique expression of Rome's commitment to the social apostolate and peace-keeping in action.[21]

Pope John Paul II spoke out repeatedly and eloquently in the same vein: "Violence destroys what it claims to defend: the dignity, the life, the freedom of other human beings". "Nothing is resolved by war; on the contrary, everything is put in jeopardy by war". "War should always be considered a defeat: the defeat of reason and of humanity."[22] John Paul II rarely referred directly to just war criteria, though it was essentially their application that obliged him to rule out modern warfare. Limited recourse to force, better described as "international policing", in situations of grave human rights violations and with the authority of the UN, was permissible. Nothing else. His inclination was to model Christian conduct on the non-violence of Christ and on the "truth of Man" seen in Christ's suffering and love.

With the exception of the US bishops who, at the height of the Cold War in 1983, published *The Challenge of Peace* promoting non-violence, Bishops Conferences have been resistant to even the most forceful peace diplomacy from Vatican diplomats when it meant speaking out against their national forces engaging in armed conflict. One of the clearest examples was the Falklands/Malvinas war between Argentina and the United Kingdom. Pope John Paul II nearly cancelled his 1982 visit to Britain at the last minute because of Cardinal Basil Hume's reluctance to condemn the war. Against a background of national jingoism, the Pope preached an unequivocal homily to thousands of English Catholics gathered for Mass at Baginton Airport. "Today, the scale and horror of modern warfare—whether nuclear or not—makes it totally unacceptable as a means of settling differences between nations," he said. "War should belong to the tragic past, to history; it should find no place in humanity's agenda for the future."[23] It would have been inconceivable for a Cardinal Archbishop of Westminster to preach such a sermon at the time.

Rome intervened no less strongly before all the wars in the Middle East, though Cardinal Jean-Louis Tauran in the Vatican Secretariat of State broke ranks by expressing understanding for "Operation Enduring Freedom" in Afghanistan as an act of self-defence. Cardinal Karl Lehmann, President of the German Bishops Conference, in Rome at the time, reacted to Tauran's reference to just war saying it was only right to speak of a "just peace". He called for the peace process in the Middle East to be restarted. Archbishop John Onaiyekan of Abuja in Nigeria called for a halt to the bombing of Afghanistan. This came only days after rioting involving Muslims in Kano that resulted in two hundred deaths, but his position was entirely within Rome's peace tradition. Lehmann's and Onaiyekan's strong support for the Vatican position was not reflected in the Bishops Conferences of the belligerent nations.[24]

The Church's teaching against war and on nuclear deterrence has notably hardened since the Council. The Holy See maintained a nuanced position during the Cold War and prior to significant proliferation of nuclear weapons. Its limited acceptance of states' possession of such weapons was conditional on deterrence being a step on the path to progressive nuclear disarmament. With the threat of further proliferation, and the US developing tactical battlefield nuclear weapons, the Vatican's stance was clearly expressed by the permanent observer of the Holy See at the United Nations, Archbishop Celestino Migliore: "The time has gone for finding ways to a "balance of terror"; the time has come to re-examine the whole strategy of nuclear deterrence. ... The Holy See has never countenanced nuclear deterrence as a permanent measure nor does it today when it is evident that nuclear deterrence drives the development of ever new nuclear arms, thus preventing nuclear disarmament." The verdict of Pope Benedict XVI in his 2006 World Day of Peace message was that a policy of nuclear deterrence had become "not only baneful but completely fallacious".[25]

On questions of non-violence and war, radical Catholics have found themselves more often than not in alliance with Rome pressuring their Bishops Conferences. The Vatican Council did not change the glaring anomalies. The US bishops condemned the Vietnam war only in November 1971. "Whatever good we hope to achieve through continued involvement in this war is now outweighed by the destruction of human life and of moral values," they finally declared after Catholics in the anti-war movement marched and burnt their draft cards in protest.[26] US Catholic Relief Services fed South Vietnamese troops. The Principal Roman Catholic Chaplain to the Fleet in Britain blessed HMS *Resolution*, the first of the UK's nuclear submarines carrying Polaris, the "UK nuclear deterrent".[27] *Pax Christi*, the official Catholic peace movement, found a sympathetic and committed bishop in each country, but support from most bishops was minimal. The movement remained small, in contrast to the Catholic development agencies which expanded rapidly in the 1980s, adding government funding to the generous giving from their Catholic constituencies.

The global vision of the Church did not diminish the affective power of national identity even as many governments in the developing world, democratic or authoritarian, became more obviously exhausted as embodiments of their peoples' hopes. Rome's influence remains intangible and patchy. Bishops Conferences, despite strenuous Vatican peace diplomacy, might today counsel against war, but never propose conscientious objection for Catholics: only to cater dutifully to the pastoral needs of troops once—what they believed to be—unjust wars began. It is as if for many bishops Rome plays mood music when it comes to peace-making, while in matters of liturgy, she becomes the great symphonic conductor who must be obeyed, or fought with, for interpretation of the score.

A consensus on the Christian practice of non-violence has escaped the Church—so far as becoming again a constitutive dimension of Catholicism. Yet there has developed something of a consensus that money spent on arms is taken from development for the poor. The emergent threats of the twenty-first century urgently require new ways for the Church to transmit its message of peace, new global solidarities and interventions such as those recently exhibited by Women Religious and development agencies. Alongside the links between war, poverty and hunger, the even more fundamental theological questions about global warming have barely been broached by Catholic teaching. They urgently need attention.

Environment and Climate Change

Outside of wartime, governments are not good at convincing their citizens of the need for privations and asceticism, of selfless concern for the Common Good. Democracies working with a "thin" account of liberalism, thus promoting few common values, do not provide more than rudimentary moral formation. It is doubtful that governments in liberal democracies will achieve a consensus on the need for radical behavioural change soon enough to avert global warming. They will find it difficult to profess a politics of radical change, and get re-elected, or win acceptance for the necessary drastic adaptations in citizens' consumption and patterns of life required to avoid the pending environmental crisis. How will they be able to avoid some degree of coercion or curtailment of civil liberties, on energy use and travel, a recourse open to authoritarian regimes? Will market forces suffice? The educational performance of government to date is not impressive. The educational potential of a global Church—or an *umma* responsive to the Prophet's call for stewardship—may be called on to prepare citizens, to model new ways of living. Otherwise loss of civil liberties are likely to occur under panic-inducing pressures, war on two fronts, against terrorism and climate change. As former US Secretary of State, Madeleine Albright, pointed out, her government had a poor record "when declaring war against nouns".[28]

Catholicism's awareness and articulation of environmental moral questions first grew out of the Church's rediscovery of the option for the poor and its encounter with the spirituality of indigenous peoples. A slow process, led by secular and lay activists and with the Protestant Churches, an applied theological ecology is still not well developed. A notable early exception was the pioneering British Catholic thinker, Barbara Ward, whose book *Only One Earth* was influential in the first UN Conference on the Environment held in Stockholm in

1972. In both Latin America and Asia, the quest for sustainability in development programmes—Church and non-Church sponsored—led to new environmental projects in the 1980s. In the face of exploitation of scarce resources to the detriment of the poor, Bishops Conferences in Guatemala and Philippines reflected their experience in two 1988 pastoral letters: *The Cry for Land* and *What is Happening to our Beautiful Land?* Both illustrated the wider phenomenon of concern for "ecojustice" and the Christian stewardship of creation—growing out of work for justice and drawing on ideas promoted by the World Council of Churches in their call for *Justice, Peace and the Integrity of Creation.* What the worst logging and mining companies did was doubly unjust; they impoverished those for whom forests and the earth provided natural wealth, and damaged God's creation. This injustice would be visited on future generations. [29]

In December 1989, Pope John Paul II issued *The Ecological Crisis: A Common Responsibility*, a call to responsible stewardship. This stimulated a number of Bishops Conferences to produce similar documents. The 1991 US Bishops' Pastoral, *Renewing the Earth*, open to the widest range of theological influences, manifested interesting trends. It called for a "sense of God's presence in nature", evoking a sacramental universe and proposing an ecological spirituality, and for solidarity to extend to the "flourishing of all earth's creatures" based on "our kinship with all that God has made". The Pope's position, expressed in *Centesimus Annus*, remained firmly in an older mode of good stewardship, critical of human domination of creation but with no suggestion of an ecological spirituality which viewed humanity in the context of Grace in the rest of creation. "Instead of carrying out his role as a co-operator with God in the work of creation, man sets himself up in place of God and thus ends up in provoking a rebellion on the part of nature, which is more tyrannised than governed by him". From essentially a reformist position, John Paul II was not sweeping away narratives of mastery and domination, rather redefining them in terms of human responsibility and solidarity.[30]

Latin America's and the Philippines' history of martyrdom in the cause of justice has now extended to those dying in the cause of ecojustice. In 2005 Sister Dorothy Stang was murdered because of her participation in resistance by local indigenous people to the destruction of the Amazonian Rain Forest, one of several "environmental martyrs" in

Latin America. Priests and lay workers have been assassinated resisting logging and mining companies in the Philippines. Such deaths coupled with the ecological spirituality of Latin America's indigenous people have been a source of inspiration and challenge, motivating a deepening of theology and focussing action. But, as with other theologies and spirituality not home grown, this has not found favour in Rome.

It remains to be seen if Catholicism will find an environmental equivalent to the seminal option for the poor or influence the key polluters among authoritarian regimes such as China. For the road to reconciliation between the Communist Party of China and the Vatican remains tortuous. The four Chinese bishops invited by the Pope to the 2005 Synod of Bishops were not given permission to attend. Rome's appointment of a strong critic of the Chinese government, Archbishop Joseph Zen of Hong Kong, as a Cardinal in February 2006, drew an immediate response, the appointment of two "patriotic" bishops by Beijing without the Pope's approval. These skirmishes disguise a genuine commitment in Rome to unite China's Catholics, and illustrate tactical responses rather than a strategic plan in Beijing. It is quite possible that some *modus vivendi* between the Vatican and China will be agreed in the next decade, with a concomitant growth in numbers of converts. Chinese Catholicism might soon be a powerful new force in the world Church. Were it prepared, this might give the Catholic Church in China some national voice in questions of ecology. Catholicism's ability to elaborate a usable ecological theology and an environmental ethics, implement them in action and speak truth to power, may prove to be its greatest test as a global Church in the twenty-first century.

The Four Churches Today

This book began with a "four Churches" metaphor, four ways of looking at Catholicism, four different voices in conversation about it. It went on to analyse a process of renewal officially sanctioned and propelled forward in the 1960s by the Second Vatican Council, a transforming moment in Catholicism that enhanced diversity and change, engaged Catholics with the problems of the twentieth century and created a world Church. The fall of the Berlin Wall gave birth prematurely to the twenty-first century, revealed the Catholic Church as a significant actor on the historical stage, and instilled in the secular West a threatening hubris coupled with a damaging forgetfulness of the need for historical humility.

So for the Catholic Church the beginning of this new century has been the best of times and the worst of times. The conversation between the four Churches—described in Chapter One—has largely been reduced to two, between the Church as it is in its human frailty and the Church as it ideally wishes itself to be as a theological construct. Hence Papal apologies for past failures, an acknowledgement in part of how others see the Church. How the Church functions as a global community is omitted from the conversation.

The trajectory on which Catholicism finds itself, in the developed world particularly, is towards a greater dissociation of laity from clergy and hierarchy, generating a fifth face of the Church, the critical lay voice—notwithstanding the importance of hierarchy-oriented lay movements such as Opus Dei. The fierce loyalty of the nineteenth-century laity and Religious, which survived well into the twentieth century, has almost dissipated, despite the lingering afterglow of Pope John Paul II and his, and countless priests', exemplary witness to priestly life unto infirmity and death. The Church's sense of deep solidarity with the whole human family, in all its frailty, remains, thanks to the Council.

The future of the Church as a force for social transformation, integral Mission, may now lie in the hands of the laity and Women Religious—who often have to treat the hierarchy as an obstacle to be overcome, appeased or instrumentalised. But the Cardinals, Bishops and priests working for peace and human rights play a vital role. Rome, the flawed but wise teacher for an age that justifies torture and makes war a first resort, remains the indispensable unifying centre of Catholicism, the fullness of the Church. Whether this antinomy, lived out daily as a dilemma by committed Catholics around the world, is a creative tension or a crushing burden will determine the future of global Catholicism. One thing is sure, the distribution of Catholics world wide means that the days of the old Eurocentric Church directed by Europeans are numbered. The future conversation about Catholicism in the twenty-first century will be conducted increasingly by Latin Americans, Africans and Asians.

NOTES

1. The Legacy of Anti-Modernism

1   It is tempting to substitute "imagine" for "said" as in Benedict Anderson's *Imagined Communities* Verso 1983, not in the sense that this community was "imaginary", only as a Catholic to capture more objectively how Catholics place themselves in a global Church.

2   Duncan, B., *The Church's Social Teaching,* Collins Dove, Victoria, 1991, 2-5. Though in a situation reminiscent of that in China two hundred years later, there were a significant number of priests who made their peace with the Revolution and continued as best they could.

3   Lash, N., "Vatican II: Of Happy Memory—and Hope?", in Ivereigh, A. (ed.), *Unfinished Journey: The Church 40 Years after Vatican II*, Continuum, London, 2003, 17.

4   Though with the termination of the Concordat the French socialist government lost control over the nomination of the Catholic bishops, see Siefer, G., *The Church and Industrial Society*, Darton, Longman, Todd, London, 1964, 27.

5   Quoted in Komonchak, J.A.,"Vatican II and the Encounter between Catholicism and Liberalism" in Bruce Douglass, R., and Hollenbach, D., *Catholicism and Liberalism: Contributions to American Public Policy,* Cambridge University Press, 1994, 78.

6   Goerres, I.F., *The Hidden Face,* Pantheon, New York, 1959, 25.

7   Ibid., 27.

8   Komonchak, J.A., " Returning from Exile: Catholic Theology in the 1930s" in Baum, G. (ed.), *The Twentieth Century: A Theological Overview*, Orbis, Maryknoll, 1999, 44. For an excellent appraisal of Newman in context of the Second Vatican Council, see Lash, N., "Tides and Twilight: Newman Since Vatican II" in Ker, I., and Hill, A.G. (eds), *Newman After a Hundred Years*, Oxford University Press, 1990, 447-64.

9   Goerres, *The Hidden Face,* 27.

10   Dries, A., *The Missionary Movement in American Catholic History* Orbis, Maryknoll, NY, 1998, 31; Langlois, L., 'Les effectifs des congrégations féminines au XIXe siècle: de l'enquête statistique à l'histoire quantitative', *Revue d'histoire de l'église de France*, 60, 1974, 56; Confederacion Latinoamericana de Religiosos (CLAR), "Etude Sociographique des Réligieux et des Réligieuses en Amerique Latine", 1973, 39.

11   Duncan, *The Church's Social Teaching,* 6-8.

12   Lammenais came out as a democrat against the Bourbon monarchy in 1829 and launched *L'Avenir* in 1830. This quote is from *L'Avenir*, 15 November 1830, on the need for separation of Church and State: "We are being paid by our enemies, by those who think us hypocrites and imbeciles, and who believe that our lives can be held ransom by their money". See O'Connell, M.R., "Politics and Prophecy, Newman and Lammenais" in Ker and Hill (eds), *Newman after a Hundred Years,* 180.

13   Duncan, *The Church's Social Teaching,* 10.

14   Schoof, M., *Breakthrough: Beginnings of the New Catholic Theology* Gill and Macmillan, Dublin, 1970, 45.

15   Siefer, *The Church and Industrial Society,* 20.

16   Duncan, *The Church's Social Teaching,* 15.

17   Mexico became part of the Vatican's "Red Triangle" after it recognised the Soviet Union under President Plutarcho Calles' "socialist" government in 1924. The Queretaro legislation modelled on the French Separation Law closed Catholic schools and convents and expelled all Spanish clergy. Over 5,000 priests, religious and lay leaders were murdered in the mid-1920s during the four year Calles Presidency and insurrection. Pius XI denounced the regime in March 1927 in *Nos es Muy Conicida.* See Daniel-Rops, H., *A Fight for God, 1870-1939,* J.M. Dent, London, 1963, 326-327 and Luxmore, J., and Babiuch, J., *The Vatican and the Red Flag: The Struggle for the Soul of Eastern Europe,* Geoffrey Chapman, London, 1999, 7-8, 14.

18   Dries, *The Missionary Movement,* 30; *Le Renouvellement intellectuel du Clergé de France au XIXe siècle,* Paris 1903, 13, quoted in Siefer, *The Church and Industrial Society,* 18. The *Instituts Catholiques* were begun in the mid-1870s as *de facto* Catholic universities as Catholic theology was forced out of the French secular university system.

19   For statistics see Sanneh, L., "Religion's Return" *The Times Literary Supplement,* 13 October 2006; Daly, G., *Transcendence and Immanence: A study in Catholic Modernism and Integralism,* Clarendon Press, Oxford, 1980. See Pius X's letter to the French bishops *Notre Charge Apostolique*: a universal society "cannot be set up unless the Church lays the foundation and supervises the work", quoted in Ruston, R., "Pacem in Terris" an unpublished paper presented at the Pax Christi Conference, 2003; Cornwell, J., *Hitler's Pope: The Secret History of Pius X11,* Penguin 1999, 35-40 for a summary of Pius X's attack on modernism; Bernardi, P., "Social Modernism: the Case of the *Semaines Sociales*" in Jodock, D. (ed.), *Catholicism Contending with Modernity,* Cambridge University Press, 2000, 277-296.

20   His letter *Aeterni Patris* on Christian Philosophy in 1879 sets this out.

21   *Summa Theologiae* II, II q.1,a 2ad 2 "Actus credentis non terminatur ad enuntiabile sed ad rem" quoted in Schoof , *Breakthrough,* 196.

22   Tyrrell, G., "The Relation of Theology to Devotion", *The Month,* 94, (1899), 473.

23   Letter to Maud Petrie 21 June 1903 quoted in "Being All Things to All People: Faith, Practice and Culture" in George Tyrrell and Liberation Theology" unpublished paper by Tim Noble, S.J. 1999.

24   Shorter, A., *African Recruits and Missionary Conscripts: The White Fathers and the Great War,* Missionaries of Africa History Project Publication, 2007, 159, 164, 168,171,175.

2. Dominican and Jesuit Pioneers

1   Taken from Shorter *African Recruits*, 175-177; Dries *The Missionary Movement*, 117.

2   Yik – Yi Chu, C. (ed.), *The Diaries of the Maryknoll Sisters in Hong Kong 1921-1966*, Palgrave-Macmillan, London, 2004, 207; Smith, S., "Maori and Mission Sisters in New Zealand since 1865: Changing Approaches", *International Bulletin of Missionary Research*, Vol. 31, 2, April 2007, 77-80.

3   Dom Cuthbert Butler's letter to *The Times* 30 September 1907 in reaction to *Pascendi* quoted in Schoof, *Breakthrough*, 187; Pollard, J., "The Pope of Peace", *The Tablet*, 27 November 2005, 10.

4   Schoof, *Breakthrough*, 158.

5   Siefer, *The Church and Industrial Society*, 37; Shorter, *African Recruits*, 58.

6   For Maritain and Christian Democracy see Lynch, E.A., *Religion and Politics in Latin America: Liberation Theology and Christian Democracy* Praeger, New York, 1991, 55-65, 69, which oddly, while applauding its promotion of civil society and the family, attributes the failure of Christian Democracy to its inadequate rejection of Marxism. The Vatican was adamantly opposed to the Marxist thinking of several of the worker priests and the militancy of most—a prelude to the mishandling of liberation theologians. Schoof, *Breakthrough*, 97; Siefer, *The Church and Industrial Society* 37-48.

7   Chenu, M.D., "Dimension nouvelle de la Chrétiénte", *La Vie Intellectuelle*, 53, 1937, 350; Schoof, *Breakthrough*, 102.

8   This culminated in *Jalons pour une théologie du laïcat* finished in 1951, translated and published in English as Congar, Y., *Lay People in the Church*, Geoffrey Chapman, London, 1959. His famous work *Chrétiens Désunis* was first published in 1937.

9   Schillebeeckx's *Mary, Mother of the Redemption*, Sheed & Ward, London, 1964, first published in Dutch in 1954, is a classic example of biblical and historical theology with ecumenical implications; see also Schoof, *Breakthrough*, 136. However, like Chenu, Schillerbeeckx never became an official Council *peritus*. Alberigo, G, and Komonchak, J.A., *History of Vatican II, Vol. I* , Orbis/ Peeters, Leuven, 1996, 457,462.

10   Stransky, T.F., "The Foundation of the Secretariat for Christian Unity" in Stacpoole, A. (ed.), *Vatican II by those who were there*, Geoffrey Chapman, London, 1986, 63.

11   De Lubac, H., *Catholicism*, Burns & Oates, London, 1961, p. vi.

12   Siefer, *The Church in Industrial Society* 41; I am grateful to Fergus Kerr O.P. for some of the details about theologians.

13   Ibid., 40-48. De Gaulle banned Suhard from a Te Deum in Notre Dame Cathedral after the allied victory in reprisal for Suhard's pro-Vichy position. His later championing of different forms of apostolate has been attributed by some to a desire to start anew after the Vichy setback -- personal communication, Geoff Chapman.

14   Hebblethwaite, P., *John XXIII: Pope of the Council*, Geoffrey Chapman, London, 1984, 222-224.

15   Maritain, J., "The Pluralist Principle in Democracy", *The Nation*, 21 April 1945, 165-171, quoted in Evans, J.W., and Ward, L.R. (eds), *The Social and Political Philosophy of Jacques Maritain*, Notre Dame Press, South Bend, 1976, 121; see also *The Rights of Man and Natural Law*, 1942 and *Christianity and*

Democracy, 1943 published by Ignatius Press, San Francisco, 1986. Maritain was essentially charting a course between liberal secular humanism and atheistic communist humanism to discover a Christian humanism based on the person in society and the mystery of the incarnation.

16   Schoof, *Breakthrough,* 108.

17   Pierre Teilhard de Chardin's bibliography begins in 1916 though his celebrity in the Anglophone world only developed during the 1950s and 1960s. *Le Milieu Divin,* alongside *The Phenomenon of Man,* his best known works, were published in 1926-1927 but only in 1960 translated into English. For a balanced account of his work see Mooney, C.F., *Teilhard de Chardin and the Mystery of Christ* Collins, London 1966. Pius XII gave him a choice between confinement in a rural Retreat House or exile in New York. Not a difficult decision.

18   Schoof, *Breakthrough,* 99.

19   Hebblethwaite, P., *John XXIII,* 221. *Essor ou Déclin de l'Eglise* (Progress or Decline of the Church) was published on 11 February 1947.

20   Ibid., 310-312.

21   Personal communiation, Fergus Kerr O.P., New Blackfriars, Oxford.

22   *Summa Theologiae,* II II q.1 a2; "Cognita sunt in cognescente secundum modum cognescentis".

23   Quoted in Schoof, *Breakthrough,* 196.

24   Ibid., 205.

25   Duffy, E., "Tradition and Reaction: Historical Resources for a Contemporry Renewal" in *Unfinished Journey* 58-60.

26   Jungmann tellingly quotes J.H. Card. Newman, "Reformation of the XIth century" in *Essays Critical and Historical,*Vol. II, 1890, 250: "...the history of the past ends in the present; and the present is our scene of trial; and to behave ourselves towards its various phenomena duly and religiously, we must understand them; and to understand them, we must have recourse to those past events which led to them. Thus the present is a text and the past its interpretation", see *The Early Liturgy,* Darton, Longman, Todd, London, 1960, 2. Jungmann, professor of pastoral theology at Innsbruck became a *peritus* on the Liturgy Commission. See also the delightful Pierre-Marie Gy, *The Reception of Vatican II Liturgical Reforms in the Life of the Church,* Marquette University Press, Milwaukee, 2003, 4. The origins of the liturgical movement are usually dated to 1909 and a speech by Lambert Beaudun at a Catholic Lay Congress in Malines, Belgium; see Jungmann, J.A., "Constitution on the Sacred Liturgy" in Vorgrimler, H., *Commentary on the Documents of Vatican II Vol. I,* Herder & Herder, 1996, 2-5; Alberigo and Komonchak *History of Vatican II Vol. III* Orbis/Peeters, Leuven, 2000, 220.

27   Comsemius, V., "The Condemnation of Modernism and the Survival of Catholic Theology" in Baum, G. (ed.), *The Twentieth Century: a Theological Overview* Orbis, 1999, 23. Karl Rahner produced his first articles on Grace in the late 1930s. His collected works in five volumes of *Schriften zur Theologie* (Theological Investigations), and *Quaestiones Disputatae,* the latter dealing among other themes with inspiration in the Bible, the episcopate and the primacy and the Church and Sacraments, came out alongside *Sendung und Gnade* (Mission and Grace) in the late 1950s and were translated into English during the critical period of Council preparations, 1958-1962, and sessions, 1962-1965. Rahner joined the Liturgy Commission as an expert, *peritus,* on the sacraments.

28   Schoof, *Breakthrough,* 100.

29   Rahner's emphasis on the "total submission" to God of the Virgin Mary, rather than on her virginity, had required intervention by Cardinal Julius Döpfner in Rome to calm troubled waters, but this did not deter Pope John XXIII who made him a *relator* on the sacraments; see Alberigo and Komonchak, *History Vol II*, 456. See also Cornwell, *Hitler's Pope*, 281-297; Stacpoole, *Vatican II*, 37.

30   The US Sister Formation Conference arose out of the National Catholic Education Association in 1954; see Koehlinger, A.L., *The New Nuns: Racial Justice and Religious Reform in the 1960s*, Harvard University Press, Cambridge, MA, 2007, 27-33, 69; Wilson, P., *My Father Took Me to the Circus: Religious Life from Within*, Darton, Longman & Todd, 1984, 64.

31   This was partly fallout from the suppression of the worker priest movement; see Siefer, *The Church in Industrial Society*, 75; Stacpoole *Vatican II*, 11.

32   Hebblethwaite, P., *The First Modern Pope*, Harper Collins, London, 1993, 253-254.

33   Ibid. 229. Given the travel limitations of the day these are extraordinary numbers to marshal for an event in Rome.

34   Hastings, A., *A History of African Christianity 1950-1975*, Cambridge, 1979, 61. When Bishop Kiwanuka returned to his vicariate from Rome in 1940 a poem, "The Hour of Africa has come", was written, more in optimism than reality, in the event; see Waliggo, J.M., *A History of African Priests: Katigondo Seminary 1911-1986,* Katigondo National Seminary/Matianum Press Consultants, Nairobi, 1988, 151.

35   Hastings, *A History,* 60.

36   Luxmore, J. and Babiuch, J., *The Vatican & the Red Flag,* Geoffrey Chapman, London, 1999, 38-44, 52.

37   Simon, G., "The Catholic Church and the Communist State in the Soviet Union and Eastern Europe" in Bociurkiw, B., and Strong, J.W. (eds), *Religion and Atheism in the USSR and Eastern Europe*, London, 1975, 208; Lernoux, P., *Hearts on Fire: The Story of the Maryknoll Sisters* Orbis, Maryknoll, 1993, 14-17. The Maryknoll Bishop, Francis Xavier Ford, died in jail after reports written to the US Consulate in Swatow were intercepted.

38   Kohen, A.S., *From the Place of the Dead: Bishop Belo and the Struggle for East Timor,* Lion Publishing, London, 1999, 76. See Pollard, J., *Money and the Rise of the Modern Papacy: Financing the Vatican 1850-1950*, Cambridge, 2005; Hastings, *A History,* 63.

39   The Apostolic letter *Maximum Illud* was published in 1919 giving a clear direction to Catholic missionary activity, in the context of the future needs of the local Churches being formed, with its view of indigenous cultures as "stepping stones" to Christian culture.

40   Bruneau, *The Political Transformation of the Brazilian Church*, 95.

41   Hastings, *A History*, 119, 169. Archbishop Denis Hurley played an important role in this development having promoted catechetical renewal in South Africa in the late 1950s; personal communication from Paddy Kearney, May 2007.

42   The difference between the African bishops leaving the council in two buses and the German purring away from St Peter's in their individual Mercedes was striking — personal communication, Geoff Chapman.

43   The differences are set out clearly in Komonchak, J.A., "Augustine, Aquinas or the Gospel *sine glossa*?" in Iverleigh, *Unfinished Journey* 102-119.

44   Hebblethwaite, *John XXIII,* 200. The Pope as nuncio in Paris had to deal with

General Charles de Gaulle's demand for the sacking of thirty-two French bishops whom he claimed had been Vichy collaborators.

45   Personal Communication, Archbishop Denis Hurley, 2002; Hebblethwaite, *The First Modern Pope*, 234.

46   The SFC, as a penalty for grassroots initiative and innovation in the social apostolate, was brought under the authority of the Conference of Major Superiors of Women's Religious Institutes (CMSW) in 1965, at the instigation of the Sacred Congregation for Religious and Secular Institutes in Rome. The impetus of their work continued in the Education Service Department of the National Catholic Conference for Interracial Justice, and later in the 1970s when CMSW became the Leadership Conference of Women Religious and the Council's priorities came into play; see Koehlinger, *The New Nuns*, 37-40, 65-72, 189-191. The first link to Peru was through a Franciscan, Sister Gretchen Berg of Rochester, Minnesota. Dries, *The Missionary Movement*, 206-207.

47   Dallek, R., *John F. Kennedy: An Unfinished Life 1917-1963*, Penguin, Harmondsworth, 2003, 231-236, 246-252, 295-296.

48   Bruneau, *The Political Transformation of the Brazilian Church*, 70, 88.

49   Statement of Campesina Grande, 1956, ibid., 75.

50   Ibid.

51   Bruneau, *The Political Transformation*, 75.

52   From his 1966 Mar del Plata CELAM Speech.

53   Quoted in Gonzalez, J.L., *The Changing Shape of Church History*, Chalice Press, St Louis, 2002, 157; Rahner, K., "Toward a fundamental theological interpretation of Vatican II" in *Theological Studies*, 40, December 1979, 717; see also his *Concern for the Church* New York, 1981. 78. This movement towards a World Church corresponds with Rahner's understanding of the "third phase" in the growth of the Church.

54   Cornwell, *Hitler's Pope*, 147-155.

55   Compare John Cornwell's *Hitler's Pope* with Cardinal I. Cardinale's "The Contribution of the Holy See to World Peace in Areas of Diplomacy, Development and Ecumenism", speech at Boston College, 27 March 1968 in Sweeney, F. (ed.), *The Vatican and World Peace*, Colin Smythe, 1970, 86-92. Two strong expressions of opposite opinions in a debate that has produced hundreds of publications for and against.

56   Lash, *Unfinished Journey*, 13; Allen, J., *Pope Benedict XVI*, Continuum Publishing, London 2000, 4.

57   Quoted in G. Gutiérrez "The Church and the Poor: A Latin American Perspective" in Alberigo, G., Jossua, J.P. and Komonchak, J.A. (eds), *The Reception of Vatican II*, The Catholic University of America Press, Washington, 1987.

58   Alberigo, G., "The Conciliar Experience: Learning on Their Own" in Alberigo and Komonchak, *History of Vatican II Vol. II*, 584.

3. The Vatican Council: Early Stages

1   Hebblethwaite, *John XXIII*, 280.

2   Ratzinger, J., *Theological Highlights of Vatican II*, Paulist Press, New York, 1966, 23.

3   Card, L.J., Suenens, "A Plan for the Whole Council" in Stacpoole, *Vatican II*, 89.

4   The new code of canon law was long in gestation and only came into effect on
    27 November 1983 Alberigo, G., and Komonchak, J.A., *History of Vatican II
    Vol I*, Orbis/Peeters, Leuven, 1996, 1, 61; Hebblethwaite, *John XXIII*, 314.

5   This may ironically have been because Cardinals Ernesto Ruffini and Alfredo
    Ottaviani had been talking to John on the night before his election about their
    attempt to get Pius XII to call a Council, and had suggested it to him; see
    Walsh, M., "The Religious Ferment of the Sixties" in McLeod, H. (ed.), *The
    Cambridge History of Christianity Vol. 9 World Christianities c. 1914 –c. 2000*,
    Cambridge University Press, 2006, 308; Capovilla, L.F., "Reflections on the 20th
    Anniversary" in Stacpoole, *Vatican II*, 11, 116-117; Alberigo and Komonchak,
    History, Vol. I, 3, 13

6   Hebblethwaite, *John XXIII*, 315-316.

7   Ibid., 323.

8   This was to Montini's old teacher, an Oratorian, Father Giulio Bevilacqua; see
    Hebblethwaite, *John XXIII*, 324.

9   Stransky, "The Foundation of the Secretariat for Christian Unity" in Stacpoole,
    Vatican II, 64; Alberigo and Komonchak, *History Vol I*, 15. This is the Pope's
    own words; the "official" Curial version used the word "communities" not
    "Churches" and made other changes.

10 See also J.H. Card. Newman to O'Neill Daunt, 7 August 1870: "It is rare for a
    Council not to be followed by great confusion" in Stacpoole, *John XXIII*, 349;
    Arch. D. Hurley, "Memories of Vatican II", ms; Wiltgen, R.M., *The Rhine Flows
    into the Tiber*, Hawthorne Books, New York, 1967, 12-14; a notable exception
    to this pessimistic view had been Celso Constantini, Apostolic Delegate to
    China who, in 1924, had been pushing the idea of a universal Council of the
    Church; Alberigo and Komonchak, *History Vol I*, 19, 68.

11 Alberigo, G., *A Brief History of Vatican II*, 2006, 11; Anderson, J.B., *A Vatican
    II Pneumatology of the Paschal Mystery: The historical doctrinal genesis of Ad
    Gentes 1, 2-5*, Editrice Pontificia Universita Gregoriana, Rome, 1988, 6.

12 Archbishop Patrick Kelly of Liverpool remembers the tensions between the
    Gregorian and Angelicum universities centred around the theologians B.
    Lonergan S.J. and R. Garrigou-Lagrange O.P. while studying in Rome in the
    late 1950s. Personal communication 2005. Why Lonergan is incompatible with
    neo-scholastic thinking, see Crowe, F.E. (ed.), *Collection*, Herder and Herder,
    New York, 1967.

13 Some 2,821 prelates and institutions were consulted, hence a 76 per cent return;
    see Hebblethwaite, *John XXIII*, 370. Pope John blocked a Curial attempt to
    have the consultation in the form of a questionnaire in favour of an open-ended
    request for suggestions; see Alberigo, *A Brief History*, 5.

14 Hurley, D., "Memories of Vatican II" in Hurley, D., *Vatican II. Keeping the
    Dream Alive*, Cluster Publications, Pietermaritzburg, 2005, 7-12 contains
    Archbishop Hurley's proposals. Alberigo and Komonchak, *History Vol I*, 98-
    140, provides a fascinating analysis of the *vota*. Perhaps the most startling is the
    absence of references to poverty and socio-economic deprivation, even from the
    Latin Americans, though some Brazilian bishops were an exception.

15 Hurley, ms 9.

16 Willebrands, J., "Christians and Jews: A New Vision" quoting Yves Congar
    and Stransky "The Foundation" in Stacpoole, *Vatican II*, 63-66, 220-221;
    Alberigo and Komonchak, *History, Vol I*, 24-25. A fourteen-page document
    produced by the Catholic Conference for Ecumenical Affairs and signed by,

among others, C.J. Dumont and J.G.M.Willebrands, played an important role in these relationships.

17   The curialists had envisaged the SPCU as merely a press office; see Stransky, "The Foundation" in Stacpoole, *Vatican II*, 69.

18   Ibid., 72-73. The intervention of Dr Chaim Wardi of the World Jewish Congress and Israeli Ministry of Religious Affairs in June 1962, announcing his self-proclaimed participation as an observer, had resulted in mounting pressure from the Arab world and a shelving of a distinct document on the Jews, *De Judaeis*. The Melkite Bishops particularly insisted on including Muslims and other religions in any document on the Jews; see Alberigo and Komonchak, *History Vol. III*, 380. John XXIII did, however, have the reference to "perfidious Jews" removed from the Good Friday liturgy; see Oesterreicher, J.M., "Declaration on the Relationship of the Church to Non-Christian Religions" in Vorgrimler, H. (ed.), *Commentary on the Documents of Vatican II. Vol. 3*, Herder and Herder, 1969, 1-42. The document was subject to considerable pressures from Arab governments. See Burigana, R., and Turbini, G., "The Intersession: preparing the Conclusion of the Council" in Alberigo and Komonchak, *History of Vatican II, Vol. IV*, 547-556.

19   Stacpoole, ibid., 73-74; Alberigo and Komonchak, *History Vol. I*, 271-272.

20   Pamphlet entitled "Council for Survival": text of a speech given on the morals of nuclear warfare at the Institute for International Relations, Spokane, Washington, March 1959.

21   Published in the United Kingdom as *The Council and Reunion*, Sheed and Ward, 1961. His book *The Living Church*, made up of talks and speeches delivered on the periphery at the Council, and reflecting on the major debates taking place, was compiled in 1962 and published in 1963. Father Joseph Ratzinger was to join him at Tübingen after the Council.

22   Bea's position was deliberately strengthened by John XXIII when he made him a Cardinal at a critical moment in late January 1960.

23   Hurley, *Vatican II*, 15.

24   Hebblethwaite, *John XXIII*, 387.

25   Ibid.

26   Hurley, *Vatican II*, 12.

27   I am grateful to the late Professor Richard Gray for pointing out the key role of Antonio Bugnini in the Council reform of the liturgy. He was punished for his belief in the vernacular in the liturgy and sacked from his chair in liturgical studies at the Lateran University until rehabilitated by Pope Paul VI.

28   *Mater et Magistra* can be traced back to the 47th French *"Semaine Sociale"* on Socialisation and the Human Person held in July 1960, and the influence of the Belgian Dominican Louis-Joseph Lebret's Economy and Humanism Centre founded in Paris in 1942. However the encyclical was in the classic format of numerous citations from the previous Pope, Pius XII, and references to theologians were absent.

29   Hebblethwaite, *John XXIII*, 397-398.

30   John XXII wrote on 5 June 1960 that the spirit of the faithful had to be: "to consider themselves, as Catholics, citizens of the whole world, just as Jesus is the adored saviour of the whole world"; see Capovilla, "Reflections" in Stacpoole, *Vatican II*, 119. M.D. Chenu highlights the importance of this: "Perhaps it takes a theologian born in the last century to feel how great have been the changes in the Church from a theology of Man that saw men and women patiently waiting

for redemption in an alien world, to one that sees them in the homeland of their redeeming, becoming redeemed and sharing in the work of their Redeemer"; see Chenu, M.D., "A Council for All Peoples" in Stacpoole, *Vatican II*, 19.

31   Suenens, "A Plan" in Stacpoole, *Vatican II*, 88. Cardinal Frings and Archbishop Hurley were also worried and suggested sub-commissions to boil down the preparatory documents into a Council agenda and plan; see Alberigo and Komonchak, *History Vol I*, 340-341.

32   Stacpoole, ibid., 89.

33   Hebblethwaite, *John XXIII*, 408-409.

34   Ibid., 462; Allen, *Benedict XVI*, 53.

35   Denis, P., "The Historical Significance of Denis Hurley's Contribution to the Second Vatican Council" in Hurley, *Vatican II*, 203. Cardinal Léger wrote to the Pope expressing his concerns about what was happening to the preparatory documents in August but by this time it was too late; see Alberigo and Komonchak, *History Vol. I*, 348-349.

36   Gutiérrez, "The Church and the Poor" in Alberigo (ed.), *The Reception*, 178-179.

37   Beckmann, J., "Roman Catholic Missions in the light of the Second Vatican Council", *International Review of Missions*, 1969, Vol. 53, 85-87; *Reception*, 179.

38   Ibid., 178.

39   The Anglican Bishop John Moorman of Ripon refers to a contribution made by a Lutheran observer, Professor Skydsgaard, concerning God's judgement on the Church, being incorporated in a text; see Moorman, J.R.H., "Observers and Guests of the Council" in Stacpoole, *Vatican II*, 42, 167 and in Girault, H. R., "The Reception of Ecumenism" in Alberigo (ed.), *The Reception* 138; interview with George Lindbeck, Lutheran Observer, New Haven, May 2006 who emphasised how most influence was indirect; the Montreal Faith and Order WCC conference in 1963, for example, gave impetus to the ecumenical movement. Lindbeck was critical of Catholic claims to be the "exclusive possessor of the fullness of unity"; see Alberigo and Komonchak, *History Vol. III*, 291.

40   Archbishop Giacomo Lercaro of Bologna, for example, as well as Montini; see Hebblethwaite, *The First Modern Pope*, 287; Alberigo and Komonchak, *History of Vatican II Vol. II*, 36. Archbishop Montini estimated that fewer than 10 per cent of the Italian bishops were in favour of reform.

41   Raguer, Hilari, "The Initial Profile of the Assembly" in Alberigo and Komonchack. *History Vol. II*, 204-207; Schoof, *Breakthrough*, 237-239; Hebblethwaite, *John XXIII*, 427.

42   Congar, Y., *Report from Rome: The First Session of the Vatican Council*, Geoffrey Chapman, London, 1963, 52; Hurley ms; Beckmann, J., "Roman Catholic Missions in the Light of the Second Vatican Council", *International Review of Missions*, 1964, vol. 53, 84.

43   Hurley, *Vatican II*, 21.

44   Both Heenan and Worlock were supportive and generous in their support for the lay apostolate; see Worlock, D., "Toil in the Lord: the Laity in Vatican II" in Stacpoole, *Vatican II*, 237-248. For an account of Worlock's role in the laity commission and *Lumen Gentium* and reflections on the English and Welsh participation in the Council, see Longley, C., *The Worlock Archive*, Geoffrey Chapman, London, 2000.

45   Schoof, *Breakthrough*, 232-233; Hebblethwaite, *John XXIII*, 423.

46   Hurley, *Vatican II*, 24.

47   This was Dr Donal Kerr; see Stacpoole, *Vatican II*.

48   See Bugnini, A., *The Reform of the Liturgy 1948-1975* (trans. O' Connell, M.J.), Collegeville, 1990; Hebblethwaite, *John XXIII*, 449.

49   In a letter to Cardinal Suenens; see Hurley, *Vatican II*, 15.

50   Hebblethwaite, *The First Modern Pope*, 311.

51   *De Duobus Fontibus Revelationis* was debated from 14-20 November 1962; see Congar, Y., "A Last Look at the Council" in Stacpoole, *Vatican II*, 346; Ratzinger, *Theological Highlights*, 20.

52   Congar, Y., *Report from Rome*, 68.

53   Hebblethwaite, *John XXIII*, 456.

54   Stacpoole, *Vatican II*, 43.

55   Hebblethwaite, *The First Modern Pope*, 307, 311, *John XXIII*, 408; Suenens, "A Plan" in Stacpoole, *Vatican II*, 89-102.

56   Ruggieri, G., "Beyond an Ecclesiology of Polemics. The Debate on the Church" in Alberigo and Komonchak, *History Vol. II*, 345-347; Hebblethwaite, *The First Modern Pope*, 312.

57   Pope John Paul II raised the question of poverty again among the Church's high-ranking officials at the inaugural mass of the 10th Synod of Bishops in October 2001; see *The Tablet*, 6 October 2001, 1431; Hebblethwaite, *John XXIII*, 453.

58   See Chapter Five.

4. The Vatican Council: A New Vision

1   Alberigo, G., *A Brief History of Vatican II*, 36.

2   Giuseppe Siri had been Pius XII's right-hand man and was a very powerful figure in the Italian Church although Laraona had, in a masterly fashion, removed the main architect of the liturgy document, Annibel Bugnini, from the conciliar Commission on the Liturgy. He was also removed from his professorship at the Lateran University and left Rome. See Lamberigts, M., "The Liturgy Debate" in Alberigo and Komonchak, *History Vol. II*, 107. Hurley ms, "Memories of Vatican II". Archbishop Hurley manages to make Laraona's heavily accented Spanish Latin sound positively sinister.

3   Hebblethwaite, *The First Modern Pope*, 297.

4   Hebblethwaite, *John XXIII*, 478, 484-487.

5   On peace see Flessati, V., "Pax: The History of the Catholic Peace Society in Britain 1936-1971" unpubl. PhD diss., University of Bradford 1991, 363-415 for an excellent overview of the peace issue at the Council; Toulat, P., "Peace: between the Good News and the Lesser Evil" in Stacpoole, *Vatican II*, 194-197. On human rights—right up until the 1930s the Church was using the language of "natural rights", see Pius XI's *Mit Brennender Sorge* of 1937. Every person: "possesses rights given by God, which must remain safe against every attempt by the community to deny them, abolish them or prevent their exercice". For a concise summary of the evolution of human rights from natural rights see Ruston, R., "Pacem in Terris", paper for a Pax Christi conference, London, May 2003.

6   Suenens is in fact himself quoting Antoine de St Exupery, quoted in

Hebblethwaite, *The First Modern Pope*, 316.

7   Ibid.

8   Hales, E.E.Y., *Pope John and His Revolution*, London, 1965, 63.

9   Hebblethwaite, *The First Modern Pope*, 331.

10   Ibid. , 344, taken from a speech to the Curia 21 September 1963.

11   Ibid., 346; Moorman, "Observers and Guests" in Stacpoole, *Vatican II*, 156-163, reveals some of the irritation caused by *Ad Petri Cathedram*'s "we cherish the hope of your return" and its mistranslation of the Biblical text "one flock, one shepherd" instead of "one fold, one shepherd"—corrected in a later edition of the *Catholic Vulgate Bible*. The equation in *Mystici Corporis* of the Mystical Body with the Catholic Church, i.e. one fold, was the root of the problem. So " *unitatis redintegratio*" was a useful formula.

12   Girault, R. , "The Reception of Ecumenism" and Ruggieri, G., "Faith and History" in *The Reception*, 101-102, 139-140; Congar, Y., "Moving towards a Pilgrim Church" and Moorman, "Observers and Guests" in Stacpoole, *Vatican II*, 136, 176.

13   *Ecclesiam Suam*, 6 August 1964, "The world will not be saved from outside. Like the word of God who became man, we have to some extent to assimilate the forms of life of those to whom we want to take the message of Christ". The role of the Chilean bishops is mentioned in Alberigo, *A Brief History*, 126. See Chapter Nine below.

14   *Vatican Council II: the Basic Sixteen Documents* ed. Flannery A., Dublin 1996, 13. The Louvain theologians led by Gérard Philips tried to build a centrist path between conflicting positions and this is most evident in the *Dogmatic Constitution on the Church*, justifying the wry title Louvain I instead of Vatican II, see Vorgrimler *Commentary* 105-307 for Philips own analysis of the text.

15   Quoted in Anderson, J.A., *A Vatican II Pneumatology of the Paschal Mystery. The Historical-Doctrinal Genesis of Ad Gentes 1, 2-5*, Editrice Pontifica Universita Gregoriana, Roma, 1988, 120; "J'entends un peuple de Dieu structuré"; Congar, Y. , "Moving Towards a Pilgrim Church in Stacpoole, *Vatican II*, 141.

16   Hebblethwaite, *The First Modern Pope*, 349-351.

17   The lay experts were mainly drawn from the *Comité Permanent des Congrès Internationaux pour l'Apostolat des Laïcs* (COPECIAL) and from the Conference of International Catholic Organisations (COIC). Worlock, "Toil in the Lord", in Stacpoole, *Vatican II*, 248; Hurley ms; Longley, *The Worlock Archive*, 183-195; Grootaers, J. , "The Drama continues between the acts" in Alberigo and Komonchak, *History Vol. II*, 419, 436, 440-442; Alberigo and Komonchak, *History Vol. V*, 273 described the final document on the laity as "outdated" within weeks of its publication, nonetheless it was the first conciliar document on the laity ever produced.

18   Alberigo and Komonchak, *History Vol. IV*, 22-23, 25-26. Ms Pilar Bellosillo, president of the World Union of Catholic Organisations—with c. 30 million members—was put forward to speak on Schema XIII, but blocked by the moderators because she was a woman. In the event Prof. Juan Vasquez from Argentina, President of the International Federation of Catholic Youth Organisations, spoke. James Norris spoke earlier in the debate probably relying extensively on the work of another woman, Barbara Ward, and her book *World Poverty and the Christian Conscience*. Despite her pre-eminence she also was not permitted to speak.

19   Anderson, *A Vatican II Pneumatology*, 24-35; Tanner, N., "The Church in the World (Ecclesia ad Extra)" in Alberigo and Komonchak, *History Vol. IV*, 340-342.

20   Alberigo and Komonchak, *History Vol. III*, 463.

21   *Lumen Gentium*, 16 and *Nostra Aetate*, 3-4 deal briefly with Islam. Anxiety was increased by a conference at St Pius X College, Goregaon, Mumbai on 25-28 November on "Christian Revelation and Non-Christian Religions" attended by Hans Küng and Raimundo Pannikar which was interpreted as saying missionaries should help people realise the riches of their own faith and therefore traditional missionary activity was redundant. Likewise, Cardinal Bea's presentation of *Nostra Aetate*: "Nevertheless they can be saved if they obey the voice of their own conscience"; see Hebblethwaite, *The First Modern Pope*, 413-414. On the other hand the influential missionary Archbishop Blomjous of Mwanza, secretary to the English-speaking group of African bishops, emphasised mission as witness rather than as quest for conversions, particularly joint ecumenical witness in the face of Islam; see Alberigo and Komonchak, *History Vol. III*, 490-491. For the consequences of this, see Chapter Nine, below.

22   Hebblethwaite, *The First Modern Pope*, 396-397.

23   Anderson, *A Vatican II Pneumatology*, 73-75, 89, 101; Beckmann, "Roman Catholic Missions", 84. "*Les peuples qui recoivent Jésus-Christ doivent pouvoir l'exprimer, le ré-incarner à leur image et ressemblance, afin qu'il soit tout pour tous*".

24   Hurley, *Vatican II*, 136.

25   Anderson, *A Vatican II Pneumatology*, 62, 67, 90.

26   Ibid., 133. ("*Hereusement il y'a Ratzinger. Il est raisonnable, modeste, désintéressé, un bon secours*").

27   Ibid., 118-124, 183.

28   Congar was attacking canon lawyers such as Professor Buijs in the Gregorian University who thought "the 'real' begins with the juridical determination... Otherwise this is just spirituality or poetry"; see Anderson, *A Vatican II Pneumatology*, 131.

29   Ibid., 199.

30   Gy, Pierre-Marie, *The Reception of Vatican II Liturgical Reforms in the Life of the Church*, Marquette University, Milwaukee, 2003, 16; Lash, "Vatican II" in Iverleigh, *Unfinished Journey*, 14.

31   I am indebted to Professor Denys Turner, at the time Norris-Hulse Professor of Divinity at Cambridge, for discussions about the reception of liturgical renewal. Reform entailed new practical steps beginning in 1965 such as the setting up of a Centre for Liturgical Research and Documentation through a collaboration between the Benedictine monasteries of Mont-Febe in Cameroon and La Bouenza in the Congo; see Turbanti, G., "Toward the Fourth Period" in Alberigo and Komonchak, *A History Vol. V*, 15.

32   Drinkwater, F.H., "Liturgy and Society", *Catholic Worker*, November 1965 (first published in the UK in the *Catholic Herald*) in which he bemoans the time wasted on such "trivialities, repeat trivialities, as concelebration, or Communion in both kinds, or the amount of vernacular to be used, or married deacons, or new definitions about Our Lady", and compares it to Pius X's emphasis on earlier first communions and more frequent communion when the *Sillon* was being banned.

33   Murray, J.C., *The Problem of Religious Freedom*, Woodstock Papers, no. 7,

Newman Press, London 1965, 54. A notable exception was Pietro Pavan, a Professor of Theology at the Lateran University in Rome, who was in favour of religious liberty and with other progressive theologians wanted to see this grounded in a theology of the human person; see Fogarty, G. P., *American Catholic Biblical Scholarship*, San Francisco, 1989, 333.

34 Murray first broached the issue in 1943 in *Theological Studies*, of which he became editor in 1941, and influenced a generation of American Catholics as Professor of Dogmatic Theology at Woodstock College. He was forbidden to speak/write on the issue from 1955 onwards and Cardinal Ottaviani cancelled his invitation to attend the first session of the Council. He was named a *peritus* on 4 April 1963 after Cardinal Spellman insisted that he go to Rome; Rynne, X., *The Third Session*, New York 1965, 31. Murray, J.C., "The Problem of Religious Freedom", *Theological Studies*, 25, 1964, 569; Murray, J.C., *We Hold these Truths*, Sheed and Ward, New York, 1960; see also Walsh, M., "Religious Freedom: the limits of Progress" in *Unfinished Journey*, 140-145 for a concise analysis of Murray's views at the time. Bishop Ddungu of Masaka and Archbishop Zoa of Yaounde felt the declaration particularly important for young Christians. Bea, Willebrands and Hamer had secretly met with Visser d'Hooft, Vischer and Nissiotis in Milan on 15 April 1964 to prepare work on the schema, and a joint working group met at Bossey in early 1965; see Alberigo and Komonchak, *History Vol. V*, 500, 504.

35 Hurley, ms., 82.

36 Ellis, J.T., "Religious Freedom: An American Reaction" in Stacpoole *Vatican II*, 295; Hebblethwaite, *The First Modern Pope*, 434. The "development of doctrine" fig leaf used was the somewhat forced argument that previous Papal condemnation of religious freedom had been in reality a contestation of the "rationalistic presupposition that the state enjoyed juridical omnipotence, i.e. that state had jurisdiction only over public order but it could not pass judgement on religion"; see Miccoli, G., "Two Sensitive Issues: Religious Freedom and the Jews" in Alberigo and Komonchak, *History Vol. IV*, 100-101, 121.

37 Walsh, "Religious Freedom", in *Unfinished Journey*, 143-144.

38 Duffy, E., "Tradition and Reaction: Historical Resources for a Contemporary Renewal", in Iverleigh, *Unfinished Journey*, 60.

39 Gutiérrez, "The Church and the Poor", in Alberigo, *Reception of Vatican II*, 176-177; Hebblethwaite, *The First Modern Pope*, 349.

40 See *Reasons for Living and Hoping: Gaudium et Spes 40 Years On*, Heythrop Institute for Religion, Ethics and Public Life, 2006.

41 Alberigo, *A Brief History*, 115; Ratzinger, *Theological Highlights*, 158; Komonchak, "Vatican II" in Douglass and Hollenbach, *Catholicism and Liberalism*, 87-89; Rahner, for example, missed a key meeting in Ariccia 1-6 February 1965, and was "semi-detached" from the process, and Bishop Wojtyla, like many eastern European bishops rejected the document's "optimism"; see Burigana, R., "The Intersession: Preparing the Conclusion of the Council" in Alberigo and Komonchak, *History Vol. IV*, 524-525; Komonchak, J., "Augustine, Aquinas or the Gospel *sine glossa*? Divisions over *Gaudium et Spes*" in *Unfinished Journey*, 104-107; Hurley ms.

42 Lebret, L., "Notations à la lecture du texte français du 26 juin 1965" quoted in Turbanti, "Toward the Fourth Session", Alberigo and Komonchak, *History Vol. V*, 41, 149; Hurley, ms.108-109.

43 Tanner, N., "The Church in the World: (*Ecclesia ad Extra*)" in Alberigo and

Komonchak, *History Vol. IV*, 290, 300, 314.

44   Hurley, ms., 110; Vorgrimmler, H. (ed.), *Commentary on the Documents of Vatican II, Vol. V*, Herder and Herder, 1996, 363-365; Alberigo and Komonchak, *History IV*, 319-320. Mahon wanted the organisation to tackle poverty, promote missionary efforts for development, channel bishops' charitable efforts and remind the world of its responsibility for international development, a farsighted agenda that was later to be partially realised; see Alberigo and Komonchak, *History Vol. V*, 170.

45   The fast began on 1 October 1965 and lasted for ten days; see Flessati, "The History", 416-417.

46   Toulat, "Peace" in Stacpoole, *Vatican II*, 194-197.

47   Flessati, "The History" , 363. Archbishop Hurley debated the issue with Archbishop Roberts at the Council and supported Pax while accepting deterrence theory.

48   *Gaudium et Spes*, 8. At a Pax Christi General Council, Cardinal Alfrink described nuclear weapons as "opposed to the dignity of the human species, even if they do not destroy it". The key opposition came from Spellman, New York, Shehan, Baltimore, and Hannan, New Orleans; see Alberigo and Komonchak, *History Vol.V*, 13, 419.

49   The point is made in Komonchak "Vatican II" in Douglass and Hollenbach, *Catholicism and Liberalism*, 82.

50   *Gaudium et Spes*, 36.

51   Ibid., 76.

52   I am grateful to James Hanvey SJ for some of the insights in this summary; see Hanvey, J., "God in the World: the Dynamic Presence of Christ and the Spirit in *Gaudium et Spes*", *The Institute Series*, 2, 29-56, Heythrop Institute for Religion, Ethics and Public Life, 2006.

53   Hebblethwaite, *The First Modern Pope*, 431.

54   Pelletier, D., "Une Marginalité engagée, le groupe 'Jésus, L'Eglise et Les Pauvres" in Lamberigts, M., Grootaers, J. (eds), *Les Commissions Conciliaires à Vatican II*, Leuven, 1996, 63-91; Gutiérrez, "The Church and the Poor" in Alberigo, *The Reception of Vatican II*, 180; interview, Geoffrey Chapman, May 2006.

55   See Chapters Five and Six below.

56   Hebblethwaite, *The First Modern Pope*, 449.

57   Gutiérrez, "The Church and the Poor" in Alberigo *The Reception of Vatican II*,182.

58   Newman, J.H., to O'Neill Daunt, 7 August 1870: "It is rare for a Council not to be followed by great confusion", quoted in Congar, Y., "A last look at the Council" in Stacpoole, *Vatican II,* 349.

59   Lash, "Tides and Twilight" in Ker and Hill, *Newman after a Hundred Years,* 459.

60   Gutiérrez, "The Church and the Poor" in Alberigo, *The Reception of Vatican II,* 176.

61   Quotes taken from Koehlinger, *The New Nuns*, 175.

62   It is telling, for example, to find Karl Rahner writing a foreword for *The Church as Mission*, a book on the Masai by the American missionary, Eugene Hillman, Herder and Herder 1965, see Dries, *The Missionary Movement*, 270; Alberigo and Komonchak, *History Vol. IV*, 630.

5. The Church of the Poor in Latin America

1   Pelletier, D.,"Une Marginalité engagée, le groupe 'Jésus, L'Eglise et Les Pauvres" in *Les Commissions Conciliaires à Vatican II*, Lamberigts, M., *et al.* (eds), Leuven, 1996, 64.

2   Siefer, G., *The Church and Industrial Society*, Darton, Longman and Todd, London, 1964 has the best history of the movement and its motivations and checks.

3   The idea of underdevelopment as a product of capitalism was spelt out by Paul Baran in 1957 and elaborated in the 1960s by André Gunder Frank. It was particularly attractive in Latin America where indigenous economists had been emphasising the problems of dependency. But the theory came under intense criticism in the 1970s after being absorbed by many Latin American theologians: see Baran, P.A., *The Political Economy of Growth* Penguin 1973 (1957) and Frank, A.G., *Capitalism and Underdevelopment in Latin America: Historical Studies of Chile and Brazil*, Monthly Review Press, New York, 1967; Dodson, M., "The Christian Left in Latin American Politics" in Levine, D. (ed.), *Churches and Politics in Latin America*, Sage, London, 1979, 120-122.

4   Alberigo and Komonchak, *History Vol. IV,* 382.

5   Dussel, E., "Populus Dei in Populo Pauperum: From Vatican II to Medellín and Puebla" in Boff, L., and Elizondo, V. (eds), *La Iglesia Popular: Between Hope and Fear* , Concilium T.T. Clark, Edinburgh, 1984, 43; Pelletier in *Commissions Conciliaires*, 65-69.

6   De Broucker, J., *The Violence of a Peacemaker: Dom Helder,* 1970, 152.

7   Pelletier in *Commissions Conciliaires*, 73.

8   Alberigo and Komonchak, *History Vol. III*, 95; ibid., *Vol. II*, 202.

9   Alberigo, G., *A Brief History of Vatican II* , Orbis, Maryknoll, 2006, 80-81; Pelletier in *Commissions Conciliaires*, 80.

10   O'Mahony, A., "Paul VI and Jerusalem: the Theology and Politics of a Papal Journey" Heythrop College, 14 February 2007.

11   Alberigo and Komonchak *History Vol. IV*, 384-386, *History Vol. V*, 5.

12   "*Une forme d'intransigeance à l'égard de la machine conciliaire*" is Pelletier's verdict on the dispute on the basis of interviews.

13   Pelletier in *Commissions Conciliaires*, 87-88.

14   Bruneau, T.C., *The Political Transformation of the Brazilian Catholic Church*, Cambridge University Press, 1974, 117; Mainwaring, Scott, *The Catholic Church and Politics in Brazil 1916-1985* Stanford University Press 1986, 96. Much of the material on Brazil in this chapter is heavily indebted to these detailed studies.

15   Beeson, T. and Pearce, J., *A Vision of Hope: The Churches and Change in Latin America*, Collins, Glasgow, 1984, 77-84. Dom Helder Camara's closeness to the government of President Goulart was used effectively against him after the coup, but support for it also came from Cardinal Carlos Carmelo Motta of São Paulo. The hierarchy in all events supported the reformist measures of both the Juscelino Kubitschek (1956-January 1961) and João Goulart (August 1961-1964) periods, while coming to denounce the transnational involvement in the Brazilian economy.

16   Bruneau, *Political Transformation,* 71.

17   Ibid., 79-84.

18   De Broucker, *The Violence of a Peacemaker*, 29.

19   Mainwaring *The Catholic Church and Politics in Brazil*, 56; Smith, B.H., *The Church and Politics in Chile: Challenges to Modern Catholicism*, Princeton University Press, 1982, 109-110.

20   Paulo Freire's *Educaçao Como Pratica de Liberdade*, written in prison under the military regime, was first published in Rio in 1967 but only appeared in English in 1972 in New York, published by Herder and Herder as *Pedagogy of the Oppressed* and in London by Sheed and Ward, in 1973. Three thousand copies of the MEB's New Primer *Viver e Lutar* (To Live is to Struggle) were confiscated in February 1964 on the orders of Carlos Lacerda, Governor of Guanabara state whose capital was Rio. It was a typical piece of conscientisation literature describing the Brazilian situation and highlighting the clash of class interests.

21   For Gramsci's evolution away from Leninism, see Laclau, E., and Mouffe, C., *Hegemony and Socialist Strategy*, Verso, London, 1985, 65-71; Mainwaring, *The Catholic Church and Politics in Brazil*, 206, 222-223. Bruneau in *Political Transformation* has a narrow view of Catholic commitment to social change solely as a product of fear of Communism that cannot be substantiated even by the data of his own excellently researched study.

22   Bruneau, *Political Transformation*, 94-98.

23   The result of this was severe criticism of Helder Camara in the press and by parts of the hierarchy, and his removal as national assistant to the Catholic student movement; see Bruneau, *Political Transformation*, 100.

24   Beeson and Pearce, *A Vision of Hope*, 90; Bruneau, *Political Transformation*, 124.

25   Lernoux, P., *Cry of the People*, Penguin, Harmondsworth, 1982, 42-44. For example a number of conservative bishops spoke out against the repression of the Catholic worker movement, and a handful of bishops suffered grievously at the hands of paramilitary and military forces, for example, Dom Adriano Hipólito, who did not have full support from his clergy, was humiliated and abused physically, and even Cardinal Aloisio Lorscheider was detained in one instance. This undoubtedly contributed to a certain solidarity in the Brazilian Church not found to the same extent in Central America; see Mainwaring, *The Catholic Church and Politics in Brazil*, 239.

26   See Mulligan, J., *The Nicaraguan Church and the Revolution*, Sheed and Ward, London, 1999, 99; Lernoux, P., *Hearts of Fire. The Story of the Maryknoll Sisters*, Orbis, Maryknoll, 1993, 152-159.

27   De Broucker, *Violence of a Peacemaker*, 42.

28   Linden, I., *Liberation Theology. Coming of Age?*, COMMENT CIIR, London, 1997, 8.

29   The statistics for Aguilares are taken from Berryman, P., *The Religious Roots of Rebellion*, SCM Press, London, 1984, 108.

30   See Gunder Frank, A., *Latin America: Underdevelopment or Revolution*, Monthly Review Press, New York, 1969.

31   Linden, *Liberation Theology*, 11.

32   *Paroles de l'Eglise Catholique sur le développement*, French Justice and Peace Commission, 1990, 75.

33   *Gaudium et Spes*, 36.

34   A.F. McGovern "Dependency Theory, Marxist Analysis and Liberation Theology" in Ellis, M. H., and O. Maduro, O. (eds), *The Future of Liberation Theology: Essays in Honour of Gustavo Gutiérrez* Orbis, Maryknoll, 1989, 272; Linden, *Liberation Theology*, 13-14.

35   Dorr, D., *Option for the Poor,* Gill and Macmillan, Dublin, 1983, 139-143 for a discussion of *Populorum Progressio* and radicalism.

36   Filibeck, G., *The Right to Development,* Pontifical Council for Justice and Peace, Vatican City, 1991, 7.

37   Lebret, Louis-Joseph, *Dynamique concrète de développement,* Economie et Humanisme, Paris, 1961, 28.

38   Dorr, *Option for the Poor,* 144.

39   *Populorum Progressio,* 21.

40   Cardenal, E., *The Gospel in Solentiname* (4 vols trans. D. Walsh), Orbis, Maryknll, 1976-1982 gives extensive insights into the life of the community before it was attacked and razed to the ground by Somoza's National Guard. See also *Basic Christian Communities,* LADOC, Washington, DC, no. 14, 1976 for a useful, short account.

41   Berryman, P., *Liberation Theology,* Pantheon, New York 1987, 67; Dries, *The Missionary Movement,* 216-221.

42   Segundo, J.L., *The Liberation of Theology,* Orbis, 1976, 8: "each new reality obliges us to interpret the word of God afresh, to change reality accordingly, and then to go back and reinterpret the word of God again". This might seem an unhelpful invitation to open the floodgates to relativism, no doubt noted in Rome. Likewise Segundo cites the Protestant theologian Bultmann here in his first chapter on hermeneutics and Gutiérrez begins his *Theology of Liberation* with a quote from Bultmann, red rags to the CDF bull.

43   Helder Camara used the phrase in a press conference as the Council drew to a close. For a more elaborate analysis, see M.A. Vasquez, *The Brazilian Popular Church and the Crisis of Modernity,* Cambridge University Press, 1998, 23-35.

44   The volume of articles entitled, somewhat inappropriately, *The Challenge of Basic Christian Communities,* from a 1980 Ecumenical Congress of Theology held in São Paulo in 1980 (Torres, Sergio, and Eagleton, John, eds, trans. John Drury) Orbis, Maryknoll, 1982 gives some indication of what a flagship CEBs had become for radical theologians.

45   Vasquez points out that it is "incorrect to reduce the popular Church to liberation theology" and that theological reflection took place at two levels each with a degree of autonomy and reciprocal influence, one involving lay pastoral agents, the other the priest and professional theologian who joined in community life. The comparison between missionary—catechist and theologian—pastoral agent is not far fetched with the Delegates of the Word/pastoral agents acting as mediators between the two levels of theological reflection, see Vasquez, *The Brazilian Popular Church,* 47.

46   *The Church in the Present-Day Transformation of Latin America in the Light of the Council: Medellín Conclusions,* CELAM, Washington, DC, Secretariat for Latin America, NCCB, 1979, 6, 177; Dussel, E., *The History of the Church in Latin America. Colonialism to Liberation 1492-1979* Eerdmans, Grand Rapids, MI, 1981, 145.

47   *The Church in the Present-Day,* 19, 59, 110.

48   Ibid., 176.

49   De Broucker, *The Violence of a Peacemaker,* speech at the inauguration of the Theological Institute of Recife, 91.

50   Interview with Cardinal Walter Kaspar, Worth Abbey, 2005, who confirmed that the events of 1968 had produced an extraordinarily strong reaction in

Joseph Ratzinger, as does John Allen in his *Benedict XVI*, Continuum, London, 2001.

51   It is important to underline that this accounts only for the Catholic origins of liberation theology. Rubem Alves, a Brazilian Presbyterian theologian, was submitting a doctoral dissertation to Princeton at the time entitled "Towards a Theology of Liberation". In 1969 it was published—but the publishers tellingly did not like the original title and changed it to *A Theology of Hope*. It reverted to *liberaçion* in Spanish translation in 1970. Alves and Gutiérrez met in SODEPAX conference in Cartigny, Switzerland, in 1969 where Gutiérrez presented a lecture based on "Notes toward a theology of liberation" and discovered they were working on similar lines. By the 1980s, the Argentinian Methodist, Miguel Bonino, had become a highly respected liberation theologian. See Tombs, D., "Latin American Liberation Theology Faces the Future" in, Porter, S.E., Hayes, M.A. and Tombs, D. (eds), *Faith in the Millennium*, Sheffield Academic Press, Sheffield, 2001, 38; Dussel, E., *The Church in Latin America 1492-1992*, Burns and Oates, 1992, 392.

52   Betto, Frei, "Gustavo Gutiérrez: A Friendly Profile" in *The Future of Liberation Theology: Essays*, 36-38, 49-53. Gutiérrez himself points to Chenu's book *The Saulchoir School* as opening up the scope of history for him during his first seminary years; see Gutiérrez, G., "The Task of Theology and Ecclesial Experience" in *La Iglesia Popular*, 61.

53   See footnote 51. There were a number of symposia on "liberation" theology throughout Latin America in the period 1969-1971. In Autumn 1970, the secretary-general of CELAM, Eduardo Pironio later cardinal, wrote a paper called "A Theology of Liberation" for the Argentine Ministry of Education; see Dussel, *The Church in Latin America*, 394. The word later used in South Africa was "contextual theology" largely as a defensive measure for survival under apartheid. Personal Communication, Father Albert Nolan.

54   See Chapter VI.

55   Sobrino, J. *Christology at the Crossroads*, SCM Press, London, 1978.

56   Gutiérrez, G., *A Theology for Today: the Option for the Poor in 2005*, CAFOD, London, 2005, 9; Gutiérrez in *La Iglesia Popular*, 63.

57   Linden, *Liberation Theology*, 5-6.

58   *The Church in the Present Day Transformation*, 175. The bishops of the North East had said this in a 14 July 1966 document: "The Church has to favour those who suffer; those who cannot earn their daily bread even with the abundant sweat of their labour, those who have been condemned to stagnation in subhuman living conditions". Publication was forbidden by the police and the document confiscated; see Scott Mainwaring, *The Catholic Church and Politics in Brazil, 1916-1985*, Stanford University Press, Stanford, CA, 1985, 98.

6. The Church in Conflict

1   Lernoux, P., *Cry of the People*, Penguin, Harmondsworth, 1982, 56.

2   Ibid. , 13, 24; Lernoux, P., *Hearts on Fire. The Story of the Maryknoll Sisters*, Orbis, 1993, 229-234. Eleven US missionaries were killed between 1959-1990; see Dries, *The Missionary Movement*, 235.

3   For the antecedents to this counter-insurgency strategy see Comblin, J., *The Church and the National Security State*, Orbis, Maryknoll, 1984, 64-74;

Beeson, T., and Pearce, J., *A Vision of Hope: The Churches and Change in Latin America*, Collins, Glasgow, 1984, 119-120; Lernoux, *Cry of the People*, 142-145. Comblin, who was Rector of the major regional seminary in North East Brazil, was himself refused entry on returning from Belgium in 1972 and thus deported. For Angelelli see Klaiber, J., *The Church, Dictatorships and Democracy in Latin America*, Orbis, Maryknoll, 1998, 82; Smith, B.H., "Churches and Human Rights in Latin America" in Levine, D. (ed.), *Churches and Politics in Latin America*, Sage, Los Angeles, 1979, 179

4   Smith, B.H., *The Church and Politics in Chile*, Princeton University Press, NJ, 1982, 231-237.

5   Ibid., 174, 186-187.

6   The CpS statement "*Mensaje a los cristianos de America Latina*", Havana 3 March 1972, had the ring of a direct challenge to the teaching authority of the hierarchies of the continent.

7   Ibid., 242; Dodson, D., "The Christian Left in Latin American Politics" in Levine, *Churches and Politics*, 1979, 11-134, provides a good comparative study of CpS with the movement of Priests for the Third World in Argentina.

8   Ibid., 254-257.

9   Lernoux, *Cry of the People*, 26-27, 291-293.

10   Ibid., 28; Vekemans, R., "*Unidad y pluralismo en la Iglesia*", Tierra Nueva, 5, 1973, 45-50; *Teologia de la Liberaçion y Cristianos por le Socialismo*, Bogota, 1976 for examples of the counter-attack. On the other hand, the US Catholic Mission Council put relatively successful pressure on the US government in 1975 to stop the CIA approaching missionaries in the field for intelligence; see Dries, *The Missionary Movement*, 231.

11   Dussel, E., "Current Events in Latin America (1972-1980) in Torres, S. , and Eagleson, J. (eds) , *The Challenge of Basic Christian Communities* Orbis, Maryknoll, 1982, 82-83; Berryman, P., *Liberation Theology*, Pantheon, 1987, 98-99.

12   Mainwaring, Scott, *The Catholic Church and Politics in Brazil* 80-93; Lernoux, *Cry of the People*, 268-277. Casaldáliga faced a situation reminiscent of the nineteenth-century Congo with land companies burning down villages, private armies, and death threats. He responded on being consecrated bishop in October 1971 with a 120 page document "A Church in the Amazon in Conflict with the Latifundia and with Social Marginalistion" and was a charismatic figure in the Latin American Church; see Bishop Pedro Casaldáliga, *Prophets in Combat*, trans/ed. Berryman, P.,Meyer Stone/CIIR, 1987.

13   Berryman, P., *The Religious Roots of Rebellion*, SCM Press, 1984, 33. For killing and explusion of Church personnel in Guatemala, see Klaiber, *The Church, Dictatorships and Democracy*, 224-229.

14   Boff, L., "A Theological Examination of the terms 'People of God' and 'Popular Church' in Boff, L., and Elizondo, V. (eds), *The People of God amidst the Poor*, Concilium, 1984, 89-98 for an example.

15   Berryman, *The Religious Roots of Rebellion*, 59-74.

16   Mulligan, J., *The Nicaraguan Church and the Revolution*, Sheed and Ward, Kansas, 1991, 123-125.

17   The Nicaraguan Bishops Conference "Message to the People of God" of 6 January 1978 itemised sixteen specific abuses suffered by the Nicaraguan people in an overwhelming indictment of *Somoçismo*; see Berryman, *The Religious Roots of Rebellion*, 77.

18   Ibid., 80-83; Mulligan, *The Nicaraguan Church*, 125-128; Klaiber, *The Church, Dictatorships and Democracy*, 197.

19   Berryman, *The Religious Roots of Rebellion*, 230-231.

20   There had been nothing moral about the Apostolic Delegate drinking champagne with Somoza on the National Holiday, 15 September 1978, while the dictator's planes bombed the poor quarters of Esteli; see Mulligan, *The Nicaraguan Church*, 129.

21   Interviews conducted with ex-combatants in Nicaragua during 1987.

22   Ezcurra, A.M., *Ideological Aggression against the Sandinista Revolution: The Political Opposition Church in Nicaragua* in Unger, L., and Kalke, D.J. (eds), CIRCUS Publications, New York, 1984, 26-57, sets out a hardline Sandinista position on the Church discourse.

23   *Guatemala Never Again! The Official Report of the Human Rights Office, Archdiocese of Guatemala. REMHI Recovery of Historical Memory Project,* CIIR/LAB/Orbis, 1999 provides an in-depth study of human rights violations until the 1991 agreement. *Quitar el Agua al pez; Analisis del terror en tres communidades rurales de Guatemala, (1980-1984)* Centro Internacional para Investigaciones en Derechos Humanos (CIIDH), 1996 focuses on three rural communities to illustrate counter-insurgency tactics.

24   Berryman, *The Roots of Religious Rebellion*, 106-109.

25   Ibid., 117-122; *Cry of the People* 77-79.

26   Ibid., 122.

27   See Comblin, *The Church and the National Security State*, 182-183. Comblin sets out three "temptations of the modern-day Church", adopting destructive revolutionary movements, secularisation and separation into a *societas perfecta.*

28   Berryman, *The Roots of Religious Rebellion*, 122-129.

29   Lernoux, P., "The Long Path to Puebla" in Eagleson, J., and Scharper, P. (eds), *Puebla and Beyond*, Orbis, 1979, 23-24.

30   Filochowski, J., "Medellín to Puebla" in *Reflections on Puebla* CIIR, London, 1980, 12-13.

31   Lernoux, *Cry of the People*, 420; "The Long Path to Puebla", 24.

32   Moises Sandoval, "Report from the Conference" in *Puebla and Beyond*, 30-31.

33   Ibid; Filochowski, "Medellín to Puebla", 18-19; Lernoux, "The Long Path to Puebla", 24.

34   Lernoux "The Long Path to Puebla", 24.

35   Sandoval, "Report from the Conference", 28-30. Lopez Trujillo's careful plans to "swing the moderates" were hindered when he inadvertently passed a letter to Archbishop Luciano Duarte of Aracaju, his man in the Brazilian Conference, to a journalist. It contained derogatory comments about a number of prominent figures from Father Arrupe, head of the Jesuits, to Cardinal Pironio, Prefect of the Vatican Congregation for Religious; see for full text Filochowski, "Medellín to Puebla", 15-16.

36   Ibid., 34-39.

37   Ibid., 32.

38   Hebblethwaite, P., "Liberation Theology and the Roman Catholic Church" in Rowland, C., *The Cambridge Companion to Liberation Theology*, Cambridge University Press, 1999, 182-183; Sobrino, J., "The significance of Puebla for the Catholic Church in Latin America" in *Reflections on Puebla*, 26; Luxmore and

Babiuch, *The Vatican and the Red Flag*, 178-180.

39 The text of the Pope's homily in Puebla can be found on pp. 77-81 of *Puebla and Beyond* with a very thoughtful commentary by Virgilio Elizondo, pp. 47-5; c.f. Wojtyla, K., *Aby Chrystus sie nami poslugiwal*, published in Krakow, 1979, 169-179, quoted in Luxmore and Babiuch *The Vatican and the Red Flag*, 90: "Without exaggeration, we can say that Jesus Christ engaged in this struggle himself —but within a dimension greater than that of those who wish to see him only as a "first Socialist".

40 The addresses at Oaxaca, Basilica of Guadeloupe and in Chiapas are found on pp. 72-87 of *Puebla and Beyond*; for the Rome speech see *Uno mas uno* in Dussel, *The History of the Church*, 235.

41 Most notably in an address to priests at the Basilica of Guadeloupe on 27 January 1979. Gustavo Guttierez wrote to the Puebla Conference via Archbishop Marcos McGrath of Panama, who chaired the presiding committee of five, to explain that the liberation theologians were in town to support the bishops not as a "parallel magisterium".

42 Lernoux, *Cry of the People*, 433.

43 Sobrino, "The Significance of Puebla", 23.

44 Erdozain, P., *Archbishop Romero: Martyr of Salvador*, Orbis, Maryknoll, 1980, 28 and Sobrino "The Significance of Puebla", 23 have slightly different versions of this remark.

45 Published on 6 August 1978, his third pastoral letter, in English translation, is contained in Sobrino, J., and Martín-Baró, I., *Archbishop Oscar Romero: Voice of the Voiceless*, Orbis, Maryknoll, 1985, 85-114.

46 Remhi Recovery of Historical Memory Project, *Guatemala Never Again! The Official Report of the Human Rights Office, Archdiocese of Guatemala* Orbis/ CIIR/LAB, 1999, 5-28, 213-214; Beeson, T., and Pearce, J., *A Vision of Hope*, 257.

47 The sub-committee was chaired by an Alabama Republican, Jeremiah Denton and heard a right-wing clerical witness, Father Enrique Rueda, describe how liberation theology was part of the Soviet Union's tactics for culturally undermining the USA and Latin America; see Allen, *Benedict XVI*, 154; Diamond, S., *Spiritual Warfare: The Politics of the Christian Right*, Pluto Press, 1989, 147-150; Mulligan, *The Nicaraguan Church*, 176-177, c.f. Brazil's Second Army report of 1974 that described the clergy as "the most active of the enemies that threaten our national security. Through decidedly subversive processes, they are promoting the substitution of the political, social and economic structures of Brazil by a new order, inspired by Marxian philosophy", quoted in Mainwaring, *The Catholic Church and Politics in Brazil*, 155.

48 Berryman, *Roots of Rebellion*, 149-150.

49 Ibid.

50 Sobrino and Martín-Baró *Voice of the Voiceless*, 191-193 for the sermon in full.

51 Allen, *Benedict XVI*, 150.

52 This included people such as Maria Elena Moyano, a mayor of Villa El Salvador, in Peru, who opposed the guerrillas. She led a massive march against Sendero Luminosa and was shortly after murdered by them. Sobrino, J., *A Crucified Peoples*, CIIR, London, 1989; Klaiber, *The Church, Dictatorships and Democracy*, 166, 175.

53 Chomsky, N., *Deterring Democracy*, Verso, London, 1991, 354; Aguilar, M.I.,

Current Issues on Theology and Religion in Latin America and Africa, Edwin Mellen Press, Lampeter, 2002, 74-85.

54   See Dussel, *The Church in Latin America*, 428. Ezcurra, *Ideological Aggression*, 30-31 offers some fascinating glimpses of the way that the wishes of the Blessed Virgin in popular piety were manipulated ideologically, a phenomenon also found in Rwanda during a period of intense civil conflict in the early 1990s, as well, of course, as in the Fatima revelations and other apparitions where "Communism" played a great role. The Virgin had appeared in Cuapa in 1980 and again to Bernardo Martinez in May 1987 calling on people to burn atheistic books; see pp. 46-53 of *Ideological Aggression* which provide an interesting analysis of what is called the "political discourse" of the Nicaraguan bishops.

55   According to David Wiley there was no Cross visible in the Plaza and Cuban cadres led the chanting; see Wiley, D., *God's Politician*, Faber and Faber, London, 1993, 123; according to Pablo Richard the content of the Pope's homily was interpreted as his supporting the anti-revolutionary forces in Nicaragua and setting up an ideological opposition, Church-people with the *Frente Sandinista*, and the demonstration voiced this concern; see Ezcurra, *Ideological Aggression*, 11-12.

56   Allen, *Benedict XVI*, 156-157; Hebblethwaite, "Liberation Theology", 186-190.

57   Ibid. , 190-195. Nicaragua as well as Cuba by now may have been specifically informing these judgements about liberation. By 1985 Nicaragua had become a touchstone for the theological disputes in the Church. On the one hand, ten foreign priests had had their residence permits revoked, Bishop Pablo Antonio Vega was about to be deported to Honduras by the Sandinistas for his support for the Contras and Bishop Obando Y Bravo was questioning the legitimacy of the government. On the other hand Bishop Pedro Casaldáliga and Gustavo Gutiérrez arrived on "pilgrimage" in Managua to support Father Miguel d'Escoto's fast for spiritual renewal in Nicaragua; see *Prophets in Combat: The Nicaraguan Journal of Bishop Pedro Casaldaliga*, CIIR, London, 1987; Mulligan, *The Nicaraguan Church*, 196; Allen, *Benedict XVI*, 157.

58   Hebblethwaite, "Liberation Theology", 191; Linden, I., *Liberation Theology Coming of Age*, CIIR Comment, 1987, 17-18; Allen, *Benedict XVI*, 161-162.

59   *Pronończiamentos do Papa no Brasil*, Petropolis, 1980, 55,57; Mainwaring, *The Catholic Church and Politics in Brazil*, 246.

60   Allen, *Benedict XVI*, 165-167, 239.

61   See Chapter Nine.

7. Radicals and Liberals in the Philippines and South Africa

1   Hebblethwaite, P., *Synod Extraordinary: the Inside Story of the Rome Synod November/December 1985*, Darton, Longman, Todd, London, 1986, 37.

2   Ibid., 58. This was taken from an article in *Concilium*.

3   Quoted from *Herder Korrespondenz* by Sobrino, J., in *Christology at the Crossroads*, SCM Press, 1978, 10.

4   Barbara Ward, later Lady Jackson, had been active in the Sword of the Spirit in the 1940s. The publication of *Populorum Progressio* (see Ward, B., "Looking back on Populorum Progressio", *Doctrine and Life*, 29 (1978), 202), was a strong motivating factor in her participation in the Pontifical Commission. Her

book, Ward, B., and Dubois, R., *Only One Earth*, Penguin, Harmondsworth, 1972, was one of the first major popular warnings of a forthcoming ecological crisis.

5   This was particularly true of the Polish Communist Party after the appointment of John Paul II; see Luxmore, J., and Babiuch, J., *The Vatican and the Red Flag*, Geoffrey Chapman, London, 1999, 203-240.

6   Gremillion, J., *The Gospel of Peace and Justice: Catholic Social Teaching Since Pope John*, Orbis, Maryknoll, 1976, 485-512.

7   During my own time at the Catholic Institute for International Relations (CIIR), a front page headline story about a Rhodesian Front political meeting, telephoned via Catholic channels, featured in first editions of *The Times* in May 1978. It was later that night "pulled" by the editor, William Rees-Mogg, as detrimental to the cause of the Smith-Muzorewa coalition. The reporting of the Wiriamu massacre in Mozambique in 1973 was an early example of the network's potential. It was thanks in part to this network that East Timor stayed in the press; see Kohen, A.S., *From the Place of the Dead: Bishop Belo and the Struggle for East Timor*, Lion Publishing, Oxford, 1999.

8   Luxmore and Babiuch, *The Vatican and the Red Flag*, 38, 172.

9   Tang, E., and Wiest, J.-P. (eds), *The Catholic Church in Modern China*, Orbis, Maryknoll, 1993 provides a useful analysis. Obituary of Bishop James Xie Shiguang, *The Independent*, 8 September 2005, 55.

10 During interviews with Catholics in Moscow in 1991 it was apparent that formal dialogue by Latin American theologians with the Communist Party of the Soviet Union, without meeting any local Christians, had caused outrage. They had heard of Cardinal Evaristo Arns but were convinced he was a Communist. Timothy Radcliffe OP remembers one contrary example, a Chilean priest dancing for joy at the arrival at the General-Chapter in 1989 of Father Dominic Duka from Czechoslavakia. Duka was a factory worker and his fellow workers covered for his absence. Another instance was dinner with a Croatian and Portuguese Dominican in Lyons and their moving sharing of their prison experiences. These tell of warmer relations, though Albert Nolan's memories are similar to mine in Moscow.

11 Polish Catholic culture, the soul of the nation, was the core of resistance, hence the political and spiritual were inextricably linked. Hence also the political significance of his prayer in Warsaw's Victory Square in 1979 "Let Your Spirit come down and renew the face of this land, *this land*". Luxmore and Babiuch, 215-216.

12 Smith, B., "The Churches and Human Rights in Latin America" in Levine, D. (ed.), *Churches and Politics in Latin America*, Sage Publications, 1979, 155-187.

13 Sr Katherine Anne Gilfeather, "Women Religious, the Poor, and the Institutional Church in Chile", *Journal of Interamerican Studies and World Affairs*, Vol. 21, No.1, February 1979, 129-155.

14 Ibid.

15 For a sensitive assessment of the problem, see Sobrino, J., "Getting Real about the Option for the Poor" in Filochowski, J., and Stanford, P., *Opening Up. Speaking Out in the Church*, Darton, Longman and Todd, London, 2005, 17-30.

16 Youngblood, R.L., *Marcos Against the Church: Economic Development and Political Repression in the Philippines*, Cornell University Press, Ithaca, NY,

1990, 4, 76.

17   Fabella, V., and Mulligan, D., *Maryknoll Sisters in the Philippines*, Maryknoll, Orbis, 2001, 119.

18   De la Torre, E., *Touching Ground, Taking Root: Theological and Political Reflections on the Philippine Struggle*, CIIR/BCC, London, 1986, 27-37.

19   Ibid., 51-77. Some of the non-Maoist Left and Social Democrats were also willing to countenance armed struggle.

20   Ibid., 114-120; Youngblood, *Marcos Against the Church*, 81-83.

21   Gomburza Declaration, 17 February 1972.

22   It was his alienation of large sections of the Filipino middle class in the early 1980s, culminating in the assassination of Aquino, that finally resulted in his overthrow in 1986.

23   Karl Gaspar complained that the CNL, even after Aquino's murder in 1983, were pushing the faith dimension of the struggle against Marcos to the "back-burner", and that "liturgy, prayer and companionship" were being neglected. Their commitment was to a politicisation of the Church, the "transformation of the Church" required for a national democratic revolution. This allowed Cory Aquino and the middle class to capture the rich repertoire of Catholic symbols and culture, so evident during the EDSA velvet revolution. Interview with Karl Gaspar in 1985.

24   The creation of Basic Christian Communities (BCCs or in Latin America CEBs), for example, was interpreted by Intelligence agents as sinister. "They are practically building an infrastructure of political power in the entire country". See Galileo C. Kintanar, "Contemporary Religious Radicalism in the Philippines" , *Quarterly National Security Review of the NDCP*, June 1979; Interviews conducted in Philippines during 1985 with Church personnel.

25   See Chapter Six.

26   *Laborem Exercens* on the nature of work was published by John Paul II in 1981. Support could vary from praying for the strikers, to making them sandwiches to confronting "goons" on the picket line itself. Youngblood, *Marcos Against the Church*, 95-119.

27   Ibid., 92.

28   Ibid., 159-161.

29   The leadership of the major grouping of the Protestant Churches by Revd Fely Cariño was instrumental in consolidating the strong WCC position throughout the 1980s.

30   There was, though, a wider spectrum of radical "contextual theology" positions in the Philippines from Carlos H. Abesamis, Catalino G. Arevalo and Antonio B. Lambino, respected theologians outside the NDF orbit, and also a distinctive Jesuit contribution; see Tano, R.D., *Theology in the Philippines. A Case study in the Contextualisation of Theology*, New Day, Quezon City, 1981.

31   This was the imbalance also found in Rhodesia; see Linden, I., *The Catholic Church and the Struggle for Zimbabwe*, Longman, Harlow, 1980.

32   Hurley, D.E., *Vatican II: Keeping the Dream Alive*, Cluster Publications, Pietermaritzburg, 2005, 3; Tobias, P., "Evolution and Theology: Teilhard de Chardin and Archbishop Denis Hurley" in Gamley, A.M. (ed.), *Denis Hurley: A Portrait by Friends*, Cluster Publications, Pietermaritzburg, 2001, 86-98.

33   Ryall, D., "Between God and Caesar: The Catholic Church in South Africa 1948-1990", unpubl. PhD diss., University of Swansea, 1998, 51.

34   Kearney, P., *Guardian of the Light: Archbishop Denis Hurley. A Life against*

Apartheid, Continuum, London, 2008.

35   Ibid.

36   Ryall, "Between God and Caesar", 143-148.

37   Walshe, P., *Church versus State in South Africa. The Case of the Christian Institute*, C. Hurst & Co., London, 1983, 76-77.

38   Hurley, D.E., *Apartheid. A Crisis of the Christian Conscience*, SAIRR, 1964, 16-18.

39   Kearney, *Guardian of the Llight*.

40   Pope Paul VI finally spoke to the UN Committee against Apartheid in 1974 rejecting recourse to violence.

41   Macmillan's full sentence ended "and whether we like it or not, this growth of national consciousness is a political fact. We must all accept it as a fact, and our national policies must take account of it".

42   Ryall, *Between God and Caesar*, 122.

43   De Gruchy, J.W., *The Church Struggle in South Africa*, SPCK, London, 1979, 149-193 and see *South Africa in the 1980s*, CIIR, 1980, 37-42.

44   The greatest Afrikaner Christian, formerly moderator of the Transvaal Synod and a member of the *Broederbond*, he was banned under the Suppression of Communism Act. Aasvolkop NG Church in Northcliff where he was pastor expelled him for his anti-apartheid theology but received his body when he died aged 89. His ashes were scattered in Alexandra Township at his request; see "Farewell to Oom Bey" , *The Star*, 20 September 2004; De Gruchy, *The Church Struggle*, 103-115 underlines the importance of the Christian Institute as beginning a process of turning away from liberal to radical solutions and seeking a "confessing Church" stance. It says a lot for Archbishop Denis Hurley that he was willing to be associated with this major project while not sharing its theology.

45   Borer, T.R., *Challenging the State Churches as Political Actors in South Africa 1980-1994*, University of Notre Dames Press, Notre Dame, IN, 1998, 39.

46   Ryall, *Between God and Caesar*, 143.

47   See Mosala, I.J., and Tlhagale, B. (eds), *The Unquestionable Right to be Free: Essays in Black Theology*, Skotaville, Johannesburg, 1986.

48   Chikane, Frank, *No Life of My Own*, CIIR, London, 1988, 38.

49   Borer, *Challenging the State*, 93.

50   Biographical data supplied by the SACBC at the time of Father Mkhatshwa's detention.

51   See *War and Conscience in South Africa: The Churches and Conscientious Objection*, CIIR, London, and Pax Christi 1982 for background. Kearney, *Guardian of the Light*.

52   The sheltering of activists on the run continued into the 1980s. The Dominican priory in Johannesburg was a popular centre.

53   Kearney, *Guardian of the Light*.

54   Ryall, *Between God and Caesar*, 175-176.

55   Kearney, *Guardian of the Light*.

56   See Chapter Eight.

57   See *Namibia in the 1980s*, CIIR/BCC, London, 198; *War and Conscience*, 11-22; *The Apartheid War Machine*, IDAF, No. 8, London, 1980.

58   Interviews with Smangaliso Mkhatshwa in 1980 and 1981. An interesting radical, but neglected, contemporary treatment of the BCM and the Bishops' reaction to the situation from a Christian Socialist perspective, with much liberation theology in a short bibliography, is contained in Cosmas Desmond *Christians*

or *Capitalists. Christianity and Politics in South Africa*, The Bowerdean Press, 1978, 116-158.

59   CIIR published a short pamphlet in 1983 entitled *Taking Sides* written by the South African Dominican theologian, Albert Nolan. It went into several reprints and clearly expressed a certain radical ecumenical consensus.

60   See *Relocations: The Churches' Report on Forced Removals in South Africa*, SACC and SACBC, 1984.

61   Nolan, A., *Jesus before Christianity: The Gospel of Liberation*, Darton, Longman and Todd, London, 1977.

62   Walshe, P., *Prophetic Christianity and the Liberation Movement in South Africa*, Cluster Publications, Pietermaritzburg, 1995, 43-83, 116-126; Borer, *Challenging the State*, 97-194.

63   During one such "study day" I observed Cardinal McCann reacting to a miner wearing a yellow helmet and imparting some contemporary Marxist verities. It was some measure of McCann, who was very committed to YCW, that he never flinched and barely missed a beat.

64   The Oblate Vicar-General of Windhoek Diocese, Father Heinz Henning, played an outstanding role in publicising human rights violations, at one point smuggling a BBC film on torture out of the country, but also by sustaining diplomatic relations with the South African Administrator-General while courageously working for justice, and supporting the new Namibian bishop, Boniface Haushiku. He participated in an ecumenical delegation to the Contact Group in Geneva in 1981. Henning wrote of a delegation of two South African Archbishops and three Bishops visiting in October 1984 treated by Van Niekerk"with contempt and like ignorant children"; H. Henning to Administrator Dr Willie van Niekerk, 8 October 1984, letter copied to CIIR.

65   Currin, B., "The Trial of an Archbishop" in Gamley, *A Portrait*, 128-133.

66   The Oblate Father Gerard Heimerijkx left Oshikuku Mission for this assignment and encountered numerous difficulties. He managed to import a pre-fabricated Swedish-built church in the SWAPO camp. His chaplaincy work was supported by the Namibian Refugee Service set up by CIIR.

67   *South Africa in the 1980s: State of Emergency*, CIIR, London, 1986, 29-34; *South Africa in the 1980s Update No.4*, CIIR, London, 1987, 9-15.

68   Borer, *Challenging the State*, 108-111. Several of the Kairos themes were elaborated and formed the basis of Albert Nolan's *God in South Africa. The Challenge of the Gospel*, Eerdmans, Grand Rapids, MI, 1988. Jacques Ellul in *Violence,* Seabury Press, 1969 had raised the issue of "institutional violence"— of which apartheid was an outstanding example.

69   At another level a number of evangelical Right wing Christians were tasked to interrogate and watch radical Church activists and theologians. The disadvantage of the signing was that it gave the apartheid regime a check list for surveillance, although by now they were completely over-stretched and more concerned with *Umkhonto we Sizwe* and its supporters in the townships.

70   Borer, *Challenging the State*, 121.

71   In Brussels, Beyers Naude represented the SACC, and in the absence of Smangaliso Mkhatshwa, Ian Linden from CIIR represented the SACBC. The assembled European Union officials were openly amazed—though they complied—to be told under which conditions the Churches in South Africa would accept EC monies. The funding initiative, of course, was a substitute for EC sanctions which were opposed by several member states. The Swedish

Government worked through Horst Kleinschmidt of IDAF for the SACC and through Ian Linden for the SACBC and other recipients of funds such as the Release Mandela Campaign internally.

72   Whether or not the bishops realised when they launched it what the paper would be like, is another matter. But once launched, and rapidly reaching a circulation of over 60,000, they had to live with it. They did defend it. Albertina Sisulu, Zwelakhe's mother, was a leader of the ANC's women's league, and the pro-ANC bias of the paper would not have come as a surprise. The comparison with the Communist world is instructive. For example, *The Chronicle of the Catholic Church in Lithuania* from 1972-1977 was arguably also of comparable national importance though produced underground, lay and clergy led, and addressed to a better educated Catholic readership; see Vardys, V.S., *The Catholic Church, Dissent and Nationality in Soviet Lithuania*, Columbia University Press, New York, 1978, 84, 128, 150, 160. *Tygodnik Powszechny* (Universal Weekly) in Poland during the 1970s is a closer comparison bringing together a non-Catholic left opposition with critical Catholic nationalists such as the historian Adam Michnik, though the paper had a more intellectual readership; see Scott Appleby, R., *The Ambivalence of the Sacred: Religion, Violence and Reconciliation,* Roman and Littlefield, Lanham, MD, 2000, 233.

73   Both Germany and Britain seemed to want Inkatha to develop into a rival to the ANC, feared because of its SACP links, an irresponsible policy that led to the beginnings of civil war. Only at the end of the 1980s, when the overwhelming support for the ANC was beyond doubt, did their tactics switch to trying to divide the SACP from the "nationalist" or "Africanist" elements—as they hopefully dubbed them—of the ANC. The Natal-Kwazu bishops had legitimate fears about Chief Buthelezi's Inkatha.

74   Archbishop Hurley was very sensitive about being photographed in front of the Red Flag as he saw it undeniably as a symbol of the Soviet regime rather than of the local South African Communist Party; see Kearney, *Guardian of the Light.*

75   This was because the poison, absorbed through undergarments, produced its worst effect, not in Namibia where it was intended, but a few streets from a major teaching hospital in the USA which managed to save his life. He had been very clear that his life was in danger when he worked on his autobiographical book *No Life of My Own* with me from 1987-1988.

76   Rob Lambert and Sr Brigid Flanagan were lucky to escape, the former saving the latter who was asleep, but both stranded on a balcony. The Security police responsible for the 12 October 1988 arson claimed they did not know anyone was sleeping there. This might just be true as the rooms, above offices, were used for visitors during meetings, and not always occupied.

77   Archbishop Edward Cassidy, his Australian substitute, was very different: he was liked, played tennis, and even joined in some protest marches.

78   Albert Nolan was at this time effectively a chaplain to an informal group of pro-ANC activists who had arrived at their position from a Christian motivation, and contributed to a strong spirituality of struggle that permeated their work. He was elected Superior-General of the Dominicans, but declined, and was given permission from the Friars to stand down in order to pursue his work in South Africa.

79   *The Road to Damascus Kairos and Conversion,*CIIR and Christian Aid, London, 1989, 3-4. The preparation of the document, lasting more than two years, was coordinated by CIIR and funded by Christian Aid.

8. Democracy and Nationalism in Africa

1　Perraudin, A., *Un Evèque au Rwanda Témoignage*, Editions Saint-Augustin, St. Maurice, 2002, 17-19.

2　Ibid., 99-100.

3　The analysis of these changes is contained in the first nine chapters of Linden, I., *Church and Revolution in Rwanda*, Manchester University Press, 1974. From 1925 onwards the Belgians dealt with Tutsi and Hutu differences in a "Race Policy" while recognising that the Banyarwanda did not see the distinction in that way; see Gatwa, T., *The Churches and Ethnic Ideology in the Rwandan Crises 1900-1994*, Regnum Books, 2005, 39-40.

4　Perraudin, *Un Evequê*, 19, 132-134; Gatwa, *The Churches and Ethnic Ideology*, 71-74.

5　Linden, I., *Christianisme et pouvoirs au Rwanda*, Karthala 1999, 265-267.

6　The non-aligned "Third World" Bandung Conference took place in 1955 and Ghana became independent in 1957. Political change was in the air. Perraudin took over in Kabgayi in 1956, inaugurating change in the Church.

7　*Kinyamateka* was started in 1933. Perraudin, *Un Evèque*, 106-114, 136; Linden, *Christianisme et pouvoirs*, 321-322.

8　Contrary to several later publications, Kayibanda was never Perraudin's secretary. The Archbishop's predecessor appointed him as editor in chief of *Kinyamateka,* not Perraudin, who removed him in early October 1959 when he formally assumed a party political role in Rwanda.

9　His colleague on the other hand, Aloys Munyangaju in *L'Actualité politique au Rwanda*, 1959, offered overwhelming reasoned and detailed evidence of forms of discrimination against the Hutu, both politically and in schools. Gitera should not be confused with the future military coup leader.

10　Linden, *Christianisme et pouvoirs*, 325-326.

11　Perraudin, *Un Evèque*, 187-192, 194. He repeated his basic conclusion on Catholic principles on 25 August 1959: "the present situation in Ruanda Urundi, entrenching a sort of monopoly of power in the hands of one group does not correspond to the norms of a healthy structuring of society".

12　Linden, *Christianisme et Pouvoirs*, 348-356, covers this crisis period.

13　Perraudin, *Un Evèque*, 181-182.

14　Linden, *Christianisme et pouvoirs*, 316-317. This is not to say that these bodies were in any sense "front organisations for a political movement", merely that they were existing gatherings that brought together active Catholics in Rwanda.

15　It was therefore hardly surprising that it appealed more to both the Belgians and Archbishop Perraudin than the rival APROSOMA and UNAR.

16　Gitera used the phrase "Hitlerism". Perraudin also accused the UNAR of Communism, not untypical of responses to anti-colonial movements, but in this case given due cause by the support of the Soviet Union in the United Nations for the anti-Church stand of the UNAR.

17　Prunier, G., *The Rwanda Crisis: History of a Genocide*, Hurst, London, 1995, 47-58.

18　This was Michel Kayihura, brother of Bishop Jean-Baptiste Gahamanyi of Butare, and chief in Bugoyi Province; see Perraudin, *Un Evèque*, 358-413, for a point by point rebuttal of his accusations.

19　Linden, *Christianisme et pouvoirs*, 356.

20   Perraudin to Cauwe, 8 November 1959, White Fathers Archives, dossier 738, quoted in Linden, *Christianisme et pouvoirs*, 354.
21   Ibid., 372-375.
22   Ibid., 375-377.
23   The flagrantly partisan role of the Archbishop of Kigali was later used to discredit the entire Catholic Church by President Kagame's administration.
24   The editor of *Kinyamateka* from 1980-1986, Abbé Silvio Sindambiwe died in an unexplained car crash. His successor from 1988, the courageous Hutu Abbé André Sibomana was arrested and charged after a series of challenging articles on corruption, but the case was tried on the eve of the Pope's arrival and he was unexpectedly acquitted; see Sibomana, A., *Gardons Espoir pour le Rwanda. Entretiens avec Laure Guilbert et Hervé Déguine*, Deselle de Breuwer, Paris, 1997; Longman, T., "Christianity and Democratisation in Rwanda: Assessing Church responses to political crisis in the 1990s" in Gifford, P. (ed.), *The Christian Churches and the Democratisation of Africa*, E.J. Brill, Leiden, 1995, 191-192.
25   Prunier's *The Rwanda Crisis* is the best account of the immediate antecedents to the genocide.
26   The Diocese of Kabgayi's 40-pp. pamphlet *Twivugurure tubane mu mahoro* (Let us reform ourselves to live together peacefully) resulted in Bishop Thaddee's relations with Vincent Nsengiyumva deteriorating. This was hastened by his opening up of the diocese to human rights organisations and movements for peace and reconciliation.
27   With the support of the Apostolic Delegate, Bishop Thaddée co-chaired the ecumenical *Comité de Contacts* that attempted from 1991 to mediate in the crisis but stalled after the failure of a major symposium in Mombassa. In early 1994 he hosted at Kabgayi a Rwandan Patriotic Front Youth delegation from Uganda, escorted by UN troops; see Gatwa, *The Churches and Ethnic Ideology*, 206-208, 214.
28   Prunier, *The Rwanda Crisis* 213-229 speculates on who fired the missile and why.
29   Linden, "The Church and Genocide: Lessons from the Rwandan Tragedy" in Baum, G., and Wells, H. (eds) , *The Reconciliation of Peoples: Challenge to the Churches*, Orbis, Maryknoll, 1997, 53.
30   The publications of *African Rights* have highlighted and detailed the limited number of cases of Church personnel complicit in acts of genocide. The question of whether or not the Roman Catholic Church in Rwanda was complicit in genocide remains moot unless a precise definition of the different categories of complicity is made explicit: it may apply from a mass-goer wielding a machete, or a soldier using a gun, through an array of clergy and Sisters who showed cowardice and/or aided and abetted in some way, to Archbishop Vincent Nsengiyumva. Walsh, D., "Genocide's Dark Shadow" , *The Tablet*, 17 July 2004 for specific instances including that of Bishop Misago arrested in 1999 but later acquitted.
31   Linden, I., *The Catholic Church and the Struggle for Zimbabwe*, Longman, Harlow, 1980, 44.
32   Lamont, D., *Speech from the Dock*, CIIR and Kevin Mayhew, London, 1977, 28.
33   Only 1,000 English copies were printed and most of those sold in the Salisbury—Protestant—SPCK bookshop. It was not printed in either Shona or Nde-

bele and made very little impact outside government circles.

34   Plangger, A., *Rhodesia: The Moral Issue*, Mambo Press, Gweru, 1968, 27-30, 37.

35   See Chapter Two.

36   *Peace through Justice* follows this reference to natural rights with a quote directly from Pius XI's 1937 *Mit brennender Sorge* directed at the Nazis; see Plangger, *Rhodesia*, 59.

37   McClaughlin, J., *On the Frontline: Catholic Missions in Zimbabwe's Liberation War,* Baobab Books, Harare, 1996, 12, 14. This is a fascinating book with original research that I have drawn on extensively in this section.

38   Ibid.,14; Linden, *The Catholic Church,* 69-71.

39   Ibid.

40   Blake, A., *A History of Rhodesia,* Eyre Methuen, London, 1977, 361.

41   McClaughlin, *On the Frontline,* 15.

42   Harold-Barry, D., *Knocks on the Door,* Silveira House, 2004; Linden, *The Catholic Church,* 76.

43   Ibid., 89.

44   The Land Tenure Act divided up Rhodesia into an irregular chessboard of black and white land, 45 million acres apiece with the worst land in the African squares; see RCBC, *The Land Tenure Act and the Church,* Mambo Press, Gweru, 29 March 1970, and Randolph, R.J., *Church and State in Rhodesia,* Mambo Press, Gweru, 1971 for the official Church response to this first wave of legislation.

45   In addition to *Moto's* special issue, Mike Traber produced a supplement to the *Shield*. Both carried the Bishops' detailed rejection of the new constitution in their pastoral, a *Call to Christians*. In *Moto* a mock ballot paper helpfully carried a cross in the "No" box.

46   These remarks came in a reply to a broadcast attack on Lamont by the leading Catholic in the RF, Mark Partridge, in a letter to the *Rhodesia Herald,* 20 March 1970. Lamont had on a number of occasions used the concept of institutional violence, and replied in the same vein about the attack on the RBC (Rhodesia Broadcasting Corporation).

47   Linden, *The Catholic Church,* 57, 141-142, 154.

48   This he did mainly through the Catholic Institute for International Relations (CIIR) whose general-secretary Mildred Nevile invited him to London in 1972. The CIIR was an offshoot of the wartime Sword of Spirit after a change of name in 1963. Its Africa secretary, Tim Sheehy, conducted a major campaign against the Smith-Hume proposals in the early 1970s, and the relationship was consolidated by strong links with the Rhodesian Justice and Peace Commission.

49   Linden, *The Catholic Church,* 163.

50   Auret, D., *Reaching for Justice: the Catholic Commission for Justice and Peace 1972-1992,* Mambo Press, Gweru, 1992 provides a full history.

51   The article appeared in the August 1972 issue of *Moto* and Plangger received a five months suspended sentence in Salisbury regional court. Bishop Haene afterwards recommended he use a legal adviser or exerted some self-censorship. Later, on legal advice, he turned down an article from Lamont calling the government "the real terrorists"; see Auret, *Reaching for Justice,* 173, 185.

52   Linden, The Catholic Church, 174.

53   Rhodesia's first two black priests had been ordained exactly a quarter century before. Prior to being consecrated bishop, Father Chakaipa accompanied Bish-

op Haene and Fr Richard Randolph to meetings with Sir Alec Douglas-Hume when they protested against the new 1969 constitution. His novels were *Rudo Ibofu* (Love is Blind), Mambo Press, Gweru, 1961, *Garandichauya* (Wait I will come) Longman, Salisbury, 1963, and *Dzasukwa Mwana-asina-Hembe* (Beer-for-Sale), Longman, Salisbury, 1964, all about urban moral collapse contrasted with the solidarities of country life, a stock-in-trade of the African novel at the time but also a missionary theme; see Kahari, G.P., "Missionary influences in Shona Literature" in Bourdillon, M.F.C., *Christianity South of the Zambesi*, Vol. 2, Mambo Press, Gweru, 1977, 87-101. Chakaipa never adopted a strong public position or led from the front. He was not first choice of the Zimbabwean clergy and was hampered to some extent by not being so.

54   The chair of the Commission, Alexander Graham, a politically and religiously conservative thoracic surgeon had been selected by the bishops. The background to his resignation in August 1974 was the Commission's decision to go public on their human rights dossiers, but Graham had also repeatedly clashed with Lamont on such issues. One of the RJPC's legal advisers, Mr Lardner-Burke, left and joined the RF, and became a judge. Sylvester Maluza, a young Zimbabwean advocate, took over as Chair. Sister Janice McClaughlin later worked with Zimbabwean refugees in Mozambique under ZANU control, and Dieter Scholz, now Bishop of Sinoia, after deportation directed the Zimbabwe Project for refugees from the London office of CIIR. Internally the RJPC forged a strong bond with Chief Tangwena as they tried to block forced removals resulting from the Land Tenure Act and looked after children and families who were victims of it.

55   The RJPC programmes were funded, by, among other donors, the European and Canadian Catholic development agencies in CIDSE. One of its most immediately practical outcomes was a booklet entitled *The Rights and Duties of a Citizen When Arrested and Tried* produced in Shona, Ndebele and English.

56   *Reconciliation in Rhodesia*, was read in churches on 20 January 1974; see Linden, *The Catholic Church*, 192-193.

57   A young Jesuit scholastic, Roger Riddell, later to join CIIR, applied Segundo's thought to Rhodesia; see *The Month*, May 1977.

58   McClaughlin, *On the Frontline*, 24.

59   Ibid., 26-27. Chief Tangwena organised their passage across the border itself.

60   Ibid., 79-80.

61   McClaughlin, *On the Frontline*, 133-134.

62   In two dioceses, Salisbury and Sinoia, the Sisters stayed at their missions when male clergy had been withdrawn, in both at considerable personal risk as priests had been killed. The LCBLs were founded by Archbishop Aston Chichester SJ in 1932, interestingly four years before Chishawasha seminary was opened.

63   The CIIR—RJPC link enabled rapid transmission of information to British newspapers such as the *Sunday Times* and *Guardian* whose own journalists were working under government accreditation and censorship restrictions in Rhodesia. *The Times* favoured the Internal Settlement and blocked stories. In one notable instance the first edition of 8 May 1978 carried a story discreditable to the fiction of power-sharing between Smith and Muzorewa; it disappeared completely from subsequent editions after being read at his home in Bath by the editor, William Rees-Mogg, late a night. The analysis coming from the CIIR was undoubtedly influential with the British Foreign Secretary, Dr David Owen, and his American equivalent, Andrew Young, and the focus on London was tac-

tically well directed and effective; see Linden, *The Catholic Church*, 264-265.

64   Ibid., 225.

65   Several priests in Umtali Diocese did not support or agree with Lamont, one defying him and reporting the presence of *vakomana* to Security Forces. The thirty-five Irish Franciscans, mostly in Wedza Tribal Trust Land, were more supportive as they did not have Lamont's authoritarian leadership to contend with in times of trouble, but did have his inclinations. The RJPC could not have had much influence; they had become a small dedicated group working at times in a semi-autonomous manner.

66   Linden, *The Catholic Church*, 252-255.

67   McClaughlin, *One the Frontline*, 225.

68   Ibid.

69   The RJPC created a sub-committee to deal with guerrilla human rights violations but, as McClaughlin illustrates in numerous examples in her fascinating study, this work depended on information from courageous Church personnel at mission stations. She also makes a convincing case that some of the mission-trained ZANLA platoon commanders showed exceptional mercy to "sell-outs" and moderated the violence of their forces. The effectiveness of the Church communications network stretching to Maputo as well as London was impressive.

70   "Dickie" Randolph, known affectionately as "Lord" Randolph in the Society of Jesus, personified the gentleman Jesuit of the English Province, loyal to a fault to the bishops and deeply suspicious of the "Communism" of the African nationalist movement and guerrillas. This was motivated mainly by the anti-religious attitudes of the more ideologically trained but minority ZIPA forces. These drew on both ZIPRA and ZANLA combatants and were formed in 1975, genuinely "nationalist" rather than ethnic forces. His abiding suspicion proved historically correct but, unless what is meant by "Communism" is emptied virtually of all political content, his diagnosis of the moral problem was wrong. ZANLA ideology appealed mostly to historical claims to the land; *vakomana* killed witches and consulted spirit mediums, hardly a Leninist vanguard, though Stalin's show trials bore similarities to witch trials.

71   The point was that the Church was arguably suffering *de facto* schism, a point Lamont acknowledged; see McClaughlin, *On the Frontline*, 126.

72   See for details the second half of Auret's book, *Reaching for Justice*.

73   During the 1980 elections that brought Mugabe to power under a British governor, Lord Soames, Lord Pratap Chitnis and Eileen Sudworth, working with the CIIR and RJPC, shuttled between Nkomo and Mugabe attempting to stop armed conflict breaking out during the disarmament and decommissioning of the different guerrilla forces. It was apparent that the "dirty tricks" department of both the Rhodesian, South African and—possibly—British intelligence services were doing the opposite. CIIR was threatened with deportation by the British interim authorities.

74   Mike Auret who had fled the country in the late 1970s for fear of imprisonment by the Smith regime, left the Commission to the join the political opposition, the MDC (Movement for Democratic Change) in the 1990s. The bishops had been very unenthusiastic about having a showdown with the Mugabe regime by publishing the full dossier. The CCJPIZ as an episcopal Commission had to fall into line; see Auret, *Reaching for Justice*, 147-166. For the full dossier, see *Gukurahundi in Zimbabwe: A Report on the Disturbances in Matabeleland*

and the Midlands 1980-1988 Hurst, London, 2007. In my own correspondence with the Attorney-General with whom I had once broadcast on the topic of the human rights violations of the Smith government, I was invited to travel with him in Matabeleland "to show you that the reports were false". I declined.

75   Fady, J., *Un Fils d'Alsace*, Saint-Paul à Bar-le-Duc, France, 1975, 159. His reply on 24 February 1953 was the somewhat coy: "notre politique est celle du Baptême".

76   Nyassa Apostolic Vicariat, *Status Synodaux,* Likuni, 1950, 25, White Fathers Archives, Lilongwe.

77   Reijnaerts, H., Nielsen, A., and Schoffeleers, M., *Montfortians in Malawi. Their Spirituality and Pastoral Approach,* Kachere Series 5, Christian Literature Association in Malawi (CLAIM), Blantyre, 1997, 377.

78   Schoffeleers, M., *In Search of Truth and Justice: Confrontation between Church and State in Malawi: 1960-1994,* Kachere Series No. 8, CLAIM, 1999, 19-20.

79   Ibid., 21-27.

80   "The History of Mzuzu Diocese", Mzuzu, 1989, in White Fathers Archives, Lilongwe, 88. There was very little reaction by seminarians to the 1959 crisis and detentions; c.f. Zimbabwe and South Africa. Interview with Father Jacques de l'Eprévier, Lilongwe, April 2001. But the defacing of a picture of Dr Banda by a Zambian student resulted in Zambian and Mozambican students being expelled from the seminary at Easter 1973.

81   Schoffeleers, *In Search of Truth*, 28-29.

82   Fady, *Un Fils d'Alsace*, 188-195. According to Fady he had warned Theunissen about getting religion involved in politics but Theunissen incredibly believed such a Party could win 75 per cent of the votes. Banda at least feigned—and certainly spoke of—an affection for Fady until the latter retired.

83   Schoffeleers, *In Search of Truth*, 31-33, 85-88.

84   Ibid., 44-49.

85   Ibid., 33-38.

86   The statement was interestingly strong on human and civil rights and the Church's role in defending them, an implicit criticism of the MCP's violence. Theunissen had been condemning it explicitly three days earlier in the *Nyasaland Times*; see J.C. Chakanza,"The Pro-Democracy Movement in Malawi: The Catholic Church's Contribution" in *Religion in Malawi,* No.4, February 1994. An American Montfort priest, Francis Crimmins, died in a motor-cycle accident while distributing the statement to different dioceses; see Schoffeleers, *Search for Truth*, 40. A letter from G. Van Asdonk (Montfort Education Secretary) to J. O'Leary (Vicar-General, White Fathers) points out the need for advice to be given to WF missionaries on voting. "It is absolutely forbidden for any missionary to register on the Special Roll," he insists, because of the racial nature of the Special Voters Roll; see "History of "Mzuzu Diocese", 88-89.

87   See the fascinating chapter on Chizisa and Pondeponde in Schoffeleers, *Search for Truth*, 61-90.

88   Malawi was still mainly a matrilineal, matrilocal society—though beginning to change -in which the uncle had authority in the extended family (*mbumba*). Banda presented himself in public always as the "uncle" surrounded by ullulating and dancing members of the Malawi Women's League, the symbolic women of his village, representing the national family (*mbumba*) that he "owned", ruled and protected as *mwini mbumba*.

89   "Common Document of AMRIMA and AMRIM on Justice and Evangelisa-

tion", 9-11 March 1983, submitted to the Bishops' Conference and pressing for the formation of a Justice and Peace Commission; see Schoffeleers, *Search for Truth*, 109-111.

90   O'Maille, P., *Living Dangerously. A memoir of political change in Malawi*, Dudu Nsomba publications, Glascow, 1999 gives a sense of what such a commitment meant for an expatriate priest.

91   Interviews with Fr Denis-Paul Hamelin WF, Lilongwe, April 2001; interview with Bishop Method Kilaini, auxiliary bishop of Dar-es-Salaam, February 2008; Maille, *Living Dangerously*,106-108.

92   Jacques de l' Eprévier, interview; Schoffeleers, *Search for Truth*, 113-115.

93   Hamelin and l' Eprévier interviews.

94   The full text of the letter is in Schoffeleers, *Search for Truth*, 344-354. It was produced at the Montfort Mission in Balaza where the secondary school pupils helped put it together in great secrecy. Every photocopying machine at Chancellor College was put to use in copying it; see Maille, *Living Dangerously*, 156.

95   The transcript used by Schoffeleers, ibid. 132-135, is as published in the *Malawi Democrat* for 24 September 1992 and makes extraordinary reading.

96   Ibid., 140-145.

97   The coordination of a successful campaign of international support for the bishops took place via the White Fathers' provincialate in Lilongwe. The government cut off all mission faxes but this one, improbably because it was for some reason mistakenly registered centrally under the name of "Padzuwa Garage" which doubled as a brothel; Hamelin interviews.

98   Schoffeleers, *Search for Truth*, 168, 173-174. De Andrea had served in East Timor. Accustomed to dealing with a small Catholic community under acute pressure from a hostile government (Indonesia), he misread the situation.

99   Ibid., 175.

100   Englund, H., "The Dead Hand of Human Rights; contrasting Christianities in post-transition Malawi", *The Journal of Modern African Studies*, Vol. 38, No.4, December 2000, 590, relates how, despite priests exerting maximum caution stopping all Church meetings before the referendum, Catholics organised their own prayer meetings and sometimes went directly from them to vote. The bishops issued two pastorals, *Choosing our Future*, before the referendum, reviewing advantages of different systems, multi-party and one party, and *Building our Future*, endorsing democracy and educating citizens on their role in it.

101   Gifford, P., *African Christianitty Its Public Role*, Hurst, London, 1998, 21; Okoko-Esseau, A., "The Christian Churches and Democratisation in the Congo" in Gifford, P. (ed.), *The Christian Churches*, 156-158. The first president of the Congo had been a priest, Abbé Fulbert Youlou.

9. Inculturation and Dialogue with Islam

1   Agenzia Internazionale Fides no.3441 19 October 2001, 582-584.

2   Amaladoss, M., "Dialogue between Religions in Asia Today", *East Asian Pastoral Review*, Vol. 42, 2005, 57; Phan, P., " 'Reception or Subversion' of Vatican II by the Asian Churches?" in Madges, W. (ed.), *Vatican II: Forty Years Later*, Orbis, Maryknoll, 2005, 36-40. Pope John Paul II in other contexts had been highly sympathetic to cultural difference, see his moving speech to Maoris: "For thousands of years you have lived in this land and fashioned a culture that

endures to this day. And during all this time, the Spirit of God has been with you. Your 'dreaming', which influences your lives so strongly that, no matter what happens, you remain forever the people of your culture, is your way of touching the mystery of God's Spirit in you and in creation...It is as a Maori that God calls you." Pope John Paul II speaking in Alice Springs, Australia, 1986.

3   Their thinking was influential with the Jesuit theologian, Jacques Dupuis; Mosse, D., "Catholic Saints and the Hindu Village Pantheon in Rural Tamil Nadu", *Journal of the Royal Anthropological Institute (Man)*, Vol. 29, No. 2, June 1994, 301-303; Trapnell, J., "Catholic Engagement with India and its theological implications" in O'Mahony, A., and Kirwan, M., *World Christianity: Politics, Theology, Dialogues*, Melisende, London, 2004, 257-284.

4   Hastings, A., *African Catholicism*, SCM Press, London, 1989, 138-155.

5   These are direct quotes from John Paul II, "Ecclesia in Africa", no. 62 in *L'Osservatore Romano*, 38, 20 September 1995, vii. It was promulgated in Johannesburg, Nairobi, and Yaounde in September 1994.

6   Magesa, L., *Anatomy of Inculturation: Transforming the Church in Africa*, Orbis, Maryknoll, 2004, 5. Shorter, A., *Evangelization and Culture*, Geoffrey Chapman, London, 1994 provides the best and clearest account of contemporary thinking on inculturation, and is drawn on here.

7   *Fides* statistics on missionaries and total Catholic population unfortunately do not disaggregate North and South America. "Oceania" contains Australia and New Zealand as well as Pacific Island nations with dramatically different cultural and economic profiles. There are a considerable number of Asian Catholic missionaries now in Africa and elsewhere. The point is that the "South" fields high numbers and inevitably feels resentment that this is not reflected in influence. It also has high indebtedness to the "North" which can and does have money, resources and Rome's central control that weigh during pastoral and theological arguments.

8   This is not to say that the concept of "Christian culture" was suddenly invented in the context of the growing appreciation of diversity in the twentieth century. A ninth-century Russian would probably not have preferred his own Slavic culture to what was on offer from a new universal "Christian culture". It is incarnation understood through the prism of inculturation that provides a theology of diversity—thus seen as a positive value.

9   I am grateful to Father Aylward Shorter for alerting me to this strange development of the former monocultural, Eurocentric, approach. Professor Richard Gray of the School of Oriental and African Studies, University of London, asked Father Shorter to take the matter up with Cardinal Ratzinger. He was about to become principal of the Catholic Tangaza College in Nairobi and wisely did not think it the moment to lock horns with the CDF; personal communication, Father Aylward Shorter, 12 March 2005; Allen, *Benedict XVI*, 237.

10   *L'Osservatore Romano*, No.17, 26 April 1995, V-VIII.

11   Ratzinger, J., and Messori, V., *The Ratzinger Report*, Leominister, 1985, 103, quoted in Shorter, A., *The African Synod: A Personal Response to the Outline Document*, St. Paul's Publications, Nairobi, 1991, 58. Shorter's book showed no reluctance to challenge Rome on inculturation, notably about the way that the vision of the Zairean bishops of an "African Council", mooted in an *ad limina* visit to Pope John Paul II, was blocked and slowly subverted into an African Synod held in Rome; Allen, *Benedict XVI*, 237.

12   See "Response to the *Lineamenta* for the Special Assembly for Africa on the theme 'Evangelizing Mission of the Church in Africa'" , 1992, WF Lilongwe Archives. Father Pedro Arrupe, head of the Society of Jesus and a missionary in Japan for many years, did attempt to provide a strong steer to the Jesuits in 1978 in a letter to the Society of Jesus on inculturation. He also promoted the concept of a *polycentric Church*. Likewise pastoral institutes such as Gaba, in Uganda, were actively exploring concrete ideas in practice; see Hastings, *African Catholicism*, 20, 122-137; Shorter, *The African Synod*, 60, *Culture and Evangelization*, 32.

13   Mosse, "Catholic Saints and the Hindu Village Pantheon", 302.

14   See Delumeau, J., *Catholicism between Luther and Voltaire*, Burns and Oates, London, 1977, 154-202 charts the "folklorisation of Christianity" and post-Tridentine reform efforts.

15   Sanneh, L., *Translating the Message: the Missionary Impact on Culture*, Orbis, Maryknoll, 1990; Magesa, *Anatomy of Inculturation*, 2.

16   See Chapter Four.

17   Kohen, *From the Place of the Dead*, 314-316; Parker, C., *Popular Religion and Modernisation in Latin America*, Orbis, Maryknoll, 1996; Mosse, D., "Possession and Confession. Affliction and Sacred Power in Colonial and Contemporary Catholic South India" in Cannell, F. (ed.), *The Anthropology of Christianity*, Duke University Press, Durham, NC, 2006, 99-125.

18   Mosse, "Possession and Confession", 125.

19   Mosse, D., "South Indian Christians, Purity/Impurity, and the Caste System: Death Ritual in a Tamil Roman Catholic Community", *Journal of the Royal Anthropological Institute (Man)*, Vol. 29, 2, June 1994, 476-477.

20   Santo Domingo Final Document No. 36, cited in Bamat, T., and Wiest, J-P, *Popular Catholicism in a World Church*, Orbis, Maryknoll, 1999, 2.

21   In the preparation of the Damascus document, coordinated in the late 1980s by CIIR in London, it took almost two years before the Latin American delegates thought to request an indigenous theologian to participate. He expressed considerable annoyance at the late invitation. The push for promotion of an indigenous voice came from the Latin American bishops, as much as from *ladino* clergy and Religious and this was reflected at Santo Domingo in a caucus around the issue in opposition to the Vatican's promotion of "Christian culture". Interviews in London 1988 and Santo Domingo, 1991.

22   Parker, *Popular Religion*, 135, 231.

23   Ibid., 13-15, 99.

24   Shorter, *Evangelisation and Culture*, 83.

25   Parker, *Popular Religion*, 132. The *Falun Gong* in China and *Hindutva* in India are two spectacular examples of new forms of constructed religion arising in reaction to secularity.

26   Phone Interview with Edmund Tang, Birmingham, February 2008; Phan, P., "Popular Religion, the Liturgy and the Cult of the Dead" in *East Asian Pastoral Review*, Vol. 42, Nos.1 and 2, 2005, 134. Christian celebrations in Vietnam of Tet, the Lunar New Year, also included a welcome to the ancestors. Shorter, *Evangelization and Culture*, 26. See Fasholé-Luke, E., "Ancestor Veneration and the Community of Saints" in Glasswell, M. and Fashole-Luke, E. (eds), *New Testament Essays for Africa and the World*, London 1974, 209-221; Bujo, B., *African Theology in Its Social Context*, Maryknoll, Orbis, 1992 both discussed in Parratt J. *Reinventing Christianity African Thelology Today*, Wm.

Eerdmans, Grand Rapids, 1996, 95-98, 122-136.

27   Kumbirai, J., "Kurova Guva and Christianity" in Bourdillon, M.F.C. (ed.), *Christianity South of the Zambesi*, Mambo Press, Gweru, 1977, 123-130; Shorter, *Evangelisation and Culture*, 128-129.

28   Linden, I., "Chisumphi Theology in the religion of Central Malawi" in Schof-feleers, J.M. (ed.), *Guardians of the Land*, Mambo Press, Gweru, 1978, 187-209.

29   Linden I and Schoffeleers J.M "The Resistance of the Nyau Societies to the Roman Catholic Missions in Colonial Malawi" in Ranger, T.O., and Kimambo, I. (eds), *The Historical Study of African Religion*, Heinemann, London, 1972, 252-277; Linden, I., "Chewa Initiation Rites and Nyau Societies: the use of religious institutions in local politics at Mua" in Ranger, T.O., and Weller, J. (eds), *Themes in the Christian History of Central Africa* Heinemann, London, 1974, 30-44; Linden, I., *Catholics, Peasants and Chewa Resistance in Nyasaland,1889-1939* Heinemann, London, 1974, 117-137; Schoffeleers, J. M., "The Nyau Societies: Our Present Understanding", *The Society of Malawi Journal*, Vol. 29/1, 1976, 59-68.

30   See Chapter 8. The remarkable collection of masks is contained in the Kungoni Centre, Mua Mission, Malawi, the work of Father Claude Boucher WF.

31   Hastings, *African Catholicism*, 138-155; interviews with Denis-Paul Hamelin, Lilongwe, April 200; for a positive view of Milingo's work see Ter Haar, G., and Ellis, S., "Spirit Possession and Healing in Modern Zambia: an Analysis of Letters to Archbishop Milingo", *African Affairs*, 87, April 1988, 185-206; Ter Haar, G., "Healing as Liberation. The Concept of Healing according to Archbishop Milingo", *Colloque "Eglises et Santé dans le Tiers-Monde, hier et aujourd'hui"*, Louvain le-Neuve, 19-21 October 1989.

32   Taken from title of Diamond, S., *Spiritual Warfare*, Pluto Press, London, 1989; Comoro, C., and Sivalon, J.,"Marian Faith Healing Ministry" in *Popular Catholicism*, 157-182.

33   Prof. Paul Gifford's inaugural lecture at the School of Oriental and African Studies (SOAS), University of London, 2007, "Africa's Inculturation Theology: Observations of an Outsider" offers a particularly caustic account of the state of contemporary African theology. It was published as Gifford, P., "Africa's Inculturation Theology: Observations of an Outsider", *Hekima Review*, No. 35, May 2008, 18-34.

34   Gaba Pastoral Paper 7, 1969, 7 quoted in Shorter, *The African Synod*, 14. This was in a speech marking the establishment of SECAM, The Symposium of Episcopal Conferences of Africa and Madagascar, after the Pope's visit to Kampala in 1969. Cardinal Zougrana was made President of SECAM.

35   Kalilombwe, P.A., "My Life, My faith, My Theology and My Country. In the footsteps of the incarnate and missionary Cosmic Christ" Typed MSS, WF archives, Lilongwe; Donders, J., *Non-Bourgeois Christianity*, Orbis, Maryknoll, 1985, 37.

36   Nothomb, D., *Un Humanisme Africain: Valeurs et Pierres d'Attente* Lumen Vitae, Brussels, 1969.

37   See for example Ela, J.-M., *Le Cri de l'Homme Africain*, Harmattan, Paris, 1980 translated as *African Cry* by Orbis in 1986.

38   *A Man for All People: The Message of Mandlenkhosi Zwane*, CIIR, London, 1983; Elsebernd, A., *The Story of the Catholic Church in the Diocese of Accra*, Catholic Book Centre, Accra, 2000, 278; Magesa, Anatomy, 185.

39   Shorter, *Evangelization and Culture*, 92.

40   In an Address to the Pontifical Council for Culture, see *L'Osservatore Romano*, 28 June 1982.

41   *Lumen Gentium* 16 in Flannery, A. (ed.), *The Basic Sixteen Documents: Vatican Council II*, 1996, 22.

42   Sullivan, F., *Salvation Outside the Church*, Paulist Press, 1992, 192-195.

43   Nonetheless, O'Mahony, A., and Siddiqui, A., *Christians and Muslims in the Commonwealth*, Altajir World of Islam Trust 2001, 109 highlights the analysis of the Jesuit, Christian Troll, who points out that Christians do not use the same names for God nor necessarily mean the same thing by the names they give.

44   *Nostra Aetate*, 3; O'Collins, G., *Salvation for All:God's Other Peoples*, Oxford University Press, 2008 emphasises the ground-breaking character of the Declaration.

45   Sullivan, *Salvation outside the Church*, 186-189; *Dominum et Vivificantem*, 1986; Clarke, P.B., "Christian Approaches to Islam in West Africa in the post-Independence Era (c.1960-1983): From Confrontation to Dialogue", *Bulletin on Islam and Christian-Muslim Relations in Africa*, Vol.1, April 1983, No. 2, 3-5.

46   *Redemptoris Missio*, 55; transcript of conversation between Cardinal König and Jacques Dupuis in 2003; see "Dialogue at the Deepest Level", *The Tablet*, 22 March 2008.

47   Sullivan, *Salvation outside the Church*, 192-194.

48   See Charlesworth, Max, "The Diversity of Revelations" in *Religious Inventions: Four Essays*, Cambridge University Press, 1997, 23-51 for this position.

49   From my experience of two meetings of the Pontifical Council, there was also a third dialogue, with the local Church, whose attitude to Islam was often more hostile to the local expression of state and civil society Islam.

50   Dialogue with WICS began in the 1970s and a 1976 Rome meeting ran into major procedural difficulties; see Isizoh C. (ed.), *Milestones in Interreligious Dialogue*, Lagos, 2002, 56.

51   For a diplomatic presentation of the PCID's workings see "Dialogue and Proclamation", Fitzgerald, M., *Milestones*, 209-217. Fitzgerald provided a strong cover endorsement to the hardcover edition of Dupuis' *Towards a Christian Theology of Religious Pluralism*. This disappeared from the paperback edition indicating official disapproval had been expressed. Dupuis resigned from the *Dialogue and Proclamation* editorial team because of what he saw as the incoherence in it created by interventions from the Vatican dicastery on missions; see Allen, *Benedict XVI*, 247-248; Borelli, J., "In the Spirit of Assisi", *The Tablet*, 23 September 2006.

52   Joblin, J., "Réciprocité. Chrétiens en terre d'Islam, chrétiens en terre laïque", *La Revue Liberté Politique*, 2006, No. 35, 1-5 highlights these points in an authoritative way. I am grateful to the Apostolic Nuncio to the European Communities, S.E. Monsignor André Dupuy, for making this article available to me.

53   McCabe, H., *Love, Law and Language*, Sheed and Ward, London 1968, 99.

54   See below why the Vatican might be expected to wish negotiation to improve the situation of Christians in predominantly Muslim countries. Pope John Paul II had raised the lack of liberty of Christian minorities with the Diplomatic Corps on 12 January 1985 and 17 January 1999, not naming but referring to the situation in Saudi Arabia, a priority concern for the Vatican.

55   A translation from the German by Christa Pongratz-Lippit was published in
      The Tablet, 23 September 2006. Russell, N., "Regensburg Revisited", *The Tab-
      let*, 8 September 2007, suggests that instead of "evil" *cheiron* in the original
      would have best been translated—into German—as "inferiority".
56   Russell, ibid.
57   www.zenith.org/article 5 March 2008.
58   O'Mahony, A., "Exodus under Fire", *The Tablet*, 12 August 2006, 4-5.
59   Foucher, V., "Church and Nation. The Catholic Contribution to War and Peace
      in Casamance (Senegal)", *LFM* (*Le Fait Missionaire*), October 2003, No. 13,
      11-41.
60   I am grateful to Archbishop Michael Fitzgerald for details of his visit to Ka-
      duna. The Biafran regime tried and failed to use anti-Muslim propaganda as a
      way of bringing religion into the conflict though, of course, the Biafran cause
      had considerable support from Holy Ghost missionaries and Catholics around
      the world.
61   Interviews with Rev Dr Matthew Kukah 2005, 2006. The Pope told a plenary
      session of those drafting *Dialogue and Mission*, a publication produced for the
      twentieth anniversary of *Nostra Aetate*, that "Dialogue is fundamental for the
      Church. No local Church is exempt from this duty"; see Machado, F.A., "Dia-
      logue and Mission" in Isizoh, *Milestones*, 171, 178.
62   Interview with Rev Dr Thomas Michel SJ, Chicago, 2006.
63   Viviano, R., "Responses of the Catholic Church to Islam in the Philippines from
      the Second Vatican Council to the Present Day" in O'Mahony and Kirwan
      (eds), *World Christianity*, 393-403.

10. A Global Church in the Twenty-First Century

1   Leddy, M.J., *Reweaving Religious Life: Beyond the Liberal Model* Twenty
     Third Publications, Connecticut, 1991, 47-78. For a good overview of official
     positions on changes in a Men's Religious Order, see *Initialis Formatio Fratrum
     Ordinis Praedicatorum: Documenta Recentoria*, Santa Sabina, Rome 1999
     (French & English); *To Praise, to Bless to Preach: Words of Grace and Truth*,
     Dominican Publications, Dublin, 2004.
2   Carroll, A., "Secularisation of European Identity", *The Institute Series*, 1, Hey-
     throp Institute for Religion, Ethics and Public Life, London, 2005, 25-39.
3   The phrase is taken from Ricour, P., "Prospective et Utopie. Prévision économique
     et choix ethique", *Esprit*, February 1966, 178-193 and the term "metapolitics"
     from a paper to COMECE by Bp. Arianus H. van Luyn of Rotterdam, 2008.
4   Niederberger, O., *The African Clergy in the Catholic Church of Rhodesia*,
     Mambo Press, Gwelo, 1973, 35-36.
5   Personal Communication, Prof. Richard Gray, SOAS, 2005.
6   Interviews conducted in Malawi by Jane Linden, April 2001; Ian Linden with
     Sr Maura O'Donohue, April 2008; Hastings, A., *African Catholicism: Essays in
     Discovery*, SCM Press, London, 1989, 13, refers to some dioceses in Uganda
     where "hardly a priest is without children of his own"; Cornwell, J., *The Pope in
     Winter,* Viking (Penguin), London, 2004, 243-245. Pope John Paul II did eventu-
     ally send a confidential letter to all the bishops in the world on the problem.
7   These were the statistics given in an official Church report published in 2004;
     see King, J., "Vatican II's ecclesiology and the Sexual Abuse Scandal" in (ed.)
     Madges W. *Vatican II Forty Years Later* Orbis, 2005, 146-147; Pemberton C.

"Whose Face in the Mirror? Personal and Post-Colonial Obstacles in Researching Africa's Contemporary Women's Voices" in (eds) King. U. & Beattie T. *Gender, Religion & Diversity* Continuum 2004, 254-256.

8   Excerpt from Stourton, E., *John Paul II*, Hodder & Stoughton, London, 2006, reprinted in *The Tablet*, 25 March 2006, 6-7.

9   Paul Gifford, SOAS Seminar, 2007 laments that most of these are in the luxury suburb of Langata rather than in the slums of Kibera; Linden, I., *A New Map of the World*, Darton, Longman, Todd, London, 2004, 110-111.

10   SECAM has its office in Accra with a department for advocacy that is setting up a branch in Addis Ababa to develop a permanent relationship with the African Union Secretariat. COMECE is an acronym for *Commissio Episcopatuum Communitatis Europensis*.

11   Sanchez, J.A., *The Community of the Holy Spirit: A Movement of Change in a Convent of Nuns in Puerto Rica*, University Press of America, Lanham, MD, 1983, 55-173, gives a narrative account of an indigenous community's evolution through and after the Council showing a change from a high degree of the prevailing infantilism of obedience to a maturer spirituality and social apostolate.

12   *SRTV Transactions* fourth annual newsletter of August 2003, 2-3. I am very grateful to Valerie Flessati for sending me material on Religious and sex trafficking, including emails from Sister Eugenia.

13   Bonetti, E., "Sex Slaves from Africa", *The Tablet*, 28 August 1999.

14   Speech of Welcome to Mrs Stella Obasanjo, *Caritas Italiana*, 12 September 2000; Sr Patricia Ebegbulem's report emailed to Sr Eugenia Bonetti, 15 September 2000.

15   Ibid.

16   Catholic Secretariat of Nigeria *Restoring the Dignity of the Nigerian Woman*, 20 February 2002, 17; Presentation of Pastoral Letter by Archbishop John Oneiyekan, 29 April 2002.

17   Ebegbulem, P., "News from Italy 15 May-8 June" on high cost of Nigerian visas; "Report on 'Trafficking", USMI (*Unione Superiore Maggiori D'Italia*), November-December 2003; Bonetti, E., "The Success of Important Projects in Nigeria", 29 June 2006; interview with Valerie Flessati.

18   Luckman, H.A., "Vatican II and the Role of Women" in Madges, W. (ed.), *Vatican II Forty Years Later*, 86-93.

19   Sniegocki, J., "Catholic Teaching on War, Peace and Non-violence Since Vatican II" in *Vatican II*, op. cit., 228.

20   The Iraq quote is from a little more than two years before Cardinal Ratzinger became Pope; the non-violence quote is from 18 February 2007, an allocution given at a midday Angelus in St Peter's Square; Sniegocki, "Catholic Teaching", 237.

21   *Evangelii Nuntiandi*, 37.

22   Sniegocki, J., 229-232.

23   Ibid., 229.

24   *The Tablet*, 20 October 2001, 1506.

25   Sniegocki, "Catholic Teaching on War", 244n.

26   Flessati, "The History of a Catholic Peace Society in Britain", 463.

27   Ibid., 413, 441; Cardinal Spellman famously called for "total victory" during a Christmas visit to US troops in Vietnam.

28   Quoted in Mortimer, E., "Big Ideas for a New President", *New York Review*

of Books, Vol. LV, 6, 17 April 2008, 32. The Church has tried to undertake such education. *Climate Change: A Focal Point of Global, Intergenerational and Ecological Justice* produced by the Commission for Society and Social Affairs and Commission for International Church Affairs of the German Bishops' Conference, September 2006, with a foreword by Cardinal Karl Lehmann, its President, and drawing on expert lay advice, illustrates a typical contemporary—official—European Catholic response: excellent analysis of the practical problem, only rudimentary indication of a theology and ethics. But no single official Church body solely dedicated to the major question confronting the world in the twenty-first century, and no permanent staff member. See also *The Call of Creation*, produced by a part-time worker in the Department of International Affairs of the Bishops' Conference of England and Wales in 2002. The USCC has nevertheless done some concentrated lobbying of Congress and Senate on climate change with its permanent lobbyists who cover mainly "Catholic issues". Catholic EarthCare, Australia, as a dedicated organisation, would be an exception to this meagre commitment of resources.

29   For an outstanding exploration of the three Christian strands, ecojustice, stewardship and ecological spirituality, making up environmental theology and ethics, see Jenkins, W., *Ecologies of Grace: Environmental Ethics and Christian Theology*, Oxford University Press, 2008.

30   French, W., "Greening *Gaudium et Spes*" in Madges, W. (ed.),*Vatican II Forty Years Later*, 203; Pope John Paul II, *Centesimus Annus*, 1991, section 37.

INDEX